Other Books and Series

Compilation of History of the Cherokee Indians by Emmet Starr with Combined Full Name Index

1901-1907 Native American Census Seneca, Eastern Ottawa, Peoria, Quapaw, and Wyandotte Indians (Under Seneca School, Indian Territory)

1932 Census of The Standing Rock Sioux Reservation with Births and Deaths 1924-1932

Kiowa, Comanche, Apache, Fort Sill Apache, Wichita, Caddo and Delaware Indians Birth and Death Rolls 1924-1932

Census of The Blackfeet, Montana, 1897- 1901 Expanded Edition

Eastern Cherokee by Blood, 1906-1910, Volumes I thru XIII

Choctaw of Mississippi Indian Census 1929-1932 with Births and Deaths 1924-1931 Volume I
Choctaw of Mississippi Indian Census 1933, 1934 & 1937, Supplemental Rolls to 1934 & 1935 with Births and Deaths 1932-1938, and Marriages 1936-1938 Volume II

Eastern Cherokee Census Cherokee, North Carolina 1930-1939 Census 1930-1931 with Births And Deaths 1924-1931 Taken By Agent L. W. Page Volume I
Eastern Cherokee Census Cherokee, North Carolina 1930-1939 Census 1932-1933 with Births And Deaths 1930-1932 Taken By Agent R. L. Spalsbury Volume II
Eastern Cherokee Census Cherokee, North Carolina 1930-1939 Census 1934-1937 with Births and Deaths 1925-1938 and Marriages 1936 & 1938 Taken by Agents R. L. Spalsbury And Harold W. Foght Volume III

Seminole of Florida Indian Census, 1930-1940 with Birth and Death Records, 1930-1938

Texas Cherokees 1820-1839 A Document For Litigation 1921

Starr Roll 1894 (Cherokee Payment Rolls) Districts: Canadian, Cooweescoowee, and Delaware Volume One
Starr Roll 1894 (Cherokee Payment Rolls) Districts: Flint, Going Snake, and Illinois Volume Two
Starr Roll 1894 (Cherokee Payment Rolls) Districts: Saline, Sequoyah, and Tahlequah; Including Orphan Roll Volume Three

Cherokee Intruder Cases Dockets of Hearings 1901-1909 Volumes I & II

Indian Wills, 1911-1921 Records of the Bureau of Indian Affairs Books One thru Seven
Native American Wills & Probate Records 1911-1921

Other Books and Series by Jeff Bowen

Turtle Mountain Reservation Chippewa Indians 1932 Census with Births & Deaths, 1924-1932

Chickasaw By Blood Enrollment Cards 1898-1914 Volume I thru *V*

Cherokee Descendants East An Index to the Guion Miller Applications Volume I
Cherokee Descendants West An Index to the Guion Miller Applications Volume II (A-M)
Cherokee Descendants West An Index to the Guion Miller Applications Volume III (N-Z)

Applications for Enrollment of Seminole Newborn Freedmen, Act of 1905

Eastern Cherokee Census, Cherokee, North Carolina, 1915-1922, Taken by Agent James E. Henderson   Volume I (1915-1916)
Volume II (1917-1918)
Volume III (1919-1920)
Volume IV (1921-1922)

Eastern Cherokee Census, Cherokee, North Carolina, 1923-1929, Taken by Agent James E. Henderson   Volume I (1923-1924)
Volume II (1925-1926)
Volume III (1927-1929)

Complete Delaware Roll of 1898

Applications for Enrollment of Seminole Newborn Act of 1905 Volumes I & II

North Carolina Eastern Cherokee Indian Census 1898-1899, 1904, 1906, 1909-1912, 1914   Revised and Expanded Edition

1932 Hopi and Navajo Native American Census with Birth & Death Rolls (1925-1931) Volume 1 - Hopi
1932 Hopi and Navajo Native American Census with Birth & Death Rolls (1930-1932) Volume 2 - Navajo

Western Navajo Reservation Navajo, Hopi and Paiute 1933 Census with Birth & Death Rolls 1925-1933

Cherokee Citizenship Commission Dockets 1880-1884 and 1887-1889 Volumes I thru *V*

Applications for Enrollment of Chickasaw Newborn Act of 1905 Volumes I thru *VII*
Cherokee Intermarried White 1906 Volume I thru *X*

Applications for Enrollment of Creek Newborn Act of 1905 Volumes I thru *XIV*

Other Books and Series by Jeff Bowen

Applications for Enrollment of Choctaw Newborn Act of 1905 Volumes I thru XX

Choctaw By Blood Enrollment Cards 1898-1914 Volumes I thru XX

Oglala Sioux Indians Pine Ridge Reservation 1932 Census Book I
Oglala Sioux Indians Pine Ridge Reservation Birth and Death Rolls 1924-1932 Book II

Census of the Sioux and Cheyenne Indians of Pine Ridge Agency 1896 - 1897 Book I
Census of the Sioux and Cheyenne Indians of Pine Ridge Agency 1898 - 1899 Book II

Northern Cheyenne Tongue River, Montana 1904 - 1932 Census 1904-1916 Volume I
Northern Cheyenne Tongue River, Montana 1904 - 1932 Census 1917-1926 Volume II
Northern Cheyenne Tongue River, Montana 1904 - 1932 Census 1927-1932 Volume III

Sac & Fox - Shawnee Estates 1885-1910 (Under Sac & Fox Agency) Volumes I-VIII
Sac & Fox - Shawnee Estates 1920-1924 (Under The Sac & Fox Agency, Oklahoma) & Wills 1889-1924 Volume IX
Sac & Fox - Shawnee Deaths, Cemetery, Births, & Marriage Cards (Under The Sac & Fox Agency, Oklahoma) 1853-1933 Volume X
Sac & Fox - Shawnee Marriages, Divorces, Estates Log Books Volumes 1 & 2, Log Book Births & Deaths (Under Sac & Fox Agency, Oklahoma)1846-1924 Volume XI
Sac & Fox - Shawnee Guardianships Part 1 (Under Sac & Fox Agency, Oklahoma) 1892-1909 Volume XII
Sac & Fox - Shawnee Guardianships, Part 2 (Under The Sac & Fox Agency, Oklahoma) 1902-1910 Volume XIII
Sac & Fox - Shawnee Guardianships, Part 3 (Under The Sac & Fox Agency, Oklahoma) 1906-1914 Volume XIV

Census of the Pima, Tohono O'odham (Papago), and Maricopa Indians of the Gila River, Ak Chin & Gila Bend Reservations 1932 with Birth and Death Rolls 1924-1932

Identified Mississippi Choctaw Enrollment Cards 1902-1909 Volumes I, II, III
Identified Mississippi Choctaw Enrollment Cards' Dawes Packets 1902-1909 Volumes IV, V, VI & VII

Census of the Northern Navajo, Navajo Reservation, New Mexico, 1930 Volume I
Census of the Northern Navajo, Navajo Reservation, New Mexico, 1931 Volume II

Other Books and Series by Jeff Bowen

Crow Agency Montana 1898-1905 Census Volume I 1898-1901 with Illustrations

Memoirs of a White Crow Indian (Thomas H. Leforge) As told by Thomas B. Marquis with Full Index and Illustrations

Visit our website at **www.nativestudy.com** to learn more about these other books and series by Jeff Bowen

CHEROKEE GRANTED ENROLLMENT CARDS & DAWES PACKETS 1900 - 1907 VOLUME I

TRANSCRIBED BY
JEFF BOWEN
NATIVE STUDY
Gallipolis, Ohio
USA

Copyright © 2024
by Jeff Bowen

ALL RIGHTS RESERVED
No part of this publication may be reproduced, distributed, or transmitted in any form or by any means, without the prior written permission of the publisher.

Native Study LLC
Gallipolis, OH
www.nativestudy.com

Library of Congress Control Number: 2024922411

ISBN: 978-1-64968-172-0

Bookcover and Title Page: Tuch-ee or "Dutch" By George Catlin (1796-1872) Date 1852/1860 Drawing No. 212. Portrait of a chief of a band of the Cherokee Indians, also a warrior. He wears a tunic with fringe, a large belt and carries his gun powder horn. He also wears a feathered turban, face paint and holds a rifle.
The Newberry Library (NL004918_o2.jpg)

Made in the United States of America.

"It is dangerous to be right in matters on which the established authorities are wrong."
Voltaire

Table of Contents

Notices in the Cherokee Nation	vii
Citizenship Rolls Governed by this Provision of an Act of Congress	xi
Copy of Original Treaty	xiii
Copy of Transcribed Miscellaneous Letters	lxxiii
Copy of Transcription of Treaty	lxxxi
Introduction	xcvii
Cherokee Granted Enrollment Cards & Dawes Packets	1
Index	351

DEPARTMENT OF THE INTERIOR,
Commission to the Five Civilized Tribes.

CENSUS NOTICE.

The Commission to the Five Civilized Tribes will hear at MUSKOGEE, Indian Territory, from THURSDAY, JANUARY 10, 1901, to THURSDAY, FEBRUARY 28, 1901, inclusive, applicants for enrollment as citizens of the Cherokee Nation. During that time all Cherokee citizens who have not heretofore appeared before the Commission should present themselves for enrollment.

This work is done preparatory to making final rolls of Cherokee citizens under provisions of the Act of Congress, approved June 28th, 1898, viz:

That in making rolls of citizenship of the several tribes, as required by law, the Commission to the Five Civilized Tribes is authorized and directed to take the roll of Cherokee citizens of eighteen hundred and eighty (not including freedmen) as the only roll intended to be confirmed by this and preceding Acts of Congress, and to enroll all persons now living whose names are found on said roll, and all descendants born since the date of said roll to persons whose names are found thereon; and all persons who have been enrolled by the tribal authorities who have heretofore made permanent settlement in the Cherokee Nation whose parents, by reason of their Cherokee blood, have been lawfully admitted to citizenship by the tribal authorities, and who were minors when their parents were so admitted; and they shall investigate the right of all other persons whose names are found on any other rolls and omit all such that may have been placed thereon by fraud or without authority of law, enrolling only such as may have lawful right thereto, and their descendants born since such rolls were made, with such intermarried white persons as may be entitled to citizenship under Cherokee laws.

* * * * Said commission shall make such rolls descriptive of the persons thereon, so that they may be thereby identified, and it is authorized to take a census of each of said tribes, or to adopt any other means by them deemed necessary to enable them to make such rolls. They shall have access to all rolls and records of the several tribes, and the United States court in Indian Territory shall have jurisdiction to compel the officers of the tribal governments and custodians of such rolls and records to deliver same to said commission, and on their refusal or failure to do so to punish them as for contempt; as also to require all citizens of said tribes, and persons who should be so enrolled, to appear before said commission for enrollment, at such times and places as may be fixed by said commission, and to enforce obedience of all others concerned, so far as the same be necessary, to enable said commission to make rolls as herein required, and to punish any one who may in any manner or by any means obstruct said work.

* * * *

No person shall be enrolled who has not heretofore removed to and in good faith settled in the nation in which he claims citizenship.

* * * *

The rolls so made, when approved by the Secretary of the Interior, shall be final, and the persons whose names are found thereon, with their descendants thereafter born to them, with such persons as may intermarry according to tribal laws, shall alone constitute the several tribes which they represent.

The members of said commission shall, in performing all duties required of them by law, have authority to administer oaths, examine witnesses, and send for persons and papers; and any person who shall willfully and knowingly make any false affidavit or oath to any material fact or matter before any member of said commission, or before any other officer authorized to administer oaths, to any affidavit or other paper to be filed or oath taken before said commission, shall be deemed guilty of perjury, and on conviction thereof shall be punished as for such offense.

No applicants for enrollment as Cherokee Freedmen will be heard at this appointment.

TAMS BIXBY,
T. B. NEEDLES,
C. R. BRECKINRIDGE,
COMMISSIONERS.

Muskogee, Indian Territory, December 12, 1900.

CHEROKEE ENROLLMENT NOTICE.

THE COMMISSION TO THE FIVE CIVILIZED TRIBES
WILL BE IN SESSION AT
TAHLEQUAH, INDIAN TERRITORY,
From Monday, NOVEMBER 4, Until Wednesday, DECEMBER 4, 1901, Inclusive,

For the purpose of hearing applications for enrollment of Cherokee citizens who have not heretofore applied; and also, for the purpose of hearing rebuttal and supplemental testimony with respect to applications made for enrollment as Cherokee citizens.

TAMS BIXBY,
T. B. NEEDLES,
C. R. BRECKINRIDGE,
Commissioners.

DEPARTMENT OF THE INTERIOR,

Commission to the Five Civilized Tribes.

Closing of Citizenship Rolls

OF THE MUSKOGEE OR CREEK NATION.

WHEREAS, on June 13, 1904, the Secretary of the Interior, under the authority in him vested by the provisions of the act of Congress approved March 3, 1901, (31 Stat., 1058) ordered that September 1, 1904, be and the same is hereby fixed as the time when the rolls of the Muskogee or Creek Nation shall be closed:

Notice is hereby given that the Commission to the Five Civilized Tribes will, at its office in Muskogee, Indian Territory, up to and inclusive of September 1, 1904, receive applications for the enrollment of citizens and freedmen of the Muskogee or Creek Nation, and that after that date the application of no person whomsoever for enrollment as a citizen or freedman of said nation will be received by the Commission.

Commission to the Five Civilized Tribes,
TAMS BIXBY, Chairman,
T. B. NEEDLES,
C. R. BRECKINRIDGE,
Commissioners.

Muskogee, Indian Territory,
June 25, 1904.

Citizenship Rolls Governed by this Provision of an Act of Congress

In making rolls of citizenship of the Cherokee Nation this Commission is governed by the following provision of the Act of Congress approved June 28, 1898 (30 Stats., 495);

"That in making rolls of citizenship of the several tribes, as required by law, the Commission to the Five Civilized Tribes is authorized and directed to take the roll of Cherokee citizens of eighteen hundred and eighty (not including freedmen) as the only roll intended to be confirmed by this and preceding Acts of Congress, and to enroll all persons now living whose names are found on said roll, and all descendants born since the date of said roll to persons whose names are found thereon; and all persons who have been enrolled by the tribal authorities who have heretofore made permanent settlement in the Cherokee Nation whose parents, by reason of their Cherokee blood, have been lawfully admitted to citizenship by the tribal authorities, and who were minors when their parents were so admitted; and they shall investigate the right of all other persons whose names are found on any other rolls and omit all such as may have been placed thereon by fraud or without authority of law, enrolling only such as may have lawful right thereto, and their descendants born since such rolls were made, with such intermarried white persons as may be entitled to citizenship under Cherokee laws."

[The above quote has been transcribed from Cherokee Case D-30 Nancy E. Forbes, Dawes Roll Number 21529. It will be found in similar format throughout this series.]

[Copy of the Original Treaty]

Treaty Between The United States of America And The Cherokee Nation of Indians

Concluded July 19, 1866

Proclaimed August 11, 1866

[NOTICE: Within the handwritten treaty you will find Articles 12 and 13 combined, and 14 through 16 combined following up to Article 17 and continuing.]

Andrew Johnson,

President of the United States of America,

To all and singular to whom these presents shall come, greeting:

Whereas a Treaty was made and concluded at the city of Washington, in the District of Columbia, on the nineteenth day of July, in the year of our Lord one thousand eight hundred and sixty-six, by and between Dennis N. Cooley and Elijah Sells, Commissioners, on the part of the United States, and Smith Christie, White Catcher, James McDaniel, S. H. Benge, Daniel H. Ross, and J. B. Jones, Delegates of the Cherokee Nation appointed by resolution of the National Council, on the part of said Cherokee Nation, which Treaty is in the words and figures following, to wit:

Articles of agreement and Convention at the city of Washington on the nineteenth day of July in the year of our Lord One thousand Eight hundred and Sixty six, between the United States, represented by Dennis N. Cooley, Commissioner of Indian affairs, Elijah Sells, Superintendent of Indian affairs for the Southern Superintendency, ~~and~~ ~~Col Ely S Parker~~. and the Cherokee Nation of Indians, represented by its delegates, James McDaniel, Smith Christie, White Catcher, S.H. Benge, J.B. Jones and Daniel H. Ross — John Ross, Principal Chief of the Cherokees, being too unwell to join in these negotiations —

Preamble.

Whereas existing treaties between the United States and the Cherokee Nation are deemed to be insufficient. The said Contracting parties agree as follows viz

Article 1

The pretended treaty made with the so-called Confederate States, by the Cherokee Nation on the Seventh day of October 1861, and repudiated by the National Council of the Cherokee Nation on the 18th day of February 1863 is hereby declared to be void.

Article 2

Amnesty is hereby declared by the United States and the Cherokee Nation for all Crimes and

& www
misdemeanors committed by one cherokee on the person or property of another cherokee. or of a citizen of the United States. prior to the 4th day of July 1866. and no right of action arising out of wrongs committed in aid or in suppression of the rebellion shall be prosecuted or maintained in the courts of the United States or in the courts of the Cherokee Nation. But the cherokee nation stipulate &c

Article 3.

The confiscation laws of the cherokee Nation shall be repealed, & the same. and all sales of farms. and improvements on real estate, made or pretended to be made in pursuance thereof are hereby agreed. and declared to be null and void and the former owners of such property so sold. their,

Article 4

All the Cherokees and freed persons who were formerly Slaves to any Cherokee, and all free Negroes not having been such Slaves, who resided in the Cherokee Nation, prior to June 1st 1861. who may within two years elect not to reside North East of the Arkansas River and South East of Grand River shall have the right to settle in and occupy the Canadian District South West of the Arkansas River and also all that tract of Country lying North West of Grand River and bounded on the South East by Grand River and west by the Creek reservation to the North East Corner thereof, from thence west on the North line of the Creek reservation to the Ninety sixth degree of

West Longitude and thence North on said line of Longitude so far that a line due East to Grand River will include a quantity of land equal to 160 acres for each person who may so elect to reside in the Territory above described in this article. Provided that that part of said District North of the Arkansas River shall not be set apart until it shall be found that the Canadian District is not sufficiently large to allow One hundred & Sixty acres to each person desiring to obtain settlement under the provisions of this Article.

Article 5

The inhabitants electing to reside in the District described in the preceding article shall have the right to elect all their local officers and Judges, and the number of delegates to which by their numbers they may be entitled in any general Council to be established in the Indian Territory under the provisions of this treaty as stated in Article 12 - and to Control all their local affairs, and to establish all necessary police regulations, and rules for the administration of justice in said District, not inconsistent with the Constitution of the Cherokee Nation, or the laws of the United States. Provided the Cherokees residing in said District shall enjoy all the rights and privileges of other Cherokees who may elect to settle in said District as hereinbefore provided, and shall hold the same rights and privileges, and be subject to the same liabilities as those who elect to settle in said District under the provisions of this treaty

Provided also that if any such police regulations or rules be adopted which in the opinion of the President bear oppressively on any citizen of the Nation, he may suspend the same. And all rules or regulations in said District or in any other District of the Nation, discriminating against the citizens of other Districts, are prohibited, & shall be void

Article 6

The inhabitants of the said District herein before described shall be entitled to representation according to numbers in the National Council, and all laws of the Cherokee Nation shall be uniform throughout said Nation. And should any such law either in its provisions or in the manner of its enforcement.

in the opinion of the President of the United States operate unjustly or injuriously in said District, he is hereby authorized and empowered to correct such evil, and to adopt the means necessary to secure the impartial administration of justice as well as a fair and equitable application and expenditure of the National funds as between the people of this and of every other District in said Nation—

Article 7

The United States Court to be created in the Indian Territory, and until such court is created therein the United States District Court the nearest to the Cherokee Nation shall have exclusive original jurisdiction of all causes, civil and criminal, wherein an inhabitant of the District hereinbefore described shall be a party and where an inhabitant outside of said District in the Cherokee Nation shall be the other party as plaintiff or defendant in a civil Cause, or shall be defendant or prosecutor in a Criminal Case, and all process issued in said District by any officer of the Cherokee Nation to be executed on an inhabitant residing outside of said District, and all process issued by any officer of the Cherokee Nation Outside of said District to be executed on an inhabitant residing in said District, shall be to all intents and purposes Null & void unless endorsed by the District Judge for the District where such process is to be Served, and

13

said person so arrested shall be held in custody by the Officer so arresting him. Until he shall be delivered over to the United States Marshall. or consent to be tried by the Cherokee Courts.

Provided that any or all the provisions of this treaty which make any distinction in the rights and remedies between the Citizens of any District, and the Citizens of the rest of the Nation, shall be abrogated whenever the President shall have ascertained by an election duly ordered by him, that a majority of the voters of such District desire them to be abrogated; and he shall have declared such Abrogation. And pro-

vided futher, that No law or regulation to be hereafter enacted within said Cherokee Nation or any District thereof prescribing a penalty for its violation shall take effect or be enforced until after 90 days from the date of its promulgation either by publication in one or more newspapers of general circulation in said Cherokee Nation or by posting up copies thereof in the Cherokee and english languages in each District where the same is to take effect, at the usual place of holding District Courts.

Art 8.

No license to trade in goods wares or merchandize

Merchandize shall be granted by the United States to trade in the Cherokee Nation unless approved by the Cherokee National Council. except in the Canadian District & such other District North of Arkansas River & West of Grand River occupied by the so called Southern Cherokees. as provided in Article 4 of this treaty –

Article 9

The Cherokee Nation, having voluntarily in February 1863 by an Act of their National Council forever abolished Slavery hereby Covenant and agree that never hereafter shall either slavery or involuntary servitude exist in their Nation otherwise than in the punishment of Crime whereof the party shall have been duly Convicted, in accordance with laws applicable to all the members of said tribe alike. They further agree that all freedmen who have been liberated, by voluntary act of their former owners or by law as well as all free –

colored persons who were in the Country at the commencement of the rebellion, and are now residents therein, or who may return within six months, and their descendants, shall have all the rights of native Cherokees, Provided that owners of slaves so emancipated in the Cherokee Nation shall never receive any compensation or pay for the slaves so emancipated.

Article 10

Every Cherokee & freed person, resident in the Cherokee Nation shall have the right to sell any products of his farm including his or her, live stocks or any Merchandize or Manufactured products and to ship & drive the same to market, without restraint, paying any tax thereon which is now or may be levied by the United States, on the quantity sold outside of the Indian Territory

Article 11

The Cherokee Nation hereby grant a right of way not exceeding two hundred feet wide. except at stations, switches, water stations, or crossing of rivers when more may be indispensible to the full enjoyment of the franchise herein granted, and then, only two hundred additional feet shall be taken; and only for such length as may be absolutely necessary, through all their lands, to any Company or corporation, which shall be duly authorized by Congress to construct a rail road from any point North to any point South, and from any point East to any point West of, and which may pass through the Cherokee Nation. Said Company or corporation and their employees and laborers while constructing and repairing the same and in operating said road or roads, including all necessary agents on the line, at stations, switches, water tanks and all others, necessary to the successful operation of a rail road, shall be protected, in the discharge of their duties, and at all times subject to the Indian intercourse laws, now or which may hereafter be enacted and be in force in the Cherokee Nation.

Article 12.

The Cherokees agree that a general Council consisting of delegates elected by each nation or tribe lawfully residing within the Indian Territory, may be annually convened in said Territory, which Council shall be organized in such manner and possess such powers as hereinafter prescribed.

First,- After the ratification of this treaty, and as soon as may be deemed practicable by the

Secretary of the Interior, and prior to the first session of said Council a census or enumeration of each tribe lawfully resident in said Territory shall be taken under the direction of the Commissioner of Indian Affairs, who for that purpose is hereby authorized to designate and appoint competent persons, whose compensation shall be fixed by the Secretary of the Interior, and paid by the United States.

Second,— The first general Council shall consist of one member from each tribe and an additional member for each one thousand Indians, or each fraction of a thousand greater than five hundred, being members of any tribe lawfully resident in said Territory, and shall be selected by said tribes respectively, who may assent to the establishment of said general Council, and if none should be thus formally selected by any Nation or tribe so assenting, the said Nation or tribe shall be represented in said General Council, by the Chief, or Chiefs & headmen of said tribes, to be taken in order of their rank as recognized in tribal usage, in the same number, and proportion as above indicated. After the said Census shall have been taken and completed, the Superintendent of Indian Affairs shall publish and declare to each tribe assenting to the establishment of such Council the number of members of such Council, to which they shall be entitled under the provisions of this article, and the persons entitled to represent said tribes shall meet at such time and place as he shall approve: but thereafter the time, and places of the sessions of said Council shall be determined by its action. Provided that no session in any one year shall exceed the term of thirty days. And provided, that special sessions of said Council may be called by the Secretary of the Interior, whenever in his judgment the interest of said tribes shall require such special session.

Third — Said General Council shall have power to legislate upon matters pertaining to the intercourse and relations of the Indian tribes, and Nations, and Colonies of Freedmen resident in said Territory, the arrest and extradition of Criminals and offenders escaping from one tribe to another, or into any Community of Freedmen, the administration of justice between members of different tribes of said Territory and persons other than Indians and members of said tribes or nations, and the Common defense and safety of the Nations of said Territory.

All laws enacted by said Council shall take effect at such time as may therein be provided, unless suspended by direction of the President of the United States — No law shall be enacted inconsistent with the Constitution of the United States or laws of Congress or existing treaty stipulations with the United States — nor shall said Council legislate upon matters other than those above indicated — Provided however, that the legislative power of such General Council may be enlarged, by the Consent of the National Council of each nation or tribe assenting to its establishment with the approval of the President of the United States

Fourth. Said Council shall be presided over by such person as may be designated by the Secretary of the Interior

Fifth — The Council shall elect a Secretary whose duty it shall be to keep an accurate record of all the proceedings of said Council and who shall transmit a true copy of all such proceedings duly certified by the presiding officer of such Council, to the Secretary of the Interior, and to each tribe or nation represented in said Council, immediately after the sessions of said Council shall terminate. He shall be paid out of the Treasury of the United States an annual salary of five hundred dollars.

Sixth. The members of said Council shall be paid by the United States the sum of four dollars per diem during the term actually in attendance on the sessions of said Council, and at the rate of four dollars for every twenty miles necessarily travelled by them in going from and returning to their homes respectively from said Council, to be certified by the Secretary and President of the said Council.

Article 13th The Cherokees also agree that a Court or Courts may be established by the United States in said Territory, with such jurisdiction and organized in such manner as may be prescribed by law. provided that the Judicial tribunals of the Nation shall be allowed to retain exclusive jurisdiction in all civil and criminal cases arising within their country in which members of the Nation by nativity or adoption shall be the only parties, or where the cause of action shall arise in the Cherokee Nation, except as otherwise provided in this treaty.

Article 14

The right to the use and occupancy of a quantity of land not exceeding one hundred and sixty acres to be selected according to legal subdivisions in one body, and to include their improvements

25

and not including the improvements of any member of the Cherokee Nation, is hereby granted to any Society or denomination which has erected, or which with the consent of the National council may hereafter erect buildings within the Cherokee country for missionary or educational purposes. But no land thus granted, nor buildings which have been or may be erected thereon shall ever be sold or otherwise disposed of, except with the consent and approval of the Cherokee National Council and of the Secretary of the Interior. And whenever any such lands or buildings

dings shall be sold or disposed of. the proceeds thereof shall be applied by said Society or societies for like purposes within said Nation subject to the approval of the Secretary of the Interior

Article 15th The United States may settle any civilized Indians friendly with the Cherokees and adjacent tribes within the Cherokee country on unoccupied lands east of 96°, on such terms as may be agreed upon by any such tribe and the Cherokees, subject to the approval of the President of the United States which shall be consistent with the following provisions viz: should any such tribe or band of Indians settling in said country, abandon their tribal organization, there being first paid into the Cherokee national fund a sum of money which shall sustain the same proportion to the then existing National fund that the number of Indians sustain to the whole number of Cherokees then residing in the Cherokee Country they shall be incorporated into and ever after remain a part of, the Cherokee Nation, on equal terms in every respect with native citizens.

And should any such tribe thus settling in said country decide to preserve their tribal organizations and to maintain their tribal laws, customs and usages, not inconsistent with the Constitution and laws of the Cherokee Nation, they shall have a district of country set off for their use by metes and bounds equal to 160 acres if they should so decide for each man, woman and child of said tribe and shall pay for the same into the National fund such price as may be agreed on by them and the Cherokee Nation subject to the approval of the President of the United States and in cases of disagreement the price to be fixed by the President—

And the said tribe thus settled shall also pay into the National fund a sum of money to be agreed on by the respective parties not greater in proportion to the whole existing National fund and the probable proceeds of the lands herein ceded or authorized to be ceded or sold. them their numbers bear to the whole number of Cherokees then residing in said country, and thence afterwards they shall enjoy all the rights of native Cherokees. But no Indians who have no tribal organizations or who shall determine to abandon their tribal organizations shall be permitted to settle east of the 96° of longitude without the consent of the Cherokee National Council or of a Delegation duly appointed by it being first obtained. And no Indians who have and determine to preserve their tribal organizations shall be permitted to settle as herein provided east of the 96° of Longitude without such consent being first obtained: unless the President of the United States after a full hearing of the objections offered by said Council or Delegation to such settlement shall determine that the objections are insufficient, in which case he may authorize the settlement of such tribe east of the 96° of longitude

Article 16. The United States may settle friendly Indians in any part of the Cherokee country west of 96° to be taken in a compact form in quantity not exceeding 160 acres for each member of each of said tribes thus to be settled: the boundaries of each of said Districts to be distinctly marked and the land conveyed in fee simple to each of said tribes to be held in common or by their members in severalty as the United States may decide.

Said lands thus disposed of to be paid for to the Cherokee Nation at such price as may be agreed on between the said parties in interest, subject to the approval of the President and if they should not agree, then the price to be fixed by the President.

The Cherokee Nation to retain the right of possession of and jurisdiction over all of said country west of 96° of Longitude until thus sold and occupied, after which their jurisdiction and right of possession to terminate forever as to each of said districts. thus sold and occupied.

Article 17

The Cherokee Nation hereby cedes in trust to the United States, the tract of land in the State of Kansas, which was sold to the Cherokees by the United States under the provisions of the 2nd article of the treaty of 1835: and also that strip of the land ceded to the Nation by the 4th article of said treaty which is included in the State of Kansas, and the Cherokees consent that said lands may be included in the limits and jurisdiction of the said State.

The lands herein ceded shall be surveyed as the Public Lands of the United States are

#34—

Surveyed, Under the direction of the Commissioner of the General Land Office, and shall be appraised by two disinterested persons, one to be designated by the Cherokee National Council and one by the Secretary of the Interior, and in Case of disagreement by a third person to be mutually selected by the aforesaid appraisers. The appraisement to be not less than an average of One dollar and a quarter per acre exclusive of improvements.

And the Secretary of the Interior Shall from time to time as such

35

surveys and appraisements are approved by him, after due advertisement for sealed bids, sell such lands to the highest bidders for cash in parcels not exceeding one hundred and sixty acres, and at not less than the appraised value Provided that whenever there are improvements of the value of $50 made on the lands, not being mineral, and owned and personally occupied by any person for agricultural purposes at the date of the signing hereof, such person so owning and in person residing on such improvements, shall after due proof made under such regulations as the Secretary of the Interior may prescribe X be entitled to buy at the appraised value the smallest quantity of land in legal subdivisions which will include his improvements not exceeding in the aggregate one hundred and sixty acres. The expenses of survey and appraisement to be paid by the Secretary out of the proceeds of sale of said land. Provided that nothing in this article shall prevent the Secretary of the Interior from selling the whole of said neutral lands in a body to any responsible party for Cash for a sum not less than Eight hundred Thousand dollars-] Provider &c

Article 18

That any lands owned by the Cherokees in the State of Arkansas and in states East of the Mississippi. May be sold by the Cherokee Nation in such manner as their National Council May prescribe, all such sales. being first approved by the Secretary of the Interior.

Article 19

All Cherokees being heads of families residing at the date of the ratification of this treaty On any of the lands herein Ceded. or authorized to be sold and desiring to remove

38–

to the reserved country, shall be paid by the purchasers of said lands the value of such improvements to be ascertained and appraised by the Commissioners who appraise the lands. Subject to the approval of the Secretary of the Interior. And if he shall elect to remain on the land, now occupied by him shall be entitled to receive a patent from the United States in fee simple, for 320 acres of land to include his improvements. and thereupon he and his family shall cease to be members of the Nation

Article 20

Whenever the Cherokee National Council shall request it the Secretary of the Interior shall cause the country reserved for the Cherokees to be surveyed and allotted among them at the expense of the United States.

Article 21

It being difficult to learn the precise boundary line between the Cherokee Country and the States of Arkansas, Missouri and Kansas it is agreed that the United States shall at its own expense cause the same to be run as far west as the

Arkansas, and marked by permanent and conspicuous monuments, by two Commissioners, one
of whom shall be designated by
the Cherokee National Council.

Article 22 The Cherokee National Council
or any duly appointed Delegation
thereof shall have the privilege
to appoint an agent to examine
the accounts of the Nation with
the Government of the United States,
at such time as they may see
proper, and to continue or discharge such agent and to appoint
another, as may be thought best

by such Council or Delegation, and such agent shall have free access to all accounts and books in the Executive Departments relating to the business of said Cherokee Nation and an opportunity to examine the same in the presence of the officer having such books and papers in charge.

Article 23

All funds now due the Nation or that may hereafter accrue from the Sale of their lands by the United States as herein before provided for shall be invested in United States registered Stocks at their current value, and the interest on all said funds, shall be paid semi annually on the order of the Cherokee Nation and shall be applied to the following purposes, towit. Thirtyfive percent shall be applied for the support of the common schools of the Nation, and educational purposes, fifteen percent for the orphan fund and fifty percent for general purposes, including reasonable salaries of District officers. And the Secretary of the Interior with the approval of the President of the United States may pay out of the funds due the Nation on the order of the National Council or a delegation duly authorized by it, such amount as he may deem necessary to meet outstanding obligations of the Cherokee Nation Caused by the suspension of the payment of their annuities, not to exceed the sum of one hundred & fifty thousand dollars—

Article 24

As a slight testimony for the useful and arduous services of the Rev Evan Jones for forty years a Missionary in the Cherokee Nation, now a cripple, old, and poor, it is agreed that the sum of three thousand dollars be paid to him under the direction of the Secretary of the Interior out of any Cherokee fund in or to come into his hands not otherwise appropriated.

Article 25

A large number of the Cherokees who served in the Army of the United States, having died, leaving no heirs entitled to receive bounties and arrears of pay on account of such service – It is agreed that all bounties and arrears for service in the Regiments of Indian United States Volunteers, which shall remain unclaimed by any person legally entitled to receive the same, for two years from the ratification of this treaty, shall be paid as the National Council may direct to be applied to the foundation and support of an asylum for the education of Orphan children, which Asylum shall be under the control of the National Council or of such benevolent society as said Council may designate, subject to the approval of the Secretary of the Interior.

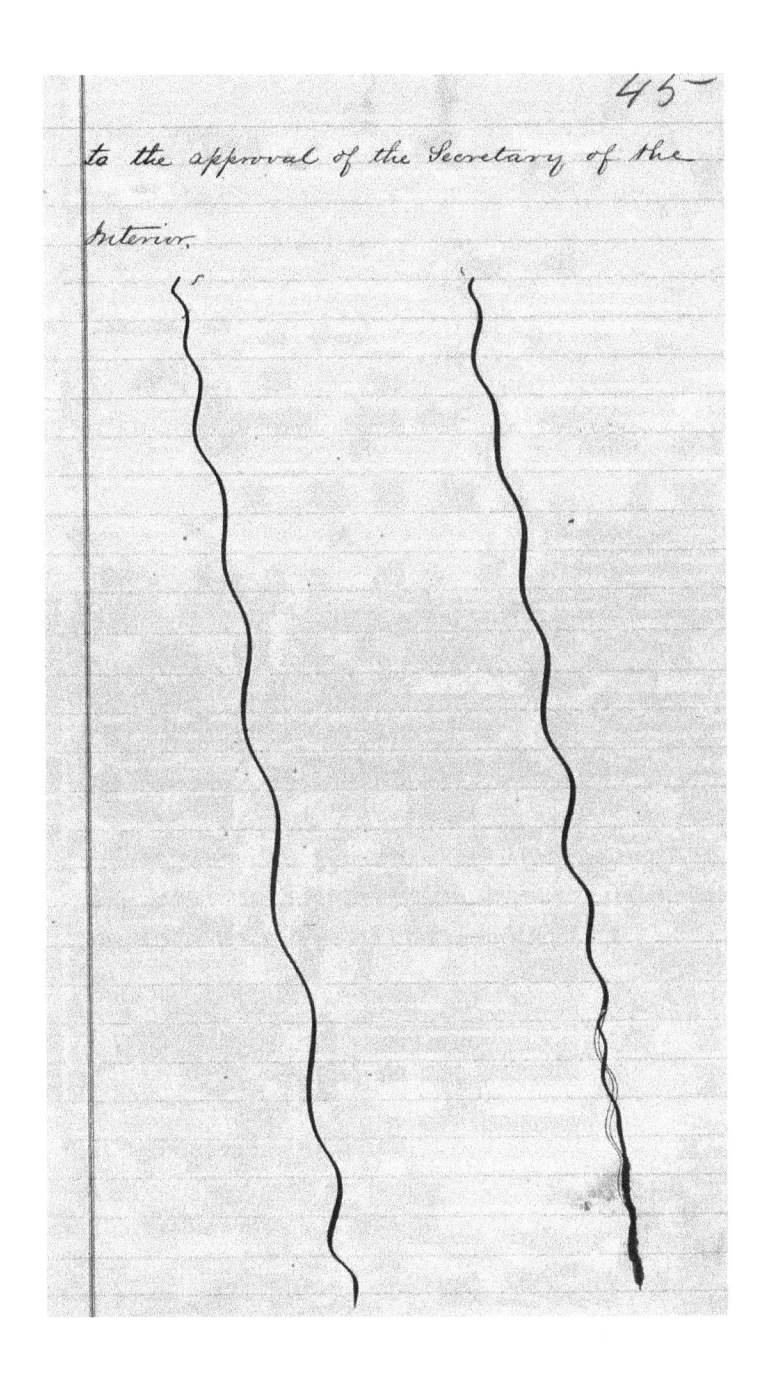

<u>Article 26</u>

The United States guarantee to the people of the Cherokee nation the quiet and peaceable possession of their country and protection against domestic feuds and insurrections and against hostilities of other tribes. They shall also, be protected against interuptions or intrusion from all unauthorized citizens of the United States who may attempt to settle on their lands or abide in their territory. In case of hostilities among the Indian tribes, the United States agree that, the party or parties commencing the same shall so far as practicable make reparation for the damages done.

<u>Article 27.</u>

The United States shall have the right to establish one or more military posts or stations in the Cherokee nation as may be deemed necessary for the proper protection of the citizens of the United States lawfully residing therein and the Cherokees and other citizens of the Indian Country. But no sutler or other person connected therewith either in or out of the military organization shall be permitted to introduce any spiritous, vinous or malt liquors into the Cherokee nation, except the medical department, proper, and by them only for strictly medical purposes. And all persons not in the military service of the United States, not citizens of the Cherokee nation, are to be prohibited from coming into the Cherokee nation or remaining in the same, except as herein otherwise provided, and it is the duty of the United States Indian Agent for the Cherokees to have such persons not lawfully residing or sojourning therein in removed from the nation as they now are, or hereafter may be required by the Indian intercourse laws of the United States

Article 2~~7~~ 28

The United States hereby agree to pay for provisions and clothing furnished the army under Appothlehala in the winter of 1861 and 1862, not to exceed the sum of ten thousand dollars, the accounts to be ascertained and settled by the Secratary of the Interior.

Article In 29

The sum of ten thousand, or as much thereof as may be necessary, to pay the expenses of the delegates and representatives of the Cherokees, invited by the Government to visit Washington for the purposes of making this treaty, shall be paid by the United States on the ratification of this treaty, and the Secretary

Article ~~29~~ 30.

The United States agree to pay to the proper claimants all losses of property by Missionaries or Missionary Societies resulting from their being ordered or driven from the country by United States agents, and from their property being taken and occupied or destroyed by by United States troops, not exceeding in the aggregate, twenty thousand dollars, to be ascertained by the Secretary of the Interior

Article ~~30~~ 31.

All provisions of treaties, heretofore ratified and in force, and not inconsistent with the provisions of this treaty are hereby re-affirmed and declared to be in full force; and nothing herein shall be construed as an acknowledgement by the United States, or as a relinquishment by the Cherokee ration of any claims or demands under the provisions of former treaties except as herein expressly provided.

In testimony whereof the said Commissioners on the part of the United States, and the said delegation on the part of the Cherokee Nation, have hereunto set their hands and seals, at the City of Washington this ninth day of July, A. D. one thousand eight hundred and sixty-six.

N. Cooley,
Com'r Ind Affairs

Elijah Sells
Supt Ind affs

Smith Christie
White Catcher
James McDaniel
S. H. Benge
Dan'l H. Ross
J. B. Jones

Delegates of the Cherokee Nation, Appointed by Resolution of the National Council.

In presence of
W. H. Watson
J. W. Wright

Signatures witnessed by the following named persons, the following interlineations being made before signing:— On page 6th the word "the" interlined, on page 11 the word "the" struck out and to said page 11 a sheet attached, requiring publication of laws, and on page 34th the word "Ceded" struck out and the words "Neutral lands" inserted. Page 47½ added relating to expenses of treaty.

Thomas Ewing Jr
W. A. Phillips
J. W. Wright

Forty-ninth

lxiv

And whereas, the said Treaty having been submitted to the Senate of the United States for its constitutional action thereon, the Senate did, on the twenty-seventh day of July, one thousand eight hundred and sixty-six, advise and consent to the ratification of the same, with amendments, by a resolution in the words and figures following, to wit:

In Executive Session,
Senate of the United States,
July 27, 1866

Resolved, (two thirds of the Senators present concurring,) That the Senate advise and consent to the ratification of the Articles of Agreement and Convention made at the City of Washington on the nineteenth day of July, in the year of our Lord one thousand eight hundred and sixty-six, between the United States, and the Cherokee nation of Indians, with the following

<u>Amendments.</u>

1st Insert at the end of Article 2 the following:— But the Cherokee nation stipulate and agree to deliver up to the United States or their duly authorized agent any or all public property, particularly ordnance, ordnance stores, arms of all kinds and quartermasters stores, in their possession or control, which belonged to the United States or the so-called Confederate States, without any reservation.

over

2nd Strike out the last proviso in Article 17, and insert in lieu thereof the following:—
Provided, That nothing in this Article shall prevent the Secretary of the Interior from selling the whole of said lands not occupied by actual Settlers at the date of the ratification of this Treaty, not exceeding 160 acres to each person entitled to pre-emption under the preemption laws of the United States; in a body to any responsible party, for Cash, for a sum not less than one Dollar per acre.

3 Insert at the end of Article 29 the following:—
— And the Secretary of the Interior shall also be authorized to pay the reasonable costs and expenses of the Delegates of the Southern Cherokees.

The moneys to be paid under this Article shall be paid out of the proceeds of the sales of the National lands in Kansas.

Attest,

J. W. Power
Secretary.

And whereas, the foregoing amendments having been fully explained and interpreted to the aforenamed Delegates of the Cherokee nation, they did, on the thirty-first day of July, one thousand eight hundred and sixty-six, give, on behalf of said nation, their free and voluntary assent to said amendments, in the words and figures following, to wit:

Whereas the Senate of the United States did on the 27th day of July 1866 advise and consent to the ratification of the Articles of Agreement and Convention made at the City of Washington on the nineteenth day of July, in the year of our Lord, one thousand eight hundred and sixty six, between the United States, and the Cherokee nation of Indians with the following,

Amendments, towit:

1st Insert at the end of Article 2 the following:— But the Cherokee nation stipulate and agree to deliver up to the United States or their duly authorized agent any or all public property particularly ordnance, ordnance stores, arms of all kinds and quartermasters stores, in their possession or control, which belonged to the United States or the so-called Confederate States, without any reservation.

2nd Strike out the last proviso in Article 17. and insert in lieu thereof the following:— Provided, That nothing in this Article shall prevent the Secretary of the Interior from selling the whole of said lands not occupied by actual settlers at the date of the ratification of this Treaty, not exceeding

160 acres to each person entitled to pre-emption under the pre-emption laws of the United States; in a body to any responsible party, for cash, for a sum not less than one Dollar per acre.

3ᵈ Insert at the end of Article 29, the following: And the Secretary of the Interior shall also be authorized to pay the reasonable costs and expenses of the Delegates of the Southern Cherokees

The moneys to be paid under this article shall be paid out of the proceeds of the sales of the National lands in Kansas.

Now therefore, we, the delegates on the part of the said Cherokee Nation, do hereby assent and agree to the said amendments above written, the same having been explained to us and being fully understood by us.

Witness our hands and seals this 31st day of July A.D. 1866 at Washington D.C.

In presence of:
D. N. Cooley
Cenis 25 O'Bois
J. Harlan, U.S. Indian agent
Charles E. Mix
T. W. Wright
W. R. Irwin

Smith Christie
White Catcher
James McDaniel
H. H. Bertge
Dan'l H. Ross
J. B. Jones

Now, therefore, be it known that I, Andrew Johnson, President of the United States of America, do, in pursuance of the advice and consent of the Senate, as expressed in its resolution of the twenty-seventh of July, one thousand eight hundred and sixty-six, accept, ratify, and confirm the said Treaty with the amendments as aforesaid.

In testimony whereof I have signed my name hereto, and have caused the seal of the United States to be affixed.

Done at the city of Washington this eleventh day of August, in the year of our Lord one thousand eight hundred and sixty-six, and of the Independence of the United States of America the ninety-first.

Andrew Johnson

By the President:
Henry Stanbery
Acting Secretary of State.

[Transcribed Miscellaneous Letters with Treaty]

Treaty Between The United States of America And The Cherokee Nation of Indians

Concluded July 19, 1866

Proclaimed August 11, 1866

Miscellaneous Letters - July, Part II, 1866.

DEPARTMENT of the INTERIOR,
WASHINGTON D. C. July 31 1866

Sir

    I have the honor to transmit for promulgation, the treaty negotiated on the 19$^{\underline{th}}$ inst., with the Cherokee Indians together with certain amendments thereto, made by the Senate, which amendments having been submitted to said Indians, have been assented to by them as will appear from the accompanying paper signed by their duly authorized delegates.

                  I am sir very respect'y
                      Your obt servt
                        Jas Harlan
                          Secretary

Hon. W$^{\underline{m}}$ H Seward
  (*&c*)
 Secretary of War.

#358.

Domestic Letters, Volume 73, page 551.

Department of State,
Washington August 4, 1866

Hon. O. H. Browning,
　　Secretary of the Interior.

Sir:

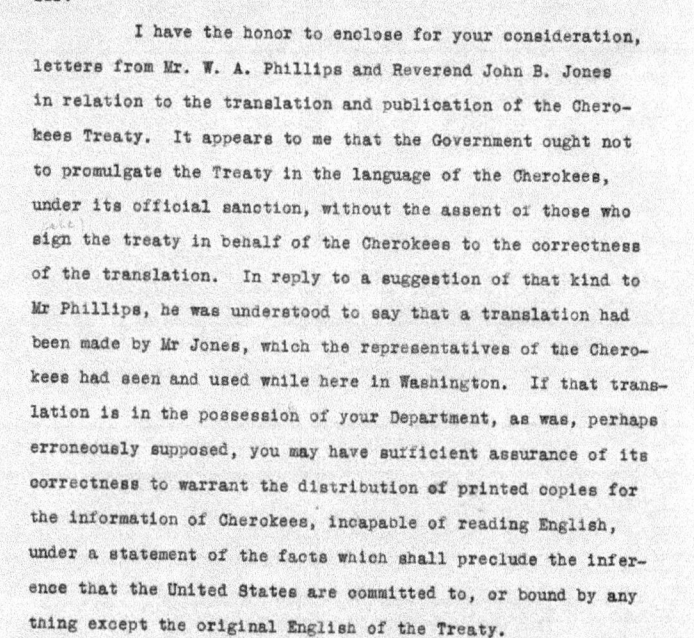

　　I have the honor to enclose for your consideration, letters from Mr. W. A. Phillips and Reverend John B. Jones in relation to the translation and publication of the Cherokees Treaty. It appears to me that the Government ought not to promulgate the Treaty in the language of the Cherokees, under its official sanction, without the assent of those who sign the treaty in behalf of the Cherokees to the correctness of the translation. In reply to a suggestion of that kind to Mr Phillips, he was understood to say that a translation had been made by Mr Jones, which the representatives of the Cherokees had seen and used while here in Washington. If that translation is in the possession of your Department, as was, perhaps erroneously supposed, you may have sufficient assurance of its correctness to warrant the distribution of printed copies for the information of Cherokees, incapable of reading English, under a statement of the facts which shall preclude the inference that the United States are committed to, or bound by any thing except the original English of the Treaty.

　　　　　　I have the honor to be Sir
　　　　　　　　Your obedient servant,
　　　　　　　　　　Henry Stanbery
　　　　　　　　　　Acting Secretary.

#358.

Miscellaneous Letters - August, Part I, 1866.

Rec'd 4th Aug:

                DEPARTMENT of the INTERIOR,
                   WASHINGTON D. C. Aug 4 1866

Sir

      I have the honor to state in reply to the letter of your Department of this date, that this Department will pay the reasonable expenses occasioned by the translation and publication in the Cherokee language and character, of the recent treaty between the United States and Cherokees, on the presentation of proper vouchers approved by the Department of State.

                  Very respectfully
                  Your ob't servt
                  Jas Harlan
                  Secretary

Hon W. H. Seward
  Secretary of State.

#358.

Domestic Letters, Volume 73, page 583.

Department of State,
Washington August 9. 1866.

William J. McDonald
    Chief Clerk Office Secretary of Senate

Sir:

    With a view of facilitating the promulgation of the following named treaties with Indians, I have to request that you will cause six of the printed copies of each of them to be transmitted to this Department, viz: Treaty with the Chippewas of Saginaw Swan Creek, and Black River in Michigan, of October 18, 1864. #333

    Treaty with the Seminoles, of March, 21, 1866. #352
        do   do do Creeks, of June, 14, 1866. #356
        do   do do Delawares of July 4, 1866. #357
        do   do do Cherokees of July 19. 1866. #358

    I am, Sir, your obedient servant,
        R. S. Chew.
        Acting Chief Clerk.

#358.

Miscellaneous Letters - August, Part I, 1866.

RECEIVED,
Dept. of State
Aug 10 1866

Office of Secretary of U. S. Senate,
Washington, August 10 1866.

R. S. Chew Esq
  Acting Chief Clerk,
    State Department,
      Sir,

In compliance with the request contained in your communication of the 9th instant, I herewith enclose six of the printed copies of each of the Indian Treaties therein named.

Yours Respectfully,
W: J: McDonald
Chief Clerk

#358.

Domestic Letters - Volume 74, pages 66 and 67.

Department of State,
Washington August 24, 1866.

Hon James Harlan,
　　Secretary of the Interior.

Sir:

　　Agreeably to a request contained in your letter of the 22^d instant, received today, I have the honor to transmit to you herewith, 250 copies of each of the following named Treaties with Indians, viz:

　　Treaty with the Delawares concluded July 4, 1866. #357
　　　　do　　do　　do Creeks　　do　　June 14, do #356
　　　　do　　do　　do Cherokees　do　　July 9, do #358

Be pleased to acknowledge their receipt. A copy of these Treaties has been sent respectively to the editors of the newspapers designated by you for their promulgation.

　　　　　　　　I am, sir, your obedient servant,
　　　　　　　　　　　　William H. Seward.

#358.

[Transcription of the Original Treaty]

Treaty Between
The United States of America
And The
Cherokee Nation of Indians

Concluded July 19, 1866

Proclaimed August 11, 1866

TREATY

BETWEEN

THE UNITED STATES OF AMERICA

AND THE

CHEROKEE NATION OF INDIANS.

CONCLUDED JULY 19, 1866.
RATIFICATION ADVISED, WITH AMENDMENTS, JULY 27, 1866.
AMENDMENTS ACCEPTED JULY 31, 1866.
PROCLAIMED AUGUST 11, 1866.

ANDREW JOHNSON,

PRESIDENT OF THE UNITED STATES OF AMERICA,

TO ALL AND SINGULAR TO WHOM THESE PRESENTS SHALL COME, GREETING:

Whereas a Treaty was made and concluded at the city of Washington, in the District of Columbia, on the nineteenth day of July, in the year of our Lord one thousand eight hundred and sixty-six, by and between Dennis N. Cooley and Elijah Sells, Commissioners, on the part of the United States, and Smith Christie, White Catcher, James McDaniel, S. H. Benge, Daniel H. Ross, and J. B. Jones, delegates of the Cherokee nation, appointed by resolution of the national council, on the part of said Cherokee nation, which treaty is in the words and figures following, to wit:

> Articles of agreement and convention at the city of Washington on the nineteenth day of July, in the year of our Lord one thousand eight hundred and sixty-six, between the United States, represented by Dennis N. Cooley, Commissioner of Indian Affairs, [and] Elijah Sells, superintendent of Indian affairs for the southern superintendency, and the Cherokee nation of Indians, represented by its delegates, James McDaniel, Smith Christie, White Catcher, S. H. Benge, J. B. Jones, and Daniel H. Ross—John Ross, principal chief of the Cherokees, being too unwell to join in these negotiations.

PREAMBLE.

> Whereas existing treaties between the United States and the Cherokee nation are deemed to be insufficient, the said contracting parties agree as follows, viz:

ARTICLE 1.

> The pretended treaty made with the so-called Confederate States by the Cherokee nation on the seventh day of October, 1861, and repudiated by the national council of the Cherokee nation on the 18th day of February, 1863, is hereby declared to be void.

ARTICLE 2.

> Amnesty is hereby declared by the United States and the Cherokee nation for all crimes and misdemeanors committed by one Cherokee on the person or property of another Cherokee, or of a citizen of the United States, prior to the 4th day of July, 1866; and no right of action arising out of wrongs committed in aid or in the suppression of the rebellion shall be prosecuted or maintained in the courts of the United States or in the courts of the Cherokee nation.

ARTICLE 3.

The confiscation laws of the Cherokee nation shall be repealed, and the same, and all sales of farms, and improvements on real estate, made or pretended to be made in pursuance thereof, are hereby agreed and declared to be null and void, and the former owners of such property so sold, their heirs or assigns, shall have the right peaceably to reoccupy their homes, and the purchaser under the confiscation laws, or his heirs or assigns, shall be repaid by the treasurer of the Cherokee nation from the national funds, the money paid for said property, and the cost of permanent improvements on such real estate, made thereon since the confiscation sale; the cost of such improvements to be fixed by a commission, to be composed of one person designated by the Secretary of the Interior and one by the principal chief of the nation, which two may appoint a third in cases of disagreement, which cost so fixed shall be refunded to the national treasurer by the returning Cherokees within three years from the ratification hereof.

ARTICLE 4.

All the Cherokees and freed persons who were formerly slaves to any Cherokee, and all free negroes not having been such slaves, who resided in the Cherokee nation prior to June 1st, 1861, who may within two years elect not to reside northeast of the Arkansas river and southeast of Grand river, shall have the right to settle in and occupy the Canadian district southwest of the Arkansas river, and also all that tract of country lying northwest of Grand river, and bounded on the southeast by Grand river and west by the Creek reservation to the northeast corner thereof; from thence west on the north line of the Creek reservation to the ninety-sixth degree of west longitude; and thence north on said line of longitude so far that a line due east to Grand river will include a quantity of land equal to 160 acres for each person who may so elect to reside in the territory above described in this article: *Provided*, That that part of said district north of the Arkansas river shall not be set apart until it shall be found that the Canadian district is not sufficiently large to allow one hundred and sixty acres to each person desiring to obtain settlement under the provisions of this article.

ARTICLE 5.

The inhabitants electing to reside in the district described in the preceding article shall have the right to elect all their local officers and judges, and the number of delegates to which by their numbers they may be entitled in any general council to be established in the Indian territory under the provisions of this treaty, as stated in article 12; and to control all their local affairs, and to establish all necessary police regulations and rules for the administration of justice in said district, not inconsistent with the constitution of the Cherokee nation or the laws of the United States: *Provided*, The Cherokees residing in said district shall enjoy all the rights and privileges of other Cherokees who may elect to settle in said district as hereinbefore provided, and shall hold the same rights and privileges and be subject to the same liabilities as those who elect to settle in said district under the provisions of this treaty: *Provided also*, That if any such police regulations or rules be adopted which, in the opinion of the President, bear oppressively on any citizen of the nation, he may suspend the same. And all rules or regulations in said district, or in any other district of the nation, discriminating against the citizens of other districts, are prohibited, and shall be void.

Article 6.

The inhabitants of the said district hereinbefore described shall be entitled to representation according to numbers in the national council, and all laws of the Cherokee nation shall be uniform throughout said nation. And should any such law, either in its provisions or in the manner of its enforcement, in the opinion of the President of the United States, operate unjustly or injuriously in said district, he is hereby authorized and empowered to correct such evil, and to adopt the means necessary to secure the impartial administration of justice, as well as a fair and equitable application and expenditure of the national funds as between the people of this and of every other district in said nation.

Article 7.

The United States court to be created in the Indian territory; and until such court is created therein, the United States district court, the nearest to the Cherokee nation, shall have exclusive original jurisdiction of all causes, civil and criminal, wherein an inhabitant of the district hereinbefore described shall be a party, and where an inhabitant outside of said district, in the Cherokee nation, shall be the other party, as plaintiff or defendant in a civil cause, or shall be defendant or prosecutor in a criminal case, and all process issued in said district by any officer of the Cherokee nation, to be executed on an inhabitant residing outside of said district, and all process issued by any officer of the Cherokee nation outside of said district, to be executed on an inhabitant residing in said district, shall be to all intents and purposes null and void, unless endorsed by the district judge for the district where such process is to be served, and said person, so arrested, shall be held in custody by the officer so arresting him, until he shall be delivered over to the United States marshal, or consent to be tried by the Cherokee court: *Provided*, That any or all the provisions of this treaty, which make any distinction in rights and remedies between the citizens of any district and the citizens of the rest of the nation, shall be abrogated whenever the President shall have ascertained, by an election duly ordered by him, that a majority of the voters of such district desire them to be abrogated, and he shall have declared such abrogation: *And provided further*, That no law or regulation, to be hereafter enacted within said Cherokee nation or any district thereof, prescribing a penalty for its violation, shall take effect or be enforced until after 90 days from the date of its promulgation, either by publication in one or more newspapers of general circulation in said Cherokee nation, or by posting up copies thereof in the Cherokee and English languages in each district where the same is to take effect, at the usual place of holding district courts.

Article 8.

No license to trade in goods, wares, or merchandise *merchandise* shall be granted by the United States to trade in the Cherokee nation, unless approved by the Cherokee national council, except in the Canadian district, and such other district north of Arkansas river and west of Grand river occupied by the so-called Southern Cherokees, as provided in article 4 of this treaty.

Article 9.

The Cherokee nation having, voluntarily, in February, 1863, by an act of their national council, forever abolished slavery, hereby covenant and agree that never hereafter shall either slavery or involuntary servitude exist in their nation othererwise than in the punishment of crime, whereof the party shall have been duly convicted, in accordance with laws applicable to all the members of said tribe alike. They further agree that all freedmen who have been liberated by voluntary act of their former owners or by law, as well as all free colored persons who were in the country at the commencement of the rebellion, and are now residents therein, or who may return within six months, and their descendants, shall have all the rights of native Cherokees : *Provided*, That owners of slaves so emancipated in the Cherokee nation shall never receive any compensation or pay for the slaves so emancipated.

ARTICLE 10.

Every Cherokee and freed person resident in the Cherokee nation shall have the right to sell any products of his farm, including his or her live stock, or any merchandise or manufactured products, and to ship and drive the same to market without restraint, paying any tax thereon which is now or may be levied by the United States on the quantity sold outside of the Indian territory.

ARTICLE 11.

The Cherokee nation hereby grant a right of way not exceeding two hundred feet wide, except at stations, switches, water stations, or crossing of rivers, where more may be indispensable to the full enjoyment of the franchise herein granted, and then only two hundred additional feet shall be taken, and only for such length as may be absolutely necessary, through all their lands, to any company or corporation which shall be duly authorized by Congress to construct a railroad from any point north to any point south, and from any point east to any point west of, and which may pass through, the Cherokee nation. Said company or corporation, and their employés and laborers, while constructing and repairing the same, and in operating said road or roads, including all necessary agents on the line, at stations, switches, water tanks, and all others necessary to the successful operation of a railroad, shall be protected in the discharge of their duties, and at all times subject to the Indian intercourse laws, now or which may hereafter be enacted and be in force in the Cherokee nation.

ARTICLE 12.

The Cherokees agree that a general council, consisting of delegates elected by each nation or tribe lawfully residing within the Indian territory, may be annually convened in said territory, which council shall be organized in such manner and possess such powers as hereinafter prescribed.

First. After the ratification of this treaty, and as soon as may be deemed practicable by the Secretary of the Interior, and prior to the first session of said council, a census or enumeration of each tribe lawfully resident in said territory shall be taken under the direction of the Commissioner of Indian Affairs, who for that purpose is hereby authorized to designate and appoint competent persons, whose compensation shall be fixed by the Secretary of the Interior, and paid by the United States.

Second. The first general council shall consist of one member from each tribe, and an additional member for each one thousand Indians, or each fraction of a thousand greater than five hundred, being members of any tribe lawfully resident in said territory, and shall be selected by said tribes respectively, who may assent to the establishment of said general council ; and if none should be thus formally selected by any nation or tribe so assenting, the said nation or tribe shall be represented in said general council by the chief or chiefs and headmen of said tribes, to be taken in the order of their rank as recognized in tribal usage, in the same number and proportion as above indicated. After the said census shall have been taken and completed, the superintendent of Indian affairs shall publish and declare to each tribe assenting to the establishment of such council the number of members of such council to which they shall be entitled under the provisions of this article, and the persons entitled to represent said tribes shall meet at such time and place as he shall approve; but thereafter the time and place of the sessions of said council shall be determined by its action: *Provided,* That no session in any one year shall exceed the term of thirty days : *And provided,* That special sessions of said council may be called by the Secretary of the Interior whenever in his judgment the interest of said tribes shall require such special session.

Third. Said general council shall have power to legislate upon matters pertaining to the intercourse and relations of the Indian tribes and nations and colonies of freedmen resident in said territory; the arrest and extradition of criminals and offenders escaping from one tribe to another, or into any community of freedmen; the administration of justice between members of different tribes of said territory and persons other than Indians and members of said tribes or nations; and the common defence and safety of the nations of said territory.

All laws enacted by said council shall take effect at such time as may therein be provided, unless suspended by direction of the President of the United States. No law shall be enacted inconsistent with the Constitution of the United States, or laws of Congress, or existing treaty stipulations with the United States. Nor shall said council legislate upon matters other than those above indicated : *Provided, however,* That the legislative power of such general council may be enlarged by the consent of the national council of each nation or tribe assenting to its establishment, with the approval of the President of the United States.

Fourth. Said council shall be presided over by such person as may be designated by the Secretary of the Interior.

Fifth. The council shall elect a secretary, whose duty it shall be to keep an accurate record of all the proceedings of said council, and who shall transmit a true copy of all such proceedings, duly certified by the presiding officer of such council, to the Secretary of the Interior, and to each tribe or nation represented in said council, immediately after the sessions of said council shall terminate. He shall be paid out of the treasury of the United States an annual salary of five hundred dollars.

Sixth. The members of said council shall be paid by the United States the sum of four dollars per diem during the term actually in attendance on the sessions of said council, and at the rate of four dollars for every twenty miles necessarily travelled by them in going from and returning to their homes, respectively, from said council, to be certified by the secretary and president of the said council.

ARTICLE 13.

The Cherokees also agree that a court or courts may be established by the United States in said territory, with such jurisdiction and organized in such manner as may be prescribed by law : *Provided,* That the judicial tribunals of the nation shall be allowed to retain exclusive jurisdiction in all civil and criminal cases arising within their country in which members of the nation, by nativity or adoption, shall be the only parties, or where the cause of action shall arise in the Cherokee nation, except as otherwise provided in this treaty.

ARTICLE 14.

The right to the use and occupancy of a quantity of land not exceeding one hundred and sixty acres, to be selected according to legal subdivisions in one body, and to include their improvements, and not including the improvements of any member of the Cherokee nation, is hereby granted to every society or denomination which has erected, or which with the consent of the national council may hereafter erect, buildings within the Cherokee country for missionary or educational purposes. But no land thus granted, nor buildings which have been or may be erected thereon, shall ever be sold or [o]therwise disposed of except with the consent and approval of the Cherokee national council and of the Secretary of the Interior. And whenever any such lands or buildings shall be sold or disposed of, the proceeds thereof shall be applied by said society or societies for like purposes within said nation, subject to the approval of the Secretary of the Interior.

ARTICLE 15.

The United States may settle any civilized Indians, friendly with the Cherokees and adjacent tribes, within the Cherokee country, on unoccupied lands east of 96°, on such terms as may be agreed upon by any such tribe and the Cherokees, subject to the approval of the President of the United States, which shall be consistent with the following provisions, viz: Should any such tribe or band of Indians settling in said country abandon their tribal organization, there being first paid into the Cherokee national fund a sum of money which shall sustain the same proportion to the then existing national fund that the number of Indians sustain to the whole number of Cherokees then residing in the Cherokee country, they shall be incorporated into and ever after remain a part of the Cherokee nation, on equal terms in every respect with native citizens. And should any such tribe, thus settling in said country, decide to preserve their tribal organizations, and to maintain their tribal laws, customs, and usages, not inconsistent with the constitution and laws of the Cherokee nation, they shall have a district of country set off for their use by metes and bounds equal to 160 acres, if they should so decide, for each man, woman, and child of said tribe, and shall pay for the same into the national fund such price as may be agreed on by them and the Cherokee nation, subject to the approval of the President of the United States, and in cases of disagreement the price to be fixed by the President.

And the said tribe thus settled shall also pay into the national fund a sum of money, to be agreed on by the respective parties, not greater in proportion to the whole existing national fund and the probable proceeds of the lands herein ceded or authorized to be ceded or sold than their numbers bear to the whole number of Cherokees then residing in said country, and thence afterwards they shall enjoy all the rights of native Cherokees. But no Indians who have no tribal organizations, or who shall determine to abandon their tribal organizations, shall be permitted to settle east of the 96° of longitude without the consent of the Cherokee national council, or of a delegation duly appointed by it, being first obtained. And no Indians who have and determine to preserve their tribal organizations shall be permitted to settle, as herein provided, east of the 96° of longitude without such consent being first obtained, unless the President of the United States, after a full hearing of the objections offered by said council or delegation to such settlement, shall determine that the objections are insufficient, in which case he may authorize the settlement of such tribe east of the 96° of longitude.

ARTICLE 16.

The United States may settle friendly Indians in any part of the Cherokee country west of 96°, to be taken in a compact form in quantity not exceeding 160 acres for each member of each of said tribes thus to be settled; the boundaries of each of said districts to be distinctly marked, and the land conveyed in fee simple to each of said tribes to be held in common or by their members in severalty as the United States may decide.

Said lands thus disposed of to be paid for to the Cherokee nation at such price as may be agreed on between the said parties in interest, subject to the approval of the President; and if they should not agree, then the price to be fixed by the President.

The Cherokee nation to retain the right of possession of and jurisdiction over all of said country west of 96° of longitude until thus sold and occupied, after which their jurisdiction and right of possession to terminate forever as to each of said districts thus sold and occupied.

ARTICLE 17.

The Cherokee nation hereby cedes, in trust to the United States, the tract of land in the State of Kansas which was sold to the Cherokees by the United States. under the provisions of the 2nd article of the treaty of 1835; and also that strip of the land ceded to the nation by the 4th article of said treaty which is included in the State of Kansas, and the Cherokees consent that said lands may be included in the limits and jurisdiction of the said State.

The lands herein ceded shall be surveyed as the public lands of the United States are surveyed, under the direction of the Commissioner of the General Land Office, and shall be appraised by two disinterested persons, one to be designated by the Cherokee national council and one by the Secretary of the Interior, and, in case of disagreement, by a third person, to be mutually selected by the aforesaid appraisers. The appraisement to be not less than an average of one dollar and a quarter per acre, exclusive of improvements.

And the Secretary of the Interior shall from time to time, as such surveys and appraisements are approved by him, after due advertisement for sealed bids, sell such lands to the highest bidders for cash in parcels not exceeding one hundred and sixty acres, and at not less than the appraised value: *Provided*, That whenever there are improvements of the value of $50 made on the lands not being mineral, and owned and personally occupied by any person for agricultural purposes at the date of the signing hereof, such person so owning, and in person residing on such improvements, shall, after due proof, made under such regulations as the Secretary of the Interior may prescribe, be entitled to buy, at the appraised value, the smallest quantity of land in legal subdivisions which will include his improvements, not exceeding in the aggregate one hundred and sixty acres; the expenses of survey and appraisement to be paid by the Secretary out of the proceeds of sale of said land: *Provided*, That nothing in this article shall prevent the Secretary of the Interior from selling the whole of said neutral lands in a body to any responsible party, for cash, for a sum not less than eight hundred thousand dollars.

ARTICLE 18.

That any lands owned by the Cherokees in the State of Arkansas and in States east of the Mississippi may be sold by the Cherokee nation in such manner as their national council may prescribe, all such sales being first approved by the Secretary of the Interior.

ARTICLE 19.

All Cherokees being heads of families residing at the date of the ratification of this treaty on any of the lands herein ceded, or authorized to be sold, and desiring to remove to the reserved country, shall be paid by the purchasers of said lands the value of such improvements, to be ascertained and appraised by the commissioners who appraise the lands, subject to the approval of the Secretary of the Interior; and if he shall elect to remain on the land now occupied by him, shall be entitled to receive a patent from the United States in fee simple for 320 acres of land to include his improvements, and thereupon he and his family shall cease to be members of the nation.

ARTICLE 20.

Whenever the Cherokee national council shall request it, the Secretary of the Interior shall cause the country reserved for the Cherokees to be surveyed and allotted among them, at the expense of the United States.

ARTICLE 21.

It being difficult to learn the precise boundary line between the Cherokee country and the States of Arkansas, Missouri, and Kansas, it is agreed that the United States shall, at its own expense, cause the same to be run as far west as the Arkansas, and marked by permanent and conspicuous monuments, by two commissioners, one of whom shall be designated by the Cherokee national council.

ARTICLE 22.

The Cherokee national council, or any duly appointed delegation thereof, shall have the privilege to appoint an agent to examine the accounts of the nation with the government of the United States at such time as they may see proper, and to continue or discharge such agent, and to appoint another, as may be thought best by such council or delegation; and such agent shall have free access to all accounts and books in the executive departments relating to the business of said Cherokee nation, and an opportunity to examine the same in the presence of the officer having such books and papers in charge.

ARTICLE 23.

All funds now due the nation, or that may hereafter accrue from the sale of their lands by the United States as hereinbefore provided for, shall be invested in United States registered stocks at their current value, and the interest on all said funds shall be paid semi-annually on the order of the Cherokee nation, and shall be applied to the following purposes, to wit: Thirty-five per cent. shall be applied for the support of the common schools of the nation and educational purposes; fifteen per cent. for the orphan fund, and fifty per cent. for general purposes, including reasonable salaries of district officers; and the Secretary of the Interior, with the approval of the President of the United States, may pay out of the funds due the nation, on the order of the national council or a delegation duly authorized by it, such amount as he may deem necessary to meet outstanding obligations of the Cherokee nation, caused by the suspension of the payment of their annuities, not to exceed the sum of one hundred and fifty thousand dollars.

Article 24.

As a slight testimony for the useful and arduous services of the Rev. Evan Jones, for forty years a missionary in the Cherokee nation, now a cripple, old and poor, it is agreed that the sum of three thousand dollars be paid to him, under the direction of the Secretary of the Interior, out of any Cherokee fund in or to come into his hands not otherwise appropriated.

Article 25.

A large number of the Cherokees who served in the army of the United States having died, leaving no heirs entitled to receive bounties and arrears of pay on account of such service, it is agreed that all bounties and arrears for service in the regiments of Indian United States volunteers which shall remain unclaimed by any person legally entitled to receive the same for two years from the ratification of this treaty, shall be paid as the national council may direct, to be applied to the foundation and support of an asylum for the education of orphan children, which asylum shall be under the control of the national council, or of such benevolent society as said council may designate, subject to the approval of the Secretary of the Interior.

Article 26.

The United States guarantee to the people of the Cherokee nation the quiet and peaceable possession of their country and protection against domestic feuds and insurrections and against hostilities of other tribes. They shall also be protected against inter[r]uptions or intrusion from all unauthorized citizens of the United States who may attempt to settle on their lands or reside in their territory. In case of hostilities among the Indian tribes, the United States agree that the party or parties commencing the same shall, so far as practicable, make reparation for the damages done.

Article 27.

The United States shall have the right to establish one or more military posts or stations in the Cherokee nation, as may be deemed necessary for the proper protection of the citizens of the United States lawfully residing therein and the Cherokees and other citizens of the Indian country. But no sutler or other person connected therewith, either in or out of the military organization, shall be permitted to introduce any spirit[u]ous, vinous, or malt liquors into the Cherokee nation, except the medical department proper, and by them only for strictly medical purposes. And all persons not in the military service of the United States, not citizens of the Cherokee nation, are to be prohibited from coming into the Cherokee nation, or remaining in the same, except as herein otherwise provided; and it is the duty of the United States Indian agent for the Cherokees to have such persons, not lawfully residing or sojourning therein, removed from the nation, as they now are, or hereafter may be, required by the Indian intercourse laws of the United States.

Article 28.

The United States hereby agree to pay for provisions and clothing furnished the army under Appotholehala in the winter of 1861 and 1862, not to exceed the sum of ten thousand dollars, the accounts to be ascertained and settled by the Secretary of the Interior.

Article 29.

The sum of ten thousand [dollars,] or so much thereof as may be necessary to pay the expenses of the delegates and representatives of the Cherokees invited by the government to visit Washington for the purposes of making this treaty, shall be paid by the United States on the ratification of this treaty.

Article 30.

The United States agree to pay to the proper claimants all losses of property by missionaries or missionary societies, resulting from their being ordered or driven from the country by United States agents, and from their property being taken and occupied or destroyed by *by* United States troops, not exceeding in the aggregate twenty thousand dollars, to be ascertained by the Secretary of the Interior.

Article 31.

All provisions of treaties, heretofore ratified and in force, and not inconsistent with the provisions of this treaty, are hereby reaffirmed and declared to be in full force; and nothing herein shall be construed as an acknowledgment by the United States, or as a relinquishment by the Cherokee nation of any claims or demands under the guaranties of former treaties, except as herein expressly provided.

In testimony whereof, the said commissioners on the part of the United States, and the said delegation on the part of the Cherokee nation, have hereunto set their hands and seals, at the city of Washington, this *ninth* [nineteenth] day of July, A. D. one thousand eight hundred and sixty-six.

         D. N. COOLEY,
           Com'r Ind. Affairs.
         ELIJAH SELLS,
           Sup't Ind. Affs.
         SMITH CHRISTIE,
         WHITE CATCHER,
         JAMES McDANIEL,
         S. H. BENGE,
         DANL. H. ROSS,
         J. B. JONES,
    Delegates of the Cherokee Nation, appointed by Resolution of the National Council.

In presence of—
  W. H. Watson.
  J. W. Wright.

Signatures witnessed by the following named persons, the following interlineations being made before signing: On page 1st the word "the" interlined, on page 11 the word "the" struck out, and to said page 11 a sheet attached requiring publication of laws; and on page 34th the word "ceded" struck out and the words "neutral lands" inserted. Page 47½ added relating to expenses of treaty.
          THOMAS EWING, Jr.
          WM. A. PHILLIPS.
          J. W. WRIGHT.

And whereas, the said treaty having been submitted to the Senate of the United States for its constitutional action thereon, the Senate did, on the twenty-seventh day of July, one thousand eight hundred and sixty-six, advise and consent to the ratification of the same, with amendments, by a resolution in the words and figures following, to wit:

IN EXECUTIVE SESSION, SENATE OF THE UNITED STATES,
July 27, 1866.

Resolved, (two-thirds of the Senators present concurring,) That the Senate advise and consent to the ratification of the articles of agreement and convention made at the city of Washington, on the nineteenth day of July, in the year of our Lord one thousand eight hundred and sixty-six, between the United States and the Cherokee nation of Indians, with the following

AMENDMENTS:

1st. Insert at the end of article 2 the following:
But the Cherokee nation stipulate and agree to deliver up to the United States, or their duly authorized agent, any or all public property, particularly ordnance, ordnance stores, arms of all kinds, and quartermasters' stores, in their possession or control, which belonged to the United States or the so-called Confederate States, without any reservation.

2nd. Strike out the last proviso in article 17, and insert in lieu thereof the following:
Provided, That nothing in this article shall prevent the Secretary of the Interior from selling the whole of said lands not occupied by actual settlers at the date of the ratification of this treaty, not exceeding 160 acres to each person entitled to pre-emption under the pre-emption laws of the United States, in a body, to any responsible party, for cash, for a sum not less than one dollar per acre.

3d. Insert at the end of article 29 the following:
And the Secretary of the Interior shall also be authorized to pay the reasonable costs and expenses of the delegates of the southern Cherokees.
The moneys to be paid under this article shall be paid out of the proceeds of the sales of the national lands in Kansas.
Attest:

J. W. FORNEY,
Secretary.

And whereas the foregoing amendments having been fully explained and interpreted to the aforenamed delegates of the Cherokee nation, they did, on the thirty-first day of July, one thousand eight hundred and sixty-six, give, on behalf of said nation, their free and voluntary assent to said amendments, in the words and figures following, to wit:

Whereas the Senate of the United States did, on the 27th day of July, 1866, advise and consent to the ratification of the articles of agreement and convention, made at the city of Washington, on the nineteenth day of July, in the year of our Lord one thousand eight hundred and sixty-six, between the United States and the Cherokee nation of Indians, with the following

AMENDMENTS, to wit:

1st. Insert at the end of article 2 the following:
But the Cherokee nation stipulate and agree to deliver up to the United States, or their duly authorized agent, any or all public property, particularly ordnance, ordnance stores, arms of all kinds, and quartermasters' stores, in their possession or control, which belonged to the United States or the so-called Confederate States, without any reservation.

2nd. Strike out the last proviso in article 17, and insert in lieu thereof the following:
Provided, That nothing in this article shall prevent the Secretary of the Interior from selling the whole of said lands not occupied by actual settlers at the date of the ratification of this treaty, not exceeding 160 acres to each person entitled to pre-emption under the pre-emption laws of the United States, in a body, to any responsible party, for cash, for a sum not less than one dollar per acre.

3d. Insert at the end of article 29 the following:
And the Secretary of the Interior shall also be authorized to pay the reasonable costs and expenses of the delegates of the Southern Cherokees.
The moneys to be paid under this article shall be paid out of the proceeds of the sales of the national lands in Kansas.

Now, therefore, we, the delegates on the part of the said Cherokee nation, do hereby assent and agree to the said amendments above written, the same having been explained to us and being fully understood by us.
Witness our hands and seals, this 31st day of July, A. D. 1866, at Washington, D. C.

SMITH CHRISTIE. [SEAL.]
WHITE CATCHER. [SEAL.]
JAMES McDANIEL. [SEAL.]
S. H. BENGE. [SEAL.]
DANL. H. ROSS. [SEAL.]
J. B. JONES. [SEAL.]

In presence of—
  D. N. COOLEY,
    Com'r Ind. Affairs.
  J. HARLAN,
    U. S. Ind. Agent.
  CHARLES E. MIX.
  J. W. WRIGHT.
  W. R. IRWIN.

Now, therefore, be it known that I, ANDREW JOHNSON, President of the United States of America, do, in pursuance of the advice and consent of the Senate, as expressed in its resolution of the twenty-seventh of July, one thousand eight hundred and sixty-six, accept, ratify, and confirm the said treaty with the amendments as aforesaid.

In testimony whereof I have signed my name hereto, and have caused the seal of the United States to be affixed.

Done at the city of Washington, this eleventh day of August, in the year of [SEAL.] our Lord one thousand eight hundred and sixty-six, and of the Independence of the United States of America the ninety-first.

ANDREW JOHNSON.

By the President:
  HENRY STANBERY,
    Acting Secretary of State.

INTRODUCTION

It was found that the material within these pages had to contain three separate stipulations in order to be transcribed. Every page to be typed or packet to be considered for each individual involved had to be "Granted." They had to have, #1: a "D" card (Doubtful to be reconsidered); #2: had to have a follow up of a Cherokee by Blood Enrollment Card and #3; had to be entered upon the final Dawes Roll (with a Dawes Number) for the Cherokee.

Not all packets will be transcribed for this series; out of the 3,207 packets only those applying for citizenship under the Doubtful listings and fully accepted while meeting the three stipulations will fall within these pages.

Individuals fully rejected cover a lot of ground and contain no ability for searching out factual receipts in changing a decision from so long ago. "Rejected" cases being added to the "Granted" materials could only over burden these volumes being transcribed while undermining the purpose of searching the accepted bloodlines of true Cherokee descendants.

The rejections cover so much time and testimony even though maybe sometimes treated unfairly or unjustly through the Commission or Government representatives a party's circumstance at this moment can't be overturned and need not be involved with the records transcribed.

These cases are fascinating, it can easily be seen that the authorities in charge of researching the Cherokee people scrutinized these people almost with every intention of disallowing their claims whether blood or no blood. To put it bluntly it would make your blood boil.

There is no doubt that the Cherokee were being overrun by a horde of various groups all with one motive in mind; wanting a share of the take which belonged to only those that truly carried Cherokee blood in their veins.

The circumstances thrown towards the Cherokee as well as the Commission had to have been overwhelming. While at the same time making it easier to incur favor from those in power; those with ample resources sometimes likely slipped through the cracks only to create more wealth for themselves while leaving some in the cold when rightfully citizens.

The theme throughout these cases came to one final conclusion, a stamp; applied on every card in most cases, "Granted."

Time and again you will notice many stamps, Refused; Denied; Citizenship Certificate Issued; Action Approved By Secretary of Interior; Notice of Departmental Action Forwarded Attorney for The Cherokee Nation; Copy of Decision Forwarded Applicant; Record Forwarded Department; Decision Rendered; Granted Decision Rendered; Applicate Granted and Applicants Ordered Enrolled.

The confusion can be seen while many of these stamps were repeatedly applied on a single decision page time and again. So a rule of acceptance or stipulations ("Granted" as applied to the series title) for transcription had to be followed as explained in the first paragraph. In most cases the decisions are made for citizenship concerning individuals from the Western Cherokee.

The whole thing was mass hysteria. The Cherokee were being flooded with every sort of governmental intrusion imaginable. They wanted their own government run by their own laws, their own courts. It's necessary that a brief history be provided below to understand how these historically valuable papers came to be.

They just wanted the U.S. government to keep up their end of the bargain by Treaty; which was to keep the intruders out while the Cherokees took care of building their own lives. But the Government representatives told the Cherokees you either take care of the problem or we take care of the whole thing and take charge of your government thus denying Cherokee sovereignty. When the Cherokee Nation formed its own decision making policies and authorizations the Department of Interior openly overrode many of their decisions with delay tactics as well as overturning legitimate decisions in favor of following in many ways cronyism, bribery or selfish power.

To reiterate, the Cherokee relied upon their leaders to guide them but they ended up hanging in the balance after the Civil War, with their loyalties split worse than ever and their country ravished. Fathers and brothers were off fighting a war that didn't even concern them. By the time the war was over the Cherokee people had lost any form of stability. The men fighting the war came back to the same old political hatreds and in-fighting. The Nation was being overrun with many that claimed they were Cherokee, hoping to benefit from false claims of citizenship. These people, known as intruders, did nothing but make it more difficult for the Cherokees because of the pressures from the Government to control their boundaries. The blood Cherokees that were seeking their homeland were again in question as to who they were. They found nothing but scrutiny and distrust, the war had made them choose a side, and the U.S. Government didn't care for the choice of the majority.

Intruder after intruder was encroaching on Cherokee land and what was to seem like a never ending battle. Many Cherokee citizens lost their rights while intruders that didn't belong stayed using up what little resources there were. The government was telling the Cherokee leaders to settle their own intruder problems or else they would have to intercede. In an effort to clarify who were true Cherokee citizens and who were not, or who had been wrongfully taken off of the rolls, was a problem.

There were part-bloods, full-bloods, and no bloods along with mass confusion, prejudice, vendettas, and deceptions. The intruders wanted a free ride and were willing to use the confusion as a camouflage to achieve their purpose and greed.

This was a situation where the government was threatening to come in and turn the Cherokee Nation into a Federal Territory because it appeared to them that the Tribal Council would not be able to organize an effort to control the problem. But this wasn't the issue at hand as far as the Cherokee were concerned. They felt as if, according to their treaty stipulations, the United States was responsible for intruder removal. They felt as if the United States had let things get out of hand and that the government had not lived up to its contractual agreement. According to treaty stipulations this was true, but, they were told to either come up with a solution or lose their rights as a sovereign nation. Realizing the same things have been stated over and over again it needs to be repeated. The Government moved the natives to Indian Territory, they suffered and many died and now the Government intended on stealing the rest of not only their human rights but their homes forever more.

From William G. McLoughlin's book, *After the Trail of Tears, The Cherokees Struggle for Sovereignty 1839-1880,* it references on page 354, "Still, the Nation remained very uneasy about the fundamental question of its right to define who were its own citizens and its right to expect the United States to remove those who the Nation judged were not. Ever since 1872, federal agents had refused to expel from the Nation those former slaves whom the Nation considered 'aliens' and since 1874, federal agents had been under instructions from the Bureau of Indian Affairs to compile their own list of black or white persons who, in their opinion, had some claim to citizenship despite previous rulings of the Cherokee Courts on their claims."

On page 355-356, "On the basis of the affidavits and reports submitted, the Secretary of the Interior, Zachariah Chandler, sent E.C. Watkins to the Nation in 1875, to investigate the citizenship problem and gather information that Chandler could use to ask Congress to take action on behalf of these 'men without a country.' Watkins reported in February, 1876, that many of those on Ingall's list were 'clearly entitled' to Cherokee citizenship. Oochalata denied it. He counter charged that Ingalls was meddling in Cherokee affairs and wrote to the Bureau of Indian Affairs to complain. Receiving no satisfactory response, he wrote directly to President Grant on November 13, 1876, enclosing a petition from the Cherokees in Cooweescoowee District, complaining that the agent had not removed thousands of intruders in their area though ordered to do so by the Council. Some of these intruders were former slaves from the Deep South, but most were white U.S. citizens from Kansas, Missouri, and Arkansas.

Grant referred this letter to Commissioner J.Q. Smith. Annoyed that Oochalata had gone over the head of the Interior Department to the President, on December 8, Smith wrote Oochalata a long, assertive, and highly provocative letter outlining for the first time the department's position on this question. Smith said that from the evidence he had received, both from various federal agents and from the investigations of E.C. Watkins, the Cherokee Nation had failed to deal consistently and impartially with the problems of former slaves and others who claimed Cherokee citizenship. Therefore, the Bureau of Indian Affairs would continue to compile its own list of those who had "prima facie" evidence for citizenship (whether the Cherokee courts had acted negatively on their claims or not), and it would take no action to remove them until the Cherokees carried out four stipulations to resolve the issue. First, the Council must establish a clear, legal procedure providing due process for adjudicating all prima facie claims. Second, the rules by which such cases were decided must be approved by the Secretary of the Interior to ensure their impartiality.

Third, he suggested that the Cherokee Circuit Courts be designated as the appropriate bodies for such hearings. Finally, claimants' appeals of the decisions of the Cherokee Circuit Courts must be forwarded to the Secretary of the Interior, and no claimant for citizenship should be removed from the Nation until the Secretary had made his own ruling. In effect, Smith asserted the right of the Bureau of Indian Affairs to decide who was and was not a Cherokee citizen. A crucial decision concerning the issue of the sovereignty of Indian nations was about to be reached.

Oochalata was stunned and wrote a 139-page letter to Smith explaining why this procedure was totally unacceptable and contrary to law, treaties, precedent, and the U.S. Constitution."

On page 357, "Acting on instructions from Oochalata, the Cherokee Delegation sent another letter to President Grant on January 9, 1877, insisting that treaty rights, the Trade and Intercourse Act, and precedent gave the Nation the right 'to determine the question as to who are and who are not intruders.' The president referred their letter to Secretary of the Interior, Carl Schurz, who, on April 21, 1877, told the delegation that he supported Smith's four stipulations for settling the matter. Oochalata ignored this response and in August, 1877, sent to the new Commissioner of Indian Affairs, Ezra A. Hayt, a list of all the intruders whom the Cherokees wished to be immediately removed. On Nov. 7, Hayt replied flatly that the Bureau of Indian Affairs would not do so: 'while the department reserves to itself the right to finally determine who are and are not intruders under the law, **it expects the Cherokee Nation Council to enact some general and uniform law by which the Cherokee courts shall hear and determine the rights of claimants to citizenship,** subject only to the review of the Secretary of Interior after a final adjudication has been reached.'"

On page 358-9, "The department's claim that it had the right to judge intruders was, in Oochalata's opinion, 'a new doctrine for construing treaty or contracts in writing, to add to it verbally, a new clause, after the expiration of 92 years from date of that compact or treaty and without the consent of [one] party. . . . It is a dangerous doctrine to which I can never agree.'

While he urged the Council to send a protest through its delegation, Oochalata also asked it to enact a law that would establish a court to decide citizenship claims in a legal and uniform manner. The Council complied on Dec. 5, 1877, but the compromise was fatally weakened by the Council's failure to address two aspects of the law governing the Citizenship Court's actions.

First, the law provided no guidelines for deciding cases that would meet the demands of the Bureau of Indian Affairs, and consequently, in cases involving former slaves, the Citizenship Court relied, as the Cherokee Supreme Court had in 1870-71, simply on the wording in the Treaty of 1866. Second, the Council explicitly refused to allow the right of the Secretary of the Interior to review the decisions of the Court, stating that the Cherokee Citizenship Court was 'a tribunal of last resort.' The three persons appointed to the court, were John Chambers, O.P.H. Brewer, and George Downing. Also referred to as the Chamber's Commission, the Court began to hold hearings early in 1878. All persons claiming to have grounds for citizenship were required to present them or to be declared intruders."

On pages 359-360, McLoughlin continues, "By the end of 1878, Oochalata was struggling to find some new approach to the problem. On Dec. 3, he went over the head of the Bureau of Indian Affairs again, and wrote to Pres. Rutherford B. Hayes, forwarding a complete account of all of the cases adjudicated by the Citizenship Court and asking him to order the expulsion of those rejected and all other intruders. He told Hayes that the Cherokee Nation had an 'inherent national right' to define its own citizens, while the United States had a well-established obligation to expel non-citizens. Suspecting that Hayes would reject this request, Oochalata approached Commissioner Ezra A. Hayt and tried to work out a compromise. He said that the Cherokees would stop confiscating the property of those former slaves judged to be intruders pending the appointment of a joint commission of Cherokees and members of the Bureau to review the rejected claims. Hayt agreed only on the condition that decisions of this commission must be unanimous or the Bureau would retain the right to make its own decision in each case. Oochalata and the delegation could not accept such a condition, and the negotiations broke down. Finally, as a last resort, the council decided to submit a series of questions to the Secretary of the Interior, Carl Schurz, about their right to determine citizenship and the obligation of the United States to accept their determinations. They asked Schurz to present these questions to Attorney General Charles Devens for his opinion. They sent the letter on March 3, 1879, and after Hayt informed Devens of his views on the matter, Devens held hearings at which both sides presented their views. Realizing the importance of the decision, the Cherokees spent the money necessary to hire the best lawyers they could find to assist them. Hayt said that the status of at least one-thousand persons was at issue; the Council argued that there were over twice that many intruders whom the Department was refusing to remove. Throughout the dispute, the Bureau of Indian Affairs declined to act against intruding squatters from Kansas who made no pretense to citizenship.

"The three questions that the Council asked Devens to answer were: Did the Cherokee Nation have the right to determine its own citizenship? Did the former slaves who were citizens have any claim to share in the use of Cherokee land or in the money derived from the sale of the Cherokee land? Was it, or was it not, the duty of the Federal government to remove intruders under treaty stipulations and The Trade and Intercourse Act? By the time Devens sent his reply to Shurz in December, 1879, the citizenship court had heard 416 claims for citizenship and rejected 338."

Devens' opinion was clearly in the negative as far as the Cherokee Nation's sovereignty and decision processes were concerned. On page 364, McLoughlin observes, "Clearly, as since the days of Andrew Jackson, Federal refusal to honor the requirement of removing intruders was to be the means of forcing the Indian nations to do what they did not want to do." Oochalata would not run again as the election of August 1879 neared and Dennis W. Bushyhead became the new chief on August 4, 1879 but in the end it didn't matter who was chief the fight to keep Cherokee sovereignty along with self-government was all but lost by 1880.

On pages 365-366, McLoughlin wrote, "The turning point was reached in 1887 when Congress passed the Dawes Severalty Act. The act expressed what was now the national consensus among white voters (including Indian reformers, railroad magnates, and entrepreneurs)--that the solution to 'the Indian question' was to denationalize the tribes in the Indian Territory, survey and allot their land in severalty, and establish a white-dominated territorial government over 'Oklahoma' the Choctaw word for 'red man.'"

The sovereignty of the Western Cherokee tribe was taken, and to this day they still don't have a true land base as a nation. Even though others were able to take away the land that was promised to remain theirs forever; nobody was able to take away their right and ability to choose who was a true citizen and who was not. The packets transcribed within this series are exactly as they appeared on the microfilm copies from the original court records.

These cases are fascinating because of the generational bloodlines that can be verified by documentation rather than just word of mouth. From Kent Carter's book, *The Dawes Commission,* "The tribe also, continued to oppose the enrollment of whites who had married into the Cherokee tribe. That controversy dragged through the U.S. Court of Claims and then the Supreme Court, which finally ruled in favor of the tribe on November 05, 1906. The court upheld the Cherokee citizenship laws that denied rights to any white who had married into the tribe after November 1, 1877. It also upheld an 1839 law which stated that anyone who moved out of the nation lost their citizenship unless they were readmitted. The applications of 3,341 persons were rejected as a result of this ruling, and the allotment clerks were forced to undo a great deal of their work. With the issue finally settled by the courts, the commission was able to send the first schedule of Cherokees by intermarriage, containing fifty-five names, to the secretary of interior on June 10, 1907. Eventually only 286 people were enrolled as intermarried whites----far fewer than the number put on the rolls of the Choctaw and Chickasaw tribes, which had much more liberal laws on rights based on marriage."[1]

In Cohen's *Handbook of Federal Indian Law* he states, "In the *Cherokee Intermarriage Cases,* the Supreme Court considered the claims of certain white persons, intermarried with Cherokee Indians, who wanted to participate in the common property of the Cherokee Nation. Such persons were permitted by tribal law to be tribal citizens with limited rights in tribal property. The tribe had also provided for the revocation of citizenship rights of a white person who intermarried with a Cherokee if the Cherokee spouse were abandoned or if a widower or widow married a non-Cherokee. The Court found that the Cherokee Nation had authority to qualify the rights of citizenship which it offered to its 'naturalized' citizens. Such tribal action defeated the claims of the plaintiffs:

The laws and usages of the Cherokees, their earliest history, the fundamental principles of their national policy, their constitution and statutes, all show that citizenship rested on blood or marriage; that the man who would assert citizenship

---

[1] The Dawes Commission and the Allotment of the Five Civilized Tribes, 1893-1914 by Kent Carter, pg. 121, para. 2.

must establish marriage; that when marriage ceased (with a special reservation in favor of widows or widowers) citizenship ceased; that when an intermarried white married a person having no rights of Cherokee citizenship by blood it was conclusive evidence that the tie which bound him to the Cherokee people was severed and the very basis of his citizenship obliterated."[2]

An important footnote that Cohen published within his pages for the above paragraph also needs to be studied. He noted, "Under Cherokee law white persons intermarrying with Cherokees before 1875 were tribal citizens for most purposes, including allotment of tribal land, but had no interest in tribal funds except those funds derived from tribal lands. A Cherokee law that became effective in 1875 provided that whites marrying Cherokees had no rights to tribal property but could obtain full citizenship by the payment of $500 to the tribe. In 1877 the tribe provided that no intermarried citizen could obtain any rights to tribal land or funds."[3]

You will also find many of the Doubtful "D" cards as well as "Straight" Cherokee By Blood Roll cards within these pages, establishing each parties "Granted" status.

During many years of study this author has found cases that should have been accepted, especially with the particular documentation presented. It's obvious that reading a little Cherokee history you'd find the problems between the Cherokee and the Government started and continued on for decades from pre-Civil War excelling after and into the early 1900's the troubles continued to brew.

All in all the outcome of the many decisions made should have rendered a different result, not counting the misery of those that wouldn't live to see justice through. Also there have been many cases that would numb the minds of so many. How spent and frail they'd become wondering over and over how their lives could have gotten to this point with such a lack of conversation when they just wanted what was theirs. The years of struggle had given many the hopes that their ancestors were one of those that had a decent claim and an honest consideration. Like any time in history there are political struggles and the human factor that points out man is not perfect. These pages were transcribed with the wish that another person somewhere along the line will find their relation from the past and give them the answers long hoped for. These Cherokee packets or testimonies fill the genealogical curiosity to the brim in helping a descendant to understand part of what their ancestor had to endure at the hands of a bureaucrat following the will of the mindless government and the mindless questioner likely in many cases maybe not all, but with prejudice towards the Native People.

Under a select catalog of National Archive microfilm publication, covering, under a film explanation on page 73, paragraph 2, for M-1186, "The commission enrolled individuals as 'citizens' of a tribe under the following categories: Citizens by Blood, Citizens by Marriage, New Born Citizens by Blood (enrolled under an act of Congress approved March 3, 1905, 33 Stat.1071), Minor Citizens by Blood (enrolled

---

[2] Felix S. Cohen's Handbook of FEDERAL INDIAN LAW 1982 ED. pgs 20-21.
[3] Felix S. Cohen's Handbook of FEDERAL INDIAN LAW 1982 ED. pg 21 footnote16.

under an act of Congress approved April 28, 1906, 34 Stat. 137), Freedmen (former black slaves of Indians, later freed and admitted to tribal citizenship), New Born Freedmen, and Minor Freedmen. Delaware Indians adopted by the Cherokee tribe were enrolled as a separate group within the Cherokee. Within each enrollment category the commission generally maintained three types of cards: 'Straight' cards for persons whose applications were approved, 'D' cards for persons whose applications were considered doubtful and subject to question, and 'R' cards for persons whose applications were rejected. Persons listed on 'D' cards were subsequently transferred to either 'Straight' or 'R' cards depending on the commission's decisions."

Two more points can be made from paragraph 4 on page 73 also. "An applicant's census card number can be determined only by using the final rolls and the accompanying indexes reproduced on roll 1."[4]

"No indexes have been located for the majority of the "D" and "R" cards."[5]

The actual packets transcribed in this series come from National Archive film M-1301, rolls 27-31.

Jeff Bowen
Gallipolis, Ohio
NativeStudy.com

---

[4] American Indians; pg. 73, Para. 4
[5] American Indians; pg. 73, Para. 5

CHEROKEE GRANTED ENROLLMENT CARDS & DAWES PACKETS 1900-1907 VOLUME I

Cherokee D1 - Mary Elizabeth Wicket

CHEROKEE GRANTED ENROLLMENT CARDS & DAWES PACKETS 1900-1907 VOLUME I

Commission to the Five Civilized Tribes,

Muskogee, Indian Territory,

May 11th, 1900

In the matter of the application of Mary Elizabeth ~~Nickel~~ Wicket for enrollment as a Cherokee Indian; being sworn and examined by Commissioner McKennon, she testifies as follows, to-wit:

Q What is your name? A Mary Elizabeth ~~Nickel~~ Wicket.

Q How old are you? A Forty.

Q You are a Cherokee by blood? A Yes sir.

Q Were you born and raised in the Cherokee Nation? A Yes sir.

Q Have you ever been enrolled anywhere else except in the Cherokee Nation? A No sir.

Q You have been on the rolls all your life? A Yes sir I have been on the rolls.

Q Was your mother a citizen by blood? A Yes sir,

Q Was your father also? A Yes sir.

Q Have you any children? A No sir.

Q Where is your present home? A Here in Muskogee.

Q How long have your lived here? A I have been here nine years I think.

Q Were you born in Arkansas? A No sir, I was born in the Cherokee Nation; my parents died, and so I went out to the state of Arkansas and lived with a family out there.

Q How long did you live there, about twenty years? A Yes sir.

Q How old were you when you went out there? A I don't know, - I was about twelve or thirteen years old.

Q And you live there until 1890 and went then to the Territory? A Yes sir.

Q You came to Muskogee then did you? A Yes sir I came to Muskogee.

Q During this time that you were out there did you have any property in the Cherokee Nation? A No sir.

Q When did you first acquire property in the Cherokee Nation? A It has been over a year ago since I got the place in Canadian District

Q How did you get the place there? A I bought it.

CHEROKEE GRANTED ENROLLMENT CARDS & DAWES PACKETS 1900-1907 VOLUME I

Q When? A A year ago last October.

Q From whom,- a citizen or a non-citizen? A He was a citizen.

Q What kind of a place is it- has it got improvements on it? A Yes sir, it has a house and a good well of water.

Q Have ever you lived on it? A No myself, no sir.

Q You have lived here in Muskogee ever since you returned from Arkansas? A Yes sir.

Department of the Interior,
Commission to the Five Civilized Tribes

I hereby certify, upon my official oath as stenographer to above named Commission, that this transcript is a true, full and correct translation of my stenographic notes.

.....M.D. Green.....

Supl.-C.D. #1.

Department of the Interior,
Commission to the Five Civilized Tribes,
Muskogee, I. T., January 15, 1902.

SUPPLEMENTAL TESTIMONY In the matter of the enrollment of MARY E. WICKET as a citizen by blood of the Cherokee Nation

Said Mary E. Wicket being duly sworn by Commissioner T. B. Needles, testified as follows: Examination by the Commission:

Q What is your name? A Mary Elizabeth Wicket.
Q How old are you? A I am 40; I don't know exactly.
Q What is your post office address? A My post office is Muskogee.
Q You appeared before the Commission in May, 1900, and made application for enrollment as a citizen by blood? A Yes, sir.
Q What was the name of your father? A Charles Wicket.
Q Is he living? A No, sir.
Q Was he a Cherokee? A Yes, sir.
Q Were you born in the Cherokee Nation? A Yes, sir.
Q Have you always made the Indian Territory your home? A No, I left the Territory.
Q About how old were you when you left the Territory? A Well, 14 I expect.
Q How long were you gone before you came back? A I stayed twenty years.
Q About how long had it been since you came back? A Been ten years.

CHEROKEE GRANTED ENROLLMENT CARDS
& DAWES PACKETS 1900-1907 VOLUME I

Q After you returned to the Cherokee Nation did you apply to the Council to be readmitted to citizenship? A Yes, sir, I did.
Q Did the Council admit you? A Yes, sir.
Q Have you anhy[sic] evidence of your admission, or have you a certificate? A Yes, sir.
Q Have you the certificate with you? A Yes, sir.

There is offered in evidence a certificate from the Cherokee Commission on citizenship certifying that Mary Elizabeth Williams was admitted to citizenship in the Cherokee Nation on the 7th day of January, 1888. The certificate is signed by J. T. Adair, Chairman of the Commission on Citizenship, C. C. Lipe, Clerk of the Commission on Citizenship; approved and endorsed by J. B. Mayes, Principal Chief of the Cherokee Nation. This document bears the seal of the Cherokee Nation. It will be filed herewith.

Q Now, since your admission to citizenship in 1888, have you resided in the Cherokee Nation continuously? A Not in the Cherokee Nation.
Q Well, in the Indian Territory? A Yes, sir.
Q Were you living here when you were admitted to citizenship? A No, sir, I got citizenship before I come to the Territory.
Q How long was it after your admission before you came here? A I came here in '90.
Q In 1890? A Yes, sir.
Q Well, did you ever come here between the time you were admitted and 1890; is that the first time you came here after you were admitted? A First time I came here to live.
Q Were you living in the Cherokee Nation about 21 years ago? A Twenty-one? Yes? A No, I don't think I was.
Q Then, you don't think your name is on the roll of 1880? A My name wasn't on the roll until I got citizenship.
Q Since your admission have you always been recognized as a citizen? A Yes, sir.
Q Have you always drawn money? A Yes, sir, since I was admitted.

BY MR. W. W. HASTINGS, of Counsel for Cherokee Nation:
Q Where have you lived since 1890? A I have lived here in Muskogee.
Q Come from the State of Texas? A I came from Arkansas.
Q To Muskogee in 1890? A Yes, sir.
Q You have lived here continuously since that time? A Yes, sir.

1896 Census roll of citizens of the Cherokee Nation examined and name of applicant identified thereon, page 82, #2293, Mary E. Widked[sic], Canadian district.
COMMISSION: Did you draw Cherokee strip money? A Yes, sir.
Q Did you draw the money at the time the payment was made to all the other citizens? A What you call the strip money?
Q Yes. A Yes, sir, I drew that money.
Q Did you draw it at the time they were making the payment to all the other citizens?

CHEROKEE GRANTED ENROLLMENT CARDS
& DAWES PACKETS 1900-1907 VOLUME I

A   Yes, sir.
Q   Who drew this money for you? A Mr. W. N. Martin.

1894 Strip Payment roll of Cherokee citizens examined and name of applicant found thereon, page 110, #2319, Bettie M. Wicket, Canadian district.

MR. HASTINGS: Have you any property in the Cherokee Nation?
A   Yes, sir, I own a place in the Cherokee Nation.
Q   When did you acquire it? A It has been three years ago.
Q   Was that the first property you owned in the Cherokee Nation? A Yes, sir.
Q   Three years ago? A Three years ago.
Q   Where is the farm? A Canadian.
Q   How far from here? A Ten Miles.
Q   Did you make it on the public domain or purchase it? A I purchased it.
Q   From whom? A From a Mr. Haines.
Q   You receive rents from it this last year? A Yes, sir, it is not very much of an improvement, not very much land.

COMMISSION: On the 11th day of May, 1900, Mary E. Wicket made application for the enrollment of herself as a citizen by blood of the Cherokee Nation. The testimony taken at that time was found to be incomplete, and the applicant was notified to appear before the Commission again which she does this day in person and makes application to be enrolled. She makes satisfactory proof of her admission to Cherokee citizenship by the Cherokee Commission on Citizenship on the 7th day of January, 1888. She avers that she has been living in the Indian Territory continuously since 1890. She is duly identified on the census roll of 1896 and on the strip payment roll of 1894, and she will be listed for enrollment as a citizen by blood. This testimony will be filed and made a part of the record in Cherokee case No. D.1.

J. O. Rosson, being first duly sworn, states that as stenographer to the Commission to the Five Civilized Tribes he correctly recorded the testimony and proceedings in this case, and that the foregoing is a true and complete transcript of his stenographic notes thereof.

JO Rosson

Subscribed and sworn to before me this February 5th, 1902.

TB Needles
Commissioner.

CHEROKEE GRANTED ENROLLMENT CARDS & DAWES PACKETS 1900-1907 VOLUME I

Department of the Interior,
Commission to the Five Civilized Tribes,
Muskogee, I.T., January 27, 1902.

In the matter of the application of Mary E. Wicket for enrollment as a citizen of the Cherokee Nation.

Upon a review of the testimony in this case, and a consideration of the evidence submitted to the Commission since the date of the original application, it is ordered that the card upon which this applicant was original listed, Cherokee Roll Card Field No. D-1, be cancelled, and that the name of this applicant, Mary E. Wicket, be transferred to regular Cherokee Roll Card, and that she be listed for enrollment as a citizen by blood of the Cherokee Nation.

TB Needles
Commissioner.

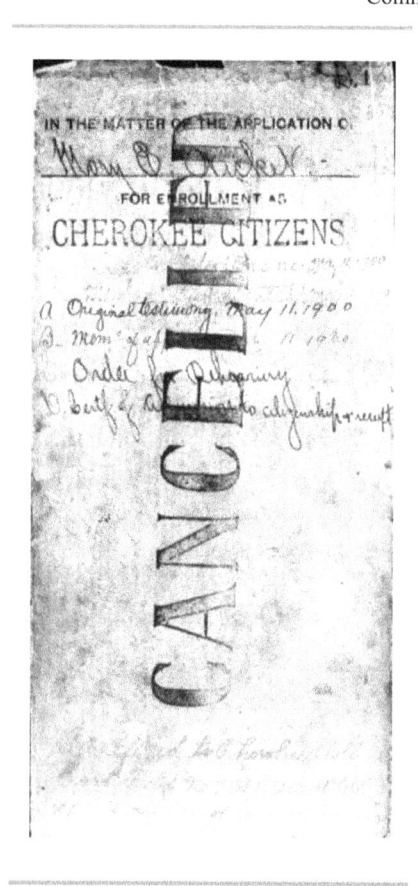

CHEROKEE GRANTED ENROLLMENT CARDS & DAWES PACKETS 1900-1907 VOLUME I

CHEROKEE GRANTED ENROLLMENT CARDS
& DAWES PACKETS 1900-1907 VOLUME I

Cherokee D3 - Gilbert T. Thompson

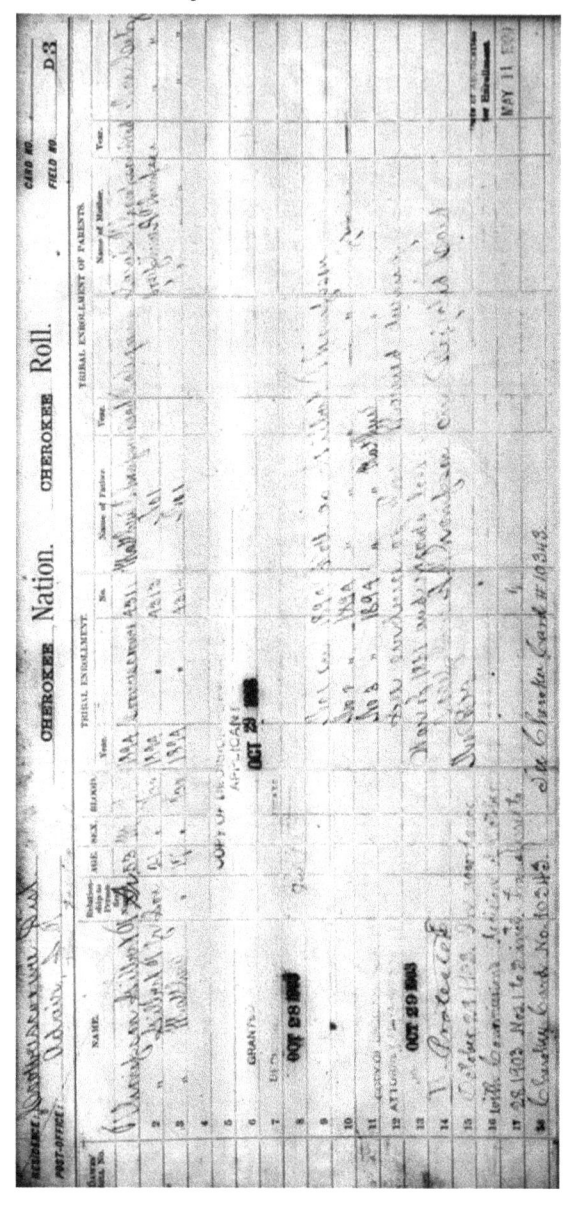

CHEROKEE GRANTED ENROLLMENT CARDS & DAWES PACKETS 1900-1907 VOLUME I

File with C D #4, #5, #6.

MEMORANDUM OF AGREEMENT made and entered into between Francis B. Fite, agent of G. T. Thompson & Sons, of the first and Charles Hawkins of the second part, Witnesseth, That in consideration of the agreement and covenant hereinafter made, the party of the first part demises and leases unto the party of the second part all that farm and improvements known as "Squaw Hollow Ranch", situated near the M. K. & T. Ry., between the towns of Pryor Creek & Adair, containing between 450 and 500 acres in cultivation.

And the said party of the second part stipulates that he will pay for land rented for the year 1897, the sum of $500.00 in cash. Said sum to be paid as soon as the said party of the second part can reasonably gather and sell his crops, all to be paid by Dec. 31 of each year.

It is further stipulated and agreed that said contract may be renewed each year for five consecutive years, each of said years and renewals to end on the 31st day of December. Said renewals to take effect without further covenant or agreement, except that said contract may be terminated, and said right of renewal done away with and abrogated at the instance and desire of either party of this contract. But either party desiring not to renew said contract but to abrogate the same must give the other party 60 days notice of his said intention and desire, otherwise said contract is to remain in full force and effect.

Said Fite further agrees to furnish the said Hawkins with stock-cattle of from one to two hundred head, the said Hawkins at his own expense to feed, care for and maintain said cattle as a compensation for which he is to have one-half of the net profit of said cattle, and at the termination or abrogation of this contract he is to tunr[sic] back to the said Fite the equivalent in number and value of the cattle originally turned over to him by the said Fite. All cattle on said place to belong to F. B. Fite.

It is further agreed and understood between the parties hereto that the said party of the second part is to keep said place in good repair and is to make all reasonable and necessary improvements and all repairs at his own expense, furnishing all material of every kind and description, except that where it is necessary to repair the fences around the fields, that said party of the first part is to furnish the materials

CHEROKEE GRANTED ENROLLMENT CARDS & DAWES PACKETS 1900-1907 VOLUME I

for that purpose. And the said Fite hereby agrees to give the said Hawkins orders upon the proper authorities for all necessary permits for himself and employees, and to do whatever is necessary for him to procure and obtain the same except to pay the necessary sum for their procurement and the said Hawkins hereby covenants and agrees that he is to pay for all permits for himself and employees, and that upon his failure so to do he is to forfeit and pay to the said Fite the sum of $50.00 in each case, the same to be collected and to be a part of the rent of said place, during the whole time that the relation of landlord and tenant may exist between them. The said Hawkins stipulates that in the management and control of said cattle, that he will comply with the laws of the Cherokee Nation in such cases made and provided.

Witness our hands this the 28th day of July A. D. 1896[sic] This Contract is subject to the laws of the Cherokee Nation.

signed, F. B. Fite.
signed, Chas. Hawkins.

I, the undersigned, as stenographer to the Commission to the Five Civilized Tribes, do certify that the above and foregoing is a true and correct copy of the original.

Ella Mieleng

DEPARTMENT OF THE INTERIOR,
COMMISSION TO THE FIVE CIVILIZED TRIBES,
MUSCOGEE[sic], MAY 17th, 1900.

-----o-----

In the matter of the application of the application for enrollment as a Cherokee Citizen by Gilbert T. Thompson.

-----o-----

Mr. Gilbert T. Thompson, being duly sworn, made the following statement, in addition to testimony already taken:

Capt. McKennon: You may just state anything you want to say now.

CHEROKEE GRANTED ENROLLMENT CARDS
& DAWES PACKETS 1900-1907 VOLUME I

A - The statement I wish to make is this; that we felt all the while that we were complying with the Cherokee law in regard to maintaining our citizenship. We would have lived here, only that our profession took us out. We had no charge of our denomination here and couldn't get any work. Myself and two sons are ministers and we had no work to keep us here. We would have live here, only that our profession took us out. We had no charge of our denomination here and couldn't get any work. Myself and two sons are ministers and we had no work to keep us here. We maintained our property right and our citizenship as to voting nowhere also except here, and we felt that we had complied with the law in that particular. If at any time we could have gotten work here in the Cherokee Nation in our church, or even in the Northern branch of the Prasbyterian[sic] Church, we would have moved here. According to the agreement between the Northern and Southern churches, we occupy the Choctaw and the Chickasaw, and the Northern preachers occupy the Creek Nation and the Cherokee and the Seminoles. That is the agreement between us, just as we do in foreign countries. Owing to that fact it has been impossible for me to get work here. The Northern brethren always give their own applicants the preference, and it has just kept us out in that way, but we have from time to time visited the Nation and voted in the Nation and maintained our property rights all the while.

Mr. Bixby: What do you mean by maintaing[sic] your property rights?

A - We understand that when one moves out of the Nation with their effects that they forfeit citizenship, but we did not move our effects, that is our property.

Q - You have a farm here? A - Yes, sir.

Q - What personal property have you in the Cherokee Nation; any personal property?

A - We have cattle and horses and things of that kind, and farm implements.

Q - You own a farm stocked with cattle and horses?

A - Yes, sir, most of the while we have had it stocked. Sometimes we would run out of cattle to a limited extent, but we had a few all the time.

Q - When you would come back to the Nation do you go to this place and live there?

A - Yes, sir, every time we come back we go there and remain there the while. Of course I can't say that we lived there in the sense that one would live a month or two or three, but we would stay a week or ten days; that is about all the living we did there.

Q - How did you first become a citizen of the Cherokee Nation?

A - Regularly before a citizenship court or commission, I don't remember the technical name, of the Cherokee Nation.

Q - How many years ago? A - 17 years ago, in August or September. The record will show.

Q - How much of that 17 years have you lived in the Cherokee Nation?

A - I can't say that we have lived here more than about a year and a half, I have stayed here and worked here. I preached one year at Tahlequah, had charge of the Presbyterian Church there.

Q - How long is it since you have been here preceding this trip?

A - It has been about three yeats[sic]; but I would have been here every year, but I suppose you know that ministers are poorly paid and have no money to travel on. It would suit me very well to come here every year, but our work is such we can't live here and not having the money to travel on we couldn't come just when we would like to.

Capt. McKennon: You are a minister of the Presbyterian Church, how long have you been?

A - Been a minister of the Presbyterian Church I suppose 25 or 30 years.

Q - Continuously in the ministry?

A - I haven't done a thing but preach the Gospel.

Q - you[sic] have two sons who are minister too? A - yes, sir.

Q - How long have they been preaching?

A - One of them has been preaching about ten years, and the other about four.

Q - They have regular charges, have they? A - Yes, sir.

Q - During all that time?

A - Yes, sir, all the while and they were in school; they had to go to a seminary and colleges, and they both made trips to Europe to school, the studied in Edinburgh during a year, and the youngest one has just returned a few months ago. The church gave him the vacation and he has gone back to work. The spirit of the government of the Presbyterian Church requires all of the ministers to keep at work. We have to

CHEROKEE GRANTED ENROLLMENT CARDS
& DAWES PACKETS 1900-1907 VOLUME I

have churches, and report twice a year where we are and what we are doing, and we do not allow any idlers in our church or any local preachers. We require all to have churches and we have tried to comply with the requirements of our church and also as we understood it, the laws of the Nation, in maintaining our rights. If we failed, we didn't aim to do it.

-----o-----

Bruce C. Jones, being duly sworn, says that as Stenographer to the Commission to the Five Civilized Tribes, he reported in full the testimony of the above named witness, and that the foregoing is a true and complete transcript of his stenographic notes.

<u>Bruce C Jones</u>

Subscribed and sworn to before me this 17th day of May, 1900.

<u>A S McKennon</u>
Comm

Commission to the Five Civilized Tribes,
Muskogee, Indian Territory,
May 11th, 1900.

In the matter of the application of Gilbert T. Thompson for enrollment as a Cherokee citizen; being sworn and examined by Commissioner McKennon he testified as follows:

Q   What is your name? A Gilbert T. Thompson.
Q   How old are you? A Fifty-three years old.
Q   Were you ever enrolled in Cooweescoowee District? A My property is there.
Q   When were you admitted? A It was up before the Council in 1883.
Q   You have been recognized as a citizen all the while since that time?
A   Yes sir, all along; my property is here, and I have voted here.
Q   What is your wife's name? A Josephine A.
Q   Have you got a marriage certificate? A No sir, I married in the State.
Q   She was never admitted? [sic] Well she has been admitted like they admit the all of them I suppose; she is not a citizen by blood.
Com'r McKennon: If she is a white woman you would have to marry her according to Cherokee law in order that she might be enrolled. If they had admitted her with you that would have been different.
Q   What are the names of your children living with you? A Cleo Thompson, she is married.
Q   What is the next child? A Gilbert Thompson Jr.
Q   Next? A Matthew, aged seventeen.

CHEROKEE GRANTED ENROLLMENT CARDS & DAWES PACKETS 1900-1907 VOLUME I

Department of the Interior,
Commission to the Five Civilized Tribes

I hereby certify, upon my official oath as stenographer to above named Commission, that this transcript is a true, full and correct translation of my stenographic notes.

....M.D. Green......

PT "R"

Cherokee D-3

Department of the Interior,
Commission to the Five Civilized Tribes,
Muskogee, I.T., February 3, 1902.

SUPPLEMENTAL TESTIMONY ON BEHALF OF APPLICANT, In the matter of the application of Gilbert T. Thompson, Jr. for enrollment as a Cherokee citizen.

Appearances:
Applicant present in person;
W.W. Hastings, of attorneys for the Cherokee Nation.

GILBERT T. THOMPSON JR., being sworn and examined testified as follows:
BY COMMISSION:
Q What is your name? A Gilbert T. Thompson.
Q How old are you? A I am 23.
Q What is your post-office address? A Muskogee.
Q Did your father make application for your enrollment in May 1900 as a citizen of the Cherokee Nation? A Yes sir.
Q What is your father's name? A The same as mine.
Q Gilbert T. Thompson? A Yes sir.
Q Is your father living? A Yes sir.
Q What is the name of your mother? A Josephine Amanda.
Q Is she living? A Yes sir.
Q You claim your right to enrollment through your father? A Yes sir, as a Cherokee citizen.
Q Where were you born? A In Tennessee.
Q How long did you live in Tennessee before you came to the Cherokee Nation?
A I lived there about five years; I was very small at that time.
Q Did you then come to the Cherokee Nation with your parents? A Yes sir.
Q How long did you continue to reside here? A One year I believe.
Q Where did you go then? A They went to the southern part of Missouri.
Q How long did they reside there? A Something like four or five years, about.

CHEROKEE GRANTED ENROLLMENT CARDS
& DAWES PACKETS 1900-1907 VOLUME I

Q Then where did they go? A They went back to Texas I believe, yes, went to Texas.
Q How long did they reside in Texas? A One year.
Q Where did they move to then? A Went back up to the Northern part of Missouri.
Q How long did they reside there? A I don't really remember, a year or two.
Q Where did the go then? A Went from there to Texas, no from there to Kentucky; I went to Texas to school; I didn't take that trip with them.
Q You went from Missouri to Texas to school? A Yes sir.
Q How long did you remain in Texas attending school? A I was there four years.
Q How old were you when you finished school? A I was 18 when I finished that school, then I attended another school and took the post-graduate lectures for three years.
Q In Texas? A Yes sir, from that school, I was in North Carolina however, and was taking the post graduate course in Texas all the time.
Q What were you doing when you reached your majority? A At the time I reached my majority I wasn't doing anything just at that time.
Q Where were you living at that time? A In North Carolina.
Q How long after you became of age before you came out to the Territory?
A Hardly a year.
Q How old were you when you first came here the last time? A I was [answer on curled corner of page]
Q Was your father ever admitted to citizenship in the Cherokee Nation? A Well I think, yes I think the whole family were in '82, and I was admitted about that time I believe myself, with them.
  BY COMMISSION: From the records of the Cherokee Nation on page 171 Case No. 164, from the docket of the Commission on Citizenship for the years 1880 to 1884, inclusive, it appears that Gilbert Taylor Thompson and his wife, Josephine A Thompson, together with various other persons, among whom appears the name of Gilbert Taylor Thompson Jr., were admitted to citizenship in the Cherokee Nation, on the 4th day of September 1883, by the Cherokee Commission on Citizenship.

  BY MR. HASTINGS:
Q What is the exact date of your birth? A September 11, 1878, or '9, let's see.
Q You were 23 years old last September? A Yes sir.
Q It would be '78? A Yes sir, that's right, '78.
Q How long have you been in the Indian Territory this time?
A I have been in the Indian Territory about 16 months.
Q Continuously? A Continuously.
Q You came here then about October 1900? A Yes sir, I came in October, 1900.
Q You stated that you lived here about a year in ;83 after you were admitted?
A Yes sir.
Q Then from that time until October of 1900 you have lived where you state in your testimony? A Yes sir.
  BY COMMISSION:
Q Is your father a Minister of the Gospel? A Yes sir.
Q To what denomination does he belong? A He is a Presbyterian.

CHEROKEE GRANTED ENROLLMENT CARDS
& DAWES PACKETS 1900-1907 VOLUME I

BY COMMISSION: On May 11, 1900, application was made for the enrollment of Gilbert T. Thompson, Jr., by his father, Gilbert T. Thompson, as a citizen of the Cherokee Nation. The testimony taken at that time was found to be incomplete and the applicant this day appears and gives further testimony as regards his application.

It appears that he was admitted to citizenship in the Cherokee Nation by an act of the Cherokee Commission on Citizenship on the 4th day of September, 1883, and that he resided in the Cherokee Nation about one year after his admission, since which time he has been making his home in the States, since which time he has been making his home in the States, having returned to the Cherokee Nation in October, 1900, where he has since resided.

The applicant is not identified on the Cherokee Census Roll of 1896, but is identified on the pay roll of 1894 and not on the authenticated roll of 1880. By reason of the fact that he has not resided in the Territory continuously since he reached his majority, final judgment as to his application for enrollment as a citizen of the Cherokee Nation will be suspended, and his name will remain on doubtful Cherokee card No. 3, awaiting further testimony as to the residence of his parents.

APPLICANT:
Since my majority I have been continuously in school and would have come to the Territory had I been out of school; and I have never cast a vote since I have been out of the Cherokee Nation at all. I always held this as my home here, this town, that is, Muskogee.

BY MR. HASTINGS:
Q Not married are you? A No sir. I am not married.

1894 pay roll of citizens of the Cherokee Nation examined and applicant identified on page 317 No. 4313 Gilbert Thompson Jr., Cooweesooowee[sic] District.

BY COMMISSION:
Q Were you enrolled in 1896 Mr. Thompson? A I was absent from the Territory at that time; I was too young to know anything about it. I was under age; I was at school down here in Sherman, at the time, however.

1896 census roll of citizens of the Cherokee Nation examined and applicant not identified thereon.

M.D. Green, being first duly sworn, states that as stenographer to the Commission to the Five Civilized Tribes he correctly recorded the testimony and proceedings in this case and that the foregoing is a true and complete transcript of his stenographic notes thereof.

MD Green

CHEROKEE GRANTED ENROLLMENT CARDS & DAWES PACKETS 1900-1907 VOLUME I

Subscribed and sworn to before me this February 4, 1902.

T B Needles

File in C D # 3 # 4 # 5
Cherokee D - 6

Department of the Interior,
Commission to the Five Civilized Tribes,
Muskogee, I. T. February 4, 1902.

SUPPLEMENTAL TESTIMONY ON BEHALF OF APPLICANT, In the matter of the application of James K. Thompson for enrollment as a citizen by blood of the Cherokee Nation.

Appearances:
Applicant in person,
W. W. Hastings, of attorneys for the Cherokee Nation,

JAMES K. THOMPSON, being sworn and examined testified as follows:

Q What is your name? A James K. Thompson.
Q How old are you? 28
Q What is your post office address? A Muskogee, I think it was down there before as Adair, but I am living here now; I have charge of the Presbyterian Church, regular pastor.
Q Did you appear before the Commission in 1900 and make application for yourself as a citizen of the Cherokee Nation? A Yes sir.
Q What is the name of your father? A G. T. Thompson.
Q Is he living or dead? A Living
Q What is the name of your mother? A Josephine A. Thompson.
Q Is she living? A Yes sir.
Q You claim a right for enrollment through your father or through your mother?
A Through my father.
Q Where were you born? A Born at Tunnell[sic] Hill, Georgia.
Q How long did you continue to reside there after your birth? A I don't know exactly; father moved to Tennessee when I was quite a small boy, infant.
Q How long did you reside in Tennessee? A Until '82 I believe it was.
Q Then did you come to the Cherokee Nation? A Yes sir.
Q Were you admitted to citizenship in the Nation by an Act of the Cherokee National Council? A Yes sir, I don't remember, I was only a boy then, possibly about '83, I was about nine or ten years old I think.

BY COMMISSION: It appears from the records of the Cherokee Nation, that the applicant and his father were admitted to citizenship in the Cherokee Nation on the 4th day of September 1883, by an act of the Cherokee Commission on Citizenship.

CHEROKEE GRANTED ENROLLMENT CARDS & DAWES PACKETS 1900-1907 VOLUME I

Q How long did you continue to reside in the Cherokee Nation after you were admitted to citizenship.[sic] A I don't know just how long father was here possibly about a year.
Q Where did you go then? A He went to Springfield, Missouri.
Q Did you go with him? A Yes sir, yes, I was a minor you see and had to; it was the only thing I could do.
Q How long did you reside at Springfield, Missouri? A Stayed there I think about four years.
Q Then where did you go? A He went and we went with him to Texas, to McKinney, Texas; he was a minister you know and was called to the church at McKinney, and I was about 14 I think at the time.
Q How long did he reside in Texas? A He stayed there for two, three I think that time about three years.
Q Did you accompany him when he left Texas? A He left us in College at Sherman.
Q At Sherman, Texas? A Yes, sir.
Q How long did you continue to attend school there? A I stayed there for one year after father left. I was then just eighteen years old.
Q Where did you go then? A I went to Kentucky and attended school there.
Q When did you finish your school? A My schooling in my seminary course in May 1896.
Q Did you attend school again after that? A Yes sir, I went abroad for a while in Scotland.
Q When did you return to this country, that is to the United States? A I came back in March, May, April, just about two years ago.
Q You had then reached your majority? A Yes.
Q How old were you at that time? A I was a little past 26.
Q Had you been attending school continuously from the time you left your father there in Sherman, Texas, up until the time you returned from Scotland? A Well with a little intermission while I was supplying the church in Texas. I was simply a stated supply looking to my final settlement in this country, but I was doing church work off and on. I hadn't completed it.
Q When was the frst[sic] time you came to the Cherokee Nation after your admission in '83? A You mean to live?
Q Yes, when did you come back, how long have you been here the last time?
A Oh, I have been here simply a month, to live; I came here January 1st.
Q Where did you come from? A I came from Calvert, Texas.
Q Have you attended school any since your return from Scotland? A No sir.
Q You have been a minister since that time? A Yes sir. In my profession we go where we are called, and as soon as I was called to the Nation- of course it is in the Creek Nation, I accepted; I am in charge of the Presbyterian Church.
Q As a matter of fact you have never resided in the Cherokee Nation since your admission? Up until the present time? A No sir, when the 1896 roll was made I was a stated supply in the church at Texarkana, Arkansas, and I knew nothing about any roll; I came immediately from the Seminary.

1896 roll of citizens of the Cherokee Nation examined and applicant not identified thereon.

CHEROKEE GRANTED ENROLLMENT CARDS & DAWES PACKETS 1900-1907 VOLUME I

1894 pay roll of citizens of the Cherokee Nation examined and applicant identified thereon. On page 317, No 4316, James K. Thompson, Cooweescoowee District.

BY MR. HASTINGS:
Q Are you married? A Yes sir.
Q How long have you been married? A I have been married two years let's see, married the 3rd day of October, 1899.
Q Two years last October? A Yes sir.
Q Where were you married? A Married in Texas. Calvert, Texas, where I was preaching at the time.
Q You came here the first of January to the Creek Nation, Muskogee?
A Yes sir.

BY COMMISSION: On the 11th day of May, 1900, James K. Thompson came before the Commission and made application for the enrollment of himself as a citizen by blood of the Cherokee Nation. The testimony taken at that time was found to be incomplete, and the applicant this day appears and gives further testimony as regards his application.

It appears from the records of the Cherokee Nation that he was duly admitted to citizenship by an act of the Cherokee National Council on the 4th day of September, 1883; it appears from the testimony that he only resided in the Cherokee Nation one year subsequent to his admission to citizenship, since which time he has not resided in the Cherokee Nation.

He returned to the Indian Territory in January 1902, and since that time has resided in Muskogee, Indian Territory. He is not identified on the Cherokee census roll of 1896, but is duly identified on the pay roll of 1894. By reason of the fact that the applicant has not resided in the Cherokee Nation since his admission to citizenship, final judgment as to his application will be suspended, and his name will remain on Doubtful card #6. The final decision of the Commission will be made known to the applicant when the same is rendered.

M. D. Green being first duly sworn, states that as stenographer to the Commission to the Five Civilized Tribes he correctly recorded the testimony and proceedings in this case and that the foregoing is a true and complete transcript of his stenographic notes thereof.   Signed,   M. D. Green.
Subscribed and sworn to before me this February 4, 1902.
            signed,   T. B. Needles,
                                            Commissioner.

I, the undersigned, as stenographer to the Commission to the Five Civilized Tribes, do certify that the above and foregoing is a true and correct copy of the original transcript.
                                    Ella Mieleng

CHEROKEE GRANTED ENROLLMENT CARDS & DAWES PACKETS 1900-1907 VOLUME I

File in Doubtful Cherokee #3, #4, #5.

"R"

Cherokee D - 6

Department of the Interior,
Commission to the Five Civilized Tribes,
Muskogee, I. T. February 12, 1902.

SUPPLEMENTAL TESTIMONY ON BEHALF OF APPLICANT, in the matter of the application of James K. Thompson for enrollment as a citizen of the Cherokee Nation, by blood; being sworn and examined he testified as follows:

Appearances:
Applicant in person.
BY COMMISSION:

Q What is your name? A James K. Thompson.
Q How old are you? A 28 years old.
Q What is your post office address? A Muskogee.
Q You were an applicant before this Commission for enrollment as a citizen by blood of the Cherokee Nation? A Yes sir.
Q You desire to make a statement relative to your residence? A Yes.
Q Just state briefly. A The fact that I have always considered the Indian Territory was my domicile and with that in view I have never at any time exercised the right of franchise in any of the States, though I am in my 29th year, feeling that that might jeopardise[sic] possibly the interest here which I considered always to be mine. Besides this, in 1894 I believe it was, the sum of money something over two hundred dollars that was paid to each of the Cherokee citizens, received by myself, was all turned back into our place close to Adair in the Cherokee Nation, on improvements. It was not used at all but turned back into the place for improvement.
Q Have you anything else that you desire to state relative to your enrollment? A I think these two points cover all; only that I have looked forward always to coming back and had simply waited for an opportunity to come, and when the opportunity came I returned here, at the first opportunity.
Q I believe the fact was brought out that you were a minister of the Gospel?
A Yes sir, being a minister of course I go where I have an opportunity to go and am sent; our church is'nt[sic] strong in the territory, relatively strong, of course, and the pulpits have all been filled, but now I am staying here permanently, it is of course supposed to be permanently depends on the church, at Muskogee as pastor of the First Presbyterian church.

BY COMMISSION: This testimony will be filed and made part of the record in the Cherokee case No D - 6.

CHEROKEE GRANTED ENROLLMENT CARDS & DAWES PACKETS 1900-1907 VOLUME I

M. D. Green being first duly sworn, states that as stenographer to the Commission to the Five Civilized Tribes he correctly recorded the testimony and proceedings in this case and that the foregoing is a true and complete transcript of his stenographic notes thereof.
     Signed,   M. D. Green.
Subscribed and sworn to before me this February 12, 1902.
     Signed,   T. B. Needles, Commissioner.

I, the undersigned as stenographer to the Commission to the Five Civilized Tribes do certify that the above and foregoing is a true copy of the original transcript.

          Ella Mieleng

File in C D #3, #4, #5.

Cherokee "D" - 6

      Department of the Interior,
    Commission to the Five Civilized Tribes,
     Muskogee, I. T. February 14, 1902.

SUPPLEMENTAL TESTIMONY ON BEHALF OF APPLICANT, in the matter of the application of James K. Thompson for enrollment as a Cherokee citizen.

  Appearances:
      Applicant in person.
JAMES K. THOMPSON; being sworn and examined, testified as follows:
BY COMMISSION:
Q What is your name? A James K. Thompson.
Q How old are you? A 28
Q What is your post office address? A Muskogee.
Q Are you an applicant before this Commission for enrollment as a Cherokee?
A Yes sir.
Q In answer to the question asked you when you appeared before the Commission to give supplemental testimony on the 4th day of February 1902, "Q, As a matter of fact you have never resided in the Cherokee Nation since your admission up ujtil[sic] the present time?" You answered "No sir." "When the 1896 roll was made I was a stated supply in the church at Texarkana, Ark and knew nothing about any roll; I came immediately from the seminary."
A Well, that was the question. I misunderstood the purport of it; of course I was admitted to citizenship by an act of the Council; I was a minor at the time and of course don't remember the exact transaction, but I was admitted along with the family, father's family, and he resided for twelve months in the Territory, in the Cherokee Nation, at Tahlequah.
Q That was in '83 or '84? A '83, yes sir; it was the fall of '83 or '84.

CHEROKEE GRANTED ENROLLMENT CARDS & DAWES PACKETS 1900-1907 VOLUME I

Q Any other statement you desire to make? A No, I think,-yes the point with regard to the establishment of our home, when we established our citizenship to foresee that we were establishing our home and when I individually went away I knew nothing about the whys and wherefores, I knew nothing about it; I was nine years old. And I have always felt as I grew up to manhood that I would return to take up my interest.
Q You submit this case now to the Commission for final consideration?
A Yes sir.
BY MR. HASTINGS: Cherokee Nation submits.

M. D. Green being first duly sworn, states that as stenographer to the Commission to the Five Civilized Tribes he correctly recorded the testimony and proceedings in this case and that the foregoing is [sic] true and complete transcript of his stenographic notes thereof.
signed, M. D. Green.
Subscribed and sworn to before me this February 17, 1902.
signed, T. B. Needles, Commissioner.

I, the undersigned, as stenographer to the Commission to the Five Civilized Tribes, do hereby certify that the above is a full and correct copy of the original transcript.

Ella Mieleng

File with Cherokee D- 3, Gilbert T. Thompson, et al.

"R"

Department of the Interior,
Commission to the Five Civilized Tribes,
Muskogee, I. T., February 15, 1902.

SUPPLEMENTAL TESTIMONY AND PROCEEDINGS In the matter of the application of Gilbert T. Thompson, Sr., for the enrollment of himself and children as Cherokee citizens.

APPEARANCES:
Milton K. Thompson, for the applicants;
W.W. Hastings, attorney for the Cherokee Nation.

BY COMMISSION: There is offered in evidence a memorandum of an agreement made and entered into by and between Francis B. Fite, agent of G. T. Thompson and sons, of the first part, and Charles Hawkins, of the second part, bearing date of July 28, 1896, and same will be filed.

This case is closed by agreement of the parties concerned.

CHEROKEE GRANTED ENROLLMENT CARDS & DAWES PACKETS 1900-1907 VOLUME I

By agreement of the parties concerned it is ordered that all the testimony had in the matter of the application of James K. Thompson, son of Gilbert T. Thompson, be filed and made part of the record in doubtful case No. 3, being that of Gilbert T. Thompson, et al., doubtful case No. 4, being that of Allison Thompson, et al., and doubtful case No. 5, being that of Ernest Thompson, et al.

By agreement of the parties concerned these cases are submitted for final consideration.

M. D. Green, being first duly sworn, states that as stenographer to the Commission to the Five Civilized Tribes he correctly recorded the testimony and proceedings in this case and that the foregoing is a true and complete transcript of his stenographic notes thereof.

MD Green

Subscribed and sworn to before me this February 21, 1902.

T B Needles
Commissioner.

DEPARTMENT OF THE INTERIOR

Commission to the Five Civilized Tribes,

Muskogee I. T. October 16, 1902.

In the matter of the application of Gilbert T. Thompson et al for enrollment as citizens of the Cherokee Nation.

Cherokee D. 3.

Motion to Reopen Case.

Comes now the representative of the Cherokee Nation, and upon examination of the testimony in the above case represents to the Commission that the testimony as to the residence of the applicant is insufficient and therefore moves the Commission that the applicants be again notified by the Commission to appear before the Commission at some convenient date for the purpose of giving additional testimony as to their residence prior to xxxxx and on June 28th 1898 and subsequent thereto, in as much as we deem the testimony upon the question of residence insufficient in this case.

CHEROKEE GRANTED ENROLLMENT CARDS & DAWES PACKETS 1900-1907 VOLUME I

Respectfully,

W W Hastings

Attorney for the Cherokee Nation.

DEPARTMENT OF THE INTERIOR,

COMMISSION TO THE FIVE CIVILIZED TRIBES.

Muskogee, Indian Territory, August 17, 1903.

In the matter of the application of Gilbert T. Thompson, et al. for enrollment as citizens by blood of the Cherokee Nation, consolidating the applications of

Gilbert T. Thompson, et al.,……………....Cherokee D 3
Allison Thompson, et al.,…………….…..Cherokee D 4
Ernest Thompson, et al.,………………….Cherokee D 5

O R D E R.

Motions to reopen each of the above entitled cases for the purpose of introducing additional testimony as to the residence of the applicants therein, were filed with the Commission, October 16, 1902, for and in behalf of the Cherokee Nation.

No legal grounds for reopening said cases have been assigned in said motions and such testimony not being deemed necessary at this time, it is the opinion of this Commission that the motions to reopen said cases should be denied, and it is so ordered.

TB Needles
Commissioner.

COMMISSIONERS:
TAMS BIXBY,
THOMAS B. NEEDLES,
C. R. BRECKINRIDGE,
W. E. STANLEY.

ALLISON L. AYLESWORTH,
SECRETARY.

DEPARTMENT OF THE INTERIOR,
COMMISSION TO THE FIVE CIVILIZED TRIBES.

REFER IN REPLY TO THE FOLLOWING

ADDRESS ONLY THE
COMMISSION TO THE FIVE CIVILIZED TRIBES.

Muskogee, Indian Territory, August 18, 1903.

CHEROKEE GRANTED ENROLLMENT CARDS & DAWES PACKETS 1900-1907 VOLUME I

W. W. Hastings,
    Attorney for the Cherokee Nation,
        Tahlequah, Indian Territory.

Dear Sir:

    There is herewith enclosed a copy of an order denying your motion of October 16, 1902, to reopen for further testimony Cherokee cases D 3, 4 and 5, Gilbert T. Thompson et al.

        Respectfully,

        TB Needles

        Commissioner in Charge.

Enc. D-121

DEPARTMENT OF THE INTERIOR,
COMMISSION TO THE FIVE CIVILIZED TRIBES.

In the matter of the application for the enrollment of Gilbert T. Thompson, Sr. et al. as citizens by blood of the Cherokee Nation, consolidating the applications of

    Gilbert T. Thompson, Sr.,.et al.,...Cherokee D 3
    Allison Thompson, et al.,………..   "   D 4
    Ernest Thompson, et al.,…………..   "   D 5
    James K. Thompson, et al.,………   "   D 6

D E C I S I O N.

    The record herein shows that applications for enrollment as citizens by blood of the Cherokee Nation were made to this Commission, by Gilbert T. Thompson, Sr. for himself, his adult son, Gilbert T. Thompson, Jr., and his minor son, Matthew Thompson; by Allison Thompson for himself and is minor children, Ernest W. and Mamie Thompson; that subsequent to the date of his original application an affidavit was filed with the Commission as to the birth of his minor child, Allison Archibald Thompson, and the same is made a part of the record herein; by Ernest Thompson for himself and his minor children, Allison G., Ernest T. and Hugh C. Thompson; and by James K. Thompson for himself; and that subsequent to the date of his original application an affidavit was filed with the Commission as to the birth of his minor child, Joseph G. Thompson, and the same is made a part of the record

CHEROKEE GRANTED ENROLLMENT CARDS & DAWES PACKETS 1900-1907 VOLUME I

herein. Copies of the testimony taken at Tahlequah, Indian Territory, July 28, 1903, in the case of Cleo T. Reid, et al. are made a part of the record herein.

The evidence shows that on September 7, 1883, the said Gilbert T. Thompson, Sr. and his sons, Allison Thompson, Ernest Thompson, James K. Thompson and Gilbert T. Thompson, Jr., were admitted with others, as citizens by blood of the Cherokee Nation by the duly constituted authorities of said Nation; that the said Matthew Thompson was a minor, and is considered to have been a member of the family of his father, Gilbert T. Thompson, Sr., at the time of the latter's admission to citizenship; that all the said minor applicants herein are the descendants of said Gilbert T., Sr., Allison, Ernest and James K. Thompson respectively; and that all of said descendants, except Matthew Thompson, were born since the admission of their said ancestors to citizenship, as above mentioned.

It further appears that all the applicants herein, except Allison Archibald, Ernest T., Hugh C. and Joseph G. Thompson, are identified on the 1894 Cherokee strip payment roll. The four minor applicants last mentioned are identified by birth affidavits made a part of the record herein.

The evidence further shows that the said Gilbert T., Sr., Allison, Ernest and James K. Thompson removed to and in good faith settled in the Cherokee Nation in 1883 and resided therein about one year; that about 1884 they left the Cherokee Nation and have not since that time and prior to June 28, 1898, resided in said Nation. It does not appear that they ever removed their effects from the Cherokee Nation, or became citizens of any other government. On the contrary, they have each retained interests in property in said Nation for 1883 up to the date of the applications herein. It is considered that the residence of said minor applicants has been the same as that of their said parents.

The evidence further shows that the said Gilbert T. Thompson, Jr. was a minor on June 28, 1898, and his residence up to and including said date is considered to have been the same as that of his father, Gilbert T. Thompson, Sr.

It is, therefore, the opinion of this Commission, following the decision of the Department in the cases of Joseph D. Yeargain, et al. (I. T. D. 2900-1903), and Martha Hill, et al. (I. T. D. 3886-1903), that the said Gilbert T. Thompson, Sr., Gilbert T. Thompson, Jr., Matthew Thompson, Allison Thompson, Ernest Thompson, Allison G. Thompson, Ernest T. Thompson, Hugh C. Thompson, James K. Thompson and Joseph G. Thompson should be enrolled as citizens by blood of the Cherokee Nation, in accordance with the provisions of section twenty-one of the Act of Congress, approved June 28, 1898 (30 Stats., 495), and it is so ordered.

COMMISSION TO THE FIVE CIVILIZED TRIBES.

(SIGNED). *Tams Bixby.*
Chairman.
(SIGNED). *T. B. Needles.*
Commissioner.
(SIGNED). *C. R. Breckinridge.*
Commissioner.
(SIGNED). *W. E. Stanley.*
Commissioner.

Muskogee, Indian Territory,
this **OCT 28** 1904

CHEROKEE GRANTED ENROLLMENT CARDS & DAWES PACKETS 1900-1907 VOLUME I

COMMISSIONERS:
TAMS BIXBY,
THOMAS B. NEEDLES,
C. R. BRECKINRIDGE,
W. E. STANLEY.

ALLISON L. AYLESWORTH,
SECRETARY.

DEPARTMENT OF THE INTERIOR,
COMMISSION TO THE FIVE CIVILIZED TRIBES.

REFER IN REPLY TO THE FOLLOWING
Cherokee D-3-4-5-6.

ADDRESS ONLY THE
COMMISSION TO THE FIVE CIVILIZED TRIBES

Muskogee, Indian Territory, October 29, 1903.

W. W. Hastings,
    Attorney for Cherokee Nation,
        Tahlequah, Indian Territory.

Dear Sir:
    There is herewith enclosed a copy of the decision of the Commission to the Five Civilized Tribes, dated October 28, 1903, in the consolidated case of Gilbert T. Thompson, Sr., et al., granting the applications for the enrollment of Gilbert T. Thompson, Sr., Gilbert T. Thompson, Jr., Matthew, Allison, Ernest W., Mamie, Allison Archibald, Ernest, Allison G., Ernest T., Hugh C., James K. and Joseph G. Thompson as citizens by blood of the Cherokee Nation.

    You are hereby advised that you will be allowed fifteen days from date hereof in which to file such protest as you may desire to make against the action of the Commission in this case, a copy of which protest you will be required to furnish the principal applicant. If you fail to file protest within the time allowed this decision will be considered final.

                Respectfully,

                T B Needles
Enc. D-33.   Commissioner in Charge.

DEPARTMENT OF THE INTERIOR,
    Commission to the Five Civilized Tribes,
    Muskogee I. T. Nov 12, 1903.

    In the matter of the application for the enrollment of Gilbert T. Thompson Sr et al, as citizens by blood of the Cherokee Nation, consolidating the cases of
        Gilbert T. Thompson Sr et al Cherokee ----------D   3

CHEROKEE GRANTED ENROLLMENT CARDS
& DAWES PACKETS 1900-1907 VOLUME I

Allison Thompson   et al   D   4

Ernest Thompson et al   -   -   - --D   5

James K. Thompson et al------------------------- D   6

The Cherokee Nation respectfully dissents from the opinion of the Commission that the above applicants are entitled to be enrolled as citizens of the Cherokee Nation and requests that these cases be forwarded to the Honorable Secretary of the Interior for Review.

Respectfully,

WW Hastings
Attorney for the Cherokee Nation.

J.C.S.   *JCS*

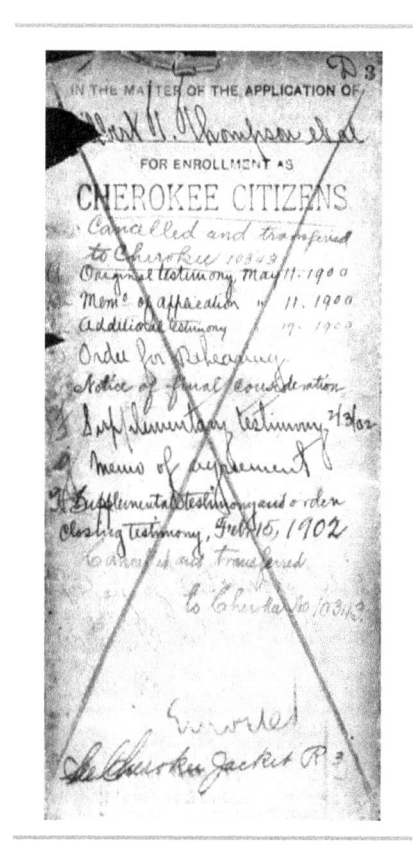

CHEROKEE GRANTED ENROLLMENT CARDS & DAWES PACKETS 1900-1907 VOLUME I

CHEROKEE GRANTED ENROLLMENT CARDS & DAWES PACKETS 1900-1907 VOLUME I

Cherokee D4 - Allison Thompson

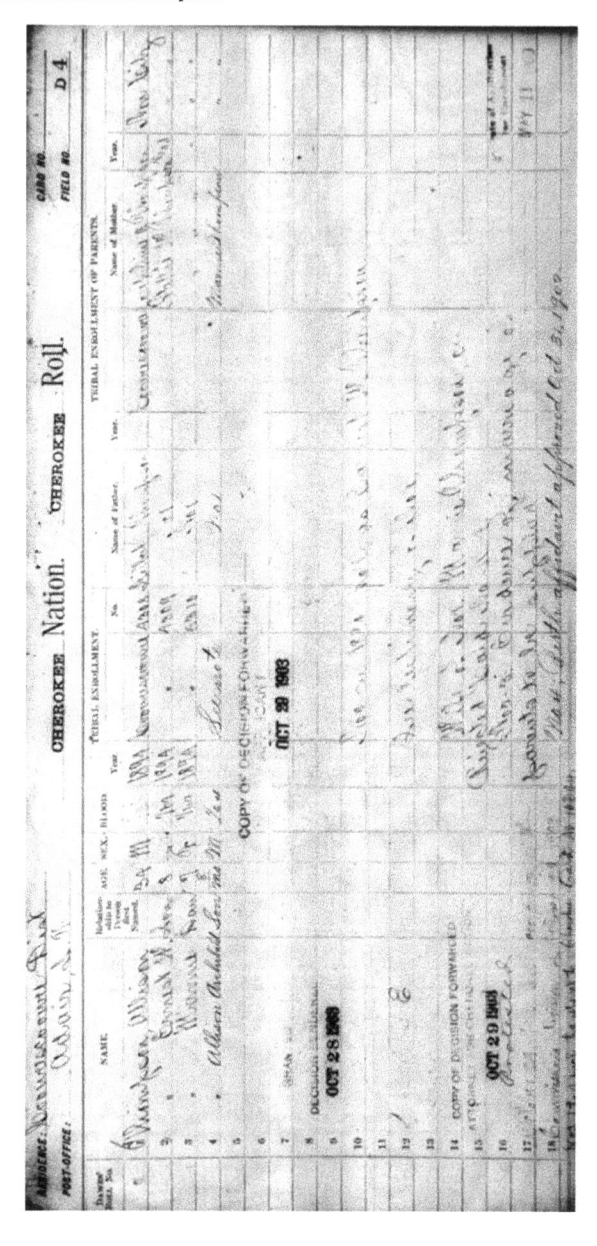

CHEROKEE GRANTED ENROLLMENT CARDS & DAWES PACKETS 1900-1907 VOLUME I

Commission to the Five Civilized Tribes,
Muskogee, Indian Territory,
May 11th, 1900.

In the matter of the application of Allison Thompson for enrollment as a citizen of the Cherokee Nation; being sworn and examined by Commissioner McKennon he testifies as follows:

Q What is your name? A Allison Thompson.
Q How old are you? A Thirty-four.
Q Where do you live? A At Sherman, Texas; I am teaching school there.
Q Where were you born and raised? A I was born in Georgia.
Q How long did you remain here? A I remained here one year, and then went off to school and stain four years, and I have been teaching in Sherman, Texas ever since.
Q You have not resided in the Territory then since 1883? A No sir. I have not been a resident; I have had property here all the time, and I always come up here and vote.
Q What property? A Ranch property up here in Cooweescoowee District and cattle and horses, and at Tahlequah too, I have a town lot over there.
Q Have you any family? A Yes sir.
Q What family? A A wife and two children.
Q What is your wife's name[sic] A Mamie A. She is my second wife.
Q What is her age? A She is twenty-seven.
Q Is she a white woman? A Yes sir.
Q Where were you married? A Mississippi.
Q Has she ever lived in the Territory? A No sir.
Q Never been here? A No sir.
Q Have you got some children? A I have two.
Q What is the name of the oldest? A Ernest W.
Q How old? A He is eight years old.
Q Did he ever live here? A No sir.
Q Your next one? A Mamie.
Q How old is she? A Seven.
Q She ever live here? A No sir.
Q The mother of these children is dead is she? A Yes sir.
Q Was she a white woman? A Yes sir.
Q Where did you marry her? A In Sherman, Texas.
Q Was your mother Cherokee? A No sir, my father was Cherokee, my mother was white.

Commissioner McKennon:
Mamie Thompson, Sherman, Texas.
Your enrollment as an intermarried Cherokee is refused, because you have never resided in the Cherokee Nation.

---   ---

Department of the Interior,
Commission to the Five Civilized Tribes

I hereby certify, upon my official oath as stenographer to above named Commission, that this transcript is a true, full and correct translation of my stenographic notes.

_____M.D. Green_____

CHEROKEE GRANTED ENROLLMENT CARDS & DAWES PACKETS 1900-1907 VOLUME I

File in C D #3, #4, #5.

Cherokee D - 5

Department of the Interior,
Commission to the Five Civilized Tribes.
Muskogee, I. T. February 4, 1902.

SUPPLEMENTAL TESTIMONY ON BEHALF OF APPLICANT, In the matter of the application of James K. Thompson for enrollment as a citizen by blood of the Cherokee Nation.
Appearances:
Applicant in person.
W. W. Hastings of attorneys for Cherokee Nation.

JAMES K. THOMPSON, being sworn and examined testified as follows:
BY COMMISSION:
Q What is your name? A James K. Thompson.
Q How old are you? A 28
Q What is your post office address? A Muskogee, I think it was down there before as Adair, but I am living here now; I have charge of the Presbyterian Church, regular pastor.
Q Did you appear before the Commission in 1900, May and make application for the enrollment of yourself as a citizen of the Cherokee Nation? A Yes sir.
Q What is the name of your father? A G. T. Thompson.
Q Is he living or dead? A Living.
Q What is the name of your mother? A Josephine A. Thompson.
Q Is she living? A Yes sir.
Q You claim a right to enrollment through your father or through your mother?
A Through my father.
Q Where were you born? A Born at Tunnell[sic] Hill, Georgia.
Q How long did you continue to reside there after your birth? A I don't know exactly, father moved to Tennessee when I was quite a small boy, infant.
Q How long did you reside in Tennessee? A Until '82 I believe it was.
Q Then did you come to the Cherokee Nation? A Yes sir.
Q Were you admitted to citizenship in the Nation by an Act of the Cherokee National Council? A Yes sir; I don't remember, I was only a boy then, possibly about '83, I was about 9 or ten years old I think.
BY COMMISSION: It appears from the records of the Cherokee Nation that the applicant and his father were admitted to citizenship in the Cherokee Nation on the 4th day of September 1823, by an act of the Cherokee Commission on Citizenship

Q How long did you continue to reside in the Cherokee Nation after you were admitted to citizenship? A I don't know just how long father was here possibly about a year.
Q Where did you go then? A He went to Springfield, Mo.

CHEROKEE GRANTED ENROLLMENT CARDS
& DAWES PACKETS 1900-1907 VOLUME I

Q Did you go with him? A Yes sir, yes I was a minor you see and had to; it was the only thing I could do.
Q How long did you reside at Springfield, Mo? A Stayed there I think about four years.
Q Then where did you go? A He went and we went with him to Texas to McKinney, Texas; he was a minister you know, and was called to the church at McKinney, and I was about 14 I think at the time.
Q How long did you reside in Texas? A He stayed there for two, three, I think that time about three years.
Q Did you accompany him when he left Texas? A He left us in College at Sherman.
Q At Sherman Texas? A Yes sir.
Q How long did you continue to attend school there? A I stayed there for one year after father left. I was then just eighteen years old.
Q Where did you go then? A I went to Kentucky and attended school there.
Q When did you finish your school? A My schooling in my seminary course in May 1896.
Q Did you attend school again after that? A Yes sir, I went abroad for a while in Scotland.
Q When did you return to this country? that is to the United States? A I came bake[sic] in March, May, April just about two years ago.
Q You had then reached your majority? A Yes.
Q How old were you at that time? A I was a little past 26.
Q Had you been attending school continuously since the time your[sic] left your father there in Sherman, Texas, or up until the time you returned from Scotland? A Well with a little intermission while I was supplying the church in Texas. I was simply a stated supply looking to my final settlement in this country, but I was doing church work off and on. I had'nt[sic] completed it.
Q When was the first time you came to the Cherokee Nation after your admission in '83? A You mean to live?
Q Yes, when did you come back; how long have you been here the last time? A Oh I have been here simply a month, to live; I came here January 1st.
Q Where did you come from? A I came from Calvert, Texas.
Q Have you attended school any since your return from Scotland? A No sir.
Q You have been a minister since that time? A Yes sir. In my profession we go where we are called, and as soon as I was called to the Nation- of course it is in the Creek Nation, I accepted; I am in charge of the Presbyterian church.
Q As a matter of fact you have never resided in the Cherokee Nation since your admission, up until the present time? A No sir, when the 1896 roll was made I was stated supply in the church at Texarkana, Arkansas, and I knew nothing about any roll; I came immediately from the Seminary.

    1896 roll of citizens of the Cherokee Nation examined and applicant not identified thereon.
    1894 pay roll of citizens of the Cherokee Nation examined and applicant identified thereon. On page 317, #4316, James K. Thompson, Cooweescoowee District.

CHEROKEE GRANTED ENROLLMENT CARDS & DAWES PACKETS 1900-1907 VOLUME I

BY MR. HASTINGS:

Q Are you married? A Yes sir.
Q How long have you been married? A I have been married two years, let's see, married the 3d day of October 1899.
Q Two years last October? A Yes sir.
Q Where were you married? A Married in Texas. Where I was preaching at the time, Calvert Texas.
Q You came here the first of January to the Creek Nation, Muskogee? A Yes sir.

BY THE COMMISSION: On the 11th day of May, 1900 James K. Thompson came before the Commission and made application for the enrollment of himself as a citizen by blood of the Cherokee Nation. The testimony taken at that time was found to be incomplete, and the applicant this day appears and gives further testimony as regards his application.

It appears from the records of the Cherokee Nation that he was duly admitted to citizenship by an act of the Cherokee National Council on the 4th day of September, 1883; it appears from the testimony that he only resided in the Cherokee Nation one year subsequent to his admission to citizenship, since which time he has not resided in the Cherokee Nation.

He returned to the Indian Territory in January 1902, and since that time has resided in Muskogee, Indian Territory. He is not identified on the Cherokee census roll of 1896, but is duly identified on the pay roll of 1894. By reason of the fact that the applicant has not resided in the Cherokee Nation since his admission to citizenship, final judgment as to his application will be suspended and his name will remain on Doubtful card #6. The final decision of the Commission will be made known to the applicant when the same is rendered.

M. D. Green being first duly sworn, states that as stenographer to the Commission to the Five Civilized Tribes, he correctly recorded the testimony and proceedings in this case and that the foregoing is a true and complete transcript of his stenographic notes thereof.

Signed, M. D. Green.

Subscribed and sworn to before me this February 4, 1902.

signed, T. B. Needles,
Commissioner.

I, the undersigned, as stenographer to the Commission to the Five Civilized Tribes, do hereby certify that the above and foregoing is a true and correct copy of the original transcript.

Ella Mieleng

CHEROKEE GRANTED ENROLLMENT CARDS & DAWES PACKETS 1900-1907 VOLUME I

File in C. D. # 3, #4, #5.
"R"
Cherokee D - 6

Department of the Interior,
Commission to the Five Civilized Tribes,
Muskogee, I. T. February 12, 1902.

SUPPLEMENTAL TESTIMONY ON BEHALF OF APPLICANT, in the matter of the application of James K. Thompson for enrollment as a citizen of the Cherokee Nation, by blood; being sworn and examined he testified as follows:

Appearances:
    Applicant in person.
BY COMMISSION:
Q What is your name? A James K. Thompson.
Q How old are you? A 28 years old.
Q What is your post office address? A Muskogee.
Q You were an applicant before this Commission for enrollment as a citizen by blood of the Cherokee Nation? A Yes sir.
Q You desire to make a statement relative to your residence? A Yes.
Q Just state briefly. A The fact that I have always considered the Indian Territory was my domicile and with that in view I have never at any time exercised the right of franchise in any of the States, though I am in my 29th year, feeling that that might jeopardize possibly the interest here which I considered always to be mine. Besides this, in 1894 I believe it was, the sum of money something over two hundred dollars that was paid to each of the Cherokee citizens, received by myself, was all turned back into our place close to Adair in the Cherokee Nation, on improvements. It was not used at all but turned back into the place for improvement.
Q Have you anything else that you desire to state relative to your enrollment? A I think these two points cover all; only that I have looked forward always to coming back and had simply waited for an opportunity to come, and when the opportunity came I returned here, at the first opportunity.
Q I believe the fact was brought out that you were a minister of the Gospel?
A Yes sir, being a minister of course I go where I have an opportunity to go and am sent; our church is'nt[sic] strong in the territory, relatively strong, of course, and the pulpits have all been filled, but now I am staying here permanently, it is of course supposed to be permanently depends on the church, at Muskogee as pastor of the First Presbyterian church.

BY COMMISSION: This testimony will be filed and made part of the record in the Cherokee case No D - 6.

M. D. Green being first duly sworn, states that as stenographer to the Commission to the Five Civilized Tribes he correctly recorded the testimony and proceedings in this

case and that the foregoing is a true and complete transcript of his stenographic notes thereof.
Signed, M. D. Green.
Subscribed and sworn to before me this February 12, 1902.
Signed, T. B. Needles,
Commissioner.

I, the undersigned as stenographer to the Commission to the Five Civilized Tribes do certify that the above is a true and correct copy of the original transcript.

Ella Mieleng

File in C D # 3, # 4, # 5.
"R"
Cherokee D. - 6
Department of the Interior,
Commission to the Five Civilized Tribes,
Muskogee, I. T. February 14, 1902.

SUPPLEMENTAL TESTIMONY ON BEHALF OF APPLICANT, in the matter of the application of James K. Thompson for enrollment as a Cherokee citizen.
Appearances:
Applicant in person.
JAMES K. THOMPSON; being sworn and examined, testified as follows:

BY COMMISSION:
Q What is your name? A James K. Thompson.
Q How old are you? A 28
Q What is your post office address? A Muskogee.
Q Are you an applicant before this Commission for enrollment as a Cherokee?
A Yes sir.
Q In answer to the question asked you when you appeared before the Commission to give supplemental testimony on the 4th day of February 1902, "Q, As a matter of fact you have never resided in the Cherokee Nation since your admission up ujtil[sic] the present time?" You answered "No sir." "When the 1896 roll was made I was a stated supply in the church at Texarkana, Ark and knew nothing about any roll; I came immediately from the seminary."
A Well, that was the question. I misunderstood the purport of it; of course I was admitted to citizenship by an act of the Council; I was a minor at the time and of course don't remember the exact transaction, but I was admitted along with the family, father's family, and he resided for twelve months in the Territory, in the Cherokee Nation, at Tahlequah.
Q And you were residing here at that time? A I was residing with him at that time, when he moved away I was still a minor; while I was here I attended the male school at Tahlequah in the Indian Territort[sic].
Q That was in '83 or '84? A '83, yes sir; it was the fall of '83 or '84.

CHEROKEE GRANTED ENROLLMENT CARDS & DAWES PACKETS 1900-1907 VOLUME I

Q Any other statement you desire to make? A No, I think, yes the point with regard to the establishing of our home, when we established our citizenship to forsee[sic] that we were establishing our home- and when I individually went away I knew nothing about the whys and wherefores, I knew nothing about it; I was nine years old. And I have always felt as I grew up to manhood that I would return to take up my interest.
Q You submit this case now to the Commission for final consideration?
A Yes sir.
           BY MR. HASTINGS: Cherokee Nation submits.

M. D. Green being first duly sworn, states that as stenographer to the Commission to the Five Civilized Tribes he correctly recorded the testimony and proceedings in this case and that the foregoing is [sic] true and complete transcript of his stenographic notes thereof.
                  signed, M. D. Green.
Subscribed and sworn to before me this February 17, 1902.
                signed,   T. B. Needles, Commissioner.
I, the Undersigned, as stenographer to the Commission to the Five Civilized Tribes, do certify that the above is a correct copy of the original transcript.

                                                           Ella Mieleng

File with Cherokee D- 4, Allison Thompson.

"R"
                        Department of the Interior,
                  Commission to the Five Civilized Tribes,
                    Muskogee, I. T., February 15, 1902.

     SUPPLEMENTAL TESTIMONY AND PROCEEDINGS in the matter of the application of Gilbert T. Thompson, Sr., for the enrollment of himself and children as Cherokee citizens.

     APPEARANCES:
          Milton K. Thompson, for the applicants;
          W.W. Hastings, attorney for the Cherokee Nation.

BY COMMISSION: There is offered in evidence a memorandum of an agreement made and entered into by and between Francis B. Fite, agent of G. T. Thompson and sons, of the first part, and Charles Hawkins, of the second part, bearing date of July 28, 1896, and same will be filed.

     This case is closed by agreement of the parties concerned.

By agreement of the parties concerned it is ordered that all the testimony had in the matter of the application of James K. Thompson, son of Gilbert T. Thompson, be filed and made part of the record in doubtful case No. 3, being that of Gilbert T. Thompson, et al., doubtful case No. 4, being that of Allison Thompson, et al., and doubtful case No. 5, being that of Ernest Thompson, et al.

By agreement of the parties concerned these cases are submitted for final consideration.

M. D. Green, being first duly sworn, states that as stenographer to the Commission to the Five Civilized Tribes he correctly recorded the testimony and proceedings in this case and that the foregoing is a true and complete transcript of his stenographic notes thereof.

MD Green

Subscribed and sworn to before me this February 21, 1902.

T B Needles
Commissioner.

DEPARTMENT OF THE INTERIOR.

Commission to the Five Civilized Tribes,

Muskogee I. T. October 16, 1902.

Cherokee D 4.

In the matter of the application of Allison Thompson et al, for enrollment as citizens of the Cherokee Nation.

Motion to Re open case.

Comes now the representative of the Cherokee Nation, and upon examination of the testimony in the above case represents to the Commission that the testimony as to the residence of the applicant is insufficient and therefore moves the Commission that the applicants be again notified by the Commission to appear before the Commission at some convenient date for the purpose of giving additional testimony as to their residence prior to and on June 28th 1898 and subsequent thereto, xxxxin[sic] as much as we deem the testimony upon the question of residence insufficient in this case.

CHEROKEE GRANTED ENROLLMENT CARDS & DAWES PACKETS 1900-1907 VOLUME I

Respectfully,

W W Hastings

Attorney for the Cherokee Nation.

Cherokee D-4

Department of the Interior,
Commission to the Five Civilized Tribes,
Cherokee Land Office,
Tahlequah, I.T., July 28, 1903.

In the matter of the application of Allison Thompson for the enrollment of himself and his children, Earnest W., Mamie and Allison Archibald Thompson, as citizens by blood of the Cherokee Nation.

SUPPLEMENTAL TESTIMONY.

ALLISON THOMPSON, being duly sworn and examined by the Commission, testified as follows:

Q What is your name? A Allison Thompson.
Q How old are you? A 37.
Q What is your postoffice address? A Cleburne, Texas, for the present.
Q Are you an applicant for enrollment as a citizen by blood of the Cherokee Nation?
A Yes.
Q You were admitted to citizenship in '83, were you not?
A Yes sir.
Q How long did you live here at that time? A About a year; I came in June.
Q Left in '84? A Yes sir.
Q When did you return to the Cherokee Nation again.[sic]
A Well, I never have made my home here.
Q Do you wish to make any statement regarding your absence from the Cherokee Nation, or affecting your residence here?
A Well, I left here to go to school and I was in college four years; left here in '84 and attended school at Springfield, Missouri; four years in college. Before leaving Springfield I was elected as a teacher in Austin College, Sherman, Texas, Presbyterian School and I taught there for twelve years. Then I taught at Calvert, Texas two years. Since then I have had nothing permanent, just temporary, like at Cleburne; not even keeping house. During all the time I was at Sherman, Texas, I considered my citizenship in the Cherokee Nation, coming up here for elections and voting and spending from one to three months every year, looking after the ranch in Cooweescoowee, and as I said, I always owned property here, except at the present time I have'nt[sic] anything to amount to. And I have an interest in the ranch, not only

CHEROKEE GRANTED ENROLLMENT CARDS
& DAWES PACKETS 1900-1907 VOLUME I

by being a son of my father, but having paid money into it. So that I have always had an interest here ever since I came to the Territory; and I don't vote in Texas.
Q Have you ever voted in any place except the Cherokee Nation?
A Well no, not in regular election.
Q What election, if any, did you vote in? A I don't remember of any. I have been particular on that point because I used to think that if a person voted on the outside he would lose his citizenship. I have never taken any interest in politics in Texas for that reason.
Q Have you ever intended to abandon the Cherokee Nation as a home? A Never have, and have been working the last ten years to get a position here. I have taught school in the nation.

By J. C. Starr:

Q How much money have you put into the farm in the Cherokee Nation?
A Well, In actual money, I put $500 at one time.
Q When was that? A In '94. We had paid in money before that but no definite amount. I bought an interest in the Squaw Hollow Ranch and paid for it; I put $500 into it and then I paid the balance in renting out the place and taking the rents to pay the notes; renting it and paying the notes.
Q Do you own this place in individual right? A No, it is the place owned by the family; we have a written agreement.
Q Prior to 1894 did you own any property in the Cherokee Nation in your own name? A Well, I had some cattle, not any land in my own name, but cattle.
Q How many cattle did you have? A Some 15 or 20.
Q How long did you own them? A Several years.
Q When did you acquire them? A When I lived here in '84.
Q How long did you keep them? A I had them in charge of Dr. Fite here; they were here several years.
Q What became of them? A He paid me for them finally.
Q Sold them to him? A Yes sir.
Q How long ago has that been? A As near as I can recollect it was about '95 or '6.
Q When you made these trips to the nation, did your wife come with you?
A No sir.
Q Keeping house there? A No, boarding.
Q Have you been keeping house there? A No sir, boarded.
Q Have you ever lived in the Cherokee Nation since 1884?
A No, I have never resided here. I have spent from one to three months here nearly every year since I left, either on the ranch or at Muskogee.

++++++++++++++++++++

Mabel F. Maxwell, being duly sworn, states that as stenographer to the Commission to the Five Civilized Tribes, she correctly recorded the supplemental testimony in this case, and that the above and foregoing is a true and complete transcript of her stenographic notes thereof.

_____Mabel F. Maxwell_____

CHEROKEE GRANTED ENROLLMENT CARDS & DAWES PACKETS 1900-1907 VOLUME I

Subscribed and sworn to before me this
30th day of July, 1903.

                                                Samuel Foreman
                                                   Notary Public.

MFM

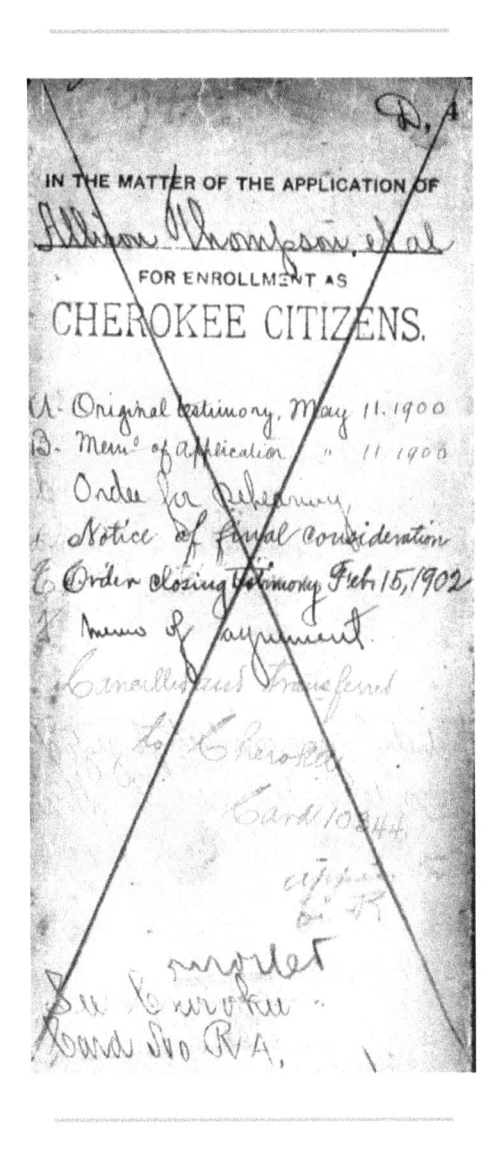

CHEROKEE GRANTED ENROLLMENT CARDS & DAWES PACKETS 1900-1907 VOLUME I

CHEROKEE GRANTED ENROLLMENT CARDS
& DAWES PACKETS 1900-1907 VOLUME I

Cherokee D5 - Ernest Thompson

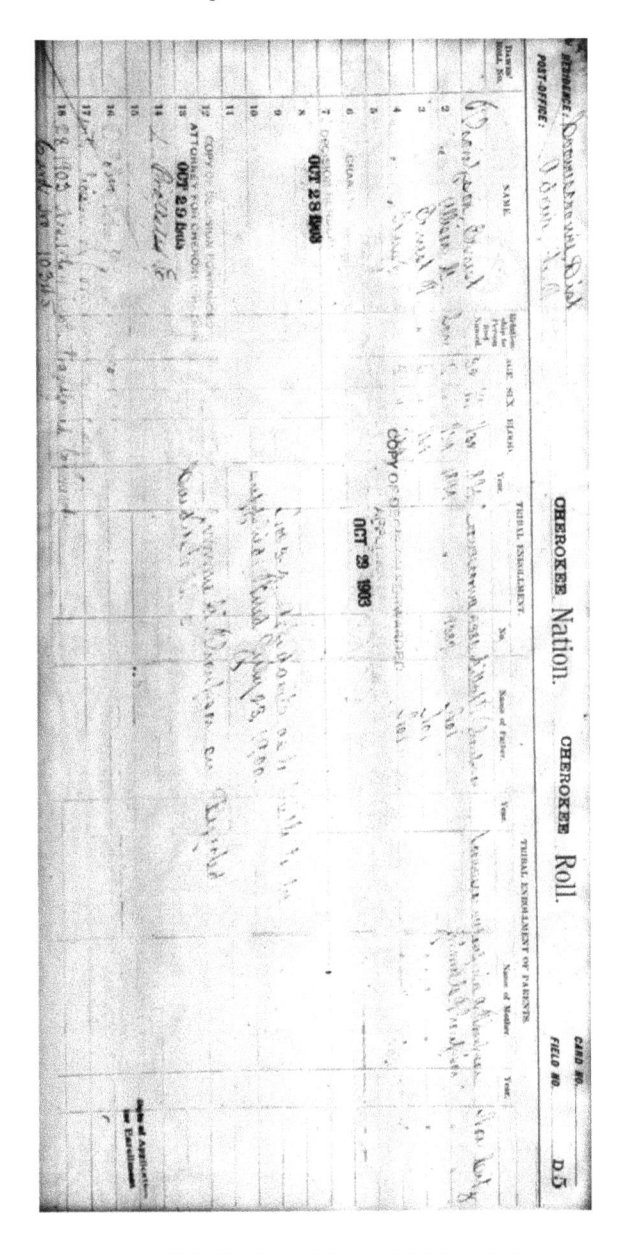

CHEROKEE GRANTED ENROLLMENT CARDS & DAWES PACKETS 1900-1907 VOLUME I

Commission to the Five Civilized Tribes,
Muskogee, Indian Territory,
May 11th, 1900.

In the matter of the application of Ernost[sic] Thompson for enrollment as a Cherokee citizen; being sworn and examined by Commissioner McKennon he testifies as follows:

Q What is your name? A Ernest Thompson
Q How old are you? A Thirty-two.
Q Where do you live? A Louisville, Kentucky.
Q Did ever you live in the Territory? A Yes sir.
Q When? A I came here in 1883.
Q How long did you remain here? A Until sometime in 1894 when I went to college.
Q About a year? A Yes sir.
Q Have you ever lived here since? A No sir, not any length of time.
Q Did you ever reside here at all since then? A No, not to make it my home; I have been here several times and staid[sic] a few weeks.
Q Have you any property in the Cherokee Nation? A Yes sir.
Q When did you acquire it? A Before I became of age. Of course my father had property, and since then I have had an interest in the ranch here, and I have invested money myself.
Q In what? A In a piece of property, real estate, in Cooweescoowee District.
Q When did you make that investment? A I don't remember just the date of that.
Q Well, the year. A I think it was some eight years ago or more, I don't remember the exact date.
Q Have you any family? A Yes sir.
Q Have you got a wife? A Yes sir.
Q What is her name? A Jimmie G. Thompson.
Q How old? A Thirty.
Q Is she a white woman? A Yes sir. I was a citizen when I married her.
Q Where did you marry her? A Pembroke, Kentucky.
Q Has ever lived here? A No sir.
Q What is her post-office address? A Louisville, Kentucky.
Q Are you in business there? A I am a minister there.
Q What children have you? A Allison G.
Q How old is he? A Seven. Ernest T., 5 years old; Hugh G., 4 years old.
Q Have these children ever lived here? A No sir.
I have also had an interest in this property at Tahlequah with my brother, and I have never voted anywhere else, and I have been back here almost every year, but I have never lived here.
Commissioner McKennon:
Jimmie G. Thompson,
510 Hill St.,
Louisville, Kentucky.

CHEROKEE GRANTED ENROLLMENT CARDS
& DAWES PACKETS 1900-1907 VOLUME I

Your enrollment as an intermarried Cherokee citizen is refused, because you have not resided in the Cherokee Nation.

Department of the Interior,
Commission to the Five Civilized Tribes

I hereby certify, upon my official oath as stenographer to above named Commission, that this transcript is a true, full and correct translation of my stenographic notes.

----M.D. Green----

File in C. D. #3, #4, #5.

Cherokee D 6

Department of the Interior,
Commission to the Five Civilized Tribes,
Muskogee, I. T. February 4, 1902.

SUPPLEMENTAL TESTIMONY ON BEHALF OF APPLICANT, in the matter of the application of James K. Thompson for enrollment as a citizen by blood of the Cherokee Nation.

Appearances:
    Applicant in person.
    W. W. Hastings, of attorneys for the Cherokee Nation.

JAMES K. THOMPSON, being sworn and examined, testified as follows:

BY COMMISSION:
Q What is your name? A James K. Thompson.
Q How old are you? A 28
Q What is your post office address? A Muskogee, I think it was down there before as Adair, but I am living here now; I have charge of the Presbyterian Church, regular pastor.
Q Did you appear before the Commission in 1900, May and make application for the enrollment of yourself as a citizen of the Cherokee Nation? A Yes sir.
Q What is the name of your father? A G. T. Thompson.
Q Is he living or dead? A Living.
Q What is the name of your mother? A Josephine A. Thompson.
Q Is she living? A Yes sir.
Q You claim a right to enrollment through your father or through your mother?
A Through my father.
Q Where were you born? A Born at Tunnell[sic] Hill, Georgia.
Q How long did you continue to reside there after your birth? A I don't know exactly, father moved to Tennessee when I was quite a small boy, infant.

CHEROKEE GRANTED ENROLLMENT CARDS
& DAWES PACKETS 1900-1907 VOLUME I

Q   How long did you reside in Tennessee? A   Until '82 I believe it was.
Q   Then did you come to the Cherokee Nation? A   Yes sir.
Q   Were you admitted to citizenship in the Nation by an Act of the Cherokee National Council? A   Yes sir; I don't remember, I was only a boy then, possibly about '83, I was about 9 or ten years old I think.

> BY COMMISSION: It appears from the records of the Cherokee Nation that the applicant and his father were admitted to citizenship in the Cherokee Nation on the 4th day of September 1823, by an act of the Cherokee Commission on Citizenship

Q   How long did you continue to reside in the Cherokee Nation after you were admitted to citizenship? A   I don't know just how long father was here possibly about a year.
Q   Where did you go then? A   He went to Springfield, Mo.
Q   Did you go with him? A   Yes sir, yes I was a minor you see and had to; it was the only thing I could do.
Q   How long did you reside at Springfield, Mo? A   Stayed there I think about four years.
Q   Then where did you go? A   He went and we went with him to Texas to McKinney, Texas; he was a minister you know, and was called to the church at McKinney, and I was about 14 I think at the time.
Q   How long did you reside in Texas? A   He stayed there for two, three, I think that time about three years.
Q   Did you accompany him when he left Texas? A   He left us in College at Sherman.
Q   At Sherman Texas? A   Yes sir.
Q   How long did you continue to attend school there? A   I stayed there for one year after father left. I was then just eighteen years old.
Q   Where did you go then? A   I went to Kentucky and attended school there.
Q   When did you finish your school? A   My schooling in my seminary course in May 1896.
Q   Did you attend school again after that? A   Yes sir, I went abroad for a while in Scotland.
Q   When did you return to this country? that is to the United States? A   I came bake[sic] in March, May, April just about two years ago.
Q   You had then reached your majority? A   Yes.
Q   How old were you at that time? A   I was a little past 26.
Q   Had you been attending school continuously since the time your[sic] left your father there in Sherman, Texas, or up until the time you returned from Scotland? A   Well with a little intermission while I was supplying the church in Texas. I was simply a stated supply looking to my final settlement in this country, but I was doing church work off and on. I had'nt[sic] completed it.
Q   When was the first time you came to the Cherokee Nation after your admission in '83? A   You mean to live?
Q   Yes, when did you come back; how long have you been here the last time? A   Oh I have been here simply a month, to live; I came here January 1st.
Q   Where did you come from? A   I came from Calvert, Texas.

CHEROKEE GRANTED ENROLLMENT CARDS
& DAWES PACKETS 1900-1907 VOLUME I

Q Have you attended school any since your return from Scotland? A No sir.
Q You have been a minister since that time? A Yes sir. In my profession we go where we are called, and as soon as I was called to the Nation- of course it is in the Creek Nation, I accepted; I am in charge of the Presbyterian church.
Q As a matter of fact you have never resided in the Cherokee Nation since your admission, up until the present time? A No sir, when the 1896 roll was made I was stated supply in the church at Texarkana, Arkansas, and I knew nothing about any roll; I came immediately from the Seminary.

   1896 roll of citizens of the Cherokee Nation examined and applicant not identified thereon.
   1894 pay roll of citizens of the Cherokee Nation examined and applicant identified thereon. On page 317, #4316, James K. Thompson, Cooweescoowee District.

   BY MR. HASTINGS:
Q Are you married? A Yes sir.
Q How long have you been married? A I have been married two years, let's see, married the 3d day of October 1899.
Q Two years last October? A Yes sir.
Q Where were you married? A Married in Texas.
                      Calvert, Texas where I was preaching at the time.
Q You came here the first of January to the Creek Nation, Muskogee? A Yes sir.
   BY THE COMMISSION: On the 11th day of May, 1900 James K. Thompson came before the Commission and made application for the enrollment of himself as a citizen by blood of the Cherokee Nation. The testimony taken at that time was found to be incomplete, and the applicant this day appears and gives further testimony as regards his application.
   It appears from the records of the Cherokee Nation that he was duly admitted to citizenship by an act of the Cherokee National Council on the 4th day of September, 1883; it appears from the testimony that he only resided in the Cherokee Nation one year subsequent to his admission to citizenship, since which time he has not resided in the Cherokee Nation.
   He returned to the Indian Territory in January 1902, and since that time has resided in Muskogee, Indian Territory. He is not identified on the Cherokee census roll of 1896, but is duly identified on the pay roll of 1894. By reason of the fact that the applicant has not resided in the Cherokee Nation since his admission to citizenship, final judgment as to his application will be suspended and his name will remain on Doubtful card #6. The final decision of the Commission will be made known to the applicant when the same is rendered.

M. D. Green being first duly sworn, states that as stenographer to the Commission to the Five Civilized Tribes he correctly recorded the testimony and proceedings in this case and that the foregoing is a true and complete transcript of his stenographic notes thereof.

CHEROKEE GRANTED ENROLLMENT CARDS & DAWES PACKETS 1900-1907 VOLUME I

          Signed, M. D. Green.
Subscribed and sworn to before me this February 4, 1902.
          signed, T. B. Needles, Commissioner.

  I, the undersigned, as stenographer to the Commission to the Five Civilized Tribes, do hereby certify that the above and foregoing is a true and correct copy of the original transcript.

                  Ella Mieleng

File in Doubtful Cherokee # 3, # 4, # 5.

Cherokee D. - 6

         Department of the Interior,
      Commission to the Five Civilized Tribes,
       Muskogee, I. T. February 12, 1902.

SUPPLEMENTAL TESTIMONY ON BEHALF OF APPLICANT, in the matter of the application of James K. Thompson for enrollment as a citizen of the Cherokee Nation, by blood; being sworn and examined he testified as follows:

  Appearances:
      Applicant in person.
BY COMMISSION:

Q What is your name? A James K. Thompson.
Q How old are you? A 28 years old.
Q What is your post office address? A Muskogee.
Q You were an applicant before this Commission for enrollment as a citizen by blood of the Cherokee Nation? A Yes sir.
Q You desire to make a statement relative to your residence? A Yes.
Q Just state briefly. A The fact that I have always considered the Indian Territory was my domicile and with that in view I have never at any time exercised the right of franchise in any of the States, though I am in my 29th year, feeling that that might jeopardize possibly the interest here which I considered always to be mine. Besides this, in 1894 I believe it was, the sum of money something over two hundred dollars that was paid to each of the Cherokee citizens, received by myself, was all turned back into our place close to Adair in the Cherokee Nation, on improvements. It was not used at all but turned back into the place for improvement.
Q Have you anything else that you desire to state relative to your enrollment? A I think these two points cover all; only that I have looked forward always to coming back and had simply waited for an opportunity to come, and when the opportunity came I returned here, at the first opportunity.
Q I believe the fact was brought out that you were a minister of the Gospel?

CHEROKEE GRANTED ENROLLMENT CARDS & DAWES PACKETS 1900-1907 VOLUME I

A Yes sir, being a minister of course I go where I have an opportunity to go and am sent; our church is'nt[sic] strong in the territory, relatively strong, of course, and the pulpits have all been filled, but now I am staying here permanently, it is of course supposed to be permanently depends on the church, at Muskogee as pastor of the First Presbyterian church.

BY COMMISSION: This testimony will be filed and made part of the record in the Cherokee case No C D - 6.

M. D. Green being first duly sworn, states that as stenographer to the Commission to the Five Civilized Tribes, he correctly recorded the testimony and proceedings in this case, and that the foregoing is a true and correct transcript of his stenographic notes thereof.
        Signed,   M. D. Green.
Subscribed and sworn to before me this February 12, 1902.
        Signed,   T. B. Needles,
                                          Commissioner.

I, the undersigned, as stenographer to the Commission to the Five Civilized Tribes, do certify that the above is a correct copy of the original transcript.

                                                          Ella Mieleng

File in C D #3, #4, #5

"R"

Cherokee D - 6
                        Department of the Interior,
                  Commission to the Five Civilized Tribes,
                    Muskogee, I. T. February 14, 1902.

SUPPLEMENTAL TESTIMONY ON BEHALF OF APPLICANT, in the matter of the application of James K. Thompson for enrollment as a Cherokee citizen.
        Appearances:
                        Applicant in person.
JAMES K. THOMPSON; being sworn and examined, testified as follows:

BY COMMISSION:
Q What is your name? A James K. Thompson.
Q How old are you? A 28
Q What is your post office address? A Muskogee.
Q Are you an applicant before this Commission for enrollment as a Cherokee?
A Yes sir.

CHEROKEE GRANTED ENROLLMENT CARDS & DAWES PACKETS 1900-1907 VOLUME I

Q In answer to the question asked you when you appeared before the Commission to give supplemental testimony on the 4th day of February 1902, "Q, As a matter of fact you have never resided in the Cherokee Nation since your admission up until the present time?" You answered "No sir." "When the 1896 roll was made I was a stated supply in the church at Texarkana, Ark and knew nothing about any roll; I came immediately from the seminary."
A Well, that was the question. I misunderstood the purport of it; of course I was admitted to citizenship by an act of the Council; I was a minor at the time and of course don't remember the exact transaction, but I was admitted along with the family, father's family, and he resided for twelve months in the Territory, in the Cherokee Nation, at Tahlequah.
Q And you were residing here at that time? A I was residing with him at that time, when he moved away I was still a minor; while I was here I attended the male school at Tahlequah in the Indian Territory.
Q That was in '83 or '84? A '83, yes sir; it was the fall of '83 or '84.
Q Any other statement you desire to make? A No, I think, yes the point with regard to the establishing of our home, when we established our citizenship to foresee that we were establishing our home- and when I individually went away I knew nothing about the whys and wherefores, I knew nothing about it; I was nine years old. And I have always felt as I grew up to manhood that I would return to take up my interest.
Q You submit this case now to the Commission for final consideration?
A Yes sir.
BY MR. HASTINGS: Cherokee Nation submits.

M. D. Green being first duly sworn, states that as stenographer to the Commission to the Five Civilized Tribes he correctly recorded the testimony and proceedings in this case and that the foregoing is a true and complete transcript of his stenographic notes thereof.
signed, M. D. Green.
Subscribed and sworn to before me this February 17, 1902.
signed,   T. B. Needles, Commissioner.

I, the undersigned, as stenographer to the Commission to the Five Civilized Tribes, do hereby certify that the above is a full and correct copy of the original transcript.

Ella Mieleng

File with Cherokee D- 5, Ernest Thompson.

"R"
Department of the Interior,
Commission to the Five Civilized Tribes,
Muskogee, I. T., February 15, 1902.

CHEROKEE GRANTED ENROLLMENT CARDS & DAWES PACKETS 1900-1907 VOLUME I

SUPPLEMENTAL TESTIMONY AND PROCEEDINGS in the matter of the application of Gilbert T. Thompson, Sr., for the enrollment of himself and children as Cherokee citizens.

APPEARANCES:
Milton K. Thompson, for the applicants;
W.W. Hastings, attorney for the Cherokee Nation.

BY COMMISSION: There is offered in evidence a memorandum of an agreement made and entered into by and between Francis B. Fite, agent of G. T. Thompson and sons, of the first part, and Charles Hawkins, of the second part, bearing date of July 28, 1896, and same will be filed.

This case is closed by agreement of the parties concerned.

By agreement of the parties concerned it is ordered that all the testimony had in the matter of the application of James K. Thompson, son of Gilbert T. Thompson, be filed and made part of the record in doubtful case No. 3, being that of Gilbert T. Thompson, et al., doubtful case No. 4, being that of Allison Thompson, et al., and doubtful case No. 5, being that of Ernest Thompson, et al.

By agreement of the parties concerned these cases are submitted for final consideration.

M. D. Green, being first duly sworn, states that as stenographer to the Commission to the Five Civilized Tribes he correctly recorded the testimony and proceedings in this case and that the foregoing is a true and complete transcript of his stenographic notes thereof.

MD Green

Subscribed and sworn to before me this February 21, 1902.

T B Needles
Commissioner.

DEPARTMENT OF THE INTERIOR.
Commission to the Five Civilized Tribes,
Muskogee I. T. October 16, 1902.

Cherokee D 5.

In the matter of the application of Ernest Thompson for enrollment as a citizen of the Cherokee Nation.

CHEROKEE GRANTED ENROLLMENT CARDS
& DAWES PACKETS 1900-1907 VOLUME I

Motion to Reopen case.

Comes now the representative of the Cherokee Nation and upon examination of the testimony in the above entitled case represents to the Commission that the testimony as to the residence of the applicant is insufficient and therefore moves the Commission that the applicants be again notified to appear before the Commission at some convenient date for the purpose of giving additional testimony as to his residence prior to and on June 28th 1898 and subsequent thereto, inasmuch as we deem the testimony upon the question of residence insufficient in this case.

                        Respectfully,
                        W W Hastings

J. C. S.   Attorney for the Cherokee Nation.
                                                JCS

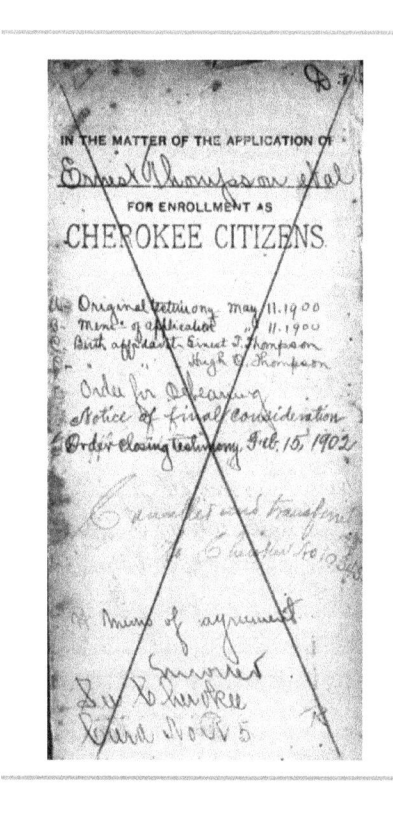

CHEROKEE GRANTED ENROLLMENT CARDS & DAWES PACKETS 1900-1907 VOLUME I

CHEROKEE GRANTED ENROLLMENT CARDS
& DAWES PACKETS 1900-1907 VOLUME I

Cherokee D6 - James K. Thompson

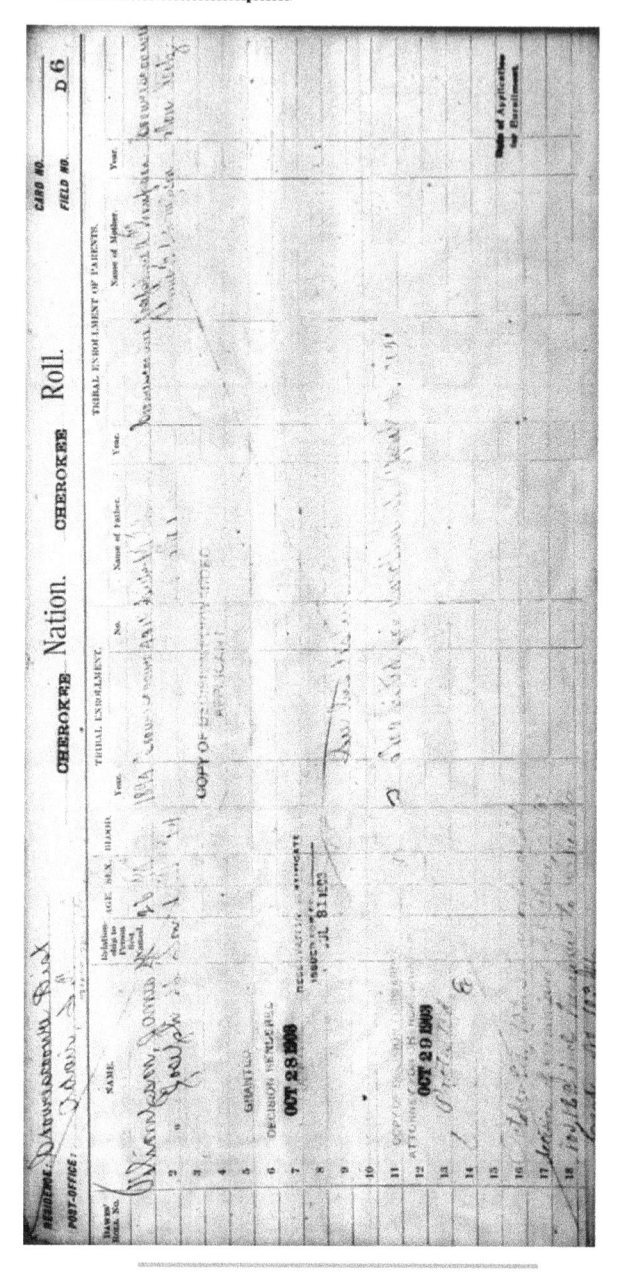

CHEROKEE GRANTED ENROLLMENT CARDS & DAWES PACKETS 1900-1907 VOLUME I

Commission to the Five Civilized Tribes,
Muskogee, Indian Territory,
May 11th, 1900.

In the matter of the application of James K. Thompson for enrollment as a Cherokee citizen; being sworn and examined by Commissioner McKennon he testifies as follows:

Q What is your name? A James K. Thompson.
Q How old are you? A Twenty-six.
Q Where are you living? A I have been living everywhere most; I have been at school, and a year or two ago graduated and am preaching now in Texas.
Q When did you first come to the Territory? A In 1883.
Q You came with your father? A Yes sir. I was then a minor.
Q And remained here about a year? A Yes sir.
Q And staid[sic] away ever since,- you have not resided here since.
A Only just like everywhere else, I hardly had a permanent residence anywhere.
Q What is your present post-office address? A Calvert, Texas.
Q Are you married? A I have just married.
Q Is your wife a white woman? A Yes sir.
Q Has she ever resided here? A No.
Q She ever been in the Cherokee Nation? A No sir. We [sic] just got back from Europe, and she hasn't had an opportunity.
I have been back repeatedly, and staid with my brother; I have considered my home just where I happened to be; I had to go away to school.
Q You have no children? A No sir.

Department of the Interior,
Commission to the Five Civilized Tribes

I hereby certify, upon my official oath as stenographer to above named Commission, that this transcript is a true, full and correct translation of my stenographic notes.

..*M.D. Green*..

"R"

Cherokee D 6

Department of the Interior,
Commission to the Five Civilized Tribes,
Muskogee, I. T. February 4, 1902.

SUPPLEMENTAL TESTIMONY ON BEHALF OF APPLICANT, in the matter of the application of James K. Thompson for enrollment as a citizen by blood of the Cherokee Nation.

CHEROKEE GRANTED ENROLLMENT CARDS & DAWES PACKETS 1900-1907 VOLUME I

Appearances:
    Applicant in person.
    W. W. Hastings, of attorneys for the Cherokee Nation.

JAMES K. THOMPSON, being sworn and examined, testified as follows:
BY COMMISSION:
Q What is your name? A James K. Thompson.
Q How old are you? A 28
Q What is your post office address? A Muskogee, I think it was down there before as Adair, but I am living here now; I have charge of the Presbyterian Church, regular pastor.
Q Did you appear before the Commission in May 1900 and make application for the enrollment of yourself as a citizen of the Cherokee Nation? A Yes sir.
Q What is the name of your father? A G. T. Thompson.
Q Is he living or dead? A Living.
Q What is the name of your mother? A Josephine A. Thompson.
Q Is she living? A Yes sir.
Q You claim a right to enrollment through your father or through your mother?
A Through my father.
Q Where were you born? A Born at Tunnell[sic] Hill, Georgia.
Q How long did you continue to reside there after your birth? A I don't know exactly, father moved to Tennessee when I was quite a small boy, infant.
Q How long did you reside in Tennessee? A Until '82 I believe it was.
Q Then did you come to the Cherokee Nation? A Yes sir.
Q Were you admitted to citizenship in the Nation by an Act of the Cherokee National Council? A Yes sir; I don't remember, I was only a boy then, possibly about '83, I was about 9 or 10 years old I think.

    BY COMMISSION: It appears from the records of the Cherokee Nation that the applicant and his father were admitted to citizenship in the Cherokee Nation on the 4th day of September 1883, by an act of the Cherokee Commission on Citizenship

Q How long did you continue to reside in the Cherokee Nation after you were admitted to citizenship? A I don't know just how long father was here possibly about a year.
Q Where did you go then? A He went to Springfield, Missouri.
Q Did you go with him? A Yes sir, yes I was a minor you see and had to; it was the only thing I could do.
Q How long did you reside at Springfield, Missouri? A Stayed there I think about four years.
Q Then where did you go? A He went and we went with him to Texas, to McKinney, Texas; he was a minister you know, and was called to the church at McKinney, and I was about 14 I think at the time.
Q How long did you reside in Texas? A He stayed there for two, three, I think that time about three years.
Q Did you accompany him when he left Texas? A He left us in College at Sherman.

CHEROKEE GRANTED ENROLLMENT CARDS
& DAWES PACKETS 1900-1907 VOLUME I

Q At Sherman, Texas? A Yes sir.
Q How long did you continue to attend school there? A I stayed there for one year after father left. I was then just 18 years old.
Q Where did you go then? A I went to Kentucky and attended school there.
Q When did you finish your school? A My schooling, in my seminary course in May 1896.
Q Did you attend school again after that? A Yes sir, I went abroad for a ~~year~~ while in Scotland.
Q When did you return to this country; that is to the United States? A I came back in March, May, April, just about two years ago.
Q You had then reached your majority? A Yes.
Q How old were you at that time? A I was a little past 26.
Q Had you been attending school continuously from the time you left your father there in Sherman, Texas up until the time you returned from Scotland? A Well with a little intermission while I was supplying the church in Texas. I was simply a stated supply looking to my final settlement in this country, but I was doing church work off and on. I hadn't completed it.
Q When was the first time you came to the Cherokee Nation after your admission in '83? A You mean to live?
Q Yes, when did you come back; how long have you been here the last time? A Oh I have been here simply a month, to live; I came here January 1st.
Q Where did you come from? A I came from Calvert, Texas.
Q Have you attended school any since your return from Scotland? A No sir.
Q You have been a minister since that time? A Yes sir. In my profession we go where we are called, and as soon as I was called to the Nation- of course it is in the Creek Nation,- I accepted; I am in charge of the Presbyterian church.
Q As a matter of fact you have never resided in the Cherokee Nation since your admission? Up until the present time? A No sir, when the 1896 roll was made I was a stated supply in the church at Texarkana, Arkansas, and I knew nothing about any roll; I came immediately from the Seminary.

    1896 census roll of citizens of the Cherokee Nation examined and applicant not identified thereon.
    1894 pay roll of citizens of the Cherokee Nation examined and applicant identifiedon[sic]
    page 317 No. 4316 James K. Thompson, Cooweescoowee District,

    BY MR. HASTINGS:
Q Are you married? A Yes sir.
Q How long have you been married? A I have been married two years, let's see, married the 3rd day of October 1899.
Q Two years last October? A Yes sir.
Q Where were you married? A Married in Texas.
Calvert, Texas, where I was preaching at the time.
Q You came here the first of January to the Creek Nation, Muskogee? A Yes sir.
    BY THE COMMISSION: On the 11th day of May 1900 James K. Thompson appeared before the Commission and made application for the enrollment

of himself as a citizen by blood of the Cherokee Nation. The testimony taken at that time was found to be incomplete, and the applicant this day appears and gives further testimony as regards his application.

It appears from the records of the Cherokee Nation that he was duly admitted to citizenship by an act of the Cherokee National Council on the 4th day of September, 1883; it appears from the testimony that he only resided in the Cherokee Nation one year subsequent to his admission to citizenship, since which time he has not resided in the Cherokee Nation.

He returned to the Indian Territory in January 1902, and since that time has resided in Muskogee, Indian Territory. He is not identified on the Cherokee census roll of 1896, but is duly identified on the pay roll of 1894. By reason of the fact that the applicant has not resided in the Cherokee Nation since his admission to citizenship, final judgment as to his application will be suspended and his name will remain on doubtful card No. 6. The final decision of the Commission will be made known to the applicant when the same is rendered.

M. D. Green, being first duly sworn, states that as stenographer to the Commission to the Five Civilized Tribes he correctly recorded the testimony and proceedings in this case and that the foregoing is a true and complete transcript of his stenographic notes thereof.

M. D. Green

Subscribed and sworn to before me this February 4, 1902.

T B Needles
Commissioner.

"R"

Cherokee D-6.

Department of the Interior,
Commission to the Five Civilized Tribes,
Muskogee, I. T. February 12, 1902.

SUPPLEMENTAL TESTIMONY ON BEHALF OF APPLICANT, in the matter of the application of James K. Thompson for enrollment as a citizen of the Cherokee Nation, by blood; being sworn and examined he testified as follows:

Appearances:
Applicant in person.

BY COMMISSION:
Q What is your name? A James K. Thompson.
Q How old are you? A 28 years old.

CHEROKEE GRANTED ENROLLMENT CARDS & DAWES PACKETS 1900-1907 VOLUME I

Q What is your post office address? A Muskogee.
Q You were an applicant before this Commission for enrollment as a citizen by blood of the Cherokee Nation? A Yes sir.
Q You desire to make a statement relative to your residence? A Yes.
Q Just state briefly. A The fact that I have always considered the Indian Territory was my domicile and with that in view I have never at any time exercised the right of franchise in any of the States, though I am in my 29th year, feeling that that might jeopardise[sic] possibly the interest here which I considered always to be mine. Besides this, in 1894 I believe it was, the sum of money something over two hundred dollars that was paid to each of the Cherokee citizens, received by myself, was all turned back into our place close to Adair in the Cherokee Nation, on improvements. It was not used at all, but turned back into the place for its improvement.
Q Have you anything else that you desire to state relative to your enrollment? A I think these two points cover all; only that I have looked forward always to coming back and had simply waited for an opportunity to come, and when the opportunity came I returned here, at the first opportunity.
Q I believe the fact was brought out that you were a minister of the Gospel?
A Yes sir, being a minister of course I go where I have an opportunity to go and am sent; our church isn't strong in the territory, relatively strong of course, and the pulpits have all been filled, but now I am staying here permanently, it is of course supposed to be permanently, depends on the church, at Muskogee as pastor of the First Presbyterian church.

BY COMMISSION: This testimony will be filed and made part of the record in the Cherokee case No D - 6.

M. D. Green being first duly sworn, states that as stenographer to the Commission to the Five Civilized Tribes he correctly recorded the testimony and proceedings in this case and that the foregoing is a true and complete transcript of his stenographic notes thereof.

M D Green

Subscribed and sworn to before me this February 12, 1902.

T B Needles
Commissioner.

"R"
Cherokee D-6

Department of the Interior,
Commission to the Five Civilized Tribes,
Muskogee, I. T., February 14, 1902.

CHEROKEE GRANTED ENROLLMENT CARDS & DAWES PACKETS 1900-1907 VOLUME I

SUPPLEMENTAL TESTIMONY ON BEHALF OF APPLICANT, in the matter of the application of James K. Thompson for enrollment as a Cherokee citizen.

Appearances:
Applicant in person.

JAMES K. THOMPSON; being sworn and examined, testified as follows:
BY COMMISSION:
Q What is your name? A James K. Thompson.
Q How old are you? A 28
Q What is your post-office address? A Muskogee.
Q You are an applicant before this Commission for enrollment as a Cherokee?
A Yes sir.
Q In answer to the question asked you when you appeared before the Commission to give supplemental testimony on the 4th day of February, 1902, "As a matter of fact, you have never resided in the Cherokee Nation since your admission up until the present time?" You answered, "No sir." "When the 1896 roll was made I was a stated supply in the church at Texarkana, Arkansas and knew nothing about any roll; I came immediately from the seminary."
A Well, that was the question. I misunderstood the purport of it; of course I was admitted to citizenship by an act of the Council; I was a minor at the time, of course don't remember the exact transaction, but I was admitted along with the family, father's family, and he resided for 12 months in the Territory, in the Cherokee Nation, at Tahlequah.
Q And were you residing here at that time? A I was residing with him at that time, when he moved away I was still a minor; while I was here I attended the male school at Tahlequah in the Indian Territory.
Q That was in '83 or '4? A '83, yes sir; it was the fall of '83 or '4.
Q Any other statement you desire to make? A No, I think,- yes the point with regard to the establishment of our home; when we established our citizenship to forsee[sic] that we were establishing our home- and when I individually went away I knew nothing about the whys and wherefores, I knew nothing about it; I was nine years old. And when I have always felt as I grew up to manhood that I would return to take up my interests.
Q You submit this case now to the Commission for final consideration?
A Yes sir.
BY MR. HASTINGS: Cherokee Nation submits.

M. D. Green, being first duly sworn, states that as stenographer to the Commission to the Five Civilized Tribes he correctly recorded the testimony and proceedings in this case and that the foregoing is a true and complete transcript of his stenographic notes thereof.

M D Green

Subscribed and sworn to before me this February 17, 1902.

T B Needles
Commissioner.

CHEROKEE GRANTED ENROLLMENT CARDS & DAWES PACKETS 1900-1907 VOLUME I

File with Cherokee D- 6, James K. Thompson.

"R"

Department of the Interior,
Commission to the Five Civilized Tribes,
Muskogee, I. T., February 15, 1902.

SUPPLEMENTAL TESTIMONY AND PROCEEDINGS in the matter of the application of Gilbert T. Thompson, Sr., for the enrollment of himself and children as Cherokee citizens.

APPEARANCES:
Milton K. Thompson, for the applicants;
W.W. Hastings, attorney for the Cherokee Nation.

BY COMMISSION: There is offered in evidence a memorandum of an agreement made and entered into by and between Francis B. Fite, agent of G. T. Thompson and sons, of the first part, and Charles Hawkins, of the second part, bearing date of July 28, 1896, and same will be filed.

This case is closed by agreement of the parties concerned.

By agreement of the parties concerned it is ordered that all the testimony had in the matter of the application of James K. Thompson, son of Gilbert T. Thompson, be filed and made part of the record in doubtful case No. 3, being that of Gilbert T. Thompson, et al., doubtful case No. 4, being that of Allison Thompson, et al., and doubtful case No. 5, being that of Ernest Thompson, et al.

By agreement of the parties concerned these cases are submitted for final consideration.

M. D. Green, being first duly sworn, states that as stenographer to the Commission to the Five Civilized Tribes he correctly recorded the testimony and proceedings in this case and that the foregoing is a true and complete transcript of his stenographic notes thereof.

MD Green

Subscribed and sworn to before me this February 21, 1902.

T B Needles
Commissioner.

CHEROKEE GRANTED ENROLLMENT CARDS & DAWES PACKETS 1900-1907 VOLUME I

DEPARTMENT OF THE INTERIOR

Commission to the Five Civilized Tribes,

Muskogee I. T. October 16, 1902.

Cherokee D # 6.

In the matter of the application of James K. Thompson for enrollment as citizens of the Cherokee Nation.

Motion to Reopen Case.

Comes now the representative of the Cherokee Nation, and upon examination of the testimony in the above case represents to the Commission that the testimony as to the residence of the applicant is insufficient and therefore moves the Commission that the applicants be again notified by the Commission to appear before the Commission at some convenient date for the purpose of giving additional testimony as to their residence prior to xxxxx and on June 28th 1898 and subsequent thereto, in as much as we deem the testimony upon the question of residence insufficient in this case.

Respectfully,
W W Hastings
Attorney for the Cherokee Nation.
JCS

J. C. S.

DEPARTMENT OF THE INTERIOR,

COMMISSION TO THE FIVE CIVILIZED TRIBES.

Muskogee, Indian Territory, August 17, 1903.

In the matter of the application for the enrollment of James K. Thompson, et al. as citizens by blood of the Cherokee Nation.

O R D E R.

A motion to reopen the above entitled case for the purpose of introducing additional testimony therein was filed with this Commission, on October 16, 1902, in behalf of the Cherokee Nation. No legal ground for reopening said case has been assigned in said motion and such additional testimony not being deemed necessary at this time, it is the opinion of this Commission that the motion to reopen said case should be denied, and it is so ordered.

(SIGNED) *T. B. Needles.*
Commissioner.

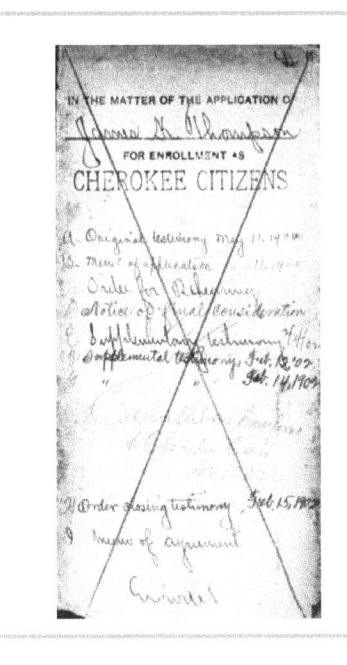

CHEROKEE GRANTED ENROLLMENT CARDS
& DAWES PACKETS 1900-1907 VOLUME I

COMMISSIONERS:
TAMS BIXBY,
THOMAS B. NEEDLES,
C. R. BRECKINRIDGE,
W. E. STANLEY.

ALLISON L. AYLESWORTH,
SECRETARY.

DEPARTMENT OF THE INTERIOR,
COMMISSION TO THE FIVE CIVILIZED TRIBES.

REFER IN REPLY TO THE FOLLOWING
Cherokee D-6

ADDRESS ONLY THE
COMMISSION TO THE FIVE CIVILIZED TRIBES.

Muskogee, Indian Territory, August 27, 1903

W. W. Hastings,
  Attorney for the Cherokee Nation,
    Tahlequah, Indian Territory.

Dear Sir:

  There is herewith enclosed a copy of the Commission's order dated August 24, 1903, denying your motion of October 16, 1902, to reopen Cherokee case D-6, James K. Thompson et al.

      Respectfully,
      Tams Bixby

Enc. D-192   Chairman.

CHEROKEE GRANTED ENROLLMENT CARDS & DAWES PACKETS 1900-1907 VOLUME I

CHEROKEE GRANTED ENROLLMENT CARDS & DAWES PACKETS 1900-1907 VOLUME I

Cherokee D7 - Milton K. Thompson

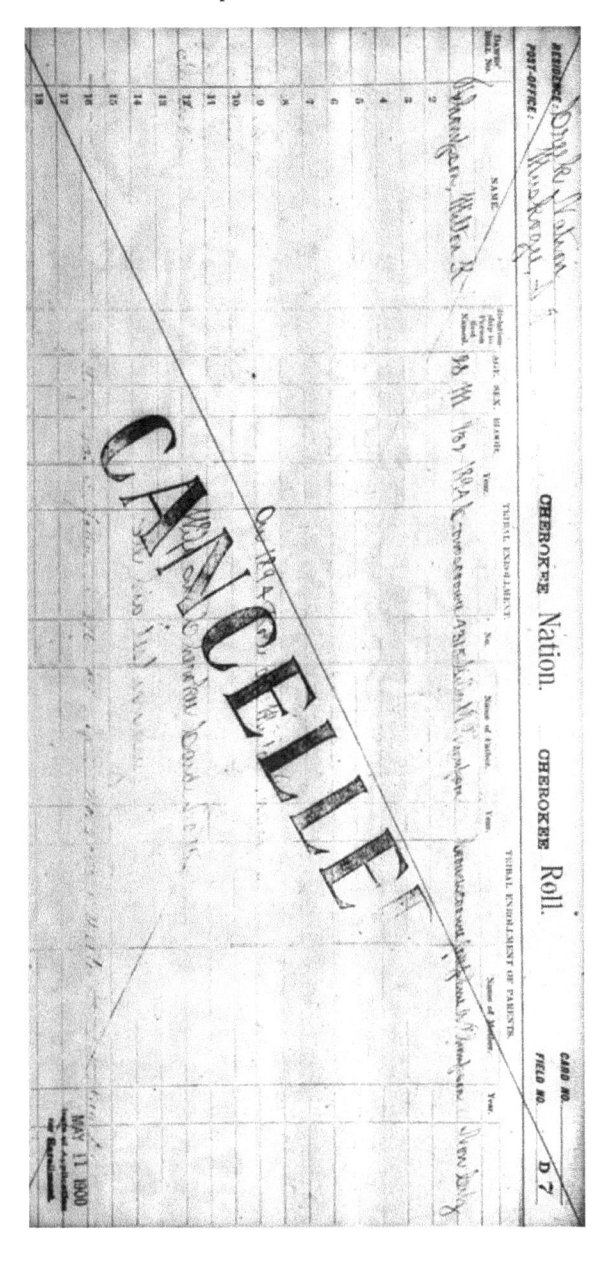

CHEROKEE GRANTED ENROLLMENT CARDS & DAWES PACKETS 1900-1907 VOLUME I

Commission to the Five Civilized Tribes,
Muskogee, Indian Territory,
May 11, 1900.

In the matter of the application of Milton Thompson for enrollment as a Cherokee Indian; being sworn and examined by Commissioner McKennon, he testifies as follows:

Q What is your name? A Milton Thompson.
Q How old are you? A Twenty-eight.
Q Where have you been living? A Ever since I got out of school I have been here at Muskogee.
Q Did you come here in 1883? A Yes sir.
Q And lived here about a year? A Yes sir.
Q Then went off to school? A Yes sir.
Q When did you return? A It is more than six years ago; I forget- ninety-three I guess, or ninety-four.
Q And you have been living in Muskogee? A I have been here ever since.
Q You were away from here all the time until 1893, and then returned, and have been living here ever since? A Yes sir. Except [illegible] at school.
Q How long have you had property in the Cherokee Nation? A My father has had property ever since 1883 and I have had property ever since,- in fact before I became of age.
Q How long? A I held it here for eight or ten years I guess.
Q What kind of property? A Real estate, and then since I have come here for seven years I have had stock and such as that and personal property. I have been here ever since I was of age practically, and wanted it understood that I have never voted anywhere else in my life, I have always voted here and have been recognized here in the Cherokee Nation all the time; I have voted in the Canadian District although I am enrolled in Cooweescoowee.

--- ---

Department of the Interior,
Commission to the Five Civilized Tribes

I hereby certify, upon my official oath as stenographer to above named Commission, that this transcript is a true, full and correct translation of my stenographic notes.

M.D. Green

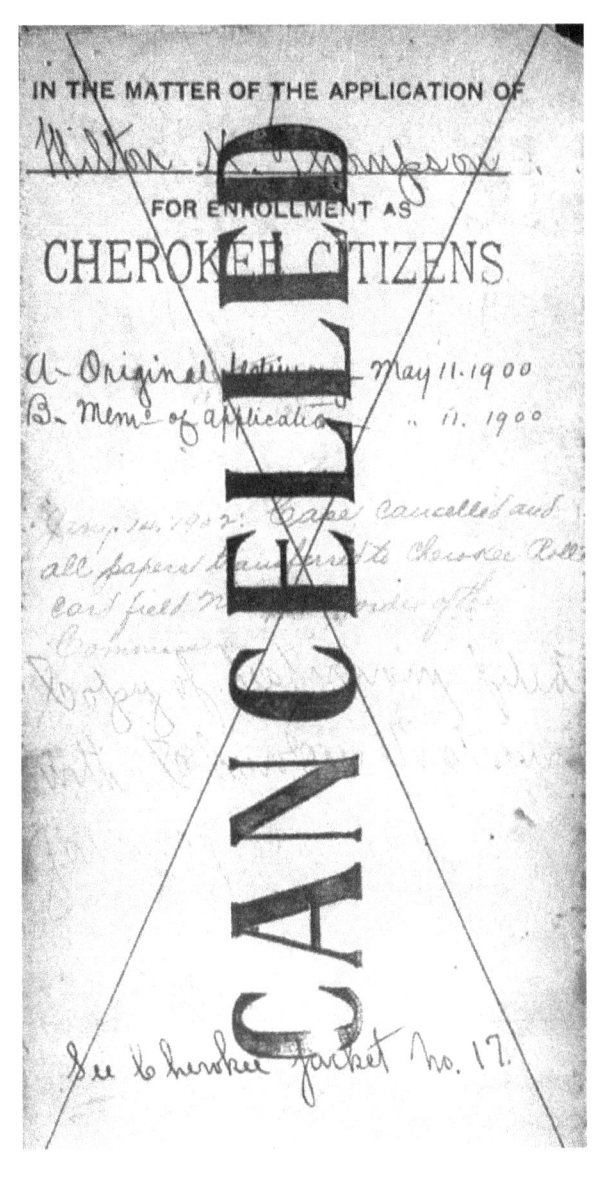

CHEROKEE GRANTED ENROLLMENT CARDS & DAWES PACKETS 1900-1907 VOLUME I

IN THE MATTER OF THE APPLICATION OF

Milton N. Thompson

FOR ENROLLMENT AS

CHEROKEE CITIZENS

A - Original Motion — May 11. 1900
B - Memo of application — " 11. 1900

CANCELLED

See Cherokee Jacket No. 17.

CHEROKEE GRANTED ENROLLMENT CARDS & DAWES PACKETS 1900-1907 VOLUME I

… CHEROKEE GRANTED ENROLLMENT CARDS
& DAWES PACKETS 1900-1907 VOLUME I

Cherokee D10 - George M. Ward for Minnie and Nellie Blevins

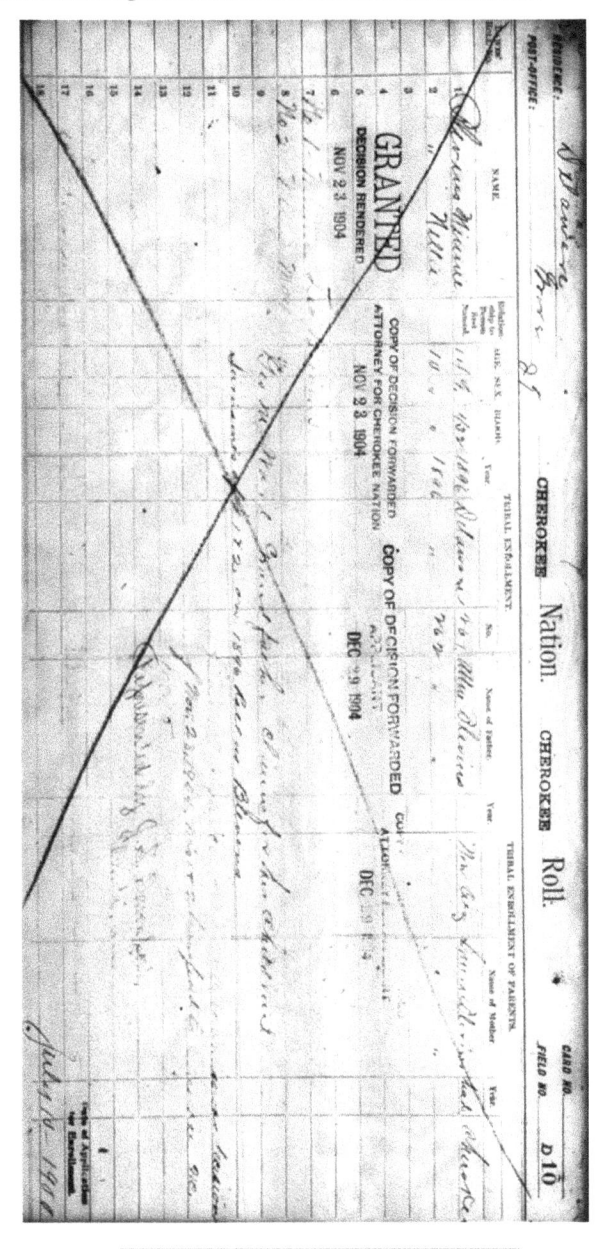

CHEROKEE GRANTED ENROLLMENT CARDS & DAWES PACKETS 1900-1907 VOLUME I

Department of the Interior,
Commission to the Five Civilized Tribes,
Fairland, I.T., July 10, 1900.

In the matter of the application of George M. Ward for the enrollment of his grandchildren, Minnie and Nellie Blevins; being duly sworn, and examined by Commissioner Needles, he testified as follows:

Q What is your name? A George M. Ward.
Q How old are you? A I am 58.
Q What is your post office address? A Grove, I. T.
Q Where do you live? A In the Delaware district.
Q You apply for the enrollment of your two grandchildren as Cherokees by blood? A Yes, sir.
Q Is their father and mother living? A No, sir; their father is alive, and lives in Arkansas; the larger one is in the Delaware district, the other is not in the district, he is going to school.
Q Is there anybody to attend to their enrollment? A I wanted to; one of the children is over at my house in the Delaware district; he stays there part of the time and part of the time at my son's, and here is a certificate that the little girl went back to California with her grandfather back to school.
Q What is the name of the one over at your house? A Minnie Blevins.
Q Their father is living? A Yes, sir he lives in Arkansas.
Q The mother is dead? A Yes, sir.
Q What is the residence of the children? A The children's residence at the present is they have just got a right in the Cherokee Nation, that is all.
Q Were the father and mother married? A Yes, sir, they were married here in this district.
Q What was the child's mother's name? A Laura Ward, her name is on those rolls.
Q Was she a citizen by blood? A Yes, sir, she was my daughter.
Q Is[sic] would be the duty of the father to register these children?
A The father isn't here.
Q Is[sic] the father doesn't live here the residence of the children would be with the father. Has he married over again in Arkansas? A Yes, sir.
Q Is he a white man? A Yes, sir; he married his rights out of here; after my daughter died he married a white woman.
Q This grandchild of yours is a child of your daughter? A Yes, sir.
Q When her father moved to Arkansas, did he take the child with him?
A Yes, sir, he took the child with him and kept it a while.
Q When did he move to Arkansas? A He moved out of the Territory it has been two or three years.
Q How old was the child when he left here? A She was probably about 10 or 11 years old, I guess.
Q She went with him? A Yes, sir.

CHEROKEE GRANTED ENROLLMENT CARDS
& DAWES PACKETS 1900-1907 VOLUME I

Q How long did she remain in Arkansas? A I guess it has been a couple of years since he first left here, he first went to Kentucky, and then went to Arkansas, I guess it has been a couple of years before he came back to this country.

Q Before he came back where? A Before he came back into Arkansas.

Q Is this child on the rolls of 1896? A Yes, sir, I think they are both on the rolls; the other one is named Nellie Blevins.

Q How old is this child Minnie Blevins now? A She is 14.

Q As I understand this, Minnie has been out of the Territory until the last two years? A Yes, sir, it has been with her father, and now she is back here with me.

Q She is back here on a visit? A No, sir, she is here living with us, she has been with us this summer; there is a great many mishaps in the world, I could make you an explanation about all these things, how they were transferred; the children are Cherokees by blood, and they were born and raised in this Territory.

Q Has she any improvements in the Nation? A Not at the present, I think they have all been disposed of, unless she has probably an interest in some of those lots by Blue Jacket. They never carried out any effects with him.

Q How old was this child when her father took her out of the Territory?

A I think it has been maybe a couple of years, when he left here; the child lived in the Territory until about two years ago, and now she has been back here about 6 or 8 months.

Q Then her father and step-mother still live in Arkansas? A Yes. she[sic], and she is living with us.

Q How long since her father lived here? A In the Nation, it has been some two or three years since he lived here; he went from here to Kentucky and from there to Arkansas, and is living there now.

Q Do you intend to keep her? A Yes, sir, that is what he wanted us to do, he wanted us to keep her and look after her land for her.

Q You haven't been appointed her legal guardian at all? A No, sir.

Q The father took this child out before June, 1898, or since; was she living here in June, 1898? A I don't recollect, she was just a minor child and he carried her off with him, and since he came back he asked me to take the child and raise her and see to her land, etc.

Q This child is alive and living with you? A Yes, sir.

Q What is the name of the other child? A Nellie Blevins.

Q Are they sisters? A Yes, sir.

Q Are they in the same condition? A Yes, sir, it is now with its grandfather in school; I brought that sworn statement; it was here last summer and went back with its grandfather to go to school.

Q Grandfather on its father's side? A Yes, sir.

Q That is Nellie Blevins? A Yes, sir, own sister to Minnie.

Q How old is Nellie? A She is 10 years old.

Q Where does she live? A She was born over here in this district, and has lived with me and her other grandfather ever since her mother died.

Q Does her other grandfather live in the District? A No, sir, he lives in California.

Q When did he take the child with him to California? A He taken it some three or four years ago, and he has got it to kinder raise and take care of and I have got this

one; it is the same blood and the same child, he came out here last summer and stayed a while and then went back to school.
Q What is the grandfather's name? A Mike Blevins.
Q He is a resident of California? A Yes, sir.
Q He has this child with him in California to raise? A Yes, sir.
Q Minnie and Nellie Blevins now are children of your daughter, Laura, who is dead? A Yes, sir.
Q Laura was an acknowledged citizen of the Cherokee Nation by blood and was upon the Cherokee rolls? A Yes, sir
(1896 Roll, page 438, Nos. 261 and 262, Minnie and Nellie Blevins, Delaware district.)
Q Is the mother of these children dead? A Yes, sir.
(The name of Laura J. Ward appears on the roll of 1880, page 334, No. 2839.)

These two children will be placed upon a doubtful card for the further consideration of the Commission, and you will be notified of the decision of the Commission in the near future, as to the citizenship of these children.

Bruce C. Jones, being duly sworn, says that as stenographer to the Commission to the Five Civilized Tribes he reported the testimony of the above names witness, and that the foregoing is a full, true and correct translation of his stenographic notes.

<u>Bruce C Jones</u>

Sworn to and subscribed before me this the 10th day of July, 1900.

<u>TB Needles</u>
Commissioner.

Supl. C.D.#10.

Department of the Interior,
Commission to the Five Civilized Tribes,
Muskogee, I. T., February 15, 1902.

SUPPLEMENTAL TESTIMONY In the matter of the enrollment of MINNIE & NELLIE BLEVINS as Cherokee citizens:

COMMISSION: this case set for hearing on the 15th day of February, 1902, and comes now the applicant represented by her Attorney, J. S. Davenport, Vinita, Indian Territory.
Mr. W. W. Hastings, present, Attorney for Cherokee Nation.

Mr. Davenport: The Attorney for the applicant desires to call the attention of the Commission to the Five Civilized Tribes fact that the mother who is a citizen by blood, died in the Cherokee Nation, and that these children were minors at the time of her death, a[sic] and the father, who was a white man, married a white woman, in the Cherokee Nation, lost his right before he moved out, and the grandfather, who applied for these children, was a bona fide citizen of the Cherokee Nation.

    Commission of Mr. Davenport: You do not desire to file a brief in this case?
A No sir.
Q Do you submit it to the Commission for final consideration?
A Yes, sir.

    Commission: By agreement of the attorney for the applicant and the representative of the Cherokee Nation this case is closed and submitted for final consideration.

---oooOOOooo---

    J. O. Rosson, being first duly sworn, states that as stenographer to the Commission to the Five Civilized Tribes he correctly recorded the testimony and proceedings in this case, and that the foregoing is a true and complete transcript of his stenographic notes thereof.

JO Rosson

Subscribed and sworn to before me this February 19, 1902.

TB Needles
Commissioner.

COMMISSIONERS:
TAMS BIXBY,
THOMAS B. NEEDLES,
C. R. BRECKINRIDGE,
W. E. STANLEY.

ALLISON L. AYLESWORTH,
    SECRETARY.

DEPARTMENT OF THE INTERIOR.
COMMISSION TO THE FIVE CIVILIZED TRIBES.

REFER IN REPLY TO THE FOLLOWING
Cherokee D-10

ADDRESS ONLY THE
COMMISSION TO THE FIVE CIVILIZED TRIBES.

Tahlequah, Indian Territory, July 13, 1903.

W. W. Hastings,
    Attorney for the Cherokee Nation,
        Tahlequah, Indian Territory.

Dear Sir:

    You are hereby notified that, before the application for the enrollment of Minnie and Nellie Blevins as citizens of the Cherokee Nation is complete, it is necessary that further evidence be introduced before the Commission, showing particularly the length of residence of each child in the Cherokee Nation and as to what effects they left in the Nation upon their removal therefrom; also as to the place of their mother's death and her residence at the time of her death and whether there was a guardian appointed for these children in the Nation.

This testimony can be presented before the Cherokee Land Office of the Commission at Tahlequah, Indian Territory, on or before the 11th of August, 1903.

Respectfully,

C. R. Breckinridge

Commissioner in Charge
Cherokee Land Office.

MFM

BCJ

Cherokee D-10

Department of the Interior,
Commission to the Five Civilized Tribes,
Cherokee Land Office,
Tahlequah, I.T., August 19, 1903.

In the matter of the application for the enrollment of Minnie and Nellie Blevins as citizens by blood of the Cherokee Nation.

SUPPLEMENTAL TESTIMONY.

Cherokee Nation represented by W.W. Hastings.

ALLEN BLEVINS, being duly sworn and examined by the Commission, testified as follows:

Q What is your name? A Allen Blevins.
Q How old are you? A 44.
Q What is your postoffice address? A Grove, Indian Territory.
Q Do you claim to be a citizen of the Cherokee Nation?
A No sir, I am not.
Q Have you two children that you claim to be citizens of that nation? A Yes sir, I have.
Q What are their names? A Minnie Lee Blevins and Nellie May Blevins.
Q Minnis[sic] is the older of the children, is she? A Yes sir.
Q You were at one time married to their mother, Laura? A Yes sir.
Q Is Laura Blevins dead now? A Yes sir.
Q She was a citizen by blood of the Cherokee Nation? A Yes sir.
Q When did she die? A She died the 29th day of October, 1890.
Q Was she living in the Cherokee Nation when she died? A Yes sir.

CHEROKEE GRANTED ENROLLMENT CARDS
& DAWES PACKETS 1900-1907 VOLUME I

Q After her death what became of these two children? A They went to live with her mother.
Q Where did her mother live? A Lived then in Arkansas.
Q When did they go over there? A Went right away after their mother died.
Q Where did you go? A I staid[sic] in the Cherokee Nation, at Bluejacket.
Q How long did you stay in the Cherokee Nation? A I was in the Cherokee Nation about 7 years.
Q You remained in the Cherokee Nation continuously for 7 years after your wife died? A Yes sir.
Q How long did the children stay with their grandmother? A Minnie, the oldest one, staid with her grandmother about 4 years; then she came back to me.
Q How long did she stay with you? A Staid with me at Bluejacket about 2 years, maybe longer; couldn't tell you just exactly.
Q She staid with you till you left the nation, did she? A Yes sir.
Q Did she go with you when you left here? A Yes sir.
Q You left here about 1897 then did you? A Yes sir, 1897.
Q Where did you go? A Kentucky.
Q Took Minnie with you? A Yes sir.
Q How long did you stay in Kentucky? A About 2 years and a half.
Q Did she stay with you all the time? A Yes sir.
Q Then where did you go? A Came back to Arkansas.
Q Did she come with you? A She came back to Arkansas but didn't stay there; came down to her uncle's, John Ward, in the Cherokee Nation, at Grove. She's been in the Cherokee Nation ever since.
Q Minnie got back to the Cherokee Nation then along about 1899 or 1900? A Yes sir, in 1899, latter part of 1899, summer.
Q How long did you stay in Arkansas? A About 4 months.
Q Then you came back to the nation? A Yes sir.
Q When you were in Kentucky, did you ever vote? A No sir.
Q What were you doing there? A Anything I could get to do; worked on the railroad about 8 months, made one crop down there; done anything I could find to do; common laborer.
Q You state, however, that you never exercised the rights of suffrage there, never voted? A No sir.
Q How long did Nellie stay with her grandmother in Arkansas?
A Ever since she was 6 months old, right after her mother died.
Q She is still with her grandmother out in California, is she? A Yes sir.
Q Mr. Blevens, when your wife died, what property did you and your children own in the Cherokee Nation? A Well sir, when she died we had quite a lot of property, 10 or 15 lots in Bluejacket, general mercantile business, about 500 acres of land on Cabin Creek.
Q Who did all that property belong to? A That property belonged to me and the children; I should judge it belonged to me, I made it.
Q Belonged to you as the head of the family? A Yes sir.
Q What became of it? A All except the town lots went to my creditors.
Q You failed in business? A Yes sir.
Q In what year? A Well, I declare, I couldn't tell you.

CHEROKEE GRANTED ENROLLMENT CARDS & DAWES PACKETS 1900-1907 VOLUME I

Q About what year? A I think about '96. '95 or '96.
Q Just a while before you went to Kentucky? A Yes sir.
Q And you disposed of all that property to pay your debts? A Yes.
Q Did you at one time claim to be a citizen by intermarriage? A I did, yes sir.
Q You married out? A Yes sir.
Q At the time you failed you still claimed to be a citizen? A I did not, now[sic] sir.
Q What have you done with the town lots, do you still own them?
A There are 7 or 8 or 10 of them I still hold deeds for.
Q Do they belong to you or your children? A They belong to me; I paid money for them; I never gave them to the children or anything of that kind; the just stand as they did.
Q When was it you married out? A '94 I believe.
Q You didposed[sic] of the farm after you yourself had ceased to be a citizen? A Yes sir, in '96 I think it was. Gave up my mercantile business and merchandise and such as that, turned it over to my creditors.
Q These children never held any property in the Cherokee Nation except through you? A Except through me, no sir.

++++++++++++++++++

Mable F. Maxwell, being duly sworn, states that as stenographer to the Commission to the Five Civilized Tribes, she correctly recorded the supplemental testimony in this case and that the above and foregoing is a true and correct transcript of her stenographic notes thereof.

Mabel F. Maxwell

Subscribed and sworn to before me
this 19th day of August, 1903.

Samuel Foreman

MFM   Notary Public.

Cherokee D-10

DEPARTMENT OF THE INTERIOR,
COMMISSION TO THE FIVE CIVILIZED TRIBES.

In the matter of the application for the enrollment of Minnie and Nellie Blevins as citizens by blood of the Cherokee Nation.

D E C I S I O N.

The record in this case shows that on July 10, 1900, George M. Ward appeared before the Commission at Fairland, Indian Territory, and made application for the enrollment of his two minor grandchildren, Minnie and Nellie Blevins, as citizens by blood of the Cherokee Nation. Further proceedings In the matter of the

CHEROKEE GRANTED ENROLLMENT CARDS & DAWES PACKETS 1900-1907 VOLUME I

application of said application were had at Muskogee, Indian Territory, on February 15, 1902, and at Tahlequah, Indian Territory, on July 16, and August 19, 1903.

The evidence shows that Minnie and Nellie Blevins are the minor children of Allen Blevins, a white man, and his wife Laura Blevins, deceased, who is identified on the Cherokee authenticated tribal roll of 1880 as a native Cherokee. Said Minnie and Nellie Blevins are identified on the Cherokee census roll of 1896.

The evidence further shows that the mother of the applicants died in 1890, being a resident at that time of the Cherokee Nation, her husband being engaged in business at Bluejacket, Indian Territory. Subsequent to her death the applicants, aged ten years and six months respectively, went to live with their maternal grandmother in the State of Arkansas, where Minnie continued to live for four years, thereafter returning to the Cherokee Nation and living therein with her father about two years when he left, going to Kentucky; remaining there two years and a half, thence to Arkansas, she remaining with her said father during all this time. It is further shown that Minnie Blevins was in her nineteenth year when she returned to the Cherokee Nation and that Nellie Blevins is still a minor and residing with her grandparents outside the limits of the Indian Territory.

It is, therefore, the opinion of this Commission that, following the decision of the Department in the case of Ora M. Camp et al (I.T.D. 1418-1903), Minnie Blevins and Nellie Blevins should be enrolled as citizens by blood of the Cherokee Nation, in accordance with the provisions of section twenty-one of the act of Congress approved June 28, 1898 (30 Stats., 495), and it is so ordered.

COMMISSION TO THE FIVE CIVILIZED TRIBES.

(SIGNED). *Tams Bixby.*
Chairman.

(SIGNED). *T. B. Needles.*
Commissioner.

(SIGNED). *C. R. Breckinridge.*
Commissioner.

Commissioner.

Dated at Muskogee, Indian Territory, this   NOV 23 1904

CHEROKEE GRANTED ENROLLMENT CARDS
& DAWES PACKETS 1900-1907 VOLUME I

COMMISSIONERS:
TAMS BIXBY,
THOMAS B. NEEDLES,
C. R. BRECKINRIDGE.

WM. G. BEALL,
SECRETARY.

DEPARTMENT OF THE INTERIOR,
COMMISSION TO THE FIVE CIVILIZED TRIBES.

Cherokee D-10.

ADDRESS ONLY THE
COMMISSION TO THE FIVE CIVILIZED TRIBES.

Muskogee, Indian Territory, November 23, 1904.

W. W. Hastings,
    Attorney for the Cherokee Nation,
        Tahlequah, Indian Territory.

Dear Sir:

    There is herewith inclosed a copy of the decision of the Commission to the Five Civilized Tribes, dated November 23, 1904, granting the application for the enrollment of Minnie Lee and Nellie May Blevins as citizens by blood of the Cherokee Nation.

    You are hereby advised that you will be allowed fifteen days from date hereof within which to file such protest as you may desire to make against the action of the Commission in this case, a copy of which you will be required to furnish the applicants. If you fail to file protest within the time allowed this decision will be considered final.

                Respectfully,

                    Tams Bixby

Incl. S-64.   Chairman.

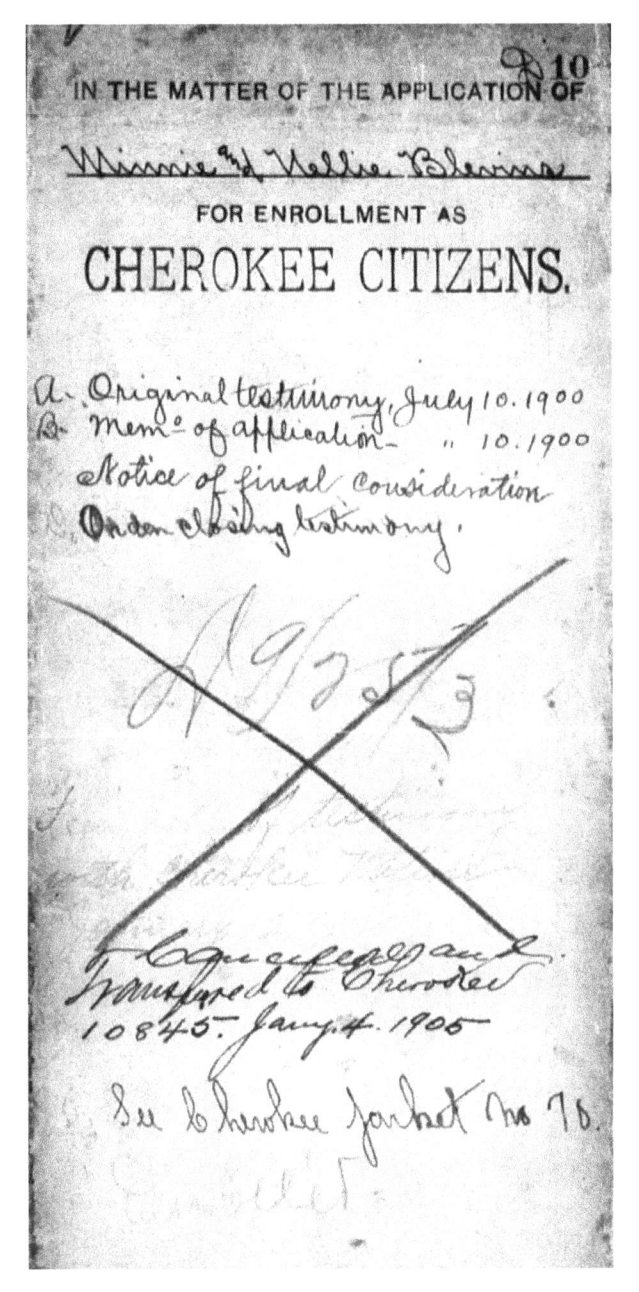

IN THE MATTER OF THE APPLICATION OF № 10

Minnie & Nellie Blevins

FOR ENROLLMENT AS

CHEROKEE CITIZENS.

a. Original testimony, July 10. 1900
b. Mem° of application— " 10. 1900
c. Notice of final consideration
d. Order closing testimony.

Transferred to Cherokee
10845— Jany 4. 1905

See Cherokee packet No 78.

CHEROKEE GRANTED ENROLLMENT CARDS & DAWES PACKETS 1900-1907 VOLUME I

CHEROKEE GRANTED ENROLLMENT CARDS & DAWES PACKETS 1900-1907 VOLUME I

Cherokee D13 - Joseph Ann Hall

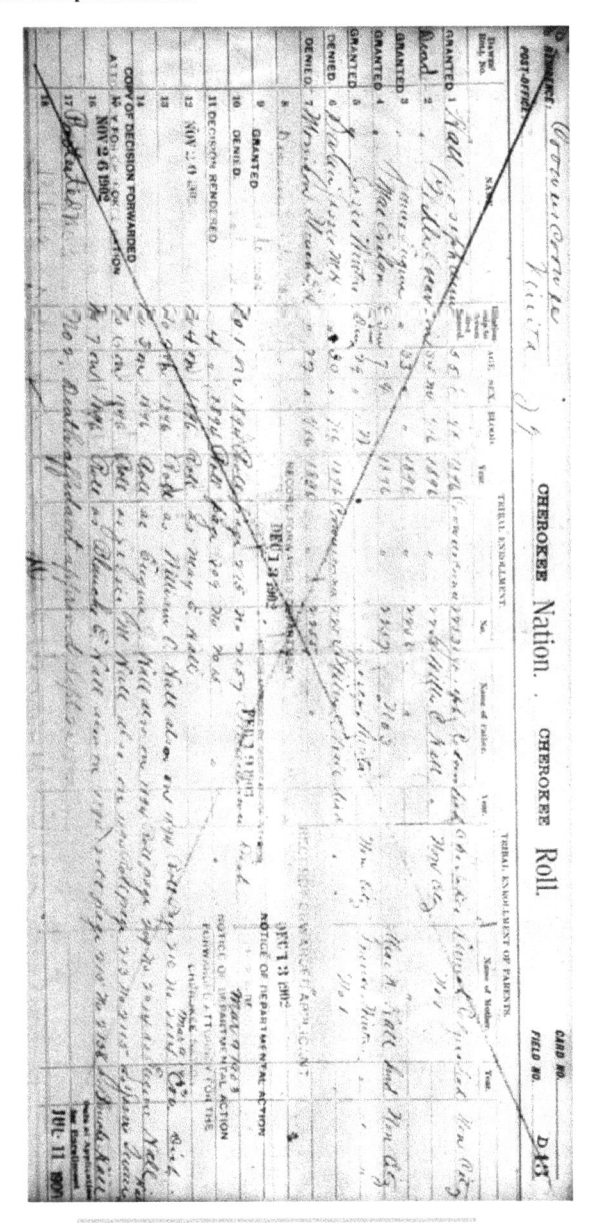

CHEROKEE GRANTED ENROLLMENT CARDS & DAWES PACKETS 1900-1907 VOLUME I

Department of the Interior,
Commission to the Five Civilized Tribes,
Fairland, I. T., July 11, 1900.

In the matter of the application of Joseph Ann Hall et. al., for enrollment as citizens by blood and intermarriage of the Cherokee Nation; being sworn and examined by Commissioner Breckenridge, she testifies as follows:

Q What is your name? A Joseph Ann Hall.
Q What is your age? A I was born in '45.
Q What is your post-office address? A Vinita Indian Territory
Q Is that where you live? A Yes sir.
Q You have made your permanent residence there? A I consider that my permanent home with the exception of times I have been away on visits with my children.
Q How long have you made that your home? A We moved there in 1888, and have made that our home, from time to time living there sometimes two years at a time, and the only time I have been away would be on visits to my children or where I would be with them.
Q Where did you live before that time? A In Saint Louis, Missouri.
Q Where were you born? A I was born on what was the Cherokee Neutral Land; in Kansas it is now, but it was then a part of the Cherokee Nation.
Q How long did you continue to reside in the Indian country before you moved out of it? A I was quite a little girl, I suppose about ten or twelve years old.
Q Where were you carried then? A To Missouri, and I was married and lived for a time, as I say, in Saint Louis, and in 1888 I removed to the Indian Territory.
Q From the time you were carried out of the Territory until 1888 you resided mostly outside of the Territory? A I was in school a great deal of the time. I was married quite young and went immediately to Saint Louis and resided there.
Q And resumed your residence in the Territory in 1888? A Yes sir.
Q Where did you first live when you resumed your residence in the Indian Territory? A Vinita.
Q Are you a Cherokee? A By blood.
Q You claim then your rights as a Cherokee by blood? A By blood.
Q What is the name of your father? A Joseph Rogers.
Q Is he living? A No sir. He died on the night of my birth.
Q Was he on any of the rolls of the Cherokee Tribe? A Yes sir, he was on the old rolls, the first rolls here.
Q The old rolls before 1860? A Yes sir.
Q In what district of the Cherokee Nation did he live? A As I have just told you, it was the Neutral Land.
Q What was the maiden name of your mother? A Hannah Foster.
Q Was she a white woman or a Cherokee? A She is a white woman.
Q Is she living? A No sir.
Q Is her name on the rolls of the Cherokee Nation? A I think so. I think I remember her drawing money at Tahlequah when I was quite a child.
Q When did she die? A Just at the commencement of the War.

CHEROKEE GRANTED ENROLLMENT CARDS & DAWES PACKETS 1900-1907 VOLUME I

Q   In what district is your home? A   Since 1888 I have considered Cooweescoowee District my home.
Q   That is the district in which Vinita is situated? A   Yes sir[sic] We have had our improvements in this District, seven miles from Vinita; my children contributed to keeping up the improvements, and considered that our home and have really never tried to make a home anywhere else.
Q   Have you been outside of the Territory during the past three years? A   Yes sir. I was away last year for a time on a visit to my children and back again.
Q   Are you keeping house at Vinita? A   No sir, not since my husband's death; I have boarded since he died.
Q   You left the Territory for the purpose of being with your children? A   Yes sir.
Q   Have you ever been enrolled by the Cherokee authorities? A   Certainly.
Q   On what rolls? A   On all the rolls since 1888.
Q   You are not on the roll of 1880? A   No sir, just escaped that by as I say being out of the Territory at that time; we were on the rolls of 1894 and 1896, all of us.
    Note: 1896 roll examined, Cooweescoowee District, page 177. #2253, is found applicant's name.
Q   When did you say your husband died? A   About five years ago.
    Note: 1894 roll examined, page 215, #2157, Joseph Ann Hall, Cooweescoowee District.
Q   Was your husband enrolled upon any of the official rolls of the Cherokee Nation? A   I don't think he was, because we were not married in the Cherokee Nation according to Cherokee laws.
Q   Your husband was not an Indian? A   No sir, he was a non-citizen. You would hardly call him an adopted citizen from the fact that we were not married according to Cherokee laws.
Q   Where were you married? A   In Warsaw, Missouri, my husband was at that time deputy clerk in that county, and I was teaching school at that time.
Q   What proportion of Cherokee blood do you claim to have?
A   My father was one-fourth, I am one-eighth.
Q   You wish to make application for yourself and your children under twenty-one years of age and unmarried? A   No sir, none except my little granddaughter who is here.
Q   Has she a father or mother to take acre[sic] of her? A   I am her natural guardian, because I have really adopted her and I have had the full care of her since she was two years old; her mother is dead.
Q   Is her father dead? A   No sir.
Q   Does she claim through her mother or her father? A   Her father.
Q   The child is not present? A   Yes sir.
Q   Where is her father? A   Her father has been traveling with my daughters in the capacity of business agent, and couldn't be present now on account of financial matters. The child's mother died in Vinita, Indian Territory four or five years ago.
Q   Was the child's mother ever on the Tribal rolls? A   Yes sir. You will find her name Alice Nancy Hall; she was a Mississippi Edwards, a non-citizen, before she was married.
Q   When were they married? A   Previous to 1896.

CHEROKEE GRANTED ENROLLMENT CARDS & DAWES PACKETS 1900-1907 VOLUME I

Examination by Cherokee Att'y Hastings:

Q This little girl's mother your daughter? A No sir, her father is my son, Eugene Hall.
   Note: 1896 roll examined for this child's mother's name, and not found.
Applicant: This child's mother died about five years ago.
Q What's your son's full name, the father of this child? A James Eugene Hall.
Q Does his name appear upon the Tribal rolls? A Yes sir.
Q On the 1880 roll? A No sir, on the rolls of 1894 and 1896, you will find his name.
Q Why was he not enrolled in 1880? A I wasn't on the rolls then, I wasn't living here then.
Q Because he wasn't in the Territory? A Yes sir.
   Note: Applicant produces certificate of admission of herself and children to citizenship in the Cherokee Nation.
Q How many children have you? A Four.
Q You have handed me here what purports to be a certificate of admission to the Cherokee Nation of yourself and Jessie Hall and Blanche Hall and James Eugene Hall and William Oscar Hall; the certificate bearing your name and the first three names following is executed the 12th day of November 1887; the certificate bearing the name of William Oscar Hall was executed the 12th day of November 1887; they all appear to be duly signed and executed by the officials of the Cherokee Nation; I pass them to the Counsel for the Cherokee Nation and ask them if they are in regular and proper order, the Counsel assents to them in due form, this makes them a matter of record, and I hand them back to you. (Hands applicant back papers)
Q Have your four children any permanent and fixed residence outside of this Territory? A No sir, they have never tried to improve or buy any home elsewhere.
Q What is the character of their occupation outside the Territory? A They are all connected with the theatrical profession; all of them are on the stage with the exception of Eugene, he is connected with them as business agent with them.
Q They are connected with a business which cause them to move outside the Territory from point to point? A Yes sir.
Q And James Eugene he acts for them in a business capacity? A Yes sir.
Q What is the name of this child of which you speak? A Mae Evelyn Hall.
Q She is the child of which one of your sons? A James Eugene Hall.
Q And her father is living? A Yes sir.
Q But you said is now out of the state on business, and finds it for business reasons impossible to come? A Yes sir, wholly impossible at present.
Q Is this child's name on any of the Tribal rolls? A Yes sir. I think you will find her on the 1894 roll, she was born just in time to be enrolled.
   Note: 1894 roll examined, on page 209, #2015, Cooweescoowee District is found name of Mae E. Hall. And 1896 roll examined and on page 177, #2257, is found name Mae E. Hall.
Q This child appears duly recorded on the roll of 1894 and 1896 as Mae E. Hall, is that the name you want it to bear in the future? A No sir, I want her full name Mae Evelyn Hall.

CHEROKEE GRANTED ENROLLMENT CARDS & DAWES PACKETS 1900-1907 VOLUME I

Q   You stated that you have had the bringing up of this child, constantly in your care, its mother is dead and its father pursuing a traveling occupation?   A   Yes sir.
Q   Which makes it impossible for him to give it a father's attention?   A   Yes sir.
Q   And you claim the right to appear for it as natural guardian and its grandmother and keeper in fact?   A   Yes sir.
Q   And this is the child that accompanies you now?   A   Yes sir.
Q   You wish to apply for tow of your sons who are absent?   A   Yes sir, one of them is sick at Hot Springs and the other one is the one we have just been discussing.
Q   What is the name of the one who is at Hot Springs?   A   William Oscar Hall. He was here for sometime until a few weeks ago, and he went out then on the road with the company and he has been playing in Little Rock and Hot Springs and has fallen ill and is too ill to be here.
Q   What is his age?   A   He was born in '66 I think. This paper will show; (Produces paper) He is I think thirty-four years of age.
Q   He is the one whose certificate of admission to Cherokee citizenship you have just shown?   A   Yes sir.
Q   You wish also to apply for another son, and that is James Eugene Hall?
A   Yes sir.
Q   He is the one whose age is given as twenty years in 1887, in the certificate of admission to Cherokee citizenship that you have just submitted?   A   Yes sir.
Q   And he is now detained in New York on business and for financial reasons finds it impossible to come?   A   Yes sir.
Q   Have you any daughters married?   A   Yes sir, two.
Q   Are either one of the sons married?   A   The oldest son, William Oscar Hall, is married.
Q   Is his wife present?   A   His wife is present.

   Examination by Cherokee Attorney Hastings:

Q   Where were you living at the time of your re-admission October 1887?
A   I was living in Saint Louis.
Q   You state that you subsequently removed to the Cherokee Nation?   A   Yes sir.
Q   Was your husband alive at that time?   A   Yes sir up until five years ago.
Q   To what point in the Cherokee Nation did you remove?   A   Vinita.
Q   What time did you remove to Vinita after your re-admission?   A   I think it was in the fall of 1888.
Q   How long did you remain in the Cherokee Nation then?   A   We removed everything that we had and settled at Vinita, Indian Territory, at the Eiffert House, and we lived there two years, and I have been back and forth to the Territory and I have lived at the Raymond House one and two and three years at different times then and my husband fell ill and I took him back to Saint Louis and he was a member of the Knights of Pythias and he was buried by the Knights of Pythias Lodge.
Q   You went back to Saint Louis in 1890?   A   Yes sir.
Q   What did you do in Saint Louis in 1890, 1891 and 1892 and 1893?
A   My husband's health failed, and he as in business for several years before he died.
Q   You had a home there in Saint Louis?   A   Only rented rooms, temporarily.

CHEROKEE GRANTED ENROLLMENT CARDS
& DAWES PACKETS 1900-1907 VOLUME I

Q   And you remained there from 1890 until he died in 1896? A No sir, I remained there until two years before his death we removed to the Indian Territory and brought him back here home, as I considered it, and he was here at the Raymond House; it wasn't a hotel, they rented rooms there, and we kept house there for about a year and a half.

 Examination by Com'r Breckenridge:

Q   When did you come? A At that time I don't remember just the year, it was a few months previous to his death that we went back to Saint Louis.
 Examination by Attorney Hastings:
Q   Do you remember the exact time of his death? A He died January 13th, it is five or six years ago, 1894 or 1895.
Q   After his death did you live in Saint Louis? A No sir immediately after his death I broke up housekeeping and I have never had a home anywhere since that; I have traveled with my children and lived back and forth with them, I have boarded where I could visit them.
Q   I want to find out where you were in 1895 and what were you doing, where did you live? A I was visiting a while with them for the first year after his death. I was traveling with them as they went around, and then in the meantime before that we was out-- I came out to the Indian Territory and spent quite a long time; I was with my son down at Adair and at Vinita a good deal of the time and then returned to my children.
Q   Have you ever had any business in Saint Louis since your husband's death?
A   No sir.
Q   Of no kind? A No sir.
Q   Do you own a home anywhere else outside the Indian Territory? A No sir.
Q   Have you ever been in business since your husband's death, since your re-admission, anywhere? A Nothing only as newspaper correspondent.
Q   What is Eugene Hall, I believe you stated he is manager of this opera? A Yes sir, he has been traveling with my daughters most of the time off and on since he left the Territory about three years ago.
Q   Has he been doing any other business except traveling with this company?
A   Nothing except occasionally a little job with his typewriter, nothing only temporarily.
Q   Does he own any business outside the Territory? A No sir.
Q   Does he own a home outside? A No sir.
Q   How about William Oscar Hall, does he won[sic] a home outside? A No sir.
Q   Has he been travelling with this company all the time? A Not all the time, but with different companies; that's his occupation.
Q   Has he made his home in the Cherokee Nation here? A Yes sir.
Q   Where was he married? A In Saint Louis.
Q   How long ago was that? A It was in 1889.
Q   Has his wife ever lived in the Cherokee Nation? A Yes sir, they have never had any other home except with me when they were there out visiting with her sisters; they have never established a home anywhere for themselves,- taken it through the authorities of the Cherokees here.

CHEROKEE GRANTED ENROLLMENT CARDS & DAWES PACKETS 1900-1907 VOLUME I

Q   Jessie and Blanche here are your two daughters? A Yes sir.
Q   This child of Eugene Hall's was born here at Adair? A Yes sir.
Q   You own any property in the Cherokee Nation? A I do.
Q   Of what character? A It is a claim of what we consider as my natural allotment all in a body, it is about seven miles north of Vinita, Indian Territory, joining the Marks' farm.
Q   That's all you own in the Indian Territory? A I have some lots at Adair.
Q   When did you acquire this property, this farm? A I guess some six or seven years ago.
Q   You have been receiving the rents off of that farm since? A Yes sir, and every one of my children have contributed to the establishment of their claim. It hasn't very much improvements on it but enough to hold it and Mr. Marks has been our agent and looking after the place for us and paying some rent on it every year.
   Com'r Breckenridge:
Q   You mean contributed to the improvements on the place? A Yes sir.
   Examination by Cherokee Attorney Hastings:
Q   Do you spend your vacations at one place all the time?
A   No sir, I usually come out here; I am here every spring; I usually stay here the greater part of my time when I am not travelling.

   Examined by Commissioner Breckenridge:

Q   You moved to Vinita in 1888? A Yes sir.
Q   Your husband died when? A Six years ago I guess, this spring 1894 or 1895, January 13th.
Q   He died in Saint Louis? A Yes sir.
Q   How long were you in Saint Louis previous to his death?
A   We went from here there when he was almost helpless.
Q   When did you leave here to go there on that occasion? A Just about three months before he died.
Q   Did you go there exclusively in the interest of his health?
A   Yes sir, and that he might be near his Lodge that they might assist me in taking care of him. I went away the following--that summer I broke up housekeeping immediately after his death and returned to the Territory that summer and was with my son at Adair and at Vinita, and I am recognized in Vinita as that being my only home, and there citizens there that will attest to the truth that I have made that my home more than anywhere else.
   Note: 1896 roll examined, page 177, #2258, William O. Hall. 1894 roll examined, Page 213, #2114, William O. Hall, Cooweescoowee District.
Applicant: My son desires to be enrolled in his full name Willis Oscar Hall, his certificate is under the name, through some mistake, of William Oscar Hall. 1896 roll, page 177, #2256, on roll as Eugene J. Hall; 1894 roll, page 209, #2014, as Eugene Hall, Cooweescoowee District.
Applicant: My son's other name is James Eugene Hall.

--   --   --

CHEROKEE GRANTED ENROLLMENT CARDS
& DAWES PACKETS 1900-1907 VOLUME I

Josie Winters Hall, appearing for herself, and being sworn and examined by Commissioner Breckenridge, testifies:

Q   What is your name? A Josie Winters Hall.
Q   What is your age? A Twenty-nine.
Q   What is your post-office address? A Vinita, Indian Territory when I am off the road.
Q   What is your permanent home? A Yes sir, with my mother.
Q   Are you of Cherokee origin? A No sir, just adopted.
Q   You claim through your husband by marriage? A Yes sir.
Q   What is the name of your husband? A Willis Oscar Hall.
Q   I hold here a certificate of admission of William Oscar Hall to citizenship in the Cherokee Nation, who was twenty-one years of age at the time of admission, the 12th day of November, 1887, is that your husband? A Yes sir.
Q   This certificate has been submitted to the representatives of the Cherokee Nation and admitted to be regular and in due form, when were you married? A In 1889.
Q   Have you your marriage certificate? A I haven't it with me, it is in Vinita.
Q   Are the ladies here present, and Mrs. Hall, the mother of William Oscar Hall, she is aware of your marriage? A Yes sir.
Q   And they are sisters of your husband? A Yes sir.
Q   And in their presence you profess your marriage to William Oscar Hall?
A   Yes sir.
Q   Have you children? A No sir.
Q   You make no application except for yourself? A For myself.
Q   What is your husband's business? A Theatrical man.
Q   Is he kept continually on the road? A Yes sir, with the exception of a few weeks in the summer.
Q   Do you consider that your husband's permanent home is in Vinita? A Vinita, Indian Territory.
Q   Has he any residence or property at any other place? A None whatever.
Q   When was he last at Vinita? A About three weeks or a month ago.
Q   Is your husband now ill at Hot Springs? A Ill at Hot Springs.
Q   The same who has had application made by his mother for admission on this roll?
A   Yes sir.
Q   Is your husband interested in any property in or about Vinita? A Yes sir.
Q   What character of property? A Farming property.
Q   Do you know when your husband was in Vinita or the Territory after his admission in 1887 as a citizen in the Cherokee Nation?
A   He was in 1890 something, 1894 or 95, and then later.
Q   When did you say you were married? A In 1889.
Q   Where were you married? A In Saint Louis.
Q   When did you first visit Vinita after your marriage? A In 1893.
Q   What connection did your husband have with Vinita or the Indian Territory after your marriage, did he often come down to the Territory? A Oh yes, this was his home you know.
Q   He did not bring you until 1893? A 1893.

CHEROKEE GRANTED ENROLLMENT CARDS
& DAWES PACKETS 1900-1907 VOLUME I

Q So far as you know he looked exclusively to the Territory as his home, political home and actual domicile? A Yes sir.
Q Have you ever had any children? A None.
Q You and your husband are living together at this time, amicably as man and wife, and have always done so? A Yes sir.

 Examined by Cherokee Attorney Hastings:

Q You say you were married in 1889 in Saint Louis? A Yes sir.
Q The first visit you paid to the Indian Territory was in 1893, four years after the marriage? A Yes sir.
Q What was your husband doing during those four years, what was his business?
A On the road, theatrical business.
Q Ever since he married? A Yes sir.
Q He is engaged in that business at this time? A Yes sir, of course now he is sick..
 Note: 1896 roll examined, page 309, #529, Josie Winters Hall, Cooweescoowee District.

    --   --   --

 Jessie Mae Hall Swan, being present, appears in person for herself, and being sworn and examined by Commissioner Breckenridge, testifies:

Q What is your name? A Jessie Mae Hall Swan.
Q What is your age? A Thirty.
Q What is your post-office address? A Vinita, Indian Territory
Q Is that your permanent residence and home? A Yes sir.
Q How long have you lived there? A Since 1888.
Q Do you stay there continually? A No.
Q What is the nature of your absence? A Theatrical business, travelling.
Q Your profession is such as takes you from point to point throughout the country?
A Yes sir.
Q Have you any other home in a permanent sense except Vinita?
[sic] No sir.
Q Do you look upon that as your fixed domicile and actual home? A Yes sir.
Q Have you any property interests in the Indian Territory? A Yes sir.
Q What is the character of your interests? A Farm land.
Q Is that farm occupied and being worked? A Yes sir.
Q Are you in receipt of any revenues from that farm? A Yes sir.
Q How long have you been interested in that farm? A Since 1896 I think, I don't know the exact year; five or six years, I don't remember the exact number of years.
Q Are you the same person as Jessie Hall, aged seventeen years mentioned in the certificate I here hold, and which has been identified as in regular and due form by the representatives of the Cherokee Nation, and which certificate is a certificate of admission to you to Cherokee citizenship on the 12th day of November 1887?
A Yes sir, I am.

CHEROKEE GRANTED ENROLLMENT CARDS & DAWES PACKETS 1900-1907 VOLUME I

Q   You are the Jessie Hall mentioned in the certificate handed me by your mother, including her and several of her children?   A   Yes sir.
Q   Does your name appear upon the Tribal rolls of the Cherokee Nation?   A   On the 1894 and 1896 roll.
      Note: 1896 roll examined, page 177, #2254, Jessie M. Hall, Cooweescoowee District. 1894 roll, page 213, #2115, Jesse Swan Hall.
Com'r Breckenridge: Upon consulting the rolls of 1894 and 1896 her name is found duly recorded as above stated.
Q   You now apply to be entered upon the roll that is being made by the Dawes Commission as Jessie Mae Hall Swan?   A   Yes sir.
Q   You are now married?   A   Yes sir.
Q   Do you apply for your husband?   A   No.
Q   When were you married?   A   In 1891.
Q   You are Cherokee by blood?   A   Yes sir.
Q   Your husband does not make his residence here?   A   He does not.
Q   You don't look upon it as his residence at all?   A   No sir.
Q   Have you children?   A   No sir.
Q   You apply only for yourself?   A   Yes sir.
Q   Have you ever had children?   A   No sir.
Q   You have no children then buried in the Territory?   A   No sir.
Q   Is your mother living in the town of Vinita?   A   Yes sir.
Q   Your mother made application for you for enrollment, do you consider that your home is with her?   A   Yes sir.
Q   And that's the only home you look to as your place of residence as in any sense a home?   [sic]   Yes sir.

    Examined by Attorney Hastings for the Cherokee Nation:

Q   Where were you married?   A   Mount Stirling[sic], Illinois.
Q   How long have you been living at Stirling when you were married?   A   I was travelling through there.
Q   What is your husband's business?   A   Theatrical.
Q   Does he travel with the same company as you?   A   Most of the time.
Q   Has he any other profession or business?   A   No sir, just as a play writer and actor.
Q   Are you living together now?   A   Yes sir.
Q   Where was his home before you married him?   A   Rockport, Indiana.
Q   Where do you spend your vacations?   A   This is about the first vacation I have had since I have been on the road, and I have been spending it in New York and here.
Q   Did you ever spend them in Indiana?   A   No sir, never have. We have played there at his home, but I have never had any vacation.
Q   Your husband had never been to the Territory?   A   Never has.
Question by Att'y Breckenridge: You claim as a Cherokee by blood?   A   Yes sir.

        --   --   --

CHEROKEE GRANTED ENROLLMENT CARDS
& DAWES PACKETS 1900-1907 VOLUME I

Blanche Evelyn Hall Morrison, being present, appears in person for herself, and being sworn and examined by Commissioner Breckenridge, she testifies:

Q   What is your name? A Blanche Evelyn Hall Morrison.
Q   What is your age? A Twenty-six.
Q   What is your post-office address? A Vinita, is my permanent address.
Q   Is that where you live? A Yes sir, that's my home.
Q   How long have you made that your residence? A Since 1887. I stated to school in 1887.
Q   Did you stay continually there? A No sir.
Q   What character of business or what occupation takes you away from there?
A   Theatrical business.
Q   Do you look to any other place as your domicile or place of residence?
A   No sir.
Q   Does your mother live there? A Yes sir.
Q   Your father is dead? A Yes sir.
Q   Have you any property interests in or around there? A Farm land.
Q   Do you derive any revenue from that farm land? A We rent it
Q   You apply for enrollment as Blanche Evelyn Hall Morrison? A Yes sir.
Q   Are you the same person mentioned as Blanche Hall, aged fourteen years in the certificate of admission to Cherokee citizenship which I now hold, and dated November 12th, 1887? A Yes sir.
Com'r Breckenridge: This certificate has been submitted to the representatives of the Cherokee Nation, and accepted as in due form and regular.
Q   When did you marry? A In 1895.
Q   Do you make application for your husband? A No sir.
Q   Only for yourself? A Only for myself.
Q   Have you children? A No sir.
Q   Has your husband ever been to this Territory? A Not since we have been married.
Q   Where were you married? A In Boone, Iowa.
Q   What is your husband's business? A Theatrical business.
Q   Is he at present engaged in this business? A No, not for a few weeks.
Q   The Territory, as I understand you, and Vinita, are the places that you look upon as your permanent home. A Yes sir.
Q   And your absence is of a temporary character according to the demands of your profession? A Yes sir.

Examined by Att'y Hastings, for Cherokee Nation:

Q   Where were you married? A Boone, Iowa.
Q   Where did your husband reside at that time? A He was traveling with me, but his home is in Portland, Maine.
Q   How long had he been traveling with you? A Just a few months, in the same company.
Q   Has he been traveling with you in the same company since that time?
A   All the time.

CHEROKEE GRANTED ENROLLMENT CARDS
& DAWES PACKETS 1900-1907 VOLUME I

Q Where is he now? A He is in Portland, Maine now.
Q Spending the summer? A Yes sir, and working there a few weeks off and on, the summer theatre there.
Q Has he been doing anything other than following the theatrical profession since your married? A No.
Q He has had no other business? A No sir.
Q He has never been to the Territory? A Not since our marriage.
Q When did you say you left the Territory? A I left in 1891.
Q When did you join the theatrical troup? A In thee same year, in 1891, the latter part of the year.
Q You have been with some theatrical troup every year subsequent to that time?
A Every year, and most of the summers.
Q You are with one now- you have been in the past? A Yes, just closed with one, and will re-open in a few weeks.
Q Have you any children? A No sir.
 Note: 1896 roll examined, page 177, #2255, Blanche E. Hall; 1894 roll, page 215, #2158, Blanche Hall, Cooweescoowee District.

-- -- --

Mrs. Joseph Ann Hall, re-called:
Com'r Breckenridge:

The decision of the Commission as to the application you make on your own behalf and in behalf of your family for enrollment as citizens of the Cherokee Nation, will be mailed to you in writing at your present post-office address as soon as practicable. The decision of the Commission will be based upon your oral testimony given at this time, and upon such written evidence as you have submitted for the consideration of the Commission, in connection with the consideration of the law bearing upon the subject.

M.D. Green, being first duly sworn, states that as stenographer to the Commission to the Five Civilized Tribes he reported the foregoing case, and that the above and foregoing is a full, true and correct transcript of his stenographic notes in said case.

MD Green

Subscribed and sworn to before me this 12th day of July 1900.

TB Needles
Commissioner.

CHEROKEE GRANTED ENROLLMENT CARDS
& DAWES PACKETS 1900-1907 VOLUME I

Cherokee by blood: Supplemental.   D - 13.

Department of the Interior.
Commission to the Five Civilized Tribes.
Vinita, I. T., May 14, 1901.

Supplemental testimony in the matter of the application of Joseph Ann Hall et al. for enrollment as Cherokee citizens.

Lemuel W. Marks, being sworn and examined by Commissioner C. R. Breckenridge, testified as follows:

Q   Give me your full name. A Lemuel W. Marks.
Q   In what case do you want to give testimony, Mr. Marks? A Joe Ann Hall et al.
Q   How old are you, Mr. Marks? A 51 years old.
Q   What is your postoffice? A Woodley.
Q   In what district do you live? A Cooweescoowee.
Q   What testimony can you give in this case of Mrs. Hall and her children that will lead to their identification as recognized and bona fide Cherokee citizens?
A   I have known them since '84.
Q   Know her and her children? A Yes sir.
Q   Where have they lived and what have they been doing? A The first I knew of them was in Vinita; her husband was alive then.
Q   When was that? A That was in the early part of '85, or latter part of '84.
Q   How long have you lived in the Cherokee Nation? A I have lived in the Cherokee Nation since '81. Her husband had a little store in Vinita when I first knew her and from there they went to Adair and done business there for a year or so, and he came back to Vinita and was sick there for some time, and was going to St. Louis to be treated, and died. The mother was with them, but the girls at that time were stopping with Willie Miller in Vinita. The son that died was off traveling.
Q   What was his name? A Oscar.
Q   He is dead now? A Yes sir.
Q   He died recently? A Yes sir.
Q   What was he travelling for, on business? A He was on the stage with a troupe.
Q   With a theatrical troupe? A Yes sir, and was only here a very short time; I only met him a few times in his life time. The two girls I mentioned, they were here at that time. The oldest boy, Eugene, was living at Adair and still lived there after his father died.
Q   And what about the girls? A They later on went off travelling with her husband.
Q   With a theatrical troupe? A Yes sir.
Q   And they followed that life ever since? A Yes sir.
Q   They had no special abiding place outside of the territory? A No stopping places at all; in vacations they would come home.
Q   What property have they had all this time in the Cherokee Nation? A They have a place of about four hundred acres in it joining my place.
Q   How long have they had that place? A They have had that since 1896.
Q   Did they have any property before that, that you know of? A On-lt[sic] town lots at Adair.

CHEROKEE GRANTED ENROLLMENT CARDS & DAWES PACKETS 1900-1907 VOLUME I

Q   Any improvement on that? A Dwelling houses I think.
Q   And they have had this farm since '96? A Yes sir, they all held it together; it is undivided.
Q   The whole family hold it? A Yes sir, I sold them the place. The deed was made out to the family and put on record at Claremore, the date I sold it to them. And Mrs. Hall sometimes goes and stays near by where the children are playing; as a general thing she makes her home here, ever since. Never been out very long at a time.
Q   Has this been her custom since you first knew her back in the eighties? A Yes sir, ever since her husband died.
Q   When did he die? A I couldn't just say what year. Its[sic] been five or six years ago, I think, or longer.
Q   That is about all you can state, is it? A Yes sir; I have rented her farm ever since I sold it.
Q   You rented it back from her? A Yes sir, paying her cash rent for it; $75.00 per year; last year I paid her only $40.00. I think that is about all I know.

Commissioner: This will be filed as additional testimony in the case of D - 13.

The undersigned, being duly sworn, states that a stenographer to the Commission to the Five Civilized Tribes, he correctly recorded the testimony and proceedings in this case, and that the foregoing is a full, true and correct transcript of his stenographic notes of said proceedings on said date. true and correct transcript of his stenographic notes thereof.

E.T. Rothenberger

Subscribed and sworn to before me this 15th day of May, 1901.

TB Needles
Commissioner.

Supl.-C.D.13.

Department of the Interior,
Commission to the Five Civilized Tribes,
Muskogee, I. T., February 15, 1902.

SUPPLEMENTAL TESTIMONY in the matter of the enrollment of JOSEPH ANN HALL, her children and grand child as citizens of the Cherokee Nation:

Appearances:
Applicant present in person;
Mr. W. W. Hastings, Cherokee Representative.

CHEROKEE GRANTED ENROLLMENT CARDS & DAWES PACKETS 1900-1907 VOLUME I

Commission: The applicant was notified by registered letter on the 30th day of January, 1902, that her application for the enrollment of herself, children and grand children would be taken up for final consideration by the Commission on the 15th day of February, 1902, and that she would on said date be given an opportunity to introduce such addition testimony that she desired affecting her case.

JOSEPH ANN HALL, the Applicant, being duly sworn and examined testified as follows: Examination by the Commission:

Q What is your name? A Joseph Ann Hall.
Q Where do you live? A Vinita, Indian Territory.
Q Is there any other statement you desire to make to the Commission relative to the children of yourself, children and grand child as citizens of the Cherokee Nation?
A I believe all the evidence is fully submitted; however, you enroll also my daughter, Josie Winters Hall.

BY MR. HASTINGS: Do you own an improvement in the Cherokee Nation, Mrs. Hall? A Yes, sir.
Q Where? A Adjoining Mr. Marshall's farm on the north.
Q When did you purchase it? A "94, the year of the strip payment.
Q Whom did you purchase it of? A Mr. Marks.
Q What did you give him for it? A I think it was in the neighborhood of $300.
Q What did the improvements consit[sic] of? A There was a house, two room house, and barn and well, and a very good fence, wire fence all around it.
Q What rent did you get off of it in 1895? A Well, I can't exactly remember the different years; I have rented it as high as $100 a year, or $50 a year.
Q Did the rent go on the improvement of the place? A Yes, keeping it up.
Q That is all you have ever got off of it, is keeping up the improvements? A Yes, sir.
Q Did you get that of Mr. Marks? A Yes, sir, and of whom he rented it; he was acking[sic] as my agent.
Q You never got any rent off of it; it went into the improvements of the place?
A Well, I have got some money off of it.
Q Well, how much? A As I told you as much as $100.
Q When did you get any money? A I received some money every year.
Q Did you receive any in 1895? A I can't state clearly; yes, I think I received money every year.
Q Do you know how much? A I have never received less than $25. cash rent.
Q Do you know you received that in 1895? A Yes.
Q Well, you are willing to swear that you redceived[sic] $25 in 1895
A No, I would not swear that; I have no recollection of not having received-
Q Well, on the other hand do you have recollection of receiving that much for that specific year? A Yes; it seems to me that I have.
Q Well, did you receive any in 1896? A Yes.
Q How much? A As I told you, I can't remember each year, how much.

CHEROKEE GRANTED ENROLLMENT CARDS
& DAWES PACKETS 1900-1907 VOLUME I

Q Did you in 1897? A I told you that I have received rent from it up to the present time.
Q Did you in 1898?
>Commission: Just answer his question, Mrs. Hall, to the best of your ability.

A Yes, I feel that I have as I can't recollect a singly[sic] year that I haven't received rent from it.
Q Well, do you know that you received it in 1898; I am trying to get an affirmative answer, not a negative answer? A Yes, I think I have, not less than $25 cash.
Q Do you know that you received that much, or over, that year? A I think I am safe in saying that I received that much.
Q But you don't have any satisfactory recollection of receiving that much? A No, sir.
Q You don't of any year? A Yes, sir.
Q Now what year? A From 1895 on.to[sic] '92; I haven't yet received the rental for '92, but I have the agreement that calls for '92.
Q By Commission: You mean 1902? A Yes, sir.
Q By Mr. Hastings: What did you get last year? A Not less that $25. cash.
Q When was it you got it, how much did you get? A Well, I received $25 in cash.
Q When? A Last year, with the understanding that the place would be kept up in good repair.
Q Mr. Marks has been keeping it up.[sic] A Yes, sir.
Q And he has been keeping the rest of the proceeds? A I don't know, it has been going in the improvements, at one time the fence had to be almost rebuilt.
Q Have you got any written transfer of this improvement?
A Yes, sir.
Q Have you got it with you? A No, sir; because I never got any notice that the Cherokee Nation would introduce any testimony; I didn't come prepared to answer any questions; I would have brought all my papers with me had I know there would be additional questions asked, but I didn't bring my papers.
>COMMISSION: Is there any other statement you desire to make to this Commission? A There was additional evidence sent down two or three weeks ago.

Q That was sent in the form of a letter and it would not, could not be considered?
A I believe it amounted to just about this, that during the time I was absent with my children, as I have stated in my evidence, during the most of the time up to the time that my husband's health failed, while he, my husband, William B. Hall, and my son, Eugene Hall, remained in the Indian Territory, at Adair, and conducted business there; they owned lots there and the building there, and they conducted business there clear on up, I think it was in '94 or '93 that his health failed, he was stricken with paralysis, and up until that year he was regularly in business there and after his health failed, he left all the business in the hands of my son there, Eugene Hall, and he remained there up until 1896, so that all the time during my absence from the Territory during that period, business was conducted in my name, by my husband and my son together. I believe that was the additional evidence stated in that letter. If you wish to refer to it and see that I have stated it in that way.
Q Is there any additional statement you desire to make?
A No, sir.

CHEROKEE GRANTED ENROLLMENT CARDS & DAWES PACKETS 1900-1907 VOLUME I

Mr. Hastings: Where are your children? A One is in New York City and the other is on the way between Chicago; they are in dramatic companies that require constant travel. They are this season with Brady's Lover"s[sic] Lane; there are two eastern Lover Lane Companies; one of them as at the head of one and the other one is at the head of the other, -William Brady's.

COMMISSION: Do you submit this case to the Commission for final consideration? A Yes, sir.

Commission) By agreement of the parties concerned, the applicant and the representatives of the Cherokee Nation, this case is submitted to the Commission for final consideration.

--- oooOOOooo---

J. O. Rosson, being first duly sworn, states that as stenographer to the Commission to the Five Civilized Tribes, he correctly recorded the testimony and proceedings in this case, and that the foregoing is a true and complete transcript of his stenographic notes thereof.

JORosson

Subscribed and sworn to before me this Febuary[sic] 19, 1902.

Commissioner.

R.

DEPARTMENT OF THE INTERIOR.
Commission to the Five Civilized Tribes.
Muskogee, Indian Territory, October 6th, 1902.

In the matter of the application of Joseph Ann Hall for the enrollment of herself; her children, Willis Oscar and James Eugene Hall, Jessie M. H. Swan and Blanch E. H. Morrison; and her grand daughter, Mae Evelyn Hall, as citizens by blood of the Cherokee Nation, and for the enrollment of her daughter-in-law, Josie Winters Hall, as a citizen by intermarriage of the Cherokee Nation.

Supplemental to D-13.

Applicant appears in person.
Cherokee Nation by J. C. Starr.

JOSEPH ANN HALL, being duly sworn, testified as follows:
Examination by the Commission.

CHEROKEE GRANTED ENROLLMENT CARDS
& DAWES PACKETS 1900-1907 VOLUME I

Q. What is your name, Mrs. Hall? A. Joseph Ann Hall.
Q. What is your age? A. 57.
Q. What is your post office? A. Vinita, Indian Territory.
Q. Do you know Josie Winters Hall, who is an applicant before this Commission for enrollment as an intermarried citizen? A. Yes, sir.
Q. What is her age at this time? A. About 31 years old.
Q. What is her husband's name? A. Her husband's name was Willis Oscar Hall.
Q. He is dead? A. Yes, sir.
Q. Was he a citizen by blood of the Cherokee Nation? A. Yes, sir.
Q. When was Josie Winters Hall and her husband Willis Oscar Hall married? A. They were married in 1891, to the best of my recollection.
Q. Where were they married? A. They were married in St. Louis. My son was in St. Louis at the time. He went to St. Louis and married this lady.
Q. Did Josie Winters Hall and her husband live together from the time of their marriage up to the time of his death as husband and wife? A. Yes, sir.
Q. Was she ever married before she married your son? A. No, sir.
Q. Was he ever married prior to his marriage to this wife? A. No, sir.
Q. Was Josie Winters Hall single on the first of September, 1902? A. Yes, sir.
Q. She has never married any other man since her marriage to your son? A. Never married any other man.
Q. How long after Josie Winters Hall was married before she came to the Cherokee Nation? A. You have that all embodied in her testimony. I couldn't give the exact date of their coming back to the Territory, but it is all in her evidence.
Q. Is she living in the Territory at this time? A. She has lived here as much as it has been possible. She has been traveling with a theatrical company. That is her profession. When it is possible she comes to the Territory. That is her only home.

Jesse O. Carr, being first duly sworn, states that as stenographer to the Commission to the Five Civilized Tribes he reported the above entitled case and that the foregoing is a true and complete transcript of his stenographic notes thereof.

Jesse O. Carr

Subscribed and sworn to before me this 4th day of November, 1902.

BCJones
Notary Public.

Cherokee D-13.

DEPARTMENT OF THE INTERIOR,
COMMISSION TO THE FIVE CIVILIZED TRIBES.

In the matter of the application of Joseph Ann Hall for the enrollment of herself, her sons Willie Oscar Hall and James Eugene Hall, her daughters, Jessie M. H. Swan and Blanche E. H. Morrison, and her grand daughter, Mae Evelyn Hall, as

CHEROKEE GRANTED ENROLLMENT CARDS
& DAWES PACKETS 1900-1907 VOLUME I

citizens by blood of the Cherokee Nation, and for the enrollment of Josie Winters Hall as a citizen by intermarriage of the Cherokee Nation.

D E C I S I O N.

The record in this case shows that on July 11, 1900, Joseph Ann Hall appeared before the Commission at Fairland, Indian Territory, and made personal application for the enrollment of herself, her sons, Willis Oscar Hall and James Eugene Hall, her daughters, Jessie M. H. Swan and Blanch E. H. Morrison, and her grand daughter, Mae Evelyn Hall, as citizens by blood of the Cherokee Nation, and for the enrollment of Josie Winters Hall as a citizen by intermarriage of the Cherokee Nation. Further proceedings in the matter of the said application were had at Vinita, Indian Territory, on May 14, 1901, and at Muskogee, Indian Territory, February 15, May 14, 1901, and at Muskogee, Indian Territory, on February 15, May 6, and October 6, 1902.

The evidence shows that the said Joseph Ann Hall, a Cherokee by blood, is the mother of the applicants, Willis Oscar Hall, James Eugene Hall, Jessie M. H. Swan (nee Hall) and Blanch E. H. Morrison (nee Hall). It appears from the records of the Cherokee Nation now in possession of the Commission that on October 12, 1887, the applicants, Joseph Ann Hall, Willis Oscar Hall, by the name of Wm. Oscar Hall, Jessie M. H. Swan, by the name of Jessie Hall and Blanch E. H. Morrison, by the name of Blanche Hall, and James Eugene Hall were re-admitted to citizenship in the Cherokee Nation by the duly constituted authorities of said Nation.

The evidence further shows that in 1889 the said Willis Oscar Hall was lawfully married to the said Josie Winters Hall (nee Winters), a non-citizen; that in 1891 the said Jessie M. H. Swan (nee Hall) was lawfully married to one Mark E. Swan, a non-citizen; that in 1895 the said Blanch E. H. Morrison (nee Hall), was lawfully married to one Lewis F. Morrison, a non-citizen; that said James Eugene Hall was lawfully married to one Alice N. Edwards, a non-citizen, some time prior to 1896. The latter has since died leaving the said Mae Evelyn Hall as the issue of such marriage.

The evidence further shows that the applicants are respectively identified on the rolls of the Cherokee Nation, as follows: Joseph Ann Hall, Willis Oscar Hall, by the name of William O. Hall, James Eugene Hall, by the name of Eugene J. Hall, Mae Evelyn Hall, Jessie M. H Swan, by the name of Jessie Swan Hall and Blanch E. H. Morrison, by the name of Blanche Hall, on the 1894 strip payment roll. Joseph Ann Hall, Willis Oscar Hall, by the name of William O. Hall, James Eugene Hall, by the name of Eugene J. Hall, Mae Evelyn Hall, Jessie M. H Swan, by the name of Jessie M. Hall and Blanch E. H. Morrison, by the name of Blanche E. Hall, on the 1896 census roll as native Cherokees; and Josie Winters Hall on said 1896 roll as an adopted white.

It appears from the evidence that the applicants, Joseph Ann Hall, Willis Oscar Hall and James Eugene Hall, have made the Cherokee Nation their permanent residence since 1888. And though temporarily absent during the greater part of that time, they never acquired a residence elsewhere. The residence of Josie Winters hall

CHEROKEE GRANTED ENROLLMENT CARDS & DAWES PACKETS 1900-1907 VOLUME I

is considered to be Cherokee as that of her husband, Willis Oscar Hall, and the residence of Mae Evelyn Hall, who is a minor, is presumed to be the same as that of her father, James Eugene Hall.

As above stated, Jessie M. H. Swan and Blanch E. H. Morrison were married respectively in 1891 and 1895, and neither has ever separated or been divorced from her husband. Under these circumstances, the rule applies that--

"A woman of whatever age acquires at marriage the domicile of her husband, and her domicile continues to be the same as his, throughout their married life. She cannot acquire a domicile separate from her husband's, and although they live apart, she still follows his domicile." 5 A&E Eneye. L.1 Ed. 868-869.

Neither Mark E. Swan, husband of Jessie M. H. Swan, nor Lewis F. Morrison, husband of Blanche E. H. Morrison, ever acquired a permanent residence anywhere within the territory of the Five Civilized Tribes, both being domiciled in foreign states. The ninth paragraph of Section twenty-one of the Act of Congress approved June 28, 1898 (30 Stats. 495), provides that-

"No person shall be enrolled who has not heretofore removed to and in good faith settled in the Nation in which he claims citizenship."

It further appears from the evidence that the applicant, Willis Oscar Hall, died prior to September, 1902.

It is, therefore, the opinion of this Commission that Joseph Ann Hall, James Eugene Hall and Mae Evelyn Hall, should be enrolled as citizens by blood of the Cherokee Nation, and that Josie Winters Hall should be enrolled as a citizen by intermarriage of said Nation, In accordance with the provisions of Section twenty-one of the Act of Congress approved June 28, 1898 (30 Stats. 493); and that the application of Jessie M. H. Swan and Blanche E. H. Morrison for enrollment as citizens by blood of the Cherokee Nation, should be denied, under the provisions of Section twenty-one of the said Act of Congress, and it is so ordered. It is further ordered that the application as to Willis Oscar Hall be, and the same is hereby dismissed.

COMMISSION TO THE FIVE CIVILIZED TRIBES.

(SIGNED) Tams Bixby.
Acting Chairman.

(SIGNED) T. B. Needles.
Commissioner.

C. R. Breckinridge
Commissioner.

Dated Muskogee, Indian Territory,
this   NOV 20 1902

CHEROKEE GRANTED ENROLLMENT CARDS & DAWES PACKETS 1900-1907 VOLUME I

DEPARTMENT OF THE INTERIOR,
Commission to the Five Civilized Tribes,
Muskogee I. T. December 10th 1902.

In the matter of the application of Joseph Ann Hall et al for enrollment as citizens of the Cherokee Nation.

Cherokee D 13.

Protest of the Cherokee Nation.

Comes now the Cherokee Nation and protests against the decision of the Commission rendered in this case on November 20th 1902 granting the applications of Joseph Ann Hall, James Eugene Hall for enrollment as citizens by blood of the Cherokee Nation and Josie Winters Hall as a citizen by intermarriage of the Cherokee Nation.

The only point involved in this case is a question of residence and we submit that the testimony in this case does not show that the applicants Joseph Ann Hall, James Eugene Hall, Mae Evelyn Hall and Josie Winters Hall have in good faith removed to and settled in the Cherokee Nation prior to the passage of the Act of Congress of June 28th 1898.

The testimony in this case shows that Josie Winters Hall was married to Willis Oscar Hall in 1889 in St. Louis Missouri and that the first visit she paid to the Cherokee Nation with her husband was in 1893 or four years after their marriage; that they merely paid visits to the Cherokee Nation, and the testimony of Joseph Ann Hall shows that " THEY HAVE NEVER ESTABLISHED A HOME ANY WHERE FOR THEMSELVES" and in fact they have never established a home for themselves in the Cherokee Nation and it is clearly shown that Willis Oscar Hall followed his occupation without the limits of the Cherokee Nation and his wife was with him and as her residence was that of her husband and the record shows that he left the Cherokee Nation prior to June 28th 1898 we submit that she is not entitled to be enrolled as a citizen of the Cherokee Nation by intermarriage. The testimony of Lemuel W. Marks taken on May 14, 1901 shows that clearly Willis Oscar Hall, husband of the applicant, Josie Winters Hall was a non resident of the Cherokee Nation on June 28th 1898 and attention is called to the following statements made by Mr. Marks: "****The son that died was off travelling." "Q What was his name?"

CHEROKEE GRANTED ENROLLMENT CARDS
& DAWES PACKETS 1900-1907 VOLUME I

"A Oscar." "Q He is dead now?" "A Yes sir." "Q He died recently?" "A Yes sir" "Q what was he travelling for, on business?" "A He was on the stage with a troupe." "Q With a Theatrical troupe?" "A Yes sir, and was ONLY HERE A VERY SHORT TIME; I ONLY MET HIM A FEW TIMES IN HIS LIFE TIME " The testimony of this witness shows that he lived near where Joseph Ann Hall claimed to have made her head quarters to wit near Vinita I. T. and that Willis Oscar Hall has not paid enough visits to the Cherokee Nation to become very well acquainted with this witness. The testimony of Joseph Ann Hall relative to the residence of Willis Oscar Hall shows that he was born in 1866 and was therefore of age when he was readmitted to citizenship in the Cherokee Nation hence his residence would not be that of his mother because he was not a minor; that Willis Oscar Hall was readmitted to Citizenship in the Cherokee Nation in 1887, when he was of age, that he married in St. Louis, Mo in 1889, that he has never established a home anywhere and in fact not in the Cherokee Nation; the testimony of Josie Winters Hall the wife of Willis Oscar Hall shows that Willis Oscar Hall was not in the Cherokee Nation, not even on a visit from the time she married him until 1893 that he was engaged in business without the limits of the Cherokee Nation and was so engaged until he took sick a short time before the original application herein was made and we submit that we do not see how, under that provision of the act of June 28th 1898, which provides:

"No person shall be enrolled who has not heretofore removed to and in good faith settled in the Nation in which he claims citizenship" that the applicant Josie Winters Hall, the wife of Willis Oscar Hall can be enrolled as a citizen of the Cherokee Nation by intermarriage.

We contend that it is shown by the testimony of James Eugene Hall was engaged in business without the limits of the Cherokee Nation prior to June 28th 1898 having left the Cherokee Nation the last time in 1897 and was absent therefrom at the date of the application here in July 11th 1900 and at the date of the supplemental testimony on May 14, 1901, *and Feb 15, 1902* and that he was also absent prior to 1897 and we submit that he has not removed to and in good faith settled in the Cherokee Nation. The residence of his daughter Mae Evelyn Hall being that of her father we most earnestly content that neither James Eugene Hall or his daughter Mae Evelyn Hall are entitled to be enrolled as citizens of the Cherokee Nation. James

CHEROKEE GRANTED ENROLLMENT CARDS & DAWES PACKETS 1900-1907 VOLUME I

Eugene Hall is not a minor nor was he a minor on June 28th 1898 and his residence is not presumed to be that of his mother. Paragraph 9 of Section 21 of the act of Congress of June 28th 1898 makes no exceptions, not even to minors and we contend that it makes no difference whether a man is with a theatrical troupe or whether he is running a general merchandise store or what business he is engaged in that he is required to have removed to and in good faith setled[sic] in the Cherokee Nation prior to the passage of the Curtis act.

The testimony in this case we contend does that[sic] show that Joseph Ann Hall the principal applicant had removed to and in good faith settled in the Cherokee Nation and we most earnestly protest against the enrollment of all of the applicant to wit: Joseph Ann Hall, James Eugene Hall, Mae Evelyn Hall and Josie Winters Hall.

         Respectfully submitted,
         W W Hastings
         Attorney for the Cherokee Nation. JCS

Cherokee R-841

        Department of the Interior,
      Commission to the Five Civilized Tribes,
         Cherokee Land Office,
        Tahlequah, I.T., July 20, 1903.

  In the matter of the application for enrollment of Willis Oscar Hall, Jessie M. H. Swan and Blanche E. H. Morrison as citizens by blood of the Cherokee Nation.

        SUPPLEMENTAL TESTIMONY.

  JOSEPH ANN HALL, being duly sworn and examined by the Commission, testified as follows:

Q What is your name? A Joseph Ann Hall.
Q What is your age? A I was born in '45.
Q What is your postoffice address? A Vinita, Indian Territory.
Q Are you the mother of Willis Oscar Hall, Jessie M. H. Swan and Blanche E. H. Morrison? A Yes sir.
Q Is Willis Oscar Hall living at this time? A No sir.

CHEROKEE GRANTED ENROLLMENT CARDS
& DAWES PACKETS 1900-1907 VOLUME I

Q When did he die? A May 1901; been dead two years.
Q Your other two children are living? A Yes sir.
Q Where does Jessie M. H. Swan live? A She is traveling; she is now on her way to California.
Q Is she with a theatrical company? A Yes sir; has been several years.
Q Is her husband living? A Yes sir; she has been divorced, however, since she first applied for enrollment, three years ago the 11th of this July.
Q How long has she been with the theatrical company? A Since '91 I believe.
Q Where did she live before that time? A She was living in Vinita, Indian Territory; she was raised principally in St. Louis.
Q Up to the time she went on the stage, had her residence been the same as your own? A Yes sir; in the Territory since 1890; I believe we removed to the Territory in '90---no, '89; we were readmitted in '87; the citizenship papers and evidence is all here if you wish to look over it; we were readmitted in '87 and came to the Territory---I think it was in '88.
Q Did your daughter Jessie live with you all her life until she went on the stage?
A Yes sir, she has never known any other home.
Q Since she left Vinita and joined the theatrical company, has she made her residence in any particular place? A No sir.
Q She has during all of that time been traveling with one theatrical company or another? A Yes sir; she had her own company four or five seasons when she first started out.
Q When you daughter Jessie left the Territory, did she have any property here?
A Well, just as everybody had; we had selected our claims and afterward decided to locate in another place and when we did take another location we gave up those claims and filed on a different claim.
Q How old was she when she left here? A She was, I think, about 17 when she was readmitted and she left when she was about 19.
Q She married after she left Vinita? A Yes sir.
Q Was her husband a member of some theatrical company? A He was her manager for several years.
Q I wish you would state, Mrs. Hall, just what property your daughter Jessie owned in Indian Territory during her absence from here. A Well, as I say, we decided to take our place all together.
Q Did you improve that place? A It was partially improved and then a few years, two or three years afterward, we decided to take another place, but still it was not nearer Vinita, but it was on the same side of Cabin Creek; the place we first selected was west of Cabin Creek and the place we last decided to take as our final allotment was improved more.
Q She has owned a home place in the Cherokee Nation all the time she has been away from here, or rather she has had in interest?
A Yes sir, she held her claim when she left and she has sent money back; her father has used some of her money to improve the place; there has never been a year since they went away that she and her sister have not sent back money; when they went away they took nothing but a trunk and wearing clothes and they never went away with any other purpose than attending to their preparations for the stage and going on

CHEROKEE GRANTED ENROLLMENT CARDS
& DAWES PACKETS 1900-1907 VOLUME I

the stage. They never had any intentions of abandoning their home in Indian Territory, never had any other home.

Q She never left any of her effects here, did she? A Yes sir; such as some household effects, pictures and money invested; her father used some of her money and some of her sister's money in business. As soon as she went on the stage, every year since she left the Territory, she has never failed to send money back here. Some of it has been invested and she has always looked upon this as the only home she had, the only place she had any interest in; never settled anywhere else.

Q Did you daughter, Blanche E. H. Morrison, leave at the same time?

A Just about. She was in school at the time Jessie left. Blanche remained until she graduated at Worcester Academy; left Vinita that summer.

Q She went on the state[sic] also? A Yes sir.

Q And she has been on the stage continuously since she left here? A Yes sir.

Q She also married I believe? A Yes sir. They never applied for enrollment for their husbands for citizenship or anything of that kind.

Q Is her husband traveling with some company also? A Yes sir, he is leading man usually in the company she is with. However, one or two seasons they had to travel separately.

Q Did you daughter Blanche also have an interest in this place? A Yes sir; it was an undivided claim for us all; I think there are several hundred acres.

Q Did she have any other interests besides the interest in this farm? A Well, just about as her sister did; they left just as anyone else would leave the Territory to go to school; she took nothing with her but what clothes she had to wear and all their personal effects they left here.

BY MR. HASTINGS:

Q What did you pay for the first claim you had on public domain?

A Well, Mr. Green attended to that for us.

Q Was anything ever done to improve it? A Yes sir, some fencing.

Q What fencing was done on the first improvement? A Well, nothing more that the place was fenced.

Q How much was fenced? A I don't know sir; there was about 600 acres I think.

Q You never gave up that first improvement, did you? A Yes sir, I beg your pardon, we did.

Q When did you give it up? A The year we moved out here----

Q What was done with that first improvement? A Mr. Green, as I say, he selected the land for us and we intended to take our allotments on it and after that decided to take the other place and after we decided to take the other place why, we just simply let it go, forfeited it. Mr. Green--there was some arrangement between him and us and we just forfeited that and took the other.

Q Went back to public domain? A Yes sir.

Q You never spent enough on the farm to care enough for it so you let it go; is that correct? A Not altogether; it was improved; afterward we selected another place.

Q Did you let it go back to public domain? A After we had selected another place we did.

Q Then you let it go back to public domain? A Well we----

CHEROKEE GRANTED ENROLLMENT CARDS
& DAWES PACKETS 1900-1907 VOLUME I

Q Well, why don't you answer yes or no? A Because we didn't let it go, didn't give it up until we had selected -- -- -- --
Q Did you let it go back to public domain? A I have answered that question fully. If you will kindly oblige me by looking at this letter you will understand----
Q Thank you, I don't care to look at the letter. Where was your daughter divorced?
A She was divorced I think while she was somewhere traveling.
Q Did she get it or he? A She got it.
Q She didn't get it in the Indian Territory? A No sir. I don't think she did, but she did give her residence as Indian Territory.
Q You are positive as to that? A Yes sir.
Q Can you file a copy of that complaint in this case? A What complaint?
Q Q The complaint upon which she secured a divorce? A Yes sir, I can.

  MR. HASTINGS: The Cherokee Nation moves that Jessie M. H. Swan be required to file a copy of the complaint upon which she secured a divorce from her husband, as stated by the witness in the testimony, for the purpose of determining where she gave her residence at the time.

  BY THE COMMISSION: Mrs. Hall, if you can possible do so, the Commission would like for you to file with this application a copy of the complain Mr. Hastings speaks of.
A Well, I have not a copy with me now.
COMMISSION: You can probably obtain it by writing to your daughter.

+++++++++++++++++++

  Mabel F. Maxwell, being duly sworn, states that as stenographer to the Commission to the Five Civilized Tribes, she correctly recorded the supplemental testimony in this case, and that the foregoing is a true and complete transcript of her stenographic notes thereof.

          Mabel F Maxwell

Subscribed and sworn to before me this 20th day of July, 1903.

          John O Rosson
MFM   Notary Public.

CHEROKEE GRANTED ENROLLMENT CARDS & DAWES PACKETS 1900-1907 VOLUME I

Cherokee R-841

Department of the Interior,
Commission to the Five Civilized Tribes,
Cherokee Land Office,
Tahlequah, I.T., July 21, 1903.

In the matter of the application for the enrollment of Willis Oscar Hall, Jessie M. H. Swan and Blanche E. H. Morrison as citizens by blood of the Cherokee Nation.

SUPPLEMENTAL TESTIMONY.

JOSEPH ANN HALL, being duly sworn and examined by the Commission, testified as follows:

Q   What is your name? A Joseph Ann Hall.
Q   What is your age? A Born in '45.
Q   What is your postoffice address? A Vinita, Indian Territory.
Q   Mrs. Hall, did you testify before the Commission on July 20, 1903, in connection with the application for the enrollment of your two daughters, Jessie M. H. Swan and Blanche E. H. Morrison?
A   Yes sir.
Q   In that testimony, in reply to the question, "She has owned a home place in the Cherokee Nation all the time she has been away from, here, or rather she has had an interest?" you make the reply, "Yes sir, she held her claim when she left and she has sent money back; her father has used some of her money to improve the place." Is that what you intended to say?
A   No sir, I intended to convey the idea that her father in business invested some money for her and her sister; he didn't use any of her money to improve her place.
Q   He did not use her money to improve her place? A No sir, we bought the improved place later; we bought the last improved place later and that we still hold.

++++++++++++++++++

Mabel F. Maxwell, being duly sworn, states that, as stenographer to the Commission to the Five Civilized Tribes, she correctly recorded the supplemental testimony in this case, and that the above is a true and complete transcript of her stenographic notes thereof.

Mabel F. Maxwell

CHEROKEE GRANTED ENROLLMENT CARDS
& DAWES PACKETS 1900-1907 VOLUME I

Subscribed and sworn to before me
this 21st day of July, 1903.

MFM

John O Rosson
Notary Public.

Cherokee D 13 (R 841).

DEPARTMENT OF THE INTERIOR,

COMMISSION TO THE FIVE CIVILIZED TRIBES.

In the matter of the application for the enrollment of Jessie Mae Hall and Blanch E. H. Morrison as citizens by blood of the Cherokee Nation.

D E C I S I O N.

The record in this case shows that on July 11, 1900, Joseph Ann Hall appeared before the Commission at Fairland, Indian Territory, and made application for the enrollment, among others, of her adult daughters, Blanch E. H. Morrison and Jessie Mae Hall, under the name of Jessie Mae Hall Swan, as citizens by blood of the Cherokee Nation. The application also included Joseph Ann Hall, James Eugene Hall and Mae Evelyn Hall who applied as citizens by blood, and Josie Winters Hall, who applied as a citizen by intermarriage, of the Cherokee Nation. Josie Winters Hall being differently classified, and the names of the said Joseph Ann Hall, James Eugene Hall and Mae Evelyn Hall being upon a partial roll of citizens by blood of the Cherokee Nation, approved by the Secretary of the Interior on July 29, 1903, at #27840, #27841 and #27842, they are therefore not embraced in this decision. Further proceedings in the matter of said application were had at Vinita, Indian Territory, May 14, 1901, and at Muskogee, Indian Territory, February 15, May 6 and October 6, 1902. The record further shows that on November 20, 1902, the Commission rendered its decision in the matter of said application which was approved by the Department on February 19, 1903; that on May 18, 1903, the Department rescinded its former action in respect to the applicants Jessie Mae Hall (formerly Jessie Mae Hall Swan) and Blanch E. H. Morrison and remanded the case for further proceedings and readjudication as to the two applicants last mentioned; and that on July 20, 1903, further proceedings were had at Tahlequah, Indian Territory, in the matter of said application as to Jessie Mae Hall and Blanche E. H. Morrison.

The evidence shows that the applicants Jessie Mae Hall, by the name of Jessie Hall, and Blanch E. H. Morrison, by the name of Blanch Hall, were readmitted to citizenship in the Cherokee Nation on October 12, 1887, by the duly constituted authorities of said Nation.

It further appears from the affidavit of the said Jessie Mae Hall, who applied for enrollment under the name of Jessie Mae Hall Swan, since the date of her application herein, and has resumed her maiden name, Jessie Mae Hall, and that she was known by that name on September 1, 1902.

The evidence further shows that the said applicants are Cherokees by blood and are identified on the Cherokee strip payment roll as follows: Jessie Mae Hall, by the name of Jessie Swan Hall, and Blanch E. H. Morrison, by the name of Blanche Hall, on the 1894 strip payment roll; and Jessie Mae Hall, by the name of Jessie M. Hall, and Blanch E. H. Morrison, by the name of Blanche E. Hall, on the 1896 census roll as native Cherokees.

The evidence further shows that Blanch E. H. Morrison removed in good faith to the Cherokee Nation about 1887; that Jessie Mae Hall removed removed[sic] in good faith to said Nation about 1888; and that the Cherokee Nation has been their permanent home ever since, though they have been absent during the greater portion of that time, being members of the theatrical profession which necessitates their travelling from place to place through the country. During their absence the said applicants have maintained ownership of certain personal effects as well as an interest in certain improvements on real estate situated in the Cherokee Nation; and since their removal to said nation, as above stated, they have never acquired a fixed abode elsewhere.

It is, therefore, the opinion of this Commission, following the decisions of the Department in the cases of Joseph D. Yeargain, et al., (I.T.D. 2900-1903) and Clement G. Clarke, et al., (I.T.D. 1370-1903), that Jessie Mae Hall and Blanche E. H. Morrison should be enrolled as citizens by blood of the Cherokee Nation, in accordance with the provisions of Section 21 of the Act of Congress, approved June 28, 1898 (30 Stats., 495), and it is so ordered.

COMMISSION TO THE FIVE CIVILIZED TRIBES.

(SIGNED). *Tams Bixby.*
Chairman.

(SIGNED). *T. B. Needles.*
Commissioner.

(SIGNED). *C. R. Breckinridge.*
Commissioner.

(SIGNED). *W. E. Stanley.*
Commissioner.

Muskogee, Indian Territory,
this _____ MAR 10 1904

CHEROKEE GRANTED ENROLLMENT CARDS & DAWES PACKETS 1900-1907 VOLUME I

DEPARTMENT OF THE INTERIOR,
Commission to the Five Civilized Tribes,
Vinita I. T. April 1st 1904.

In the matter of the application for the enrollment of Jessie Mae Hall and Blanch E. H. Morrison as citizens by blood of the Cherokee Nation

Cherokee D 13 Now R 841.

Comes now the Cherokee Nation and protests against the Decision of the Commission rendered in this case on March 10 1904 and prays an appeal to the Honorable Secretary of the Interior.

The testimony in this case shows that the applicants were readmitted to citizenship in the Cherokee Nation in 1887 but that they never lived or made their home in the Cherokee Nation except for a very short time thereafter. That they left the Cherokee Nation and have been permanent residents without the limits of the Cherokee Nation for the past ten years.

They were both married and while they follow the theatrical profession and travel from place to place yet the headquarters are outside of the Cherokee Nation; their husbands were never citizens of the Cherokee Nation and in fact never saw the Cherokee Nation and we submit that both under the Cherokee constitution and the provisions of the act of Congress approves June 28th 1898 "No person shall be enrolled who has not heretofore removed to and in good faith settled in the Nation in which he claims citizenship" that neither of these applicants should be enrolled as citizens of the Cherokee Nation. They have no property in the Cherokee Nation and their cases is in no wise parallel with the Yeargain case or the Clement G. Clark case and we submit that the Commissions[sic] decision in the case should be reversed and the applications denied.

Respectfully,

W W Hastings
Attorney for the Cherokee Nation.

CHEROKEE GRANTED ENROLLMENT CARDS & DAWES PACKETS 1900-1907 VOLUME I

JOR   Cherokee R-841

Department of the Interior,
Commission to the Five Civilized Tribes,
Cherokee Land Office,
Tahlequah, I.T. July 20, 1904.

In the matter of the application for the enrollment of Willis Oscar Hall, Jessie M. H. Swan and Blanche E. H. Morrison, as citizens by blood of the Cherokee Nation.

SUPPLEMENTAL TESTIMONY.

JOSEPH ANN HALL, being duly sworn and examined by the Commission, testified as follows:

Q What is your name? A Joseph ANN Hall.
Q How old are you? A 45.
Q What is your postt[sic] office? A Vinita.
Q You are a Cherokee by blood are you? A Yes sir.
Q Are you the mother of Jessie M. H. Swan? A Yes sir.
Q Has she married since application was made for he[sic] enrollment?
   A Yes sir, she was separated from Mr. Swan, and I think, a year after, she married Al Trahern.
Q Is his full name Albert C. Trahern.[sic] [sic] I don't know his full name, he goes by the name of Al Trahern. In this certificate book it is Al,- no it is Albert.
Q There is offered in evidence, marriage certificate signed by Charles E. Jefferson, a minister of the Gospel, certifying that on the 10th day of ~~Sept-ember~~ February, 1902, he united in matrimony, A;bert[sic] L. Trahern and Jessie Mae Hall? A She was formerly Jessie Mae Hall Swan, after she was separated from her husband her maiden name, Hall, was restored and she was afterwards married to Mr. Trahern.
Q Is the person mentioned in this marriage certificate as Jessie Mae Hall the identical person who is listed for enrollment as Jessie M. H. Swan? A Yes sir.
Q Is Mr[sic] Trahern a citizen of the Cherokee Nation? A No sir.
Q Are they living together now? A Yes sir.
Q Your daughter is living? A Yes sir.

Mary B. Risser, being duly sworn and examined states that as stenographer to the Commission to the Five Civilized Tribes, she correctly recorded the supplemental testimony in this case and that the foregoing is a true and complete transcript of her stenographic notes therein.

                                              Mary B Risser

Subscribed and sworn to before me
this July 25, 1904.

                                              JO Rosson
MBR   Notary Public.

CHEROKEE GRANTED ENROLLMENT CARDS & DAWES PACKETS 1900-1907 VOLUME I

COMMISSIONERS:
HENRY L. DAWES,
TAMS BIXBY,
THOMAS B. NEEDLES,
C. R. BRECKINRIDGE.

DEPARTMENT OF THE INTERIOR,
COMMISSION TO THE FIVE CIVILIZED TRIBES.

REFER IN REPLY TO THE FOLLOWING
Cherokee D-13.

ALLISON L. AYLESWORTH,
SECRETARY.

ADDRESS ONLY THE
COMMISSION TO THE FIVE CIVILIZED TRIBES.

Muskogee, Indian Territory, November 26, 1902.

W. W. Hastings,
    Attorney for Cherokee Nation,
        Muskogee, Indian Territory.

Dear Sir:

    There is herewith inclosed a copy of the decision of the Commission to the Five Civilized Tribes, dated November 20, 1902, granting the application of Joseph Ann Hall for the enrollment of herself, her son James Eugene Hall, and her grand-daughter, Mae Evelyn Hall, as citizens by blood, and for the enrollment of Josie Winters Hall as a citizen by intermarriage; denying her application for the enrollment of her daughters, Jessie M. H. Swan and Blanche E. H. Morrison, as citizens by blood; and dismissing her application for the enrollment of her son, Willis Oscar Hall, as a citizen by blood, of the Cherokee Nation.

    You are advised that you will be allowed fifteen days from date hereof in which to file such protest as you desire to make against the action of the Commission in this case, a copy of which protest you will be required to serve upon the applicant. If you fail to file protest within the time allowed, this decision will be considered final.   Respectfully,

                              Tams Bixby Acting Chairman.

Enc. H-175.

COMMISSIONERS:
HENRY L. DAWES,
TAMS BIXBY,
THOMAS B. NEEDLES,
C. R. BRECKINRIDGE.

DEPARTMENT OF THE INTERIOR,
COMMISSION TO THE FIVE CIVILIZED TRIBES.

REFER IN REPLY TO THE FOLLOWING
Cherokee D 13.

ALLISON L. AYLESWORTH,
SECRETARY.

ADDRESS ONLY THE
COMMISSION TO THE FIVE CIVILIZED TRIBES.

Muskogee, Indian Territory, December 13, 1902.

CHEROKEE GRANTED ENROLLMENT CARDS & DAWES PACKETS 1900-1907 VOLUME I

W. W. Hastings,

    Attorney for Cherokee Nation,

        Muskogee, Indian Territory.

Dear Sir:

    You are hereby advised that the Commission's decision, dated November 20, 1902, granting the application of Joseph Ann Hall for the enrollment of herself, her son, James Eugene Hall, her grand-daughter, Mae Evelyn Hall, as citizens by blood, her daughter-in-law, Josie Winters Hall, as a citizen by intermarriage; rejecting her application for the enrollment of her daughters, Jessie M. H. Swan and Blanch E. H. Morrison, as citizens by blood, and dismissing her application for the enrollment of her son, Willis Oscar Hall, as a citizen by blood, of the Cherokee Nation, a copy of which decision was furnished you on November 26, 1902, has this day been transmitted to the Secretary of the Interior for his review and decision.

    The action of the Secretary will be made known to you as soon as the Commission is informed of the same.

                    Respectfully,

                    Tams Bixby Acting Chairman.

COMMISSIONERS:
TAMS BIXBY,
THOMAS B. NEEDLES,
C. R. BRECKINRIDGE,
W. E. STANLEY.

ALLISON L. AYLESWORTH,
SECRETARY.

DEPARTMENT OF THE INTERIOR.
COMMISSION TO THE FIVE CIVILIZED TRIBES.

REFER IN REPLY TO THE FOLLOWING
Cherokee D-13

ADDRESS ONLY THE
COMMISSION TO THE FIVE CIVILIZED TRIBES.

Muskogee, Indian Territory, March 9, 1903.

W. W. Hastings,

    Attorney for the Cherokee Nation,

        Vinita, Indian Territory.

Dear Sir:

    You are hereby advised that the Commission's decision, dated November 20, 1902, granting the application of Joseph Ann Hall for the enrollment of herself, her son, James Eugene Hall, and her grandchild, Mae Evelyn Hall, as citizens by blood, and for the enrollment of her daughter-in-law, Josie Winters Hall, as a citizen by intermarriage; rejecting her application for the enrollment of her daughters, Jessie M. H. Swan and Blanch E. H. Morrison as citizens by blood of the Cherokee Nation; and dismissing her application for the enrollment of her son, Willis Oscar Hall, was affirmed by the Secretary of the Interior on February 19, 1903.

Respectfully,

Tams Bixby Acting Chairman.

COMMISSIONERS:
TAMS BIXBY,
THOMAS B. NEEDLES,
C. R. BRECKINRIDGE,
W. E. STANLEY.

ALLISON L. AYLESWORTH,
SECRETARY.

DEPARTMENT OF THE INTERIOR.
COMMISSION TO THE FIVE CIVILIZED TRIBES.

REFER IN REPLY TO THE FOLLOWING

Cherokee R-841

ADDRESS ONLY THE
COMMISSION TO THE FIVE CIVILIZED TRIBES.

Tahlequah, Indian Territory, July 6, 1903.

W. W. Hastings,

Attorney for the Cherokee Nation,

Vinita, Indian Territory.

Dear Sir:

You are hereby notified that, on May 18 the Secretary of the Interior reopened, for the taking of additional testimony, the application for enrollment as citizens by blood of the Cherokee Nation of Jessie May[sic] Hall Swan and Blanch Hall Morrison, Cherokee R-841 (D-13). Evidence is particularly required as to the residence of the applicants in this case.

The mother of these applicants, Joseph Ann Hall, has this day been notified that any further testimony she may have to present in this case can be introduced before the Cherokee Land Office of this Commission at Tahlequah, on or before August 4, 1903, and on that day you can, if you desire, appear and introduce additional testimony on behalf of the Cherokee Nation.

CHEROKEE GRANTED ENROLLMENT CARDS & DAWES PACKETS 1900-1907 VOLUME I

Respectfully,

TB Needles
Commissioner in Charge.

MFM

COMMISSIONERS:
TAMS BIXBY,
THOMAS B. NEEDLES,
C. R. BRECKINRIDGE,
W. E. STANLEY.

ALLISON L. AYLESWORTH,
SECRETARY.

DEPARTMENT OF THE INTERIOR.
COMMISSION TO THE FIVE CIVILIZED TRIBES.

REFER IN REPLY TO THE FOLLOWING
Cherokee D 13
(R-841)

ADDRESS ONLY THE
COMMISSION TO THE FIVE CIVILIZED TRIBES.

Muskogee, Indian Territory, March 10, 1904.

W. W. Hastings,

Attorney for the Cherokee Nation,

Tahlequah, Indian Territory.

Dear Sir:

There is herewith inclosed a copy of the decision of the Commission to the Five Civilized Tribes, dated March 10, 1904, granting the application for the enrollment of Jessie Mae Hall and Blanch E. H. Morrison as citizens by blood of the Cherokee Nation.

You are advised that you will be allowed fifteen days from the date hereof within which to file such protest as you may desire to make against the action of the Commission in this case. If you fail to file such protest within the time allowed this decision will be considered final.

Respectfully,

TB Needles
Commissioner in Charge.

Encl. V-26

COMMISSIONERS:
TAMS BIXBY,
THOMAS B. NEEDLES,
C. R. BRECKINRIDGE,

WM. O. BEALL,
SECRETARY.

DEPARTMENT OF THE INTERIOR.
COMMISSION TO THE FIVE CIVILIZED TRIBES.

REFER IN REPLY TO THE FOLLOWING
Cherokee R-841.

ADDRESS ONLY THE
COMMISSION TO THE FIVE CIVILIZED TRIBES.

Muskogee, Indian Territory, June 27, 1904.

CHEROKEE GRANTED ENROLLMENT CARDS
& DAWES PACKETS 1900-1907 VOLUME I

W. W. Hastings,

    Attorney for the Cherokee Nation,

        Tahlequah, Indian Territory.

Dear Sir:

    You are hereby advised that the Commission's decision, dated March 10, 1904, granting the application for the enrollment of Jessie Mae Hall, and Blanch E. H. Morrison as citizens by blood of the Cherokee Nation, was affirmed by the Secretary of the Interior on June 16, 1904.

                        Respectfully,
                        TB Needles
                                    Commissioner in Charge.

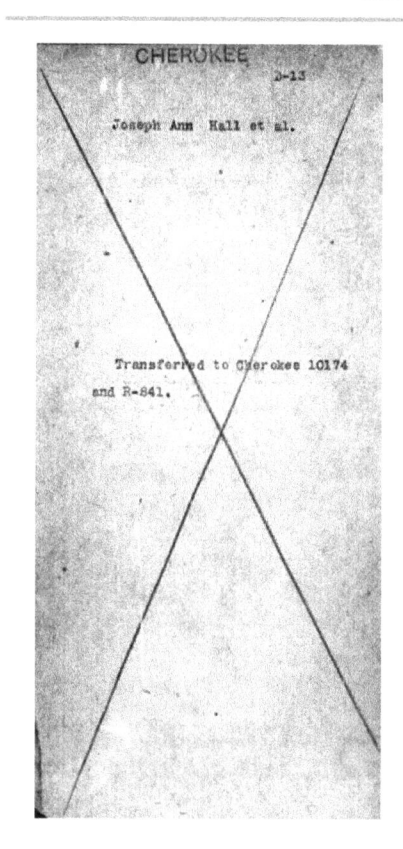

CHEROKEE 2-13

Joseph Ann Hall et al.

Transferred to Cherokee 10174 and R-841.

CHEROKEE GRANTED ENROLLMENT CARDS
& DAWES PACKETS 1900-1907 VOLUME I

CHEROKEE GRANTED ENROLLMENT CARDS & DAWES PACKETS 1900-1907 VOLUME I

Cherokee D14 – William P. Randall

CHEROKEE GRANTED ENROLLMENT CARDS & DAWES PACKETS 1900-1907 VOLUME I

DEPARTMENT OF THE INTERIOR.
COMMISSION TO THE FIVE CIVILIZED TRIBES.
FAIRLAND, I. T., JULY 11th, 1900.

IN THE MATTER OF THE APPLICATION OF William P. Randall for enrollment as a citizen of the Cherokee Nation, and he being sworn by Commissioner, C. R. Breckinridge, testified as follows:

Q What is your name? A William P. Randall.
Q What is your age? A Forty six.
Q Where do you live? A Fairland.
Q What is your Postoffice address? A Fairland,
Q Is Delaware District the place of your permanent residence? A Yes sir.
Q How long have you been living there? A Three or four months.
Q Where did you live before that? A In Kansas.
Q When did you come from Kansas? A I came the first of April.
Q What kind of application do you make here; Cherokee by blood?
A No sir; Shawnee.
Q Where have you lived for the last ten years; before you came here?
A Johnson County, Kansas.
Q How long did you live outside of the Indian Territory?
A Eighteen or twenty years.
   Q Where were you born?   Johnson County, Kansas,
Q That was your home until you came here? A No sir; I lived here about four years in 1871 - 72 - 73 & 74.
Q And before that eccept[sic] that time, you lived in Johnson County, Kansas until you came here recently? A Yes sir.
Q Does your name appear on any of the regular authenticated rolls of the Cherokee Nation? A On the regular Shawnee purchase roll; the roll of '70 or '71.
Q Does your name appear on the 1880 authenticated roll of the Cherokee Nation?
A No sir.
Q Do you appear on the 1894 Roll? A I can not say, I drawed my money.
Q Are you on the Roll of 1896? A Yes sir.
Q Are you n that roll? A Yes sir; I drawed the strip money; it was on the regular Shawnee Roll.
Q I understood you to say that you were not on the 1894 Roll? A Yes sir.
Q You were living in Kansas in 1896? A Yes sir.
Q What evidence can you present of any kind that you are, or have ever been a citizen of the Cherokee Nation? A I can refer you to a number right here, I presume; I lived here.
Q Have you any written evidence, any documentary evidence? A No, only on the Shawnee Census Roll.
Q You say you lived in Kansas a long time? A Yes sir.
Q Have you a certificate of admission to citizenship in the Cherokee Nation?
A No sir, not only as a registered Shawnee as I know of; I moved here and lived here four years: I drew that strip money in 1896 or 1897.
Q Where did you live in 1898? A Up there.

CHEROKEE GRANTED ENROLLMENT CARDS
& DAWES PACKETS 1900-1907 VOLUME I

Q Up where? A Johnson County, Kansas.
(On consulting the Shawnee Roll, approved March 30th, 1896, applicant is identified as being duly recorded as William P. Randall.[sic]
Q What time did you live in the Indian Territory before going back to Kansas?
A Spring of 1874.
Q And you stayed there about three months? A Yes sir, I moved back on account of my mother's health.
Q And there you resided continuously? A Until she died; I came back.
Q What did you do there? A Farmed.
Q Who owned the farm? A My mother.
Q And you lived with her? A Yes sir.
Q What are you doing here; farming? A Yes sir; I came down about three years ago, and bought a claim.

By Mr. W. W. Hastings - Cherokee Representative.

Q Do you own a farm up there? A No sir.
Q Your mother did? A Yes sir.

By the Commission:
Q Are you married? A No sir.
Q You apply duly for yourself? A Yes sir.

The decision of the Commission as to the application you make in your own behalf as a citizen of the Cherokee Nation, will be mailed to you in writing at your present Post-office address, as soon as practicable: The decision will be based on the oral testimony given by you and such other evidence as been adduced; and you can file any affidavits, papers or proofs that you may have, or wish to file, and they will be taken into consideration in connection with your application; and the whole matter will be forwarded to the Secretary of the Interior for his action.

R. R. Cravens, being first duly sworn, states that as stenographer to the Commission to the Five Civilized Tribes, he reported the foregoing case, and that the above and foregoing is a true, full and correct transcript of his stenographic notes in said case.

<u>   *R. R. Cravens*   </u>

Sworn to and subscribed before me this 12th day of July, 1900.

<u>   *Clifton R. Breckinridge*   </u>

COMMISSIONER.

CHEROKEE GRANTED ENROLLMENT CARDS & DAWES PACKETS 1900-1907 VOLUME I

Supl. C.D.14.

Department of the Interior,
Commission to the Five Civilized Tribes.
Muskogee, I. T., February 15, 1902.

SUPPLEMENTAL TESTIMONY in the matter of the enrollment of William P. Randall for enrollment as a citizen of the Cherokee Nation:

Appearances:
Mellette & Smith, Attorneys for Applicant;
Mr. W. W. Hastings, Cherokee Representative.

WILLIAM P. RANDALL, being duly sworn, testified as follows:
By the Commission:

Q What is your name? A William P. Randall.
Q Where do you live, Mr. Randall? A I live near Fairland.
MR. MELLETTE:
Q When did you first move to the Cherokee Nation? A I came here first in the fall of 1870; I moved in the spring of '71.
Q What month of the spring of 1871, did you move here? A In February.
Q Where did you come from? A Johnson County, Kansas.
Q Of what blood are you? A I presume I am about a quarter Shawnee. I don't know just what.
Q Is your name upon the roll of 772 Shawnees who located in the Indian Territory?
A Yes, sir.

Commission: It appears from the register of Shawnees who have moved and located in the Cherokee Nation, Indian Territory, prior to the 10th day of June, 1871, within two years from the 9th day of June, 1869, in accordance with the intered[sic] into by and between the Shawnee tribe of Indians and the Cherokee Nation of Indians, through their delegations in Washington City, D. C., on the 7th day of June, 1869, and approved by the President of the United States on the 9th day of June, 1896, that the name of William P. Randall appears upon said register as number 592.

Mr. Mellette: I would like to have the Commission refer to the certificate of the late chief of the Shawnees which is attached to that roll, certifying that those people are members of the Shawnee tribe.

Mr. Hastings: There will be no contention on the part of the Cherokee Nation on that point.

Commission: "Office of the Executive Department, Cherokee Nation, Indian Territory.
Tahlequah, Aug. 14, 1871.

CHEROKEE GRANTED ENROLLMENT CARDS & DAWES PACKETS 1900-1907 VOLUME I

   This is to certify that the foregoing is the original 'copy of the register of names of the members of the Shawnee tribe of Indians who have moved to and located in the Cherokee Nation, in accordance with the agreement made and entered into by and between the Shawnee tribe of Indians and the Cherokee Nation of Indians, through their delegates, on the 7th of June, 1869; and that a true copy of the came[sic] has been taken and retained in this office; and that on the 4th of August, the ratification of the agreement herein mentioned was proclaimed; and that the Shawnees registered had been declared to be Cherokee citizens, it being understood that the ratification is admitted by the United States government, that there is no bar to the final settlement of the agreement on the part of the United States officials, after the correction of an error in regard to the insertion of names of the delegates making the agreement. There was registered 772 persons instead of 770, as shown on the original by figures.

   The testimony of which I have hereinto set my hand and the seal of the Cherokee Nation, on this the 14th day of August, A. D. 1871.
             Lewis Downing, Principal Chief,
                    Cherokee Nation.

  MR. MELLETTE: Mr. Randall, after you moved to the Cherokee Nation in February, 1871, how long did you live here?
A Lived here about four years.
Q Where did you go then? A Went ot Johnson County, Kansas.
Q Whom did you go with? A My mother and sisters.
Q What was the condition of your sister? A My sister, one of them, was insane. I had two sisters.
Q Now, how long did you live in Kansas before you came bak[sic] here?
A I presume I lived there about 18 or 20 years, or more.
Q Did you vote in Kansas after you went back there? A Never.
Q Did you pay any poll tax? A No, sir.
Q Did you pay any kind of tax? A No, sir.
Q Did you ever hold any office in Kansas after you went back there? A No, sir.
Q When you left the Cherokee Nation did you leave any property here?
A I left a small farm, yes.
Q When did your mother die? A She died three years ago, the last October.
Q Where did she die? A Johnson County, Kansas.
Q How long after she died did you come back to the Cherokee Nation?
A About a year afterwards, a little over.
Q You have never married? A No, sir.
Q Bachelor? A Yes, sir.
  MR. HASTINGS:
Q Your mother owned a farm in Kansas? A Yes, sir.
Q And you farmed it there? A Yes, sir.
Q Made a living up there? A Yes, sir.
Q Made a living up there 15 or 20 years? A Yes, sir.
Q You never thought about her having a farm up there when you appeared before this Commission in July, 1900? A I don't know.
Q Where was that farm? A In Johnson County, Kansas.

CHEROKEE GRANTED ENROLLMENT CARDS & DAWES PACKETS 1900-1907 VOLUME I

Q Where was the farm in this country? A 18 miles from this town.
Q You mean Vinita? A Yes, sir.
Q Adjoining whose place was it? A It was adjoining, fellow by the name of Don Gooseberg.
Q And you let it go back to the Cherokee Nation? A It was jumped.
Q And you let it go back to the Cherokee Nation? A Yes, sir.
Q And you never did any more to it? A It was jumped.
Q It was abandoned by you and taken up by somebody else? A Yes, sir.
   MR. MELLETTE:
Q How was it abandoned by you? A It was abandoned on account of sickness.
Q Did you tell anybody they could take it? A No, sir.
Q Did you leave any other property here when you went to Kansas?
A Yes, sir; I left my two cows?[sic]
   MR. HASTINGS:
Q Did you find them when you came back? A No, sir; I didn't.
   COMMISSION:
Q Is there any statement you want to make in this case.[sic]

   Mr. Mellette: I want to have ten days to file a brief.

   Commission: The attorney for the applicant will be granted ten days in which to file a brief, one copy with this Commission and one copy with the Cherokee Nation, and the representatives of the Nation will also be given an opportunity in which to file a brief, one copy with the Commission and one copy with the applicant.

   By agreement between the Attorney for the applicant and the attorney for the Cherokee Nation, this case is closed and submitted as regards the testimony.

---oooOOOooo---

J. O. Rosson, being first duly sworn, states that as stenographer to the Commission to the Five Civilized Tribes, he correctly recorded the testimony and proceedings in this case, and that the foregoing is a true and complete transcript of his stenographic notes thereof.

JORosson

Subscribed and sworn to before me this February 19, 1902.

T B Needles
Commissioner.

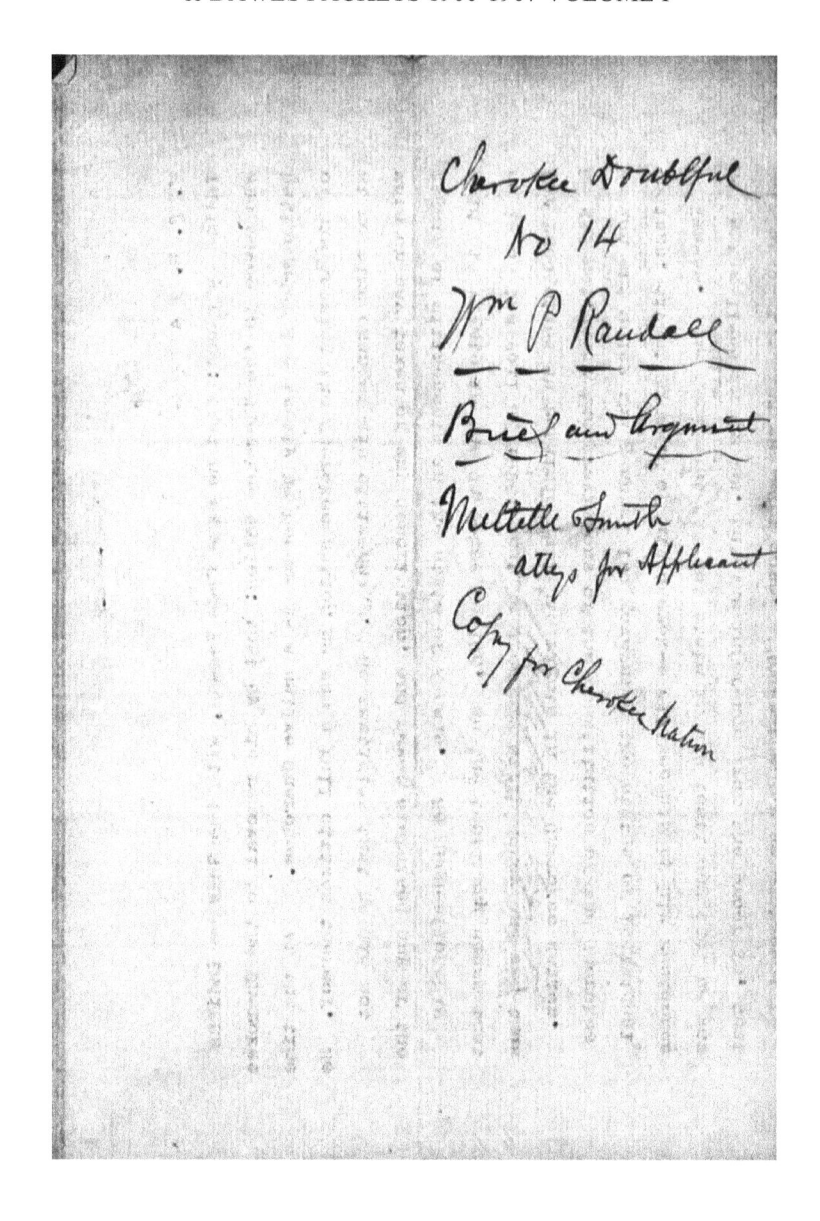

Cherokee Doubtful
No 14

Wm P Randall

Brief and Argument

Meltette Smith
attys for Applicant

Copy for Cherokee Nation

CHEROKEE GRANTED ENROLLMENT CARDS & DAWES PACKETS 1900-1907 VOLUME I

BEFORE THE COMMISSION TO THE FIVE CIVILIZED TRIBES.

IN THE MATTER OF THE APPLICATION OF WILLIAM P. RANDALL, FOR ENROLLMENT AS A CITIZEN OF THE CHEROKEE NATION. CHEROKEE DOUBTFUL. # 14.

---:BRIEF AND ARGUMENT FOR THE APPLICANT.:---

The testimony in this case shows that the applicant came to the Cherokee Nation as a member of the Shawnee tribe of Indians in Feb. 1871, under and by virtue of the treaty between the Cherokees and Shawnees.

His name appears upon the roll of the 772 Shawnees who were received into the Cherokee Tribe by the authorities of the Cherokee Nation and were registered according to the provisions of the treaty. The testimony setsforth[sic] in full the certificate of Lewis Downing, Chief of the Cherokee Nation, certifying that those 772 Shawnees were received and registered as citizens of the Cherokee Nation.

The agreement between the Shawnees and Cherokees was concluded June the 7th, 1869, and provides in substance, that the Shawnees residing in Kansas and elsewhere should be received as citizens of the Cherokee Nation in consideration of certain funds being transferred by the Shawnees for the use and benefit of the Cherokee Tribe.

Said treaty in full is to be found upon page 403 of The Laws of the Cherokee Nation Compiled in 1892. Said agreement provides, among other things, as follows:-

"And that the said Shawnees shall be incorporated into, and ever after remain a part of the Cherokee Nation, on equal terms in every respect and with all the privileges and immunities of native citizens of said Cherokee Nation; provided, that all of said Shawnees who shall elect to avail themselves of this agreement shall register their names and permanently locate in the Cherokee country within two years after the date hereof. Otherwise, they shall forfeit all rights under this agreement."

The testimony shows that the applicant resided in the Cherokee Nation for four years after coming here as a member of the Shawnee tribe; that he located an improvement upon the public domain of the Cherokee Nation and entered into the full enjoyment of his rights as a citizen of the Cherokee Nation. Four years after his arrival in the Cherokee Nation his sister became insane and it became necessary for him to go with his mother and insane sister back to the state of Kansas where he had formerly lived. When he departed from the Cherokee Nation he left behind him an improvement on the public domain of the Cherokee Nation which was afterwards entered upon by some other person. He also left a small amount of personal property, towit, two cows upon his place. After he arrived in Kansas, family conditions were which that it became necessary for him to remain with his mother and sister and he did not return to the Cherokee Nation until the fall of 1892.

The testimony shows that the applicant did not vote in the state of Kansas: that he did not pay any taxes, not even a poll tax and exercised none of the rights of a citizen of Kansas or of the United States while he resided there. He lived there from about the year 1875, to the year 1898, but all the time without identifying himself in any way as a citizen of the state of Kansas or of the United States, and exercised none of the rights of citizenship there.

The constitution of the Cherokee Nation provides, Art. 1 Sec. 2, page 12, Compiled Laws of the Cherokee Nation 1898, that:

"Whenever any citizen shall, with his effects, move out of the limits of this Nation and becomes a citizen of any other government, all his rights and privileges as a citizen of this Nation shall cease."

This provision of the constitution of the Cherokee Nation expressly provides that a citizen must leave the Nation and become a citizen of some other government before his rights and privileges shall cease. We think the facts in this case conclusively show that the applicant did not become a citizen of the state of Kansas, or of the United States while residing in Kansas, and that he remained at all times a citizen of the Cherokee Nation while residing in the state of Kansas. The mere fact of his residing outside of the Cherokee Nation did not, under the provisions of the constitution above quoted, divest him of his citizenship; it was necessary that he become a citizen of some other government, which he did not do.

The case of Elk v. Wilkens, decided by the Supreme Court of the United States, book 28, L.ed.p.643, clearly defines the status of the indians[sic] who reside outside the limits of their tribes. In that case John Elk, who was born a member of an Indian

CHEROKEE GRANTED ENROLLMENT CARDS
& DAWES PACKETS 1900-1907 VOLUME I

Tribe, residing for a number of years in the City of Omaha, state of Nebraska, presented himself before Wilkens, who was registrar in one of the ward in Omaha, and asked to have his name recorded as a legal voter. This was refused on the ground that he was not a citizen of the state of Nebraska, and although he had resided the proper length of time in Omaha, he had no right under the constitution of the United States and the state of Nebraska, to cast a vote. Action was brought for damages because of this refusal. In passing upon the case the Supreme Court of the United States used the following language:

"The petition, while it does not show of what indian[sic] tribe the plaintiff was a member, yet by the allegations that he is an indian and was born within the United States and that he had severed his tribal relations to the indian tribes, clearly implies that he was born a member of the indian tribes within the limits of the United States which still exists and is recognized as a tribe by the government of the United States. Though the plaintiff alleges that he had fully and completely surrendered himself to the jurisdiction of the United States, he does not allege that the United States accept his surrender, or that he has ever been naturalized, or taxed, or in any way treated as a citizen by the state or by the United States. Nor is it contended by his counsel that there is any statute or treaty that makes him a citizen.

The question then is whether an indian born a member of one of the indian tribes within the United States is merely by reason of his birth within the United States and afterwards voluntarily separating himself from his Tribe and taking up his residence among white citizens, a citizen within the meaning of the 1st. section of the 14th amendment of the constitution.

The Indian Tribes being within the Territory limits of the United States were not strictly speaking, foreign states but they were alien nations, distinct political communities with whom the United States may, and habitually did deal as they thought fit, either through treaties made by the President and Senate, or through acts of Congress in the ordinary forms of legislation. The members of those Tribes owed immediate allegiance to their several Tribes and were not part of the people of the United States. They were in a dependant[sic] condition, a state of pupilage resembling that of ward to his guardian. The Indians and their property exempt from taxation by treaty or a statute of the United States, could not be taxed by any state. General acts of Congress did not apply to Indians unless so expressed as to clearly manifest an intention to include them."

See authorities cited.

"The treaty of 1867, with the Kansas Indians, strikingly illustrates the principle that no one can become a citizen of the Nation without its consent, and directly contradicts the supposition that a member of the Indian Tribes can and will be alternately a citizen of the United States and a member of the Tribe..

But an Indian can not make himself a citizen of the United States without the consent and co-operation of the government. The fact that he has abandoned his nomadic life or Tribal relations, and adopted the habits and manners of civilized people may be a good reason why he should be made a citizen of the United States, but does not of itself make him one. To be a citizen of the United States is a political privilege which no one not born to can assume without its consent in some form. The Indians in origin not being born subject to the jurisdiction of the United States, were not born citizens thereof, and I am not aware of any law, or treaty by which any of them have been made so since."

The testimony in this case shows that the applicant is a Shawnee Indian by blood: that he came from Kansas, with the Shawnee Indians who moved to the Cherokee Nation: that by his removal to the Cherokee Nation under the treaty he became as a native Cherokee. At the time of his leaving the Cherokee Nation he was a full citizen thereof. He at no time changed his citizenship. He testifies that he did not vote or pay taxes of any description, and never exercised any of the rights of citizenship in the state of Kansas. He unquestionably held his rights in the Cherokee Nation, as the testimony shows that he is on the roll of 1896: that he drew his strip money and was thus far recognized as retaining all his rights in the Cherokee Nation. He did not under the provisions of the constitution of the Cherokee Nation and under the general law governing the status of individual Indians, divest himself of his Cherokee citizenship by his residence in Kansas. The applicant did not state in his testimony that he was not naturalized while in Kansas, but the inference from the proof is, that nothing of the kind was ever done. Under the law as expressed in the case of Elk vs. Wilkens, an Indian can not be naturalized and become a citizen of the United States under the general naturalization laws, but a special act of Congress is required before they can renounce their citizenship. There has been no such act in regard to the Shawnee Indians.

Respectfully Submitted.

Mellette & Smith
Attorney's for Applicant.

DEPARTMENT OF THE INTERIOR

Commission to the Five Civilized Tribes

Muskogee I. T. April 3rd 1902.

In the matter of the application of William P. Randall for enrollment as a Shawnee citizen of the Cherokee Nation.

No. D. 14.

..........................o..........................

BRIEF IN BEHALF OF THE CHEROKEE NATION.

CHEROKEE GRANTED ENROLLMENT CARDS & DAWES PACKETS 1900-1907 VOLUME I

..............................o..........................

The proof is quite clear in this case that William P. Randall is a Shawnee by blood, that he came to the Cherokee Nation with the Shawnees and that his name appears upon the register of shawnees[sic] who located in the Cherokee Nation under the provisions of the agreement entered into by and between the Cherokee Nation and the Shawnees and approved by the Government of the United States; that he remained here some three or four years and then went back to the state of Kansas where he remained until April 1900 when he returned to the Cherokee Nation; That he left no property in the Cherokee Nation although in the supplemental testimony he makes a very weak attempt to swear that he had a claim upon the public domain of the Cherokee Nation which he abandoned and a cow or two which he would have the commission to believe is wandering upon the rolling prairies of the Cherokee Nation now some twenty-five years of age. The testimony upon this proposition is too insufficient to require comment.

Had this man remained in the Cherokee Nation he would have been entitled to citizenship: "In every respect and with all the privileges and immunities of native citizens of said Cherokee Nation". When he came here in 1871 he was so entitled; he had the same rights as a full blood Indian, but according to his testimony, being forty-six years old in 1900, he would have been born in 1854 and therefore be twenty-one years of age when he left the Cherokee Nation and forty-six years of age when he returned. His name does not appear upon the roll of 1880; he was not recognized at that time as a citizen of the Cherokee Nation and his name not appearing upon that roll it certainly should be considered to mean, taken in connection with his non-residence, that it was considered by the Cherokee Nation that he had forfeited his right to citizenship in the Cherokee Nation.

Counsel for applicant relies upon the case of Elk Vs Wilkens, but this case is not at all applicable to the case at bar for the reason that section twenty-one of the Curtis Act provides that "No person shall be enrolled who has not heretofore removed to and in good faith settles in the nation in which he claims citizenship".

How it is not contended that prior to this time, since 1874 or 1875, that this man of forty-six years had removed to and became a citizen of the Cherokee Nation. The fact that this man claims as a Shawnee does not give him any greater rights than a

Cherokee by blood; we contend that he has the same, no more and no less, and that by his twenty-six years of non residence in the state of Kansas He ought not be enrolled as a citizen of the Cherokee Nation.

Respectfully Submitted,

Attorney for the Cherokee Nation.

Cherokee D 14

DEPARTMENT OF THE INTERIOR,
COMMISSION TO THE FIVE CIVILIZED TRIBES.

In the matter of the application of William P. Randall for enrollment as a citizen of the Cherokee Nation.

D E C I S I O N.

--oOo--

The record in this case shows that on July 11, 1900, William P. Randall appeared before the Commission at Fairland, Indian Territory, and then and there made application for his enrollment as a citizen of the Cherokee Nation by adoption. On February 15, 1902, applicant appeared before the Commission at its office in Muskogee, Indian Territory, and further proceedings were then and there had in the matter of this application. It appears from the evidence that the applicant is identified on the "Shawnee Register", a roll containing the names of those who located in the Cherokee Nation under the terms of a treaty concluded between the Cherokee Nation and the Shawnee tribe of Indians on June 7, 1869. It appears that applicant lived in the Cherokee Nation from 1871 to 1874, and that in the latter year he went to Kansas and resided there continuously until 1899 or 1900, when he returned to the Cherokee Nation.

CHEROKEE GRANTED ENROLLMENT CARDS & DAWES PACKETS 1900-1907 VOLUME I

He is identified on the Cherokee-Shawnee Pay roll of 1896.

The authority of the Commission herein is defined in Paragraph 9, Sec. 21, of the Act of Congress, approved June 28, 1898, (30 Stats., 495), which is as follows:

"No person shall be enrolled who has not heretofore removed to and in good faith settled in the Nation in which he claims citizenship."

It is therefore the opinion of the Commission that William P. Randall is not lawfully entitled to be enrolled as a member of the Cherokee tribe of Indians in Indian Territory, and that his application for enrollment should be denied, and it is so ordered.

COMMISSION TO THE FIVE CIVILIZED TRIBES.

Tams Bixby
Acting Chairman.

T.B. Needles
Commissioner.

C. R. Breckinridge
Commissioner.

Dated Muskogee, Indian Territory, this _____ MAY 20 1902

BEFORE THE DEPARTMENT OF THE INTERIOR
WASHINGTON.   Cherokee D #14.

September 10th 1903.

In the matter of the application for the enrollment of William P. Randall as a citizen of the Cherokee Nation.

Reply to applicants motion for a New hearing.

Comes now the Cherokee Nation and respectfully resists the motion for a new hearing in this case, filed by the applicants, for the reason that no sufficient reason is assigned insaid motion requesting that a new hearing should be granted in this case and for the further reason that the "Yeargain Case" is not a parallel case with the one at bar, because in the Yeargain cases these applicants were upon every roll made by the Cherokees since their birth, and always lived within the limits of the Cherokee Nation until three or four years ago when they went into business just across the line but always retained numerous personal property within the limits of the Cherokee Nation where they always voted and took part in Cherokee governmental affairs.

Respectfully,

W. W. Hastings   JCS
Attorney for the Cherokee Nation.

DEPARTMENT OF THE INTERIOR,
COMMISSION TO THE FIVE CIVILIZED TRIBES.

In the matter of the application of ___William P. Randall___
for enrollment as citizens of the Cherokee Nation.

No. _Cher. D 14_
UNITED STATES OF AMERICA, } ss
INDIAN TERRITORY,
NORTHERN DISTRICT.

AFFIDAVIT TO SHOW SERVICE.

This day personally appeared before me the undersigned a Notary Public within and for the Northern District of the Indian Territory, R.G. Zimmerman, who being by me first duly sworn on oath states, that his age is thirty-three years and that his postoffice is Vinita, Indian Territory, and that on the __11th__ day of __March__ 1903 he deposited in the United States postoffice at __Tahlequah, I.T.__ an envelope containing a true copy of the instrument hereto attached and he hereto attaches the receipt of the postmaster at said postoffice showing that he received said package to be duly registered and mailed to __William P. Randall__ whose postoffice is __Fairland__ Indian Territory, ~~and attached to this affidavit is the registry return receipt duly signed by the applicant showing that said envelope containing a true copy of the instrument hereto attached was received by the said applicant.~~

R.G. Zimmerman

Subscribed and sworn to before me this __11th__ day of __Sept__ 1903

J.C. Starr
Notary Public.

Cherokee D 14.

DEPARTMENT OF THE INTERIOR,
COMMISSION TO THE FIVE CIVILIZED TRIBES.

In the matter of the application of William P. Randall for enrollment as a citizen of the Cherokee Nation of Shawnee blood.

DECISION.

CHEROKEE GRANTED ENROLLMENT CARDS & DAWES PACKETS 1900-1907 VOLUME I

The record in this case shows that on July 11, 1900, William P. Randall appeared before the Commission at Fairland, Indian Territory, and made application for enrollment as a citizen of the Cherokee Nation of Shawnee blood. Further proceedings in the matter of said application were had at Muskogee, Indian Territory, on February 15, 1902. The record further shows that on May 20, 1902, the Commission rendered its decision denying said application and forwarded the same to the Department of the Interior, which decision was approved by the Department on August 1, 1902; that on May 28, 1903 the applicant filed a motion for rehearing in said case, and on July 10, 1903, the Department rescinded its former action in the matter of said application and remanded the case to the Commission for readjudication.

The evidence shows that the applicant is identified on the Shawnee Register, containing the names of the members of the Shawnee tribe of Indians who removed to and located in the Cherokee Nation, in accordance with the terms of an agreement made June 7, 1869, by and between the Shawnees and the Cherokees, and approved June 9, 1869. It further appears that the applicant is identified on the Cherokee-Shawnee pay roll of 1896.

The evidence further shows that the applicant resided in the Cherokee Nation from 1871 until 1874; that in 1874 he removed to the State of Kansas where he remained until about 1900, when he returned to the Cherokee Nation where he has since resided; that the applicant at the time of his removal to said state left some of his live stock in the Cherokee Nation; and it is not shown by the evidence that he ever assumed the obligations of citizenship in the State of Kansas during his residence there.

It is, therefore, the opinion of this Commission, following the decision of the Department in the matter of the application for the enrollment of Joseph D. Yeargain, et al. as citizens of the Cherokee Nation (I.T.D. 2900--1903), that William P. Randall should be enrolled as a citizen of the Cherokee Nation of Shawnee blood, in accordance with the provisions of section twenty-one of the act of Congress, approved June 28, 1898 (30 Stats., 495), and it is so ordered.

COMMISSION TO THE FIVE CIVILIZED TRIBES.

(SIGNED). *Tams Bixby.*
Chairman.

(SIGNED). *T. B. Needles.*
Commissioner.

Muskogee, Indian Territory, this SEP 25 1903

(SIGNED). *C. R. Breckinridge.*
Commissioner.

(SIGNED). *W. E. Stanley.*
Commissioner.

W. W. H.

Cherokee D # 14.

DEPARTMENT OF THE INTERIOR,
Commission to the Five Civilized Tribes,
Tahlequah, I. T. October 15th 1903.

In the matter of the application for the enrollment of William P. Randall as a citizen of the Cherokee Nation of Shawnee Blood.

Protest of the Cherokee Nation.

Comes now the Cherokee Nation and respectfully protests against the decision of the Commission to the Five Civilized Tribes of September 25th 1903 and asks that the record in this case be forwarded to the Honorable Secretary of the Interior for Review.

ARGUMENT.

Our reasons are fully expressed in our brief filed in this case to which reference is respectfully made. For the reasons stated in our brief we do not believe this application should be allowed and we do believe that this decision of the Commission should be reversed.

Respectfully,

W W Hastings
J.C.S.   Attorney for the Cherokee Nation.

April 5, 1902.

C. D. 14.
Vollette & Smith,
   Vinita, I. T.
Gentlemen

Enclosed herewith find a copy of the brief of the Cherokee Nation in the case Cherokee D. 14, William P. Randall. Please acknowledge receipt of same, and oblige,

Yours truly,

CHEROKEE GRANTED ENROLLMENT CARDS & DAWES PACKETS 1900-1907 VOLUME I

COMMISSIONERS:
HENRY L. DAWES,
TAMS BIXBY,
THOMAS B. NEEDLES,
C. R. BRECKINRIDGE.

DEPARTMENT OF THE INTERIOR,
COMMISSION TO THE FIVE CIVILIZED TRIBES.

REFER IN REPLY TO THE FOLLOWING
Cher. D-14.

ALLISON L. AYLESWORTH, SECRETARY.

ADDRESS ONLY THE COMMISSION TO THE FIVE CIVILIZED TRIBES.

Muskogee, Indian Territory, May 20, 1902.

W. W. Hastings, Esq.,

    Attorney for the Cherokee Nation,

        Muskogee, Indian Territory.

Sir:

    There is herewith enclosed the decision of the Commission to the Five Civilized Tribes in the matter of the application of William P. Randall for the enrollment of himself as a citizen of the Cherokee Nation.

    The decision, with a copy of the proceedings had in the case, is this day transmitted to the Secretary of the Interior for his review and decision.

    The final decision of the Secretary will be made known to you as soon as the Commission is informed of the same.

        Respectfully,

        Tams Bixby
        Acting Chairman.

Enc. R-11.

COMMISSIONERS:
HENRY L. DAWES,
TAMS BIXBY,
THOMAS B. NEEDLES,
C. R. BRECKINRIDGE.

DEPARTMENT OF THE INTERIOR,
COMMISSION TO THE FIVE CIVILIZED TRIBES.

REFER IN REPLY TO THE FOLLOWING
Cherokee D 14.

ALLISON L. AYLESWORTH, SECRETARY.

ADDRESS ONLY THE COMMISSION TO THE FIVE CIVILIZED TRIBES.

Muskogee, Indian Territory, August 16, 1902.

W. W. Hastings, Esquire,

    Attorney for the Cherokee Nation,

        Muskogee, Indian Territory.

Sir:

    You are hereby advised that the decision of the Commission to the Five Civilized Tribes, of date May 20, 1902, denying the application of William

P. Randall for the enrollment of himself as a citizen by intermarriage of the Cherokee Nation, was affirmed by the Secretary of the Interior on the 1st day of August, 1902.

       Very respectfully,

         Tams Bixby Acting Chairman.

DEPARTMENT OF THE INTERIOR.
WASHINGTON.

CMR

ITD 5235,5288,
8057-1903.

September 23, 1903.

Mr. W. W. Hastings,
  Attorney for the Cherokee Nation,
    Tahlequah, Indian Territory.

Sir:

  There is returned herewith the "reply on the part of the Cherokee Nation in the motion of applicants for a new hearing in the case of William P. Randall," applicant for enrollment as a citizen of the Cherokee Nation, as the reply has been served upon the applicant and not his attorney, Edgar Smith, of Vinita, Indian Territory.

  You are advised that on July 10, 1903, a rehearing was ordered in this case by letter to the Commission to the Five Civilized Tribes.

  If the motion to which your argument is a reply was made on some action taken by the Commission to the Five Civilized Tribes since that time the Department has no information in regard to the matter.

         Respectfully,

         Thos Ryan
1 inclosure.   Acting Secretary.

CHEROKEE GRANTED ENROLLMENT CARDS
& DAWES PACKETS 1900-1907 VOLUME I

COMMISSIONERS:
TAMS BIXBY,
THOMAS B. NEEDLES,
C. R. BRECKINRIDGE,
W. E. STANLEY.

DEPARTMENT OF THE INTERIOR.
COMMISSION TO THE FIVE CIVILIZED TRIBES.

REFER IN REPLY TO THE FOLLOWING

Cherokee D-14
(R-645).

ALLISON L. AYLESWORTH,
SECRETARY.

ADDRESS ONLY THE
COMMISSION TO THE FIVE CIVILIZED TRIBES.

Muskogee, Indian Territory, October 7, 1903.

Mr. W. W. Hastings,

    Attorney for the Cherokee Nation,

        Tahlequah, Indian Territory.

Dear Sir:

    There is herewith enclosed a copy of the decision of the Commission to the Five Civilized Tribes, dated September 25, 1903, granting the application of William P. Randall for enrollment as a citizen by blood of the Cherokee Nation.

    You are hereby advised that you will be allowed fifteen days from hereof in which to file such protest as you may desire to make against the action of the Commission in this case, a copy of which protest you will be required to furnish the applicant. If you fail to file protest within the time allowed this decision will be considered final.

        Respectfully,

        Tams Bixby

Enc. D-45   Chairman.

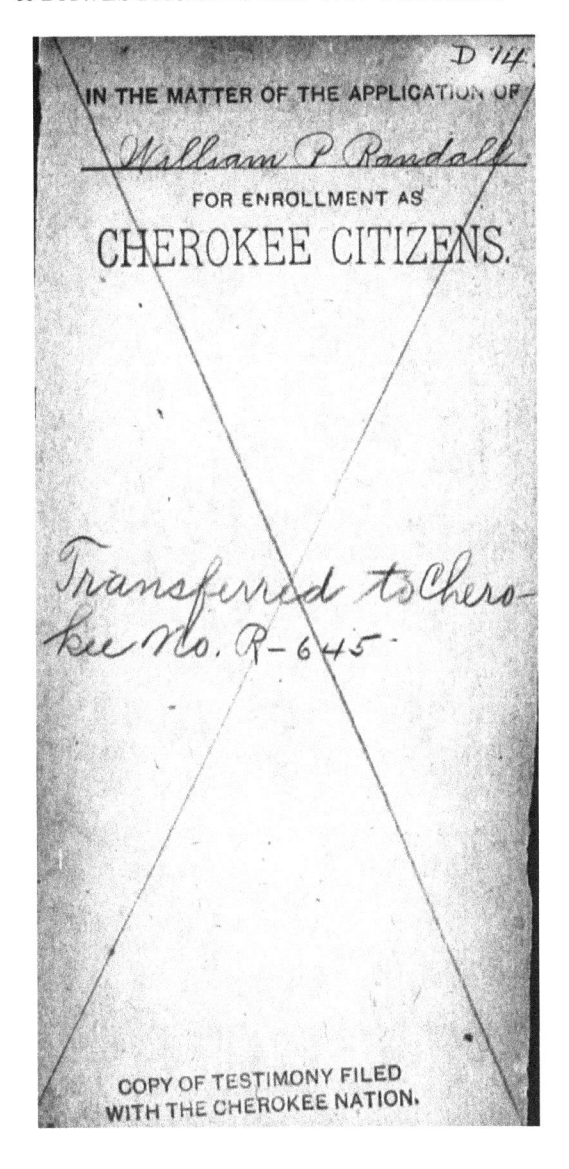

CHEROKEE GRANTED ENROLLMENT CARDS & DAWES PACKETS 1900-1907 VOLUME I

D 14

IN THE MATTER OF THE APPLICATION OF

William P Randall

FOR ENROLLMENT AS

CHEROKEE CITIZENS.

Transferred to Cherokee No. R-645.

COPY OF TESTIMONY FILED WITH THE CHEROKEE NATION.

CHEROKEE GRANTED ENROLLMENT CARDS & DAWES PACKETS 1900-1907 VOLUME I

CHEROKEE GRANTED ENROLLMENT CARDS & DAWES PACKETS 1900-1907 VOLUME I

Cherokee D18 - Napoleon B. Blythe

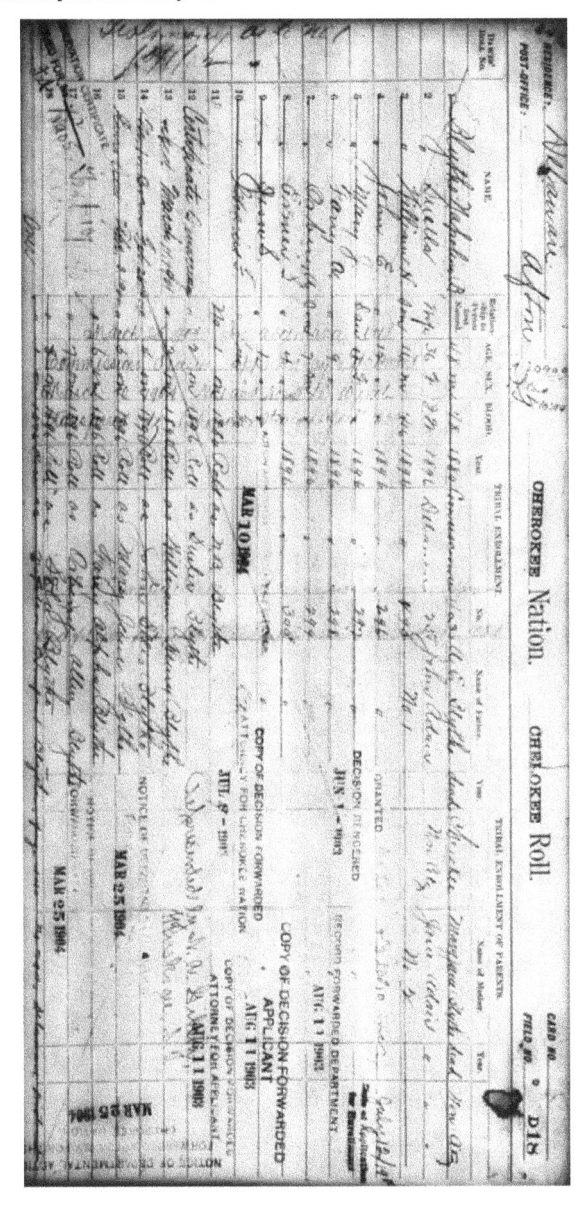

CHEROKEE GRANTED ENROLLMENT CARDS & DAWES PACKETS 1900-1907 VOLUME I

DEPARTMENT OF THE INTERIOR.
COMMISSION TO THE FIVE CIVILIZED TRIBES.
FAIRLAND, I. T., JULY 12th, 1900.

IN THE MATTER OF THE APPLICATION OF Napoleon B. Blythe et al, for enrollment as citizens of the Cherokee Nation, and he being sworn by Commissioner, T. B. Needles, testified as follows:

Q What is your name? A Napoleon B. Blythe.
Q What is your age? A Forty-eight years old.
Q What is your Postoffice address? A Afton.
Q Where do you live? A Delaware District.
Q How long have you lived there? A Six years.
Q Where did you live prior to that time? A In Missouri a while prior to that time, and before that time I lived in Cooweescoowee District.
Q Where were you born? A In the Cherokee Nation.
Q And how long did you live there before you moved to Missouri?
A I was in Cooweescoowee District eight years; first lived in Tahleuqah[sic] District, then moved to Cooweescoowee, and was there about eight years and left here in the Spring of 1882, and I was in Missouri until the Spring of 1892., I came back to the Cherokee Nation then.
Q In 1892? A Yes sir.
Q Have you been living in the Cherokee Nation since 1892? A Yes sir.
Q Are you a Cherokee? A Yes sir.
Q You make application as a citizen by blood? A Yes sir.
Q Is your name on the Roll of 1880? A Yes sir.
Roll of 1880 examined, and on Page 75 thereof, #403m Cooweescoowee District, appears the name of N. B. Blythe.
Q What District do you reside in now? A Delaware.
Q Does your name appear on the Roll of 1896? A Yes sir.
Roll of 1896 examined, and on Page 440 thereof, #294, appears the name of Napoleon B. Blythe.
Q What proportion of Cherokee blood do you claim? A About one eighth.
Q Are you married? A Yes sir.
Q Under what law did you marry? A Cherokee.
Q Is your wife a non citizen? A Yes sir.
Q Have you a marriage liscence[sic] and certificate with you? A No sir.
Q Is your wife living? A Yes sir.
Q Where were you living at the time of your marriage? A In Missouri.
Q Has your wife ever been enrolled on any of the authenticated rolls of the Cherokee Nation? A Yes sir, on the Roll of 1896.
Q What is her name? A Luella Blythe.
Roll of 1896 examined, and on Page 565 thereof, #25, Delaware District, appearsw the name of applicant's wife, Lueller Blythe.
Q When were you married? A I was married twice; first time in 1880.
Q When did you marry your present wife? A In 1887.

CHEROKEE GRANTED ENROLLMENT CARDS & DAWES PACKETS 1900-1907 VOLUME I

Q You have no certificate of marriage? A No sir, I have two witnesses here that witnessed the marriage.
Q You never had any Certificate? A No sir, never got any certificate; the clerk was busy and said you can get a certificate at any time.
Q You had a marriage liscence[sic]? A Yes sir.
Q When? A In 1887.
Q Did they require a marriage liscence in Missouri in 1887? A Yes sir.
Q What did yo pay for it? A 2.50.
Q Do you want to introduce testimony as to your marriage? A Yes sir.

Elizabeth H Hard, being sworn by Commissioner, T. B. Needles, testified as follows:

Q What is your name? A Elizabeth Hard.
Q How old are you? A Sixty-six coming October.
Q Where do you reside? A In the Nation.
Q How long have you lived in the Nation? A Four years in December.
Q Are you a citizen of the Nation? A No sir.
Q In what part of the Nation do you live? A Horse Creek, four miles south of Afton.
Q Where did you come from? A Missouri.
Q Do your know Napoleon B. Blythe? A Yes sir.
Q How long have you known him? A For about thirty years.
Q Do you know his wife? A Yes sir.
Q What is her name? A Luella Blythe.
Q Do you know whether they were married? A Yes sir, I saw their marriage.
Q Whom were they married by? A Clerk of the Court in Versailes, Missouri.
Q How did you happen to be there? A Went right there with them.
Q Kind of a wedding party? A Yes sir.
Q Do you know whether they have been living together as man an wife from that time to this? A Yes sir.
Q You have known them intimately? A Yes sir.
Q They have lived together as man and wife and have been so recognized?
A Yes sir.

John H. Sorter[sic], being sworn by Commissioner, T. B. Needles, testified as follows:

Q What is your name? A John H. Horton.
Q What is your age? A Forty four.
Q Where do you reside? A Horse Creek, four miles south of Afton,
Q Are you a citizen? A No sir.
Q Non citizen? A Yes sir.
Q How long have you lived there? A Four years.
Q Where did you come from? A Missouri.
Q Do you know the applicant, N. B. Blythe? A Yes sir,
Q Do you know Luella Blythe? A Yes sir.
Q Is she the wife of N. B. Blythe? A Yes sir.
Q Have you known them ever since their marriage? A Yes sir.
Q Have they been living together as man and wife? A Yes sir.

CHEROKEE GRANTED ENROLLMENT CARDS & DAWES PACKETS 1900-1907 VOLUME I

Q And have been so recognized? A Yes sir.

Mr. Blythe recalled:

By MR. Hutchins:
Q You were living in Missouri in 1884, were you not? A Yes sir.
Q Whom did you vote for for president, Cleaveland[sic] or Blaine? A Blaine.
Q You did vote in some of the elections there? A Yes sir.
Q And resided there nearly seven years, did you not? A Yes sir.
Q Did your voting in Missouri and married there, did you not? A Yes sir.
Q And left there in 1882? A Yes sir.
Q And did not return until 1889? A 1892, Spring of 1892.
Q You were away nine years? A Yes sir.
Q And you voted up there; acted as a citizen of Missouri for seven or eight years?
A Yes sir, I voted in one or two elections there.
By the Commission:
Q Has you a residence established in the Territory in 1898, or did you move here after 1898? A I moved here in 1892.
Q You have been here ever since 1892? A Yes sir.
Q Have you any children under twenty one years of age living at home? A Yes sir.
Q Please give their names? A My oldest one is William Henry Blythe, 16 years old.
Q Is he on the 1896 Roll? A Yes sir.
(1896 Roll examined, and on Page 295, #449)
Q Next one? A John Ellis Blythe.
Q How old? Twleve[sic] years.
(1896 Roll examined, and on Page 440 thereof, #296, Delaware District, appears the name of John Ellis Blythe.)
Q Where was John Ellis Blythe born? A In Missouri.
Q Where was William H. Blythe born? A In the State of Missouri.
Q Next one? A Mary Jane Blythe.
Q How old? A Eleven years old the 9th day of August.
Q Where was she born? A In Missouri.
(Roll of 1896 examined, and on Page 440 thereof, #297, Delaware District, appears the name of Mary Jane Blythe)
Q Next one? A Farry Alpha Blythe, (Roll of 1896 examined, and on Page 440, #298, Delaware District, appears the name of Farry Alpha Blythe.)
Q Where was she born? A In Missouri.
Q Next one? A Aubrey Allen Blythe.
Q How old? A Seven years old, fourth of February.
Q Where was he born? A In Missouri.
(Roll of 1896 examined, and on Page 440 thereof, #299, appears the name of Aubrey Allen Blythe - as Orberry Allen Blythe)
Q Next one? A Ermer Lolla Blythe.
Q How old is she? A Four years old.
(Roll of 1896 examined, and on Page 440, #300, Delaware District, appears the name of Erma Lolla Blythe - on the roll as Lolla Blythe.)
Q Where was she born? A In the Cherokee Nation.

CHEROKEE GRANTED ENROLLMENT CARDS & DAWES PACKETS 1900-1907 VOLUME I

Q What is the next one? A Jesse Louie?[sic]
Q How old? A 1 year old, the fourth of last March.
Q Where was he born? A In the Cherokee Nation.
Q What year did you move to Missouri in? A In the Fall of 1882, I think, if I am not mistaken.
Q Your wife is a white woman? A Yes sir.
Q When did you come back to the Territory?
A I came back in the Spring of 1892 I think it was.

Mr. Blythe, it appears from the records now in the possession of this Commission that you are enrolled on the authenticated rolls of the Cherokee Nation for the year 1880, which is conclusive proof of your citizenship up to the time of 1882; it also appears that in 1882 you removed from the Cherokee Nation to Missouri and there established a residence and became a regular citizen of the State of Missouri, and remained there until 1892; in 1892 you returned to the Cherokee Nation, and after that you were admitted as a citizen by the council, but present no proof as that effect; and it appears from your testimony that you married your wife, Luella Blythe, in the State of Missouri, while you were an actual resident of that State, and it appears that all your children mentioned above, except two, were born in Missouri after the year 1882; and that your two last named children were born in the Cherokee Nation after you aver to have been readmitted as a citizen of the Cherokee Nation by the Cherokee Council: The citizenship of yourself and your wife and your two younger children depends upon the fact as to whether you were actually readmitted or not. Your name, the name of your wife and the names of your children are, as cited in the evidence given by you, identified on the rolls of 1896, according to the page and number in the evidence, will be placed upon what is known as a doubtful or white card; and you will be permitted to file any other any other[sic] testimony, document, affidavits or proofs as to your citizenship, with the Commission., and upon the filing of the same, your case will be taken into consideration by the Commission, and you advised by mail of its decision as to the citizenship of yourself, wife and children.

R. R. Cravens, being first duly sworn, states that as stenographer to the Commission to the Five Civilized Tribes, he reported the foregoing case, and that the above and foregoing is a true, full and correct transcript of his stenographic notes in said case.

               R. R. Cravens

Sworn to and subscribed before me this _12_ day of July, 1900.

               TB Needles

               COMMISSIONER.

CHEROKEE GRANTED ENROLLMENT CARDS & DAWES PACKETS 1900-1907 VOLUME I

"R"

Cherokee D 18.

Department of the Interior,
Commission to the Five Civilized Tribes,
Muskogee, I. T., February 15, 1902.

SUPPLEMENTAL PROCEEDINGS, in the matter of the application of Napoleon B. Blythe et al., for enrollment as Cherokee citizens.

Appearances:
Mr. N. A. Gibson, Muskogee, I.T., Attorney for Appl'ts.
W.W. Hastings, for the Cherokee Nation.

BY COMMISSION: Attorney for the applicant will be given ten days in which to file brief in this case, a copy with the Commission and a copy with the Representatives of the Cherokee Nation.
The Representatives of the Cherokee Nation will be given due time in which to file brief in reply.

BY MR. GIBSON: I don't desire to introduce any more proof: I think everything that is necessary is here.

BY COMMISSION: Case closed so far as testimony is concerned, by agreement of the attorney for the applicant and attorney for the Cherokee Nation.

M.D. Green, being first duly sworn, states that as stenographer to the Commission to the Five Civilized Tribes he correctly recorded the testimony and proceedings in this case and that the foregoing is a true and complete transcript of his stenographic notes thereof.

MD Green

Subscribed and sworn to before me this February 18, 1902.

T B Needles

Commissioner.

CHEROKEE GRANTED ENROLLMENT CARDS & DAWES PACKETS 1900-1907 VOLUME I

DEPARTMENT OF THE INTERIOR
COMMISSION TO THE FIVE CIVILIZED TRIBES.

In the matter of the application of Napoleon B. Blythe, for enrollment as a citizen of the Cherokee Nation.

Brief of Applicant.

The proof in this case shows that the applicant is a Cherokee Indian by blood and that his name appears on the Roll of 1880, on the Strip Pay Roll of 1894, and on the Roll of 1896, and that the only objection urged against the enrollment of the applicant is because he left the Cherokee Nation about the year 1882 and did not return to live in said Nation until 1888.

The attorneys for the Cherokee Nation base their objection to his enrollment upon the provision of the Constitution of the Cherokee Nation that " whenever any citizen shall remove with his effects out of the limits of this Nation, and shall become a citizen of any other government, all his rights and privileges as a citizen of this Nation shall cease. "

This Constitution was adopted on the 6th., day of September 1839.

We respectfully submit that under the laws of the United States this provision of the Cherokee Constitution has been modified and abrogated to such an extent that it no longer bars the applicant from being enrolled, even if it ever did.

There is no proof that the applicant ever became a citizen of any other government, and hence even if he did remove with his effects from out the Cherokee Nation, the fact that he did not become a citizen of any other government will still prevent his being stricken from the Rolls of the Nation.

We respectfully refer the Commission to the opinion of Honorable William A. Little, Assistant Attorney General of the United States, rendered on September 10, 1896, and which was at said time approved by The Honorable David R. Francis, the then Secretary of the Interior, in the matter of the right of non-resident Cherokee freedmen to participate in the distribution of the fund awarded by the United States Court of Claims, in which the following language is used:-

CHEROKEE GRANTED ENROLLMENT CARDS & DAWES PACKETS 1900-1907 VOLUME I

" It remains to be seen how a citizen of the Cherokee Nation may expatriate himself-"The right of expatriation, inalienable and extends to individuals of the Indian race", United States ex rel Standing Bear vs Crook (5Dill.433).

The term includes more, however, than merely a change of domicile. There must be a renunciation of allegiance to the one, and a purpose of making a home and becoming a citizen of another country. But even the ordinary rules of International Law, the Cherokee Constitution has distinctly provided and defined what shall constitute expatriation from that Nation. "Whenever any citizen shall remove with his effects out of the limits of this Nation and become a citizen of any other government, all his rights and privileges as a citizen of this nation shall cease." He must not only remove his effects but he must become a citizen of another government. It remains to be seen how an alien, and more especially a dependent alien may become a citizen of the United States. It may be said generally that an alien may become a citizen of this country in one way only, which is strictly a judicial one, that of naturalization. By the Sixth Section of the Act of Feb 8th., 1887 ([illegible]Stat 388) it was provided, however, that:

Every indian[sic] born within the territorial limits of the United States who has voluntarily taken up within said limits his residence separate and apart from any tribe of Indians therein and has adopted the habits of civilized life, is hereby declared to be a citizen of the United States, and is entitled to all the rights, privileges and immunities of such citizen, whether said Indian has been or not by birth or otherwise a member of any tribe of Indians within the territorial limits of the United States without n any manner impairing or otherwise affecting the rights of such Indian's tribal or other property"

" The intended operation of this act is in direct conflict with the Constitution of the Cherokee Nation. That constitution provides, as has been seen, that any member of the tribe who shall become a citizen of any other country thereby forfeits all his rights and privileges as a citizen of that nation, and one of the rights so forfeited would be the right to share in the distribution of tribal property. Yet the act above quoted provides distinctly that no right to tribal property shall be forfeited thereby"

" The controlling purpose of the statute above referred to was to offer inducements to Indians to break up their tribal relations as a step in the direction of a higher civilization. This purpose would have been defeated had it not been for the guarantee that its tribal property rights should be protected."

CHEROKEE GRANTED ENROLLMENT CARDS & DAWES PACKETS 1900-1907 VOLUME I

We submit that the Act of Feb 8th., 1887 above quoted operates to abrogate the provisions of the Cherokee Constitution in conflict therewith as far as this Honorable Commission is concerned, to say the least, and that under its provisions alone the Commission should enroll the applicant.

The Act of June 10, 1896 provides:-
" That the rolls of citizenship of the several tribes as now existing are hereby confirmed,---"

The Act of June 7, 1897 provides:-
" That the words "Rolls of citizenship" as used in the act of June tenth, eighteen hundred and ninety-six making appropriations for current and contingent expenses of the Indian department and fulfilling treaty stipulations with various Indian tribes for the fiscal year ending June thirtieth, eighteen hundred and nine-ty[sic] seven, shall be construed to mean the last authenticated rolls of each tribe which have been approved by the council of the nation, and the descendants of those appearing on such rolls,-----"

Section 21 of the Act of June 28, 1898, known as the Curtis Act, under which this Roll is being made by the Commission, provides

"That in making rolls of citizenship of the several tribes as required by law, the Commission to the Five Civilized Tribes is authorized and directed to take the roll of Cherokee citizens of eighteen hundred and eighty (not including freedmen) as the only roll intended to be confirmed by this and preceeding[sic] acts of Congress, and to enroll all persons now living whose names are found on said roll, and all descendants born since the date of said roll to persons whose names are found thereon;---"

We respectfully submit that the name of the applicant appearing on the Cherokee Roll of 1880 as well as on the Rolls made by the Cherokee Nation since that date, there can be no reason for refusing to enroll him at this time upon the roll now being made by this Commission.

The rights of the applicant have been fixed absolutely and his name cannot legally be omitted from the roll.

Respectfully submitted this February 21, 1902.

N. A. Gibson
Attorney for Applicant.

Service of a copy of the foregoing brief accepted this __25__ day of February 1902.

Attorney for Cherokee Nation.

DEPARTMENT OF THE INTERIOR,
Commission to the Five Civilized Tribes
Muskogee I. T. April 3rd 1902.

Cherokee D. 18.

In the matter of the application of Napoleon B. Blythe for enrollment as a Cherokee by blood ---

Brief of the Cherokee Nation.

The applicant Napoleon B. Blythe is a Cherokee by blood, his name appears upon the roll of 1880 but the testimony shows that he moved to the state of Missouri in the year 1882, that he married there in 1887, that several of his children, all but two, were born in the state of Missouri and that he returned to the Cherokee Nation in 1892; the testimony further shows that he voted and exercised the rights of citizenship in the state of Missouri, the same as any other citizen, and the Cherokee Nation contends that by his non residence in the state of Missouri, his marriage and the exercise of the rights of citizenship in the state of Missouri that he forfeited his citizenship in the Cherokee Nation. The judgment of the commissioner in charge succinctly summarizes the testimony and makes a clear statement of the case; there is no testimony that the applicant had any effects in the Cherokee Nation from 1882 until 1892 and the presumption is that if he had he would have made a statement f all of those things favorable to himself. He states himself that he voted for presidential electors in 1884 and that he has lived without the limits of the Cherokee Nation therefore clearly comes within the provisions of the constitution of the Cherokee Nation which states "Whenever any citizen shall removed[sic] with his effects out of the limits of this nation, and becomes a citizen of any other government, all his rights and privileges as a citizen of this Nation shall cease."

He states that he removed from without the limits of the Cherokee Nation; he does not contend that he left any effects behind him and he admits that he exercised the rights of citizenship by voting and otherwise hence the Cherokee Nation contends that "All his rights and privileges as a citizen of the Cherokee Nation" were forfeited.

Respectfully Submitted,

...WW Hastings............JCS...
Attorney for the Cherokee Nationl

R.

DEPARTMENT OF THE INTERIOR.
Commission to the Five Civilized Tribes.
Muskogee, Indian Territory, October 1st, 1902.

In the matter of the application of Napoleon B. Blythe for the enrollment of himself as a citizen by blood of the Cherokee Nation; for the enrollment of his wife, Suella[sic] Blythe, as a citizen by intermarriage of the Cherokee Nation, and for the enrollment of his children, William H., John E., Mary J., Farry A., Aubrey A., Ermer[sic] L., Jesse L. and Charles F. Blythe, as citizens by blood of the Cherokee Nation.

Supplemental to D-18.

Appearances:

Benjamin C. England for Applicant.
J. C. Starr for Cherokee Nation.

BENJAMIN C. ENGLAND, being duly sworn, testified as follows:
Examination by the Commission.
Q. What is your name? A. Benjamin C. England.
Q. What is your post office? A. Afton.
Q. And your age? A. 54.

CHEROKEE GRANTED ENROLLMENT CARDS & DAWES PACKETS 1900-1907 VOLUME I

Q. Are you acquainted with Napoleon B. Blythe who is an applicant before the Commission for enrollment as a citizen by blood? A. Yes, sir.
Q. Are you acquainted with his wife, who is an applicant before the Commission for enrollment as an intermarried citizen? A. Yes, sir.
Q. How long have you know Suella[sic] Blythe? A. I have known her ever since '93, about '93.
Q. Do you know when she and Napoleon were married?
A. No, sir; I don't know.
Q. They were living together when you first knew them in 1893? A. Yes, sir.
Q. Have they lived together all the time since 1893? A. Yes, sir.
Q. Living together on September 1st, 1902? A. Yes, sir.
Q. Never separated during that time? A. No, sir.
Q. Have they lived in the Cherokee Nation since 1893? A. Yes, sir.
Q. Never lived out since that time? A. No, sir.

+++++++++++++++++++++++++++

Jesse O. Carr, being first duly sworn, states that as stenographer to the Commission to the Five Civilized Tribes he reported the above entitled case and that the foregoing is a true and complete transcript of his stenographic notes thereof.

Jesse O. Carr

Subscribed and sworn to before me this 22nd day of October, 1902.

BO Jones
Notary Public.

DEPARTMENT OF THE INTERIOR.
Commission to the Five Civilized Tribes.
Muskogee, Indian Territory, October 14th, 1902.

In the matter of the application of Napoleon B. Blythe for the enrollment of himself as a citizen by blood of the Cherokee Nation; for the enrollment of his wife, Luella Blythe, as a citizen by intermarriage of the Cherokee Nation, and for the enrollment of his children, William H., John E., Mary J., Farry A., Aubrey A., Ermer[sic] L., Jesse L. and Charles F. Blythe, as citizens by blood of the Cherokee Nation.

Supplemental to D-18.

Cherokee Nation appears by J. C. Starr.

CHEROKEE GRANTED ENROLLMENT CARDS
& DAWES PACKETS 1900-1907 VOLUME I

NAPOLEON B. BLYTHE, being duly sworn, testified as follows:
Examination by the Commission.

Q. What is your name? A. Napoleon B. Blythe.
Q. How old are you, Mr. Blythe? A. 50 years old.
Q. What is your post office? A. Afton.
Q. You are a Cherokee by blood, are you? A. Yes, sir.
Q. What is your wife's name? A. Luella.
Q. She is a white woman? A. Yes, sir.
Q. When were you married to her? A. Married January 10th, 1887.
Q. Is she your first wife? A. No, sir.
Q. You had been married before, had you? A. Yes, sir.
Q. Once or twice? A. Once.
Q. What was your first wife's name? A. Mary Ann.
Q. What was her maiden name? A. Sorter.
Q. Was she dead before you married Luella? A. Yes, sir.
Q. Has your present wife ever been married before? A. No, sir.
Q. You are her first husband? A. Yes, sir.
Q. How long have you been living in the Cherokee Nation?
A. Been living here ever since 1894.
Q. Between 1880 and 1894 where were you? A. In Missouri.
Q. You made that your home didn't you? A. Well, I was living there.
Q. You married your wife up there? A. Married my wife.
Q. Voted up there. A. Voted up there.
Q. Came back to the Nation in 1894? A. '94.
Q. You weren't readmitted to citizenship? A. I don't know. I made application for reinstatement, to the Cherokee National Council.
Q. Do you know what action the council took? A. Only what one of the council told me. Mr. Ballard told me they took the case up and it passed through the committee and they laid it aside and never took it up.
Q. How many children have you? A. Eight.
Q. All living? A. Yes, sir; all living.
Q. Your wife is living? A. Yes, sir.
Q. You and your wife have lived together ever since you married her?
A. Yes, sir.
Q. And were living together on the first day of last September? A. Yes, sir.
Examination by Mr. Starr.
Q. Did you live with your first wife until she died? A. Yes, sir.
Q. Where did she die? A. In Missouri.
Q. What was your post office? A. I didn't get mail at any regular place; sometimes Tipton, sometimes Todd, sometimes Akinsville[sic].
Q. What county? A. Morgan part of the time and part of the time Moniteau.
Q. How long had your first wife been dead when you married your second wife?
A. She had been dead about 6 months; probably a little longer.
Q. Where did you marry your second wife? A. We were married in Cooper county; the county seat of Cooper county.
Q. You have only been married twice? A. That is all.
Q. Was your present wife ever married before? A. No, sir.

CHEROKEE GRANTED ENROLLMENT CARDS & DAWES PACKETS 1900-1907 VOLUME I

Q. Where was William H. Blythe born? A. I couldn't tell you that.
Q. That is your oldest son? A. Oh, yes. He was born in Missouri.
Q. Mary J.? A. Missouri.
Q. Farry A.? A. Missouri.
Q. How about Aubrey A.? A. He was born in Missouri.
Q. Ermer L.? A. She was born here.
Q. Jesse L.? A. He was born here.
Q. Charles F.? A. He was born here.

IIIIIIIIIIIIIIIIIIIIIIIIIIIIIIIIIIIIIIIII

Jesse O. Carr, being first duly sworn, states that as stenographer to the Commission to the Five Civilized Tribes he reported the above entitled case and that the foregoing is a true and complete transcript of his stenographic notes thereof.

Jesse O. Carr

Subscribed and sworn to before me this 12th day of December, 1902.

PJ Reuter
Notary Public.

DEPARTMENT OF THE INTERIOR,
Commission to the Five Civilized Tribes
Muskogee I. T. March 20th 1903.

Cherokee D 18.

Protest of the Cherokee Nation.

Comes now the Cherokee Nation and respectfully protests against the decision of the Commission to the Five Civilized Tribes rendered in this case on March 2nd 1903 and asks that same be forwarded to the Honorable Secretary of the Interior for Review.

The testimony in this case shows that the applicant Napoleon B. Blythe removed to the State of Missouri in the year 1882, that he married there in 1887; that all of his children except two were born there (In the State of Missouri) and that he returned to the Cherokee Nation in 1894; the testimony further shows that he voted and exercised the rights of citizenship in the state of Missouri just the same as any other citizen of that state and the Cherokee Nation contends that by his non residence his living in the state of Missouri, his marriage there; and his exercising the rights of citizenship in that state that he forfeited his citizenship in the Cherokee Nation.

CHEROKEE GRANTED ENROLLMENT CARDS & DAWES PACKETS 1900-1907 VOLUME I

The Judgment of the Commissioner in charge succinctly summarizes the testimony and makes a clear statement of the case. The testimony is to the effect that the applicant had no effects in the Cherokee Nation from 1882 to 1894 during all of which time he was a citizen and resident of the State of Missouri. He states himself that he voted for the Presidential electors in 1884 and that he has lived without the limits of the Cherokee Nation and therefore he clearly comes within the provision of the clause of the Cherokee Constitution which provides that

>"Whenever any citizen shall remove with his effects out of the limits of this nation, and becomes a citizen of any other government, all of his rights and privileges as a citizen of this Nation shall cease."

He states that he moved without the limts[sic] of this nation; he does not contend that he left any effects behind him and he admits that he exercised the rights of citizenship by voting and otherwise hence the Cherokee Nation contends that "All of his rights and privileges as a citizen of this Nation" were forefeited[sic].

As to the reasoning used by the Commission in the decision referring to Article two of the treaty ratified by Congress March 3, 1893 arguing that the name of applicant does not appear upon an intruder roll we think has no bearing whatever in this case and respectfully call the attention of the Honorable Secretary of the Interior to the decision in the case of Joseph B. Ladd et al Cherokee D 470 when the Department referring to said Article two said "The Department Agrees with the Commissioner of Indian Affairs that this article of the agreement has little if any bearing on this case." The Commissioner of Indian Affairs in the same case with respect to this Article two said "The office can not see wherein the provisions of said article two of the treaty between the United States and the Cherokee Nation concluded on December 19, 1891 has anything to do with this application."

Now the applicant stated when he appeared before the Commission for enrollment in 1900 that after his return from Missouri that he was readmitted to citizenship in the Cherokee Nation as the Cherokee Constitution requires but although often urged to do so he never at any time presented any proof of his readmission to citizenship in the Cherokee Nation. Although he was a citizen in 1880, the Cherokee

Nation contends that under the above clause of the Cherokee Constitution he forfeited his citizenship in the Cherokee Nation by his ten or twelve years of actual residence in the State of Missouri; by his marriage there; and by his exercising the rights of citizenship there and by leaving no effects in the Cherokee Nation to retain his citizenship. His six children were born in Missouri and we submit that it was necessary for him to have been readmitted to citizenship in the Cherokee Nation and that his name was placed upon the Cherokee roll "Without authority of law" and that he should not be enrolled by the Secretary if[sic] the Interior and that it was an error for the Commission to decide that he was entitled to enrollment because his name did not appear upon a list of intruders provided for in Article Two of the Agreement entered into December 19, 1891 and ratified by Congress March 3rd 1893.

Respectfully, *W.W. Hastings* JCS
Attorney for the Cherokee Nation.

Cherokee D. 18.

DEPARTMENT OF THE INTERIOR,
COMMISSION TO THE FIVE CIVILIZED TRIBES.

In the matter of the application of Napoleon B. Blythe for the enrollment of himself and his eight minor children, William H., John E., Mary J., Farry A., Aubrey A., Ermer[sic] L., Jesse L. and Charles F. Blythe, as citizens by blood of the Cherokee Nation.

D E C I S I O N.

The record in this case shows that on July 18, 1900, Napoleon B. Blythe appeared before the Commission at Fairland, Indian Territory, and made application for the enrollment of himself and his seven minor children, William H., John E., Mary J., Farry A., Aubrey A., Ermer[sic] L. and Jesse L. Blythe, as citizens by blood of Cherokee Nation. Further proceedings in the matter of said application were had at Muskogee, Indian Territory, on February 15, October 1, and October 14, 1902. The application also included Luella Blythe for enrollment as a citizen by intermarriage of the Cherokee Nation, but her status as such is not passed upon at this time and she is

CHEROKEE GRANTED ENROLLMENT CARDS & DAWES PACKETS 1900-1907 VOLUME I

not embraced in this decision. Since the date of this application another child, Charles F. Blythe, has been born to Napoleon B. Blythe and his wife, Luella Blythe, and that child is now embraced in this decision.

The evidence in this case shows that Napoleon B. Blythe, a Cherokee by blood, who is identified on the Cherokee authenticated tribal roll of 1880, and Luella Blythe, a white woman, were married in the year 1887. Napoleon B. Blythe and his five minor children, William H., John E., Mary J., Farry A. and Aubrey A. Blythe, are all identified on the Cherokee strip payment roll of 1894 and on the Cherokee census roll of 1896, and Ermer L. Blythe is identified on the Cherokee census roll of 1896. The two other children, Jesse L. and Charles F. Blythe, are too young to be on any roll, but are duly identified by birth affidavits made a part of the record herein.

It further appears from the evidence that Napoleon B. Blythe was born in the Cherokee Nation and lived there continuously until the year 1882, in which he went to the State of Missouri. He remained in the State of Missouri until the year 1892, at which time he returned to the Cherokee Nation with his wife and children, and has remained in said nation ever since. The residence of the minor applicants herein is considered to be governed by that of their said father.

The evidence further shows that Napoleon B. Blythe's removal from the Cherokee Nation in 1882 was based upon expediency and not from choice, and it is considered from the surrounding facts coupled with his return to the Cherokee Nation and his continued residence therein since his said return, that he has not forfeited his rights of Cherokee citizenship, and his status as such extends to his minor children.

It is, therefore, the opinion of this Commission that, following the decision of the Department in the case of Joseph D. Yeargain, et al (I.T.D. 2900-1903), Napoleon B. Blythe, William H. Blythe, John E. Blythe, Mary J. Blythe, Farry A. Blythe, Aubrey A. Blythe, Ermer L. Blythe, Jesse L. Blythe and Charles F. Blythe, should be enrolled as citizens by blood of the Cherokee Nation, in accordance with the provisions of section twenty-one of the act of Congress approved June 28, 1898 (30 Stats., 495), and it is so ordered.

COMMISSION TO THE FIVE CIVILIZED TRIBES.

(SIGNED).   *Tams Bixby.*
_____
                              Chairman.
(SIGNED).   *T. B. Needles.*
_____
                              Commissioner.
(SIGNED).   *C. R. Breckinridge.*
_____
                              Commissioner.
(SIGNED).   *W. E. Stanley.*
_____
                              Commissioner.

Dated Muskogee, Indian Territory,
this _____JUN 1 - 1903_____

CHEROKEE GRANTED ENROLLMENT CARDS & DAWES PACKETS 1900-1907 VOLUME I

DEPARTMENT OF THE INTERIOR,
Commission to the Five Civilized Tribes,
Muskogee I. T. March 20th 1903.

In the matter of the application of Napoleon B. Blythe for the enrollment of himself and his eight minor children, William H, John E, Mary J, Farry A, Aubrey A, Ermer[sic] L, Jesse L and Charles P[sic]. Blythe as citizens of the Cherokee Nation by Blood.

Protest of the Cherokee Nation.

Cherokee D #18.

The evidence in this case shows that Napoleon B. Blythe removed with his effects to the state of Missouri in the year 1882; that he became a citizen of the State of Missouri where he voted and exercised the rights of citizenship in the State of Missouri just the same as any other citizen of that state; that he married there in 1887; and all of his children except two were born in the State of Missouri and that he resided in Missouri with his effects and exercised the rights of citizenship in Missouri until 1898.

The Cherokee Nation contends that by reason of his leaving the Cherokee Nation "With his effects" in the year 1832; his continued residence in the state of Missouri for ten years; his marriage there; and his excersising[sic] the rights of citizenship in that state and in fact becoming a citizen of the State of Missouri "Another Government" he forfeited his citizenship in the Cherokee Nation under that provision of the Cherokee Constitution which provides:

"Whenever any citizen shall remove with his effects out of the limits of this Nation, and becomes a citizen of any other Government, all of his rights and privileges as a citizen of this Nation shall cease."

The Judgment of the Commission in charge succinctly summarizes the testimony and makes clear statement of the case. The testimony is to the effect that the applicant had no effects in the Cherokee Nation from 1882 to 1894 during all of which time he was a citizen and resident of the state of Missouri; he states himself that he voted for the Presidential electors in 1884 and that he has lived without the limits of the Cherokee Nation for ten or twelve years and therefore he clearly comes within the provision of that clause of the Cherokee Constitution herein- above quoted.

The applicants[sic] states that he moved without the limits of this Nation and does not contend to have left any effects behind him and admits that he exercised yhe[sic] rights of citizenship in the State of Missouri by voting and otherwise hence the Cherokee Nation contends that "All of his rights and privileges as a citizen of this Nation" were forfeited at the moment he became a citizen of the State of Missouri.

Now the applicant stated when he appeared before the Commission in 1900 that after his return from Missouri he was readmitted to citizenship in the Cherokee Nation as the Cherokee Constitution requires but although often urged to do so he never at any time presented any proof of his re-admission to citizenship in the Cherokee Nation but on the contrary when he appeared before the Commission at Muskogee I. T. on October 14th 1902 he made the following statement:

"You weren't readmitted to citizenship?" "A I don't know. I made application for reinstatement, to the Cherokee National Council."

"Q Do you know what action the council took?" "A Only what one of the Council told me. Mr. Ballard told me they took the case up and it passed through the Committee and they laid it aside and never took it up."

It is clear then that the applicant realized himself that he had forfeited his rights and privileges of citizenship in the Cherokee Nation and therefore memmorialized[sic] the National Council for readmission but that boby[sic] did not see fit to read it him.

When the applicant left the Cherokee Nation the circumstances connected with his leaving certainly show that he intended to abandon the Cherokee Nation; that his exercising the rights of citizenship was not a matter of "expediency" but was a matter of choice with him and shows conclusively that he chose to make himself a citizen of the State of Missouri. If he intended to return to the Cherokee Nation and to retain his citizenship in the Cherokee Nation why did he voluntarily become a citizen of the State of Missouri? If his intentions are to be judged by his acts then clearly he intended to leave the Cherokee Nation and become a citizen of the State of Missouri when he exercised the rights of citizenship in that State.

CHEROKEE GRANTED ENROLLMENT CARDS & DAWES PACKETS 1900-1907 VOLUME I

The Cherokee Nation contends that there is a distinction between this case and the Yeargain case cited by the Commission (I.T.D. 2900-1903) in that case Yeargain removed from the Nation and exercised the rights of citizenship in Missouri but left his effects from the Cherokee Nation whereas Blythe removed with his effects from the Cherokee Nation and became a citizen of the State of Missouri.

The contention of the Nation is that the applicant was a citizen of the Cherokee Nation when his named[sic] was placed on the 1880 authenticated roll and he continued to be a citizen of the nation until he left the Nation and became a citizen of the State of Missouri; that he was a citizen of the Cherokee Nation up to the time he left the Nation but that he forfeited his right and privileges as a citizen of the Cherokee Nation under that clause of the Cherokee constitution herein before quoted and that upon his return to the Cherokee Nation it was necessary for him to have been readmitted to citizenship in the Cherokee Nation and hot having been readmitted there was no authority of law authorizing the census takers to place his name on the rolls of 1894 and 1896 which rolls the Cherokee National Council refused to confirm and by special act distinctly and positively stated that the Cherokee Nation would not be bound by the 1894 Strip Pay roll..[sic]

The names of the applicants are found upon the rolls of 1894 and 1896 but they were placed there "Without authority of law" because the applicant having forfeited his citizenship when he became a citizen of the State of Missouri there was no law authorizing the census takers to place their names on the Pay roll of 1894 and the Census roll of 1896.

This is a clear case of forfeiture under the Cherokee Constitution and we contend that it was error for the Commission to decide that applicants are entitled to be enrolled as citizens of the Cherokee Nation and respectfully request that the record in this case be forwarded to the Honorable Secretary of the Interior for review.

Respectfully, *W W Hastings*
Attorney Cherokee Nation. *JCS*

CHEROKEE GRANTED ENROLLMENT CARDS & DAWES PACKETS 1900-1907 VOLUME I

Cherokee D-18.

DEPARTMENT OF THE INTERIOR,
COMMISSION TO THE FIVE CIVILIZED TRIBES.
MUSKOGEE, I. T., FEBRUARY 20, 1905.

SUPPLEMENTAL PROCEEDINGS had in the matter of the application for the enrollment of LUELLA BLYTHE as a citizen by intermarriage of the Cherokee Nation.

NAPOLEON B. BLYTHE, being first duly sworn, testified as follows:

BY THE COMMISSION:
Q What is your name? A Napoleon B. Blythe.
Q Are you a Cherokee by blood? A Yes sir.
Q Is your wife a white woman? A Yes sir.
Q She claims no rights as a citizen by blood? A No sir.
Q She claims citizenship by intermarriage? A Yes sir.
Q Through whom does she claim that right? A Through me.
Q Are you her first husband? A Yes sir.
Q Is she your first wife? A No sir she is my second wife.
Q Who is your first wife? A Mary A. Sortore.
Q Was your first wife dead at the time you married Luella? A Yes sir.
Q When were you married to Luella? A January 10, 1887.
Q Have you and she lived together as husband and wife ever since your marriage in 1887? A Yes sir.
Q Any separation, abandonment or divorce during that time? A No sir.
Q And where have you and she lived? A In Delaware District.
Q In the Cherokee Nation? A Yes sir.
Q Have you lived anywhere else than in the Cherokee Nation since your marriage to her? A Yes sir.
Q Where have you lived? A I lived in Missouri after I was married to her.
Q How long did you live there? A I was there eleven years.
Q After you were married? A Yes, not long after I was married, I was in Missouri 11 years, but not after I married her.
Q I am asking after you married her? A No sir, we were married on January 10, 1887 and returned in 1893.
Q Have you lived in the Cherokee Nation since your return? A Yes sir.
Q Both of you? A Yes sir.
Q Her residence has always been the same as yours? A Yes sir.

The witness is identified on Cherokee Card Field No. 10394, and is No. 30900 upon the final roll approved by the Secretary of the Interior.

--------------------------oOo--------------------------

CHEROKEE GRANTED ENROLLMENT CARDS & DAWES PACKETS 1900-1907 VOLUME I

George H. Lessley, being first duly sworn, states that as stenographer to the Commission to the Five Civilized Tribes, he reported the proceedings had in the above entitled cause, and that the above and foregoing is a true and correct transcript of his stenographic notes thereof.

George H. Lessley

Subscribed and sworn to before me this 20th day of February, 1905.

W.S. Hawkins
Notary Public.

COPY   Cherokee D 18.

DEPARTMENT OF THE INTERIOR,
COMMISSIONER TO THE FIVE CIVILIZED TRIBES.

In the matter of the application for the enrollment of Luella Blythe as a citizen by intermarriage of the Cherokee Nation.

D E C I S I O N

THE RECORDS OF THIS OFFICE SHOW: That at Fairland, Indian Territory, July 12, 1900, Napoleon B. Blythe appeared before the Commission to the Five Civilized Tribes, and made application for the enrollment of himself and children as citizens by blood, and for the enrollment of his wife, Luella Blythe, as a citizen by intermarriage of the Cherokee Nation. The application for the enrollment of said Napoleon B. Blythe and children has been heretofore disposed of, and their rights to enrollment will not be considered in this decision.

THE EVIDENCE IN THIS CASE SHOWS: That the applicant herein, Luella Blythe, is a white woman, and neither claims nor possesses any right to enrollment as a citizen of the Cherokee Nation except such as she may have acquired by virtue of her marriage to said Napoleon B. Blythe, a citizen by blood of the Cherokee Nation, in the year 1887.

IT IS, THEREFORE, ORDERED AND ADJUDGED: That in accordance with the decision of the Supreme Court of the United States, dated November 5, 1906, in the case of Daniel Red Bird, et al., vs. the United States, Luella is not entitled, under the provisions of the Act of Congress approved June 28, 1898 (30 Stat. 495), to enrollment as a citizen by intermarriage of the Cherokee Nation, and her application for enrollment as such is accordingly denied.

(SIGNED).   *Tams Bixby.*

CHEROKEE GRANTED ENROLLMENT CARDS & DAWES PACKETS 1900-1907 VOLUME I

Dated at Muskogee, Indian Territory,
this_____JAN 8 1907_____

> April 5, 1902.
>
> C. D. 18.
> N. A. Gibson, Esq.,
>   Muskogee, I. T.
> Dear Sir:
>   Enclosed herewith find a copy of the brief of the Cherokee Nation in case Cherokee D. 18, Napoleon B. Blythe, et al. Please acknowledge receipt and oblige,
>   Yours truly,

COMMISSIONERS:
TAMS BIXBY,
THOMAS B. NEEDLES,
C. R. BRECKINRIDGE,
W. E. STANLEY.

ALLISON L. AYLESWORTH,
    SECRETARY.

DEPARTMENT OF THE INTERIOR.
COMMISSION TO THE FIVE CIVILIZED TRIBES.

REFER IN REPLY TO THE FOLLOWING

ADDRESS ONLY THE
COMMISSION TO THE FIVE CIVILIZED TRIBES.

Muskogee, Indian Territory, April 15, 1903.

W. W. Hastings,
    Attorney for the Cherokee Nation,
        Vinita, Indian Territory.

Dear Sir:

    You are hereby requested to return to the Commission copies of its decisions furnished you on March 12, 1903, in the following Cherokee cases:

        D-   18, Napoleon B. Blythe et al.,
        D-1074, John A. Reaves et al.,
        D-1208, Charles T. Ironside et al.

You are also requested to withdraw your protests heretofore filed against these decisions in order that they may be reconsidered by the Commission.

Respectfully,

Tams Bixby Chairman.

C. D. 1074 John A Reaves et al
C. D. 1076 Mollie E Parr

C. D. 1117 Charles B. Reaves et al   consolidated.

ATTORNEYS FOR THE CHEROKEE NATION
CHEROKEE ENROLLMENT

W. W. HASTINGS, Attorney
J. C. STARR, Secretary

Vinita, Muskogee Ind. Ter. April 18th 1903

Commission to the Five Civilized Tribes,
  Muskogee I. T.

Gentlemen:

In compliance with the request of the Commission of date April 15th 1903 there is herewith returned your decision in the case of Cherokee D 18 Napoleon B. Blythe et al and the request is hereby made to permit the Cherokee Nation to withdraw its protest heretofore filed in this case against this decision in order that the decision may be reconsidered by the Commission.

Respectfully,

W W Hastings

C. D. #18.   Attorney for the Cherokee Nation.

CHEROKEE GRANTED ENROLLMENT CARDS
& DAWES PACKETS 1900-1907 VOLUME I

COMMISSIONERS:
TAMS BIXBY,
THOMAS B. NEEDLES,
C. R. BRECKINRIDGE,
W. E. STANLEY.

DEPARTMENT OF THE INTERIOR.
COMMISSION TO THE FIVE CIVILIZED TRIBES.

REFER IN REPLY TO THE FOLLOWING

Cherokee D-18.

ALLISON L. AYLESWORTH,
SECRETARY.

ADDRESS ONLY THE
COMMISSION TO THE FIVE CIVILIZED TRIBES.

Muskogee, Indian Territory, July 9, 1903.

W. W. Hastings,

    Attorney for Cherokee Nation,

        Tahlequah, Indian Territory.

Dear Sir:

    There is herewith inclosed a copy of the decision of the Commission to the Five Civilized Tribes, dated June 1, 1903, granting the application of Napoleon B. Blythe for the enrollment of himself and his eight minor children, William H., John E., Mary J., Farry A., Aubrey A., Ermer L., Jesse L. and Charles F. Blythe, as citizens by blood of the Cherokee Nation.

    You are hereby advised that you will be allowed fifteen days from date hereof in which to file such protest as you may desire to make against the action of the Commission in this case, a copy of which protest you will be required to serve upon the applicant. If you fail to file protest within he time allowed, this decision will be considered final.

        Respectfully,

             T.B. Needles
            Commissioner in Charge.

Enc. H-29.

COMMISSIONERS:
TAMS BIXBY,
THOMAS B. NEEDLES,
C. R. BRECKINRIDGE,
W. E. STANLEY.

DEPARTMENT OF THE INTERIOR.
COMMISSION TO THE FIVE CIVILIZED TRIBES.

REFER IN REPLY TO THE FOLLOWING

Cherokee D 18

ALLISON L. AYLESWORTH,
SECRETARY.

ADDRESS ONLY THE
COMMISSION TO THE FIVE CIVILIZED TRIBES.

Muskogee, Indian Territory, March 25, 1904.

CHEROKEE GRANTED ENROLLMENT CARDS & DAWES PACKETS 1900-1907 VOLUME I

W. W. Hastings,

    Attorney for the Cherokee Nation,

        Tahlequah, Indian Territory.

Dear Sir:

    You are hereby advised that the Commission's decision dated June 1, 1903, granting the application of Napoleon B. Blythe for the enrollment of himself and his eight minor children, William H., John E., Mary J., Farry A., Aubrey A., Ermer L., Jesse L. and Charles F. Blythe, as citizens by blood of the Cherokee Nation, was affirmed by the Secretary of the Interior on March 10, 1904.

        Respectfully,

            TB Needles
            Commissioner in Charge.

REFER IN REPLY TO THE FOLLOWING
Cherokee D.
18.

DEPARTMENT OF THE INTERIOR,
COMMISSION TO THE FIVE CIVILIZED TRIBES.

Muskogee, Indian Territory, January 8, 1907.

W. W Hastings,

    Attorney for the Cherokee Nation,

        Muskogee, Indian Territory.

Dear Sir:

    There is enclosed herewith a copy of the decision of the Commissioner to the Five Civilized Tribes, dated January 8, 1907, denying the application for the enrollment of Luella Blythe, as a citizen by intermarriage of the Cherokee Nation.

    The decision, together with the record of proceedings had in the case, has this day been transmitted to the Secretary of the Interior for his review and decision. The Secretary's action will be made known to you as soon as this office is informed of the same.

CHEROKEE GRANTED ENROLLMENT CARDS & DAWES PACKETS 1900-1907 VOLUME I

Respectfully,

Tams Bixby

Encl.H.J.-10. Commissioner.
H.J.C.

Land
2938-1907.

DEPARTMENT OF THE INTERIOR
OFFICE OF INDIAN AFFAIRS
WASHINGTON.

COPY

February 21, 1907.

The Honorable,

The Secretary of the Interior.

Sir:

Referring to Department al letter of November 27, 1906 (I.T.D. 7606-1903) there is enclosed the record of proceedings in the matter of the application for the enrollment of Luella Blythe as a citizen by intermarriage of the Cherokee Nation, together with the decision of the Commissioner to the Five Civilized Tribes dated January 8, 1907, adverse to the applicant.

The record shows that on July 12, 1900, Napoleon B. Blythe appeared before the Commission to the Five Civilized Tribes and made application for the enrollment of Luella Blythe as a citizen by intermarriage of the Cherokee Nation.

The evidence shows that the applicant herein is a white woman and neither claims nor possesses any right to enrollment as a citizen of the Cherokee Nation except such as she may have acquired by virtue of her marriage to Napoleon B. Blythe, a citizen by blood of the Cherokee Nation, in the year 1887.

By reason of the provisions of the Act of Congress approved June 28, 1898 (30 Stat.L.,495), and following the decision of the Supreme Court of thee United States dated November 5, 1906 in the case of Danile[sic] Red Bird et al vs. the United States, the Office concurs in the decision of the Commissioner Bixby denying the enrollment of Luella Blythe as a citizen by intermarriage of the Cherokee Nation.

Very respectfully,

C.F. Larrabee

EBM.PH

Acting Commissioner.

CHEROKEE GRANTED ENROLLMENT CARDS & DAWES PACKETS 1900-1907 VOLUME I

DEPARTMENT OF THE INTERIOR,   O.K.
L.R.S.   WASHINGTON.
     I.T.D.
4306, 4332, 4334, 4368
4674, 4706, 4720, 4788,
4792, 4800--1907.   February 27, 1907.

DIRECT.

Commissioner to the Five Civilized Tribes,

        Muskogee, Indian Territory.

Sir:

        Your decisions in the following Cherokee citizenship cases adverse to the applicants are hereby confirmed. Copies of Indian Office letters submitting your reports and recommending that the decisions by affirmed are inclosed:

Title of Case.	Date of your Letter of Transmittal.
Lucile Vann (Freedman),	January 9, 1907.
Lewis Brown (Freedman),	October 17, 1906.
Manchie James,	October 17, 1906.
George E. Madden,	October 17, 1906.
Ada A. Waybourn,	February 2, 1907.
Lucy Chisholm (Katie Vann) (Freedman),	November 23, 1906.
Ethal Mary House,	November 23, 1906.
Luella Blythe,	January 8, 1907.
Frances Collins et al.,	January 7, 1907.
Alexander Alberty et al. (Freedmen),	January 8, 1907.

      A copy hereof and all the papers in the above mentioned cases have been sent to the Indian Office.

                    Respectfully,

                    Jesse E. Wilson,

10 inc. and 21   Assistant Secretary.
inc. for Ind. Of.

CHEROKEE GRANTED ENROLLMENT CARDS & DAWES PACKETS 1900-1907 VOLUME I

REFER IN REPLY TO THE FOLLOWING

Cherokee D 18.

DEPARTMENT OF THE INTERIOR,
COMMISSION TO THE FIVE CIVILIZED TRIBES.

Muskogee, Indian Territory, March 7, 1907.

W. W. Hastings,
    Attorney for the Cherokee Nation,
        Muskogee, Indian Territory.

Dear Sir:

    You are hereby advised that the decision of the Commissioner to the Five Civilized Tribes, dated January 8, 1907, rejecting the application for the enrollment of Luella Blythe as a citizen by intermarriage of the Cherokee Nation, was affirmed by the Secretary of the Interior February 21, 1907[sic]

    For your information, there is enclosed herewith a copy of Departmental letter.

        Respectfully,

        Tams Bixby

Enc I-202   Commissioner.

RPI

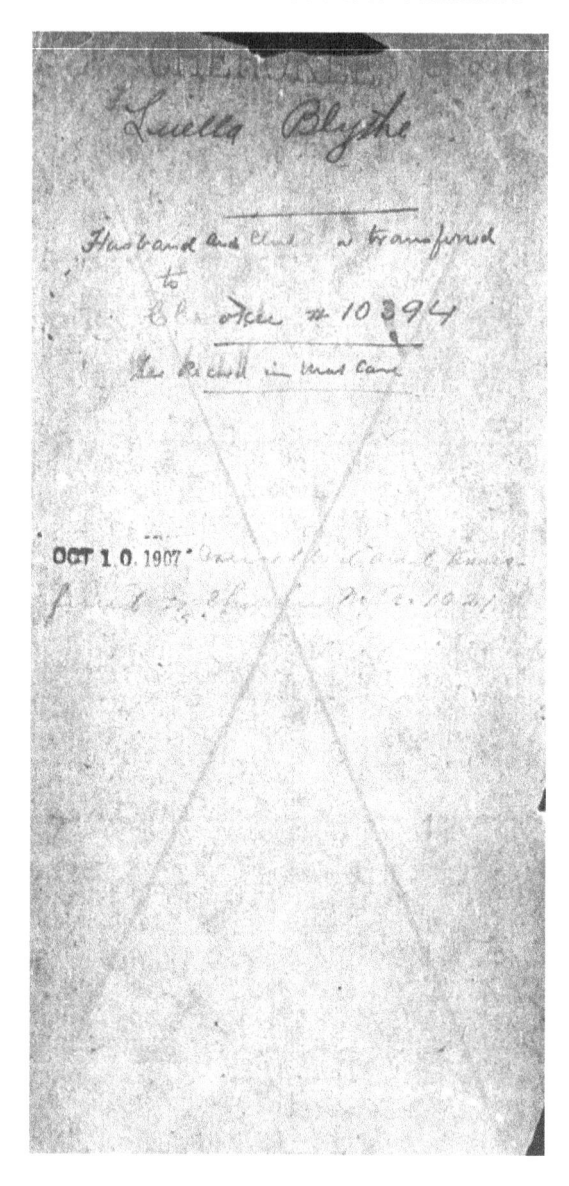

Luella Blythe

Husband and Child is transferred
to
Cherokee # 10394
See Record in that case

OCT 10 1907

… CHEROKEE GRANTED ENROLLMENT CARDS
& DAWES PACKETS 1900-1907 VOLUME I

Cherokee D19 - William W. Niemeyer

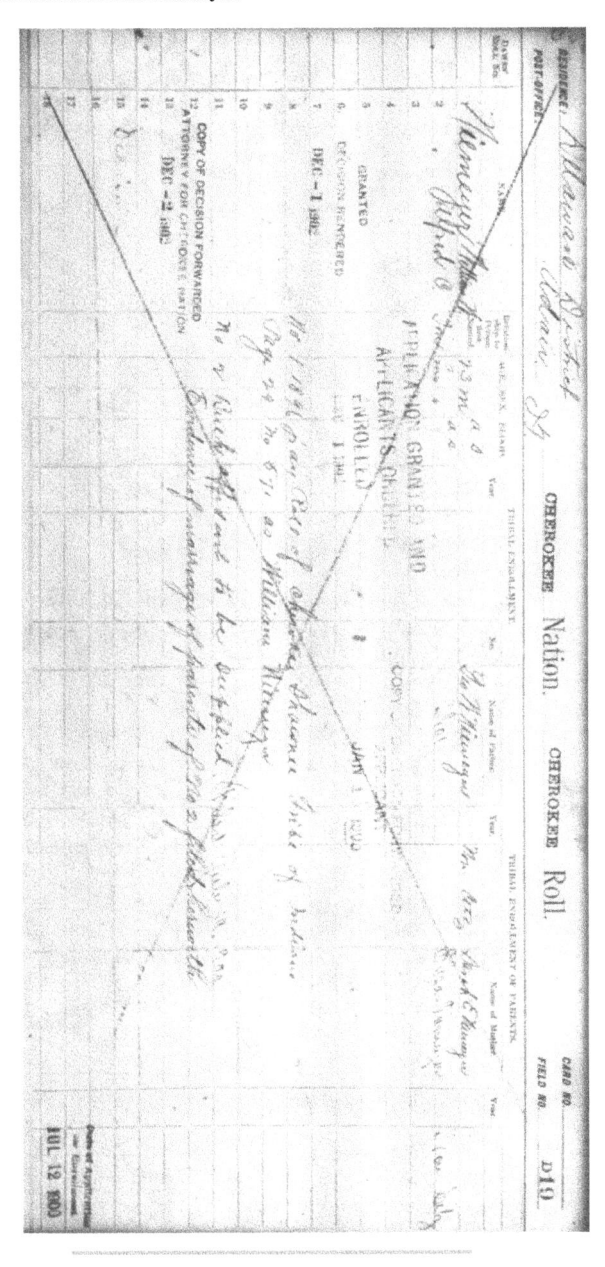

CHEROKEE GRANTED ENROLLMENT CARDS & DAWES PACKETS 1900-1907 VOLUME I

Department of the Interior,
Commission to the Five Civilized Tribes,
Fairland, I.T., July 12, 1900.

In the matter of the application of William W. Niemeyer for the enrollment of himself and child as Cherokees; being duly sworn, and examined by Commissioner Breckinridge, he testified as follows:

Q What is your name? A William W. Niemeyer.
Q What is your age? A 23 in next November.
Q What is your post office address? A Adair, I.T.
Q What is your district? A Delaware.
Q How far do you live from Adair? A I live right in town; my place is outside of town, but I live in town.
Q How long have you lived there? A For over four years.
Q Where were you born? A I was born three miles east of Vinita.
Q Where did you live before you lived at Adair? A I have lived all over the Territory; I lived at Vinita most of the time.
Q Have you lived all your life in the Territory? A Yes, sir.
Q For whom do you apply for citizenship, for yourself alone?
A Myself and one child and wife.
Q You are married? A Yes, sir.
Q Do you apply as a Cherokee by blood? A No, sir, as a Shawnee.
Q You apply for yourself as a Shawnee? A Yes, sir.
Q And you apply for your wife as an intermarried Shawnee? A Yes, sir.
Q What evidence have you of your citizenship as a Shawnee? A This paper; my mother was Sarah E. Purcell.
Q And you base your claim in part at least on this paper? A In part, you, sir.
(Applicant presents paper dated Tahlequah, Cherokee Nation, October 13, 1884, signed by W. P. Boudinot, Executive Secretary, C.N.; attested by the seal of the Cherokee Nation duly stamped into the paper; this paper contains the name of Sarah E. Purcell, opposite that name is the number 531. The applicant claims that Sarah E. Purcell is his mother. The paper stated that the list in which the name of Sarah E. Purcell appears is embraced in a list of names of Shawnees who moved and located in the Cherokee Nation prior to the 10th of June, 1871, in accordance with the agreement between the Shawnee tribe of Indians[sic] and the Cherokee Nation on June 7, 1869, approved by the President of the United States June 9, 1869, in accordance with the Cherokee Treaty of 1866, 15th article. As the said list is of record and on file in the Department and from which the above is a true and correct copy.)
Q Is your mother, Sarah E. Purcell, now living? A Yes, sir, she is right there.
Q Does your name appear upon any of the rolls of the Cherokee Nation?
A Yes, sir.
Q Upon what rolls does it appear? A I think it appears on all of them, and I don't know whether it appears on the 1880 roll or not; at the time the 1880 roll was taken my mother was sick and she sent the names in, but yesterday we hunted up a copy and in some way they are not on there.

CHEROKEE GRANTED ENROLLMENT CARDS
& DAWES PACKETS 1900-1907 VOLUME I

(The roll of 1880 examined, and the name of the applicant not found thereon. The rolls of 1894 and 1896 also examined and the name of the applicant not found.)

Q It appears that your name is not upon any of the three rolls which are now accessible to this Commission. Can you give any further evidence of your enrollment at any time? A Why my mother has always went to enroll on every roll.

Q You say that your mother's name is Sarah E. Purcell? A It was that, it is Niemeyer now.

Q What was it in 1880? A It was Sarah E. Niemeyer.

(The name of Sarah E. Niemeyer does not appear on the roll of 1880, nor on the rolls of 1894 and 1896.)

Q Do you know anything about the pay-roll of the Shawnees in 1896, did your name appear on that? A Yes, sir, it ought to be on that, I didn't put it on myself though.

(The name of William Niemeyer appears upon the Cherokee-Shawnee Pay-roll of 1896, page 29, No. 571. The name of Sarah E. Purcell appears upon the same roll, page 29, No. 570.)

Q Do you state that you are married? A Yes, sir.

Q Do you make claim for your wife through her marriage with you, or of her own right? A If she is subject to claim, I make it through marriage to me.

Q Is she an indian or a white woman? A She is a white woman.

Q When were you married? A The first day of December past.

Q The Commission is settled in its practice and opinion that that date is after the period permitted by law for people to acquire rights by intermarriage? A Well I don't know that, the reason I claimed for her.

Q Is this the only time you have ever been married? A Yes, sir.

Q You have no claim to make for anyone but yourself? A Yes, sir, one child.

Q You were married December 1st of last year? A Yes, sir.

Q And you have a child? A Yes, sir.

Q What is the name of that child? A It was born on May 14, this year.

Q What is the name of that child? A Alfred Cope Niemeyer.

Q Mr. Niemeyer, is there any other evidence which you wish to adduce in regard to your own citizenship? A I don't know, I think not; that is all I know of, I am on all the payrolls, if you will look on any pay-roll where the Shawnees are put, you will find me.

Q Are there any other pay-rolls that you can mention other than the one we have just consulted? A We drew one payment of $15 and one payment of $6 of $7.

Q You are not able to name at this time any roll that may be consulted to find that you are of record? A No, sir, only the payment rolls, I don't know the names of the rolls, only what it was paid for, therefore I can't say.

Q I will state to you at this time that you will be at liberty to submit to the Commission, if necessary, any evidence that you may be able to acquire showing your enrollment, in addition to that which has been adduced at this time.

A If I can prove that we have never been out of the Territory, isn't that all that is necessary?

Q That relates to the question of residence. A Well, this paper shows our citizenship, doesn't it?

CHEROKEE GRANTED ENROLLMENT CARDS
& DAWES PACKETS 1900-1907 VOLUME I

Q I am not prepared to give you an opinion just now on that subject, I have that incorporated in the testimony for consideration on the subject of citizenship. It also bears of course upon the question of residence. Your residence is not at this moment being called into question, but the status of your child and your citizenship are the two points that are at present being inquired into.

Mr. Hutchings, attorney for Cherokee Nation: Mr. Niemeyer, the father of your mother was R. W. Purcell, wasn't he? A I think that was his initials; I think so, I am not sure.

Q He was a white man? A I think so.

Q At the time your mother was born he belonged to no indian[sic] tribe?

A I can't answer that question.

Q Your mother's mother was recognized as a white woman?

A I think so.

Q You haven't a drop of any kind of indian blood in your veins, have you?

A I don't know.

Q You never claimed to have any? A Well, my mother was brought here as a Shawnee.

Q Which was because your father, after your mother's mother's death had married a Shawnee woman, wasn't it? A I think so.

Q You just came to this country with him and his Shawnee wife, your mother did I mean? A Yes, sir, I suppose so.

Q And your mother was never a member of the Shawnee tribe? A I can't answer those questions. That was before I was born.

Q You know she was a white woman? A No, sir, I don't know whether she was or not, only what she says, she says she was adopted, and I don't know whether she has any Shawnee blood in her or not, and she doesn't know for certain.

Q Mr. Niemeyer, do you know that you are the father of this child that you register? A I pretty near know it.

Q The child was born five months after you were married? A That doesn't make any difference, I know it is mine.

Q You do know you were the father of that child? A Yes, sir, I can swear it.

Mrs. Sarah E. Niemeyer, being duly sworn, and examined by Commissioner Breckinridge, testified as follows:

Q What is your name? A Sarah E. Niemeyer

Q What is your age? A 45.

Q What is your post office address? A Adair.

Q In what district do you live? A Delaware.

Q Is that your place of permanent residence? A Yes, sir.

Q How long have you lived there? A 4 years.

Q Where did you live before that? A In Vinita.

Q How long did you live in Vinita? A We lived there 9 years.

Q Have you lived during those nine years when you were in Vinita and the 4 years at Adair continuously in the Territory? A Yes, sir.

Q Are you the Sarah E. Purcell mentioned in this paper which I hold in my hand, and which purports to be a transcript from the Executive Department of the

CHEROKEE GRANTED ENROLLMENT CARDS
& DAWES PACKETS 1900-1907 VOLUME I

Cherokee Nation at Tahlequah, signed by W. P. Boudinot, as Executive Secretary of the Cherokee Nation? A Yes, sir.

Q Do you claim that you are the identical Sarah E. Purcell mentioned there as of the Shawnee, and known as a Cherokee-Shawnee? A Yes, sir.

Q Is R. W. Purcell, whose name is mentioned in this paper, the name of your husband at that time? A No, sir, that is my father.

Q Were you married at that time? A Yes, sir, I was married in 1876.

Q You were not married in 1871? A No, sir, I wasn't married in 1871.

Q Is your husband's name on the list? A No, sir.

Q Then the name of R. W. Purcell is the name, you state, of your father? A That is my father.

Mr. Hutchings: Your father, R. W. Purcell, was a white man, wasn't he? A As far as I know he was.

Q And at the time of your birth was a citizen of the United States? A I guess he was.

Q Your mother was a white woman and a citizen of the United States? A She was as far as I know.

Q And you have no indian[sic] blood of any kind? A Not that I know of, I can't swear to it.

Q After your birth, and after the death of your mother, your father married a Shawnee woman? A Yes, sir.

Q And when he came to this country with his Shawnee wife you came with him? A Yes, sir.

Commissioner Breckinridge?[sic] Does your name appear upon any of the tribal rolls of the Cherokee Nation? A It ought to, I can't tell you whether it did nor not, because I registered myself on every roll except the roll of 1880.

Q I will state that you are now testifying in the application of your son, and the rolls have been inquired into as regards yourself with reference to the bearing that would have upon his application, and you name has not been found upon any roll except what is known as the Shawnee pay-roll of 1896.

William W. Niemeyer, recalled, testified:

(The representatives of the Cherokee Nation desire to call the attention of the Commission to the agreement made between the Cherokees and the Shawnees which only permitted members of the Shawnee tribe to remove to the Cherokee Nation and become incorporated into the Cherokee tribe, who should remove within two years from the date of the agreement and register their names.)

Q Mr. Niemeyer, did you ever apply to the Cherokee authorities for admission to the Cherokee Nation? A No, sir.

Q Did you ever apply to the Dawes Commission for admission to the Cherokee Nation? A Only to-day.

Q Have you ever applied to any United States for admission? A No, sir.

Q Have you ever made any application for admission except the one you make now? A No, sir. I would like to know how it is, whether we are indians[sic] by blood or not; we were brought in by indians, here is evidence right here.

CHEROKEE GRANTED ENROLLMENT CARDS & DAWES PACKETS 1900-1907 VOLUME I

Q We are not prepared to give you an opinion, it is not necessary to carry on that line of inquiry. If you want to bring us any information and give any testimony, it is in order for you to do so, but it is not in order to get up a dicussion[sic]. I will take into consideration the evidence that you have submitted, the Commission will not make a decision at this time. It has invited you in the amplest manner to enlarge your evidence and testimony if you are able to do,so[sic]. You have been told that if you adduced any further testimony, it will be received and will be given very careful consideration. That applies to you and it applies likewise to the application for your child, and when a conclusion is reached by the Commission, a statement of its decision will be made to you in writing at your present post office address, and if the decision is adverse, or favorable, in either case, the papers will be forwarded to the Honorable Secretary of the Interior for his final approval or disapproval.

Q You have nothing more that you want to submit at this time?
A Nothing more than my father and mother's marriage certificate.

-----------o-----------

Bruce C. Jones, being duly sworn, says that as stenographer to the Commission to the Five Civilized Tribes he reported the testimony of the above named witness, and that the foregoing is a full, true and correct translation of his stenographic notes.

Bruce C Jones

Sworn to and subscribed before this the 13th day of July, 1900.

TB Needles
Commissioner.

File with Cherokee Doubtful #19, William W. Niemeyer.

Department of the Interior,
Commission to the Five Civilized Tribes.
Fairland, I.T., July 12, 1900.

In the matter of the application of Sarah E. Niemeyer for the enrollment of herself and children as Cherokees; being duly sworn, and examined by Commissioner Breckinridge, she testified as follows:

Q What is your name? A Sarah E. Niemeyer.
Q What is your age? A 45.
Q What is your postoffice address? A Adair.
Q In what district is that? A Delaware, I suppose you call it, we live in the Delaware district.

CHEROKEE GRANTED ENROLLMENT CARDS
& DAWES PACKETS 1900-1907 VOLUME I

Q How long have you lived there? A We have lived there 4 years, it will be this fall.
Q Where did you live before that time? A In Vinita.
Q Have you lived continuously in the Territory during the period you were at Vinita and at or near Adair? A Yes, sir.
Q For whom do you appear to make claim for enrollment, for yourself alone?
A For myself and my children.
Q How many children have you got under 21 years of age and living with you?
A I have 2,
Q Are they unmarried? A Yes, sir.
Q The older children will have to apply for themselves? A Yes, sir, that is all, this boy is the one that is 21.
Q Do you base your claim upon being a Cherokee by blood? A No, sir.
Q Upon what ground do [sic] make your claim? A I was brought here to think I was a Shawnee, and of course it is on that ground; I don't know what it is, I was brought as a Shawnee and registered as one; they brought in a certain number and I came in as a Shawnee.
Q Does your name appear upon any of the rolls of the Cherokee Nation? A It ought to, it ought to appear on every one of them; if it is not entered I can't account for it.
Q In what year was it you came in to the Territory? A In the fall of 1870.
Q What was your name in 1880? A Sarah E. Niemeyer.
Q What is your father's name? A R. W. Purcell.
(The name of the applicant does not appear on the roll of 1880, nor upon the rolls of 1894 and 1896.)
Q You say that you were brought in to the Territory as a Shawnee?
A Yes, sir, I was brought in with the tribe.
Q And you have considered yourself a Cherokee-Shawnee? A I always have.
(The name of Sarah E. Niemeyer appears on the Cherokee-Shawnee pay-roll of 1896, page 29, No. 570.)
Q That appears to be the state of facts in regard to your enrollment, as far as that data is available to the Commission at this time. Do you know of any other records where your name might appear? A None at all; I have never been out of the Cherokee Nation nowhere.
Q Was your husband an Indian? A No, sir, he was a white man.
Q If he has had any rights it was through you? A Yes, sir.
Q Will you please give the names of your minor children for whom you apply?
A Ida A. Niemeyer is the oldest, she is 19.
(The name of Ida A. Niemeyer does not appear upon the rolls of 1894 or 1896. Appears on Cherokee-Shawnee pay-roll of 1896, page 29, No. 527.)
Q Is there any further evidence in regard to the enrollment of this child that you think of? A Not that I know of.
Q What is the name of the next child? A Charles H. Niemeyer.
Q What is his age? A 15.
(The name of Charles H. Niemeyer does not appear on the Cherokee rolls of 1894 or 1896. On Shawnee-Cherokee pay-roll of 1896, page 29, No. 573.)
Q Is there any further evidence of the enrollment of your children that you know of?
A No, sir, not that I know of.

CHEROKEE GRANTED ENROLLMENT CARDS & DAWES PACKETS 1900-1907 VOLUME I

Q What was your husband's name? A George Niemeyer.
Q Was he ever enrolled upon any of the tribal rolls of the Cherokee Nation? A Yes, sir, I enrolled him when I enrolled the family.
Q What year was it? A I enrolled him in 1896, and I enrolled him in 1894.
(The name of George Niemeyer not on rolls of 1894 oe 1896. Not on Cherokee-Shawnee pay-roll of 1898,)
Q Have you ever made application for enrollment before as a Cherokee? A No, sir.
Q What evidence have you that you came into this country as a Shawnee? A Well, all the evidence I have in the world is just the old Shawnees themselves and my father's work for it.
Q Have you a copy of some record? A Just the paper that my son brought here.
Q Have you that paper? A Yes, sir, that is the paper.
Q What was your name in 1871? A It was Sarah M. Purcell.
Q You have handed me here a paper dated Tahlequah, October 13, 1864. It is signed by W. P. Boudinot, as Executive Secretary of the Cherokee Nation. It is under the seal of the Cherokee Nation. In this paper it is stated that R. W. Purcell and sundry other people of the same name, among them Sarah E. Purcell, are embraced in the list of names of Shawnee who moved and located in the Cherokee Nation prior to the 10th of June, 1871, in accordance with the agreement between the Shawnee tribe of Indians and the Cherokee Nation, on June 7, 1869, approved by the President of the United States June 9, 1869, in accordance with the Cherokee treaty of 1866, 15th article, as the said list is of record and on file in the department and from which the list written is a true and correct copy. Are you and the Sarah E. Purcell there one and the same person? A Yes, sir.
Q Was R. W. Purcell, whose name there appears, your father? A Yes.

Mr. W. T. Hutchings, attorney for the Cherokee Nation: Your father was R. W. Purcell? A Yes, sir.
Q He was a white man, and not a member of an Indian tribe? A Not that I know of.
Q Never claimed any Indian blood? A No, sir.
Q Your mother was a white woman, was she? A I can't tell you what my mother was, she died when I was 3 years old.
Q Where were you born? A I was born in Ohio.
Q Not amongst the Shawnee tribe of Indians? A Not that I know of.
Q Your father after your mother's death married a Shawnee Indian woman?
A Yes, sir.
Q And when he came to the Indian Territory with his Shawnee wife, you came with him? A Yes, sir.
Q Being a minor child? A Yes, sir.

Mrs. Niemeyer, the Commission will not render a decision at present in your application for yourself and your two children, but will take the matter under advisement. Any further evidence that may occur to you, any written evidence, affidavits, or transcripts of official records that you can furnish within a reasonable time, will be taken into consideration in connection with your case, and whatever decision the Commission arrives at, you will be informed of in writing at your present

CHEROKEE GRANTED ENROLLMENT CARDS & DAWES PACKETS 1900-1907 VOLUME I

post office. If you should for any reason change your postoffice address, you are requested to advise the Commission, or to leave proper direction at home for your mail to be forwarded. And when the Commission has rendered its decision, all the papers in the case, with the statement of the Commission's decision and reasons therefor, will be forwarded to the Honorable Secretary of the Interior at Washington, whose approval or disapproval will be necessary for making the decision final in the case.

Bruce C. Jones, being duly sworn, says that as stenographer to the Commission to the Five Civilized Tribes, and that he reported the testimony of the above named witness, and that the foregoing is a full, true and correct translation of his stenographic notes.

(Signed) Bruce C. Jones.

Sworn to and subscribed before me this the 13th day of July, 1900.

(Signed) T. B. Needles,

Commissioner.

:------------------------ooOOOOOOOOOOoo------------------------:

Department of the Interior,
Commission to the Five Civilized Tribes,
Vinita, I.T., October 22, 1901.

In the matter of the application of Sarah E. Niemeyer et al, Cherokee Doubtful case #20. SUPPLEMENTAL TESTIMONY.

Appearances:
    S. F. Parks for the applicant.
    J. L. Baugh for the Cherokee Nation.

Testimony on behalf of the applicant.

SARAH E. NIEMEYER, being first duly sworn by the Commission testified as follows in her own behalf:
    (By Mr. Parks)
Q State your name? A Sarah E. Niemeyer.

CHEROKEE GRANTED ENROLLMENT CARDS
& DAWES PACKETS 1900-1907 VOLUME I

Q Are you the Sarah E. Niemeyer who applied before this Commission at Fairland last year? A Yes, sir.
Q What was your maiden name? A Purcell.
Q What was your father's name? A Robert W. Purcell.
Q What was his citizenship? A Shawnee.
Q When did he come to this country? A In '71.
Q Did he come here within the time---- or did he avail himself of the provisions of the treaty made between the Cherokees and the Shawnees on June 9th, 1869, that is, come within two years from the making of that treaty? A Yes, sir, he come with the rest of them.
(Applicant's attorney here hands her a paper)
Q Does your name appear on that? A Yes, sir, there is my name.
Q Sarah E. Purcell? A Yes, sir.
(By Mr. Baugh)
Q What was your mother, an Indian or a white woman? A I don't know, she died before I knew.
Q Did you never hear your father say? A No, sir.
Q In fact you have no history about your mother at all? A No, sir.

Thomas Dougherty being first duly sworn by the Commission testified as follows on the part of the applicant:
(By Mr. Parks)
Q State your name? A Thomas Dougherty.
Q What is your age? A 51.
Q Where do you reside? A Here in Vinita.
Q Are you acquainted with Sarah E. Niemeyer, the applicant in this case? A Yes, sir.
Q How long have you know her? A I have known her about 15 or 20 years.
Q What was her maiden name? A Purcell.
Q Did you know her father? A Yes, sir.
Q Do you know what his name was? A Robert I think.
Q Purcell? A Yes, sir.
Q Is this lady here a daughter of Robert Purcell? A Yes, sir.
(By Mr. Baugh)
Q Do you know why Mrs. Niemeyer does not appear upon the roll of 1880?
A No, sir, I don't.
Q Has she always lived in the Cherokee Nation? A Ever since I knew her, yes, sir.
Q And you say you have known her for twenty years? A Yes, sir.
Q Did she come here with the Shawnees to the Cherokee Nation? A I can't say as to that, only by hearsay.
Q You don't know whether this lady is the same person whose name appears on that certificate or not? A No, sir, only by the name.
Q You don't know about it of your own knowledge? A No, sir.
(By Mr. Parks)
Q You know she has been recognized as the daughter of Robert Purcell?
A Yes, sir.

CHEROKEE GRANTED ENROLLMENT CARDS & DAWES PACKETS 1900-1907 VOLUME I

(By Mr. Baugh)
Q Did you know who her mother was? A No, I didn't.

HARRIETT ROSS, being first duly sworn by the Commission, testified as follows on the part of the applicant:
(By Mr. Parks)
Q State your name? A Harriett Ross.
Q What is your age? A 64.
Q What is your citizenship, Cherokee Delaware or Shawnee? A Shawnee,
Q Are you acquainted with Sarah E. Niemeyer? A Yes, sir.
Q Is this the lady here? A Yes, sir.
Q How long have you know her? A Ever since she was a baby, I raised her.
Q You did? A Yes, sir.
Q When did she come to this country, if you remember? A Time when all of us come.
Q Are you any relation of this lady? A Only by marriage.
Q What relation? A Step mother.
   (By Baugh)
Q Are you a Shawnee by blood? A Yes, sir.
Q By blood? A Yes, sir.
Q Was your husband a Shawnee by blood? A No, sir, not Purcell, he wasn't, he was a white man.
Q Are you a Shawnee direct by blood? A Yes, sir, my mother was a quarter blood Shawnee.
Q And your husband Purcell was a white man? A Yes, sir.
Q Do you know what this Mrs. Niemeyer's mother was, Indian or a white woman? A White woman.
Q And her father was a white man? A Yes, sir.
   (By the Commission)
Q This applicant does not claim to be a Shawnee b blood then? A No, sir, by adoption.

(This will be filed in the case)

Chas. von Weise, being first duly sworn states that as stenographer to the Commission to the Five Civilized Tribes he reported in full all the proceedings in the above cause and that the foregoing is a full, true and correct transcript of his stenographic notes therein.

(Signed) Chas. von Weise.

Subscribed and sworn to before me this the 30th of October, 1901.

(Signed) T. B. Needles,

Commissioner.

CHEROKEE GRANTED ENROLLMENT CARDS
& DAWES PACKETS 1900-1907 VOLUME I

Arthur G. Croninger, being duly sworn, states that as stenographer to the Commission to the Five Civilized Tribes he made the foregoing copy, and that the same is a true and complete copy of the original transcript.

Arthur G Croninger

Subscribed and sworn to before me this 25th day of November, 1901.

MD Green
Notary Public.

Department of the Interior,
Commission to the Five Civilized Tribes,
Vinita, I. T. October, 29th 1901.

SUPPLEMENTAL ORDER.

BY COM'R BRECKINRIDGE: It is ordered that a set of the testament in Cherokee Doubtful case #20, the same being the case of Sarah E. Niemeyer, be filed in Cherokee Doubtful case #19, the same being the case of William W. Niemeyer, and special attention is called to the supplemental testimony taken in Cherokee Doubtful case #20 taken on October 22, 1902, which is also desired to be filed in the records of Cherokee Doubtful case #19.

= = = = = = = =

Chas. von Weise, being sworn states that as stenographer to the Commission to the Five Civilized Tribes he reported in full all the proceedings in the above cause and that the foregoing is a full, true and correct transcript of his stenographic notes therein.

Chas won weise

Subscribed and sworn to before me this the 31st of October, 1901.

T B Needles
Commissioner.

CHEROKEE GRANTED ENROLLMENT CARDS & DAWES PACKETS 1900-1907 VOLUME I

Supl.-C.D.#19.

Department of the Interior,
Commission to the Five Civilized Tribes.
Muskogee, I. T., February 15, 1902.

SUPPLEMENTAL in the matter of the enrollment of William W. Niemeyer et al. as Cherokee citizens:

The applicant was notified by registered letter on the 30th day of January, 1902, that his case would be taken up for final consideration by the Commission on the 15th day of February, 1902, and that he would on said date be given an opportunity to introduce any further testimony in his case.

The register receipt was returned February 1, 1902. The applicant has been called three times and fails to respond either in person or by attorney, and it is directed that this case be closed.

T B Needles

Commissioner.

Cherokee D 19

DEPARTMENT OF THE INTERIOR,
COMMISSION TO THE FIVE CIVILIZED TRIBES.

In the matter of the application for the enrollment of William W. Niemeyer and his minor child, Alfred C. Niemeyer, as citizens of the Cherokee Nation.

D E C I S I O N.

--oOo--

The record in this case shows that on July 12, 1900, William W. Niemeyer appeared before the Commission at Fairland, Indian Territory, and made application for the enrollment of himself and his minor child, Alfred C. Niemeyer, as citizens of the Cherokee Nation. Further proceedings in the matter of said application were had at Vinita, Indian Territory, on October 29, 1901. A copy of the testimony taken in the matter of the application for the enrollment of Sarah E. Niemeyer et al., as citizens of the Cherokee Nation, Cherokee D. Case No. 20, is made part of the record in this case.

CHEROKEE GRANTED ENROLLMENT CARDS & DAWES PACKETS 1900-1907 VOLUME I

The evidence in this case shows that William W. Niemeyer, a white man, is the son of Sarah E. Niemeyer, whose name appears as "Sarah E. Purcell", upon the Register of Shawnees who removed to the Cherokee Nation prior to June 10, 1871, pursuant to the terms of the Cherokee-Shawnee agreement of 1869. By the provisions of that agreement the Shawnees so removing, and registered were received into the Cherokee Nation "on equal terms in every respect, and with all the privileges and immunities of native citizens of said Cherokee Nation." The name of William W. Niemeyer is found on the Cherokee Census roll of 1890, and he is identified on the Pay roll of Cherokee Shawnee citizens of 1896. Alfred C. Niemeyer, the son of the said William W. Niemeyer and his wife, Eliza Niemeyer, who were lawfully married on December 1, 1899, is too young to be on any roll but proper proof of his birth, on May 14, 1900, has been furnished this Commission.

The evidence further shows that William W. Niemeyer was born in the Cherokee Nation and has lived for the greater part of his life in said Nation. He has never lived outside of the Indian Territory, and it is considered from the evidence that Alfred C. Niemeyer has lived in the Cherokee Nation ever since his birth.

It is, therefore, the opinion of this Commission that William W. Niemeyer and Alfred C. Niemeyer should be enrolled as citizens of the Cherokee Nation in accordance with the provisions of Section twenty-one of the Act of Congress approved June 28, 1898 (30 Stats., 495), and it is so ordered.

COMMISSION TO THE FIVE CIVILIZED TRIBES.

(SIGNED). *Tams Bixby.*
Chairman.

TB Needles
Commissioner.

(SIGNED). *C. R. Breckinridge.*
Commissioner.

Dated at Muskogee, Indian Territory,
this _____ DEC -1 1902 _____

COMMISSIONERS:
HENRY L. DAWES,
TAMS BIXBY,
THOMAS B. NEEDLES,
C. R. BRECKINRIDGE.

ALLISON L. AYLESWORTH,
SECRETARY.

DEPARTMENT OF THE INTERIOR.
COMMISSION TO THE FIVE CIVILIZED TRIBES.

REFER IN REPLY TO THE FOLLOWING

Cherokee D 19.

ADDRESS ONLY THE
COMMISSION TO THE FIVE CIVILIZED TRIBES.

Muskogee, Indian Territory, December 2, 1902.

W. W. Hastings,
      Attorney for the Cherokee Nation,
           Muskogee, Indian Territory.

Dear Sir:

    There is herewith enclosed a copy of the decision of the Commission to the Five Civilized Tribes, dated December 1, 1902, granting the application of William W. Niemeyer for the enrollment of himself and his minor child, Alfred C. Niemeyer, as citizens of the Cherokee Nation.

    You are advised that you will be allowed fifteen days from date hereof in which to file such protest as you may desire to make against the action of the Commission in this case, a copy of which protest you will be required to serve upon the applicant. If you fail to file protest within the time allowed, this decision will be considered final.

          Respectfully,

                    Tams Bixby   Acting Chairman.

Enclosure H. No. 14.

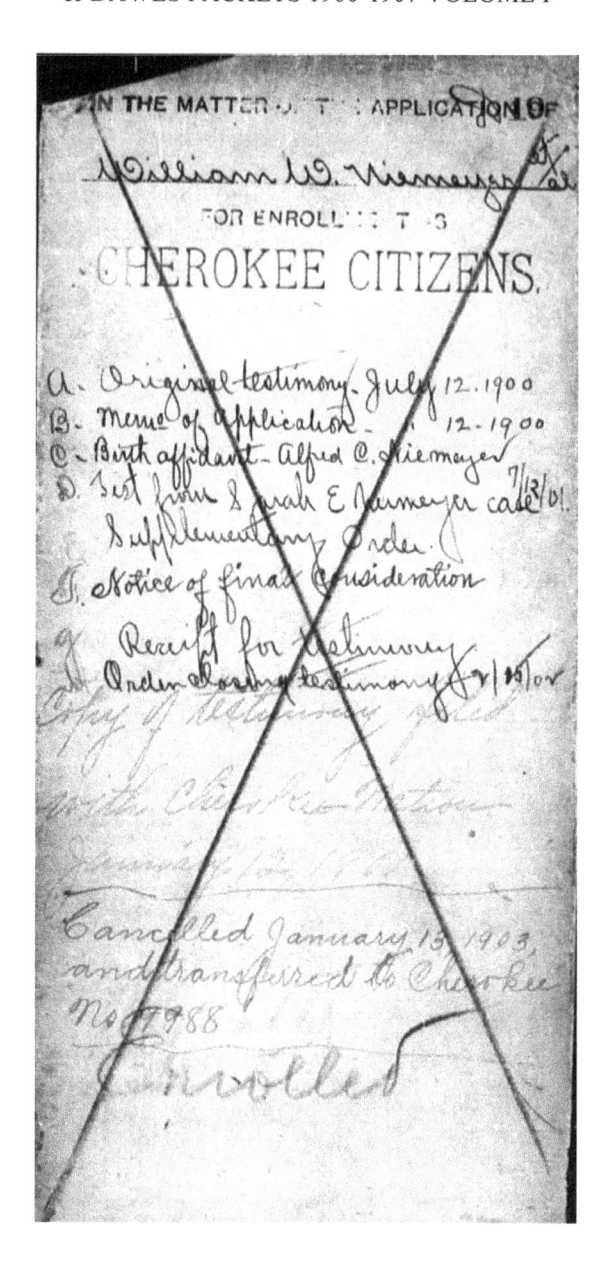

IN THE MATTER OF THE APPLICATION OF

William W. Niemeyer et al

FOR ENROLLMENT AS

CHEROKEE CITIZENS.

A - Original testimony - July 12, 1900
B - Memo of application - " 12-1900
C - Birth affidavit - Alfred C. Niemeyer
D - Test from Sarah E. Niemeyer case 7/13/01
E - Supplementary Order
F - Notice of final consideration
G - Receipt for testimony
H - Order closing testimony 8/15/0-

Copy of testimony filed
with Cherokee Nation
January 13, 1903

Cancelled January 13, 1903,
and transferred to Cherokee
No. 1988

Enrolled

CHEROKEE GRANTED ENROLLMENT CARDS & DAWES PACKETS 1900-1907 VOLUME I

CHEROKEE GRANTED ENROLLMENT CARDS & DAWES PACKETS 1900-1907 VOLUME I

Cherokee D20 - Sarah E. Niemeyer

CHEROKEE GRANTED ENROLLMENT CARDS & DAWES PACKETS 1900-1907 VOLUME I

Department of the Interior,
Commission to the Five Civilized Tribes.
Fairland, I.T., July 12, 1900.

In the matter of the application of Sarah E. Niemeyer for the enrollment of herself and children as Cherokees; being duly sworn, and examined by Commissioner Breckinridge, she testified as follows:

Q What is your name? A Sarah E. Niemeyer.
Q What is your age? A 45.
Q What is your postoffice address? A Adair.
Q In what district is that? A Delaware, I suppose you call it, we live in the Delaware district.
Q How long have you lived there? A We have lived there 4 years, it will be this fall.
Q Where did you live before that time? A In Vinita.
Q Have you lived continuously in the Territory during the period you were at Vinita and at or near Adair? A Yes, sir.
Q For whom do you appear to make claim for enrollment, for yourself alone?
A For myself and my children.
Q How many children have you got under 21 years of age and living with you?
A I have 2,
Q Are they unmarried? A Yes, sir.
Q The older children will have to apply for themselves? A Yes, sir, that is all, this boy is the one that is 21.
Q Do you base your claim upon being a Cherokee by blood? A No, sir.
Q Upon what ground do [sic] make your claim? A I was brought here to think I was a Shawnee, and of course it is on that ground; I don't know what it is, I was brought as a Shawnee and registered as one; they brought in a certain number and I came in as a Shawnee.
Q Does your name appear upon any of the rolls of the Cherokee Nation? A It ought to, it ought to appear on every one of them; if it is not entered I can't account for it.
Q In what year was it you came in to the Territory? A In the fall of 1870.
Q What was your name in 1880? A Sarah E. Niemeyer.
Q What is your father's name? A R. W. Purcell.
(The name of the applicant does not appear on the roll of 1880, nor upon the rolls of 1894 and 1896.)
Q You say that you were brought in to the Territory as a Shawnee?
A Yes, sir, I was brought in with the tribe.
Q And you have considered yourself a Cherokee-Shawnee? A I always have.
(The name of Sarah E. Niemeyer appears on the Cherokee-Shawnee pay-roll of 1896, page 29, No. 570.)
Q That appears to be the state of facts in regard to your enrollment, as far as that data is available to the Commission at this time. Do you know of any other records where your name might appear? A None at all; I have never been out of the Cherokee Nation nowhere.

CHEROKEE GRANTED ENROLLMENT CARDS & DAWES PACKETS 1900-1907 VOLUME I

Q Was your husband an Indian? A No, sir, he was a white man.
Q If he has had any rights it was through you? A Yes, sir.
Q Will you please give the names of your minor children for whom you apply?
A Ida A. Niemeyer is the oldest, she is 19.
(The name of Ida A. Niemeyer does not appear upon the rolls of 1894 or 1896. Appears on Cherokee-Shawnee pay-roll of 1896, page 29, No. 527.)
Q Is there any further evidence in regard to the enrollment of this child that you think of? A Not that I know of.
Q What is the name of the next child? A Charles H. Niemeyer.
Q What is his age? A 15.
(The name of Charles H. Niemeyer does not appear on the Cherokee rolls of 1894 or 1896. On Shawnee-Cherokee pay-roll of 1896, page 20, No. 573.)
Q Is there any further evidence of the enrollment of your children that you know of?
A No, sir, not that I know of.
Q What was your husband's name? A George Niemeyer.
Q Was he ever enrolled upon any of the tribal rolls of the Cherokee Nation? A Yes, sir, I enrolled him when I enrolled the family.
Q What year was it? A I enrolled him in 1896, and I enrolled him in 1894.
(The name of George Niemeyer not on rolls of 1894 oe 1896. Not on Cherokee-Shawnee pay-roll of 1898,)
Q Have you ever made application for enrollment before as a Cherokee? A No, sir.
Q What evidence have you that you came into this country as a Shawnee? A Well, all the evidence I have in the world is just the old Shawnees themselves and my father's work for it.
Q Have you a copy of some record? A Just the paper that my son brought here.
Q Have you that paper? A Yes, sir, that is the paper.
Q What was your name in 1871? A It was Sarah M. Purcell.
Q You have handed me here a paper dated Tahlequah, October 13, 1864. It is signed by W. P. Boudinot, as Executive Secretary of the Cherokee Nation. It is under the seal of the Cherokee Nation. In this paper it is stated that R. W. Purcell and sundry other people of the same name, among them Sarah E. Purcell, are embraced in the list of names of Shawnee who moved and located in the Cherokee Nation prior to the 10th of June, 1871, in accordance with the agreement between the Shawnee tribe of Indians and the Cherokee Nation, on June 7, 1869, approved by the President of the United States June 9, 1869, in accordance with the Cherokee treaty of 1866, 15th article, as the said list is of record and on file in the department and from which the list written is a true and correct copy. Are you and the Sarah E. Purcell there one and the same person? A Yes, sir.
Q Was R. W. Purcell, whose name there appears, your father? A Yes.

Mr. W. T. Hutchings, attorney for the Cherokee Nation: Your father was R. W. Purcell? A Yes, sir.
Q He was a white man, and not a member of an Indian tribe? A Not that I know of.
Q Never claimed any Indian blood? A No, sir.
Q Your mother was a white woman, was she? A I can't tell you what my mother was, she died when I was 3 years old.
Q Where were you born? A I was born in Ohio.

CHEROKEE GRANTED ENROLLMENT CARDS & DAWES PACKETS 1900-1907 VOLUME I

Q Not amongst the Shawnee tribe of Indians? A Not that I know of.
Q Your father after your mother's death married a Shawnee Indian woman?
A Yes, sir.
Q And when he came to the Indian Territory with his Shawnee wife, you came with him? A Yes, sir.
Q Being a minor child? A Yes, sir.

      Mrs. Niemeyer, the Commission will not render a decision at present in your application for yourself and your two children, but will take the matter under advisement. Any further evidence that may occur to you, any written evidence, affidavits, or transcripts of official records that you can furnish within a reasonable time, will be taken into consideration in connection with your case, and whatever decision the Commission arrives at, you will be informed of in writing at your present post office. If you should for any reason change your postoffice address, you are requested to advise the Commission, or to leave proper direction at home for your mail to be forwarded. And when the Commission has rendered its decision, all the papers in the case, with the statement of the Commission's decision and reasons therefor, will be forwarded to the Honorable Secretary of the Interior at Washington, whose approval or disapproval will be necessary for making the decision final in the case.

------------o------------

      Bruce C. Jones, being duly sworn, says that as stenographer to the Commission to the Five Civilized Tribes, and that he reported the testimony of the above named witness, and that the foregoing is a full, true and correct translation of his stenographic notes.

                                  Bruce C. Jones

Sworn to and subscribed before me this the 13th day of July, 1900.

                                  T. B. Needles
                                  Commissioner.

R
===

                Department of the Interior,
                Commission to the Five Civilized Tribes,
                Vinita, I.T., October 22, 1901.

In the matter of the application of Sarah E. Niemeyer et al, Cherokee Doubtful case #20. SUPPLEMENTAL TESTIMONY.

CHEROKEE GRANTED ENROLLMENT CARDS & DAWES PACKETS 1900-1907 VOLUME I

Appearances:
    S. F. Parks for the applicant.
    J. L. Baugh for the Cherokee Nation.

              Testimony on behalf of the applicant.

============

    SARAH E. NIEMEYER, being first duly sworn by the Commission testified as follows in her own behalf:
        (By Mr. Parks)
Q State your name? A Sarah E. Niemeyer.
Q Are you the Sarah E. Niemeyer who applied before this Commission at Fairland last year? A Yes, sir.
Q What was your maiden name? A Purcell.
Q What was your father's name? A Robert W. Purcell.
Q What was his citizenship? A Shawnee.
Q When did he come to this country? A In '71.
Q Did he come here within the time---- or did he avail himself of the provisions of the treaty made between the Cherokees and the Shawnees on June 9th, 1869, that is, come within two years from the making of that treaty? A Yes, sir, he come with the rest of them.
    (Applicant's attorney here hands her a paper)
Q Does your name appear on that? A Yes, sir, there is my name.
Q Sarah E. Purcell? A Yes, sir.
        (By Mr. Baugh)
Q What was your mother, an Indian or a white woman? A I don't know, she died before I knew.
Q Did you never hear your father say? A No, sir.
Q In fact you have no history about your mother at all? A No, sir.

        Thomas Dougherty being first duly sworn by the Commission testified as
        follows on the part of the applicant:
(By Mr. Parks)
Q State your name? A Thomas Dougherty.
Q What is your age? A 51.
Q Where do you reside? A Here in Vinita.
Q Are you acquainted with Sarah E. Niemeyer, the applicant in this case? A Yes, sir.
Q How long have you know her? A I have known her about 15 or 20 years.
Q What was her maiden name? A Purcell.
Q Did you know her father? A Yes, sir.
Q Do you know what his name was? A Robert I think.
Q Purcell? A Yes, sir.
Q Is this lady here a daughter of Robert Purcell? A Yes, sir.
        (By Mr. Baugh)
Q Do you know why Mrs. Niemeyer does not appear upon the roll of 1880?

CHEROKEE GRANTED ENROLLMENT CARDS & DAWES PACKETS 1900-1907 VOLUME I

A No, sir, I don't.
Q Has she always lived in the Cherokee Nation? A Ever since I knew her, yes, sir.
Q And you say you have known her for twenty years? A Yes, sir.
Q Did she come here with the Shawnees to the Cherokee Nation? A I can't say as to that, only by hearsay.
Q You don't know whether this lady is the same person whose name appears on that certificate or not? A No, sir, only by the name.
Q You don't know about it of your own knowledge? A No, sir.
   (By Mr. Parks)
Q You know she has been recognized as the daughter of Robert Purcell?
A Yes, sir.

   (By Mr. Baugh)
Q Did you know who her mother was? A No, I didn't.

HARRIETT ROSS, being first duly sworn by the Commission, testified as follows on the part of the applicant:
(By Mr. Parks)
Q State your name? A Harriett Ross.
Q What is your age? A 64.
Q What is your citizenship, Cherokee Delaware or Shawnee? A Shawnee,
Q Are you acquainted with Sarah E. Niemeyer? A Yes, sir.
Q Is this the lady here? A Yes, sir.
Q How long have you know her? A Ever since she was a baby, I raised her.
Q You did? A Yes, sir.
Q When did she come to this country, if you remember? A Time when all of us come.
Q Are you any relation of this lady? A Only by marriage.
Q What relation? A Step mother.
       (By Baugh)
Q Are you a Shawnee by blood? A Yes, sir.
Q By blood? A Yes, sir.
Q Was your husband a Shawnee by blood? A No, sir, not Purcell, he wasn't, he was a white man.
Q Are you a Shawnee direct by blood? A Yes, sir, my mother was a quarter blood Shawnee.
Q And your husband Purcell was a white man? A Yes, sir.
Q Do you know what this Mrs. Niemeyer's mother was, Indian or a white woman?
A White woman.
Q And her father was a white man? A Yes, sir.
       (By the Commission)
Q This applicant does not claim to be a Shawnee b blood then? A No, sir, by adoption.

=========

(This will be filed in the case)

****

CHEROKEE GRANTED ENROLLMENT CARDS & DAWES PACKETS 1900-1907 VOLUME I

Chas. von Weise, being first duly sworn states that as stenographer to the Commission to the Five Civilized Tribes he reported in full all the proceedings in the above cause and that the foregoing is a full, true and correct transcript of his stenographic notes therein.

Chas. von Weise

Subscribed and sworn to before me this the 30th of October, 1901.

T. B. Needles
Commissioner.

Supl.-C.D.#20.

Department of the Interior,
Commission to the Five Civilized Tribes.
Muskogee, I. T., February 15, 1902.

SUPPLEMENTAL in the matter of the enrollment of Sarah E. Niemeyer as a citizen of the Cherokee Nation:

The applicant's Attorney, S. F. Parks, of Vinita, Indian Territory, was notified by registered letter on January 30, 1902, that this case would be taken up for final consideration February 15, 1902, and that an opportunity would be given the applicant at that time to introduce any additional testimony affecting her application. Both the applicant and her attorney have been called three times and fail to respond, and the case is closed.

T B Needles
Commissioner.

R.

DEPARTMENT OF THE INTERIOR.
Commission to the Five Civilized Tribes.
Muskogee, Indian Territory, November 13th, 1902.

In the matter of the application of George W. Niemeyer for the enrollment of himself as a citizen by intermarriage of the Cherokee Nation.

Cherokee Nation appears by W. W. Hastings.

CHEROKEE GRANTED ENROLLMENT CARDS & DAWES PACKETS 1900-1907 VOLUME I

GEORGE W. NIEMEYER, being duly sworn, testified as follows:
Examination by the Commission.
Q. What is your name? A. George W. Niemeyer.
Q. How old are you? A. 50 years old the first day of last March.
Q. Where do you live? A. Prior Creek, at present.
Q. Do you desire to make application for enrollment as a Cherokee citizen by intermarriage? A. Yes, sir.
Q. What is the name of the wife through whom you claim? A. Sarah E. Purcell.
Q. Is she a Cherokee, Shawnee or white woman? A. Shawnee.
Q. Shawnee by blood? A. I don't know. The evidence is all in.
Q. When were you married to her? A. '76, August 22nd.
Q. Have you any evidence of your marriage to her under the Cherokee law?
A. I have got my license.

BY MR. HASTINGS:
Comes now the representative of the Cherokee Nation and most respectfully desires to protest against the reception of this application, for the reason that under the act of Congress approved July 1st, 1902, and ratified by the Cherokee people on August 7th, 1902, the Commission is forbidden from receiving the application of any person whomsoever for enrollment after the 31st day of October, 1902, and calls attention to Section thirty of the act herein referred to.

BY THE COMMISSION:
Q. Mr. Niemeyer, state if you have ever appeared before the Commission at any time prior to this for the purpose of making application? A. Yes, sir; I was here on the 9th.
Q. Of what? A. Of last month.
Q. Did you then ask to be allowed to make application for enrollment? A. Yes, sir; I did. In the room right back there.
Q. You were told you couldn't apply? A. My name wasn't on the roll, the said. My wife never enrolled me.
Q. Were you before the Commission when your wife made application at Fairland?
A. No, sir; I couldn't go. I was busy. She and my son and daughter went.
Q. Did you, at any time subsequent to October, receive a letter from the Commission? A. Yes, sir. I didn't receive it. It was sent to me. It was written on the 13th, and I got it the first.
Q. 13th of what? A. Last month. I didn't receive it until the first. I told J. F. Warren, at Adair--I told him to forward my mail and he held it back.
Q. Have you that letter with you? A. No, not that letter. I have it at home. I have got the envelope and when the envelope was sent to Prior Creek.
Q. When your wife appeared before the Commission she said your post office was Adair. A. Yes, sir. I explained that to that fleshy gentleman--Cherokee lawyer-- when I was here. They sent the letter to Adair and I didn't receive it. They wrote me on the 13th, it arrived at Adair on the 14th and I got it the first.
Q. Of this month; November? A. Yes, sir. October, they wrote it, on the 13th; it got to Adair on the 14th.

CHEROKEE GRANTED ENROLLMENT CARDS & DAWES PACKETS 1900-1907 VOLUME I

Q. Where was that letter addressed to you, what place? A. Adair.
Q. You had moved from there? A. Yes, sir. I live at Prior Creek. I was living at Prior Creek when I was here.

BY MR. HASTINGS:
 After the additional questions, that have been asked the applicant, the representative of the Cherokee Nation most earnestly protests, because the law does not permit, under any circumstances, the reception of any application for enrollment after *October* 31st, 1902, and even if the person were a full blood Indian, admitted as such, if no application was made for him on or before October 31st, 1902, the law permits of no action for the reception of that application subsequent to that time. It makes no difference how unfortunate the applicant may have been. It is not a matter of charity; it is a matter of absolute, strict law.

BY THE COMMISSION:
Q. Have you your license with you? A. Yes, sir. It is all torn up. I got burned out and the water got through in the trunk and it got all to pieces. Maybe it isn't all there. I don't know. I was married by J. T. Cunningham on Locust creek[sic].
Q. Is that all the paper you have? A. That is all I have. I think there is part of it gone. I can get a copy of it if you desire.
Q. Mr. Niemeyer, it is impossible to make anything out of the license, except that it is a license. You will be required to furnish a certified copy of it. These papers will be filed here but you will be required to furnish the Commission with that certified copy.
Q. When were you married to your wife? A. August 22nd, 1876.
Q. Who issued that license to you? A. J. T. Cunningham.
Q. What position was he holding at that time? A. He was district clerk at that time.
Q. Who married you? A. J. T. Cunningham.
Q. Were you ever married before you married Sarah E. Purcell.[sic]
A. No, sir.
Q. Was she ever married before? A. No, sir.
Q. Where were you living at the time? A. At Vinita; that is about 3 miles east on Locust creek.
Q. How long had you known your wife before you married her?
A. About 9 months.
Q. Isn't it a fact, Mr. Niemeyer, that she is a white woman? A. I ain't arguing that question.
Q. Now answer to the best of your knowledge. A. I suppose she is.
Q. Was she reputed to be white when you married her? A. No, sir. I got a marriage license. She claimed to be part Indian. I supposed she was.
Q. Didn't she come with the Shawnees in 1871? A. Yes, sir.
Q. What is your wife's mother's name? A. I don't know.
Q. What is your wife's father's name? A. William; W. W. I think.
Q. William Purcell? A. I think so; yes, sir.
Q. Did your wife have any brothers or sisters? A. Yes, sir.

CHEROKEE GRANTED ENROLLMENT CARDS
& DAWES PACKETS 1900-1907 VOLUME I

Q. Can you name them? A. There was Wesley---
Q. Give their full names. A. I don't know as I could.
Q. Well, their sur-names? A. Wesley Purcell, William Purcell, Charlie Purcell, Ida A. Purcell, Latham Purcell; I believe that was all of them, as near as I can remember.

There is offered in evidence a certificate bearing date October 13th, 1884, signed by W. P. Boudinot, Executive Secretary of the Cherokee Nation, bearing the seal of the Cherokee Nation, showing that among others, the name of one Sarah E. Purcell appears upon the list of Shawnees which removed to the Cherokee Nation in accordance with the agreement between the Shawnee tribe and the Cherokee Nation of June 7th, 1869.

Q. Have you ever separated from your wife since you were married? A. No, sir.
Q. Has she ever separated from you? A. No, sir.
Q. Have you, since your marriage to her, lived in the Cherokee Nation? A. Yes, sir; all but nine months I was in Colorado?
Q. When was that? A. I got back here the 25th day of April last.
Q. Why did you go to Colorado? A. For her health.
Q. Did she go with you? A. Yes, sir.
Q. With the exception of that nine months have you always resided here? A. Yes, sir.
Q. Were your children all born here? A. Yes, sir.
Q. How does it happen that your name does not appear upon any of the rolls of the Cherokee Nation? A. I don't know.
Q. Have you ever appied[sic] to the Cherokee census takers? A. Yes, sir.
Q. What did they tell you? A. They enrolled me.
Q. When was that? A. I think it was '80 or '86, I ain't sure. It was at Ballard's school house, anyway.
Q. What district? A. Delaware.
Q. Was that the only time you appear before the census enumerators?
A. No, sir; I enrolled again just before the Shawnee payment and Mr.----I can't remember his name. I enrolled and he took our names down. My wife and me was both together; witnesses by Robert Ironside and Charlie Bluejacket.
Q. That was the payment to the Shawnees in 1896? A. They got that directly afterwards.
Q. They didn't pay you anything? A. No, sir; they didn't pay any intermarried at that time.
Q. As a matter of fact they didn't enroll any intermarried people at that time?
A. No, sir.
Q. Did you apply to the census takers in '90? A. 1890? Where was that at? Yes, my wife did.
Q. Did she receive her share of the money paid at that time? A. Yes, sir; she did.
Q. What did she receive? A. Two hundred and something. I couldn't tell you exactly.

BY MR. HASTINGS:
She wasn't put on that roll? A. Shawnee pay roll?

CHEROKEE GRANTED ENROLLMENT CARDS & DAWES PACKETS 1900-1907 VOLUME I

Q. That is a blood roll. A. Oh, no. Excuse me.

BY THE COMMISSION:
I asked you if your wife participated in the payment in 1890?
A. Yes, sir; she got her strip money.
Q. That wasn't in 1890. That was quite a number of years after that. This has been some 12 years ago? A. No, sir, I don't think she did.

BY THE COMMISSION:
The tribal rolls of the Cherokee Nation in the possession of the Commission have been examined and the applicant himself is not identified thereon. His wife is identified on the 1896 pay roll of the Cherokee Shawnee tribe of Indians, page 29, number 570.

It appears that on the 12th day of July, 1900, at Fairland, Indian Territory, the applicant's wife, Sarah E. Niemeyer, appeared before the Commission and made personal application for the enrollment of herself and two children, Ida A. and Charles H. Niemeyer, as citizens of the Cherokee Nation and that they were listed for enrollment on Cherokee Doubtful card number D-20.

BY MR. HASTINGS:
The Cherokee Nation waives any cross examination for the reason that it contends that no testimony whatever ought to be taken in this case and that the Commission is without jurisdiction to receive this application, as hereinbefore stated.

BY THE COMMISSION:
The record in the matter of the application of George W. Niemeyer, including the record in the matter of the application of his wife, Sarah E. Niemeyer, will be submitted to the Commission for consideration and appropriate action and the applicant notified of such action as may be taken by the Commission.

++

Jesse O. Carr, being first duly sworn, states that as stenographer to the Commission to the Five Civilized Tribes he reported the above entitled case and that the foregoing is a true and complete transcript of his stenographic notes thereof.

Jesse O. Carr

Subscribed and sworn to before me this 13th day of November, 1902.

BC Jones
Notary Public.

CHEROKEE GRANTED ENROLLMENT CARDS
& DAWES PACKETS 1900-1907 VOLUME I

File with the case of George W. Niemeyer.

Department of the Interior,
Commission to the Five Civilized Tribes.
Fairland, I.T., July 12, 1900.

In the matter of the application of Sarah E. Niemeyer for the enrollment of herself and children as Cherokees; being duly sworn, and examined by Commissioner Breckinridge, she testified as follows:

Q What is your name? A Sarah E. Niemeyer.
Q What is your age? A 45.
Q What is your postoffice address? A Adair.
Q In what district is that? A Delaware, I suppose you call it, we live in the Delaware district.
Q How long have you lived there? A We have lived there 4 years, it will be this fall.
Q Where did you live before that time? A In Vinita.
Q Have you lived continuously in the Territory during the period you were at Vinita and at or near Adair? A Yes, sir.
Q For whom do you appear to make claim for enrollment, for yourself alone?
A For myself and my children.
Q How many children have you got under 21 years of age and living with you?
A I have 2,
Q Are they unmarried? A Yes, sir.
Q The older children will have to apply for themselves? A Yes, sir, that is all, this boy is the one that is 21.
Q Do you base your claim upon being a Cherokee by blood? A No, sir.
Q Upon what ground do [sic] make your claim? A I was brought here to think I was a Shawnee, and of course it is on that ground; I don't know what it is, I was brought as a Shawnee and registered as one; they brought in a certain number and I came in as a Shawnee.
Q Does your name appear upon any of the rolls of the Cherokee Nation? A It ought to, it ought to appear on every one of them; if it is not entered I can't account for it.
Q In what year was it you came in to the Territory? A In the fall of 1870.
Q What was your name in 1880? A Sarah E. Niemeyer.
Q What is your father's name? A R. W. Purcell.
(The name of the applicant does not appear on the roll of 1880, nor upon the rolls of 1894 and 1896.)
Q You say that you were brought in to the Territory as a Shawnee?
A Yes, sir, I was brought in with the tribe.
Q And you have considered yourself a Cherokee-Shawnee? A I always have.
(The name of Sarah E. Niemeyer appears on the Cherokee-Shawnee pay-roll of 1896, page 29, No. 570.)
Q That appears to be the state of facts in regard to your enrollment, as far as that data is available to the Commission at this time. Do you know of any other records where

CHEROKEE GRANTED ENROLLMENT CARDS
& DAWES PACKETS 1900-1907 VOLUME I

your name might appear? A None at all; I have never been out of the Cherokee Nation nowhere.
Q Was your husband an Indian? A No, sir, he was a white man.
Q If he has had any rights it was through you? A Yes, sir.
Q Will you please give the names of your minor children for whom you apply? A Ida A. Niemeyer is the oldest, she is 19.
(The name of Ida A. Niemeyer does not appear upon the rolls of 1894 or 1896. Appears on Cherokee-Shawnee pay-roll of 1896, page 29, No. 527.)
Q Is there any further evidence in regard to the enrollment of this child that you think of? A Not that I know of.
Q What is the name of the next child? A Charles H. Niemeyer.
Q What is his age? A 15.

(The name of Charles H. Niemeyer does not appear on the Cherokee rolls of 1894 or 1896. On Shawnee-Cherokee pay-roll of 1896, page 29, No. 573.)

Secretary of the Interior Is there any further evidence of the enrollment of your children that you know of?
Secretary of the Interior No, sir, not that I know of.
Secretary of the Interior What was your husband's name? Secretary of the Interior George Niemeyer.
Secretary of the Interior Was he ever enrolled upon any of the tribal rolls of the Cherokee Nation? Secretary of the Interior Yes, sir, I enrolled him when I enrolled the family.
Secretary of the Interior What year was it? Secretary of the Interior I enrolled him in 1896, and I enrolled him in 1894.

(The name of George Niemeyer not on rolls of 1894 oe 1896. Not on Cherokee-Shawnee pay-roll of 1898,)

Secretary of the Interior Have you ever made application for enrollment before as a Cherokee? Secretary of the Interior No, sir.
Secretary of the Interior What evidence have you that you came into this country as a Shawnee? Secretary of the Interior Well, all the evidence I have in the world is just the old Shawnees themselves and my father's work for it.
Secretary of the Interior Have you a copy of some record? Secretary of the Interior Just the paper that my son brought here.
Secretary of the Interior Have you that paper? Secretary of the Interior Yes, sir, that is the paper.
Secretary of the Interior What was your name in 1871? Secretary of the Interior It was Sarah M. Purcell.
Secretary of the Interior You have handed me here a paper dated Tahlequah, October 13, 1864. It is signed by W. P. Boudinot, as Executive Secretary of the Interior the Cherokee Nation. It is under the seal of the Cherokee Nation. In this paper it is stated that R. W. Purcell and sundry other people of the same name, among them Sarah E. Purcell, are embraced in the list of names of Shawnee who moved and located in the Cherokee Nation prior to the 10th of June, 1871, in accordance with the agreement between the Shawnee tribe of Indians and the Cherokee Nation, on June 7, 1869, approved by the President of the Secretary of the Interior States June 9, 1869, in accordance with the Cherokee treaty of 1866, 15th article, as the said list is of record and on file in the department and from which the list written is a true and correct copy.

CHEROKEE GRANTED ENROLLMENT CARDS & DAWES PACKETS 1900-1907 VOLUME I

Are you and the Sarah E. Purcell there one and the same person? Secretary of the Interior Yes, sir.
Secretary of the Interior   Was R. W. Purcell, whose name there appears, your father? Secretary of the Interior Yes.

Mr. W. T. Hutchings, attorney for the Cherokee Nation: Your father was R. W. Purcell? Secretary of the Interior Yes, sir.
Secretary of the Interior   He was a white man, and not a member of an Indian tribe? Secretary of the Interior Not that I know of.
Secretary of the Interior   Never claimed any Indian blood? Secretary of the Interior No, sir.
Secretary of the Interior   Your mother was a white woman, was she? Secretary of the Interior I can't tell you what my mother was, she died when I was 3 years old.
Secretary of the Interior   Where were you born? Secretary of the Interior I was born in Ohio.
Secretary of the Interior   Not amongst the Shawnee tribe of Indians? Secretary of the Interior Not that I know of.
Secretary of the Interior   Your father after your mother's death married a Shawnee Indian woman?
Secretary of the Interior   Yes, sir.
Secretary of the Interior   And when he came to the Indian Territory with his Shawnee wife, you came with him? Secretary of the Interior Yes, sir.
Secretary of the Interior   Being a minor child? Secretary of the Interior Yes, sir.

   Mrs. Niemeyer, the Commission will not render a decision at present in your application for yourself and your two children, but will take the matter under advisement. Any further evidence that may occur to you, any written evidence, affidavits, or transcripts of official records that you can furnish within a reasonable time, will be taken into consideration in connection with your case, and whatever decision the Commission arrives at, you will be informed of in writing at your present post office. If you should for any reason change your postoffice address, you are requested to advise the Commission, or to leave proper direction at home for your mail to be forwarded. And when the Commission has rendered its decision, all the papers in the case, with the statement of the Commission's decision and reasons therefor, will be forwarded to the Honorable Secretary of the Interior the Interior at Washington, whose approval or disapproval will be necessary for making the decision final in the case.

------0------

   Bruce C. Jones, being duly sworn, says that as stenographer to the Commission to the Five Civilized Tribes, and that he reported the testimony of the above named witness, and that the foregoing is a full, true and correct translation of his stenographic notes.

(Signed)   Bruce C. Jones.

CHEROKEE GRANTED ENROLLMENT CARDS & DAWES PACKETS 1900-1907 VOLUME I

Sworn to and subscribed before me this the 13th day of July, 1900.

      (Signed) T. B. Needles,
          Commissioner.

     Department of the Interior,
     Commission to the Five Civilized Tribes,
     Vinita, I.T., October 22, 1901.

In the matter of the application of Sarah E. Niemeyer et al, Cherokee Doubtful case #20. SUPPLEMENTAL TESTIMONY.

Appearances:
  S. F. Parks for the applicant.
  J. L. Baugh for the Cherokee Nation.

     Testimony on behalf of the applicant.

 SARAH E. NIEMEYER, being first duly sworn by the Commission testified as follows in her own behalf:
  (By Mr. Parks)
Q State your name? A Sarah E. Niemeyer.
Q Are you the Sarah E. Niemeyer who applied before this Commission at Fairland last year? A Yes, sir.
Q What was your maiden name? A Purcell.
Q What was your father's name? A Robert W. Purcell.
Q What was his citizenship? A Shawnee.
Q When did he come to this country? A In '71.
Q Did he come here within the time---- or did he avail himself of the provisions of the treaty made between the Cherokees and the Shawnees on June 9th, 1869, that is, come within two years from the making of that treaty? A Yes, sir, he come with the rest of them.
 (Applicant's attorney here hands her a paper)
Q Does your name appear on that? A Yes, sir, there is my name.
Q Sarah E. Purcell? A Yes, sir.
  (By Mr. Baugh)
Q What was your mother, an Indian or a white woman? A I don't know, she died before I knew.
Q Did you never hear your father say? A No, sir.
Q In fact you have no history about your mother at all? A No, sir.

CHEROKEE GRANTED ENROLLMENT CARDS
& DAWES PACKETS 1900-1907 VOLUME I

Thomas Dougherty being first duly sworn by the Commission testified as follows on the part of the applicant:

(By Mr. Parks)
Q State your name? A Thomas Dougherty.
Q What is your age? A 51.
Q Where do you reside? A Here in Vinita.
Q Are you acquainted with Sarah E. Niemeyer, the applicant in this case? A Yes, sir.
Q How long have you know her? A I have known her about 15 or 20 years.
Q What was her maiden name? A Purcell.
Q Did you know her father? A Yes, sir.
Q Do you know what his name was? A Robert I think.
Q Purcell? A Yes, sir.
Q Is this lady here a daughter of Robert Purcell? A Yes, sir.
        (By Mr. Baugh)
Q Do you know why Mrs. Niemeyer does not appear upon the roll of 1880?
A No, sir, I don't.
Q Has she always lived in the Cherokee Nation? A Ever since I knew her, yes, sir.
Q And you say you have known her for twenty years? A Yes, sir.
Q Did she come here with the Shawnees to the Cherokee Nation? A I can't say as to that, only by hearsay.
Q You don't know whether this lady is the same person whose name appears on that certificate or not? A No, sir, only by the name.
Q You don't know about it of your own knowledge? A No, sir.
   (By Mr. Parks)
Q You know she has been recognized as the daughter of Robert Purcell?
A Yes, sir.

(By Mr. Baugh)
Q Did you know who her mother was? A No, I didn't.

HARRIETT ROSS, being first duly sworn by the Commission, testified as follows on the part of the applicant:

(By Mr. Parks)
Q State your name? A Harriett Ross.
Q What is your age? A 64.
Q What is your citizenship, Cherokee Delaware or Shawnee? A Shawnee,
Q Are you acquainted with Sarah E. Niemeyer? A Yes, sir.
Q Is this the lady here? A Yes, sir.
Q How long have you know her? A Ever since she was a baby, I raised her.
Q You did? A Yes, sir.
Q When did she come to this country, if you remember? A Time when all of us come.
Q Are you any relation of this lady? A Only by marriage.
Q What relation? A Step mother.
        (By Baugh)
Q Are you a Shawnee by blood? A Yes, sir.

CHEROKEE GRANTED ENROLLMENT CARDS
& DAWES PACKETS 1900-1907 VOLUME I

Q By blood? A Yes, sir.
Q Was your husband a Shawnee by blood? A No, sir, not Purcell, he wasn't, he was a white man.
Q Are you a Shawnee direct by blood? A Yes, sir, my mother was a quarter blood Shawnee.
Q And your husband Purcell was a white man? A Yes, sir.
Q Do you know what this Mrs. Niemeyer's mother was, Indian or a white woman?
A White woman.
Q And her father was a white man? A Yes, sir.
   (By the Commission)
Q This applicant does not claim to be a Shawnee b blood then? A No, sir, by adoption.

(This will be filed in the case)

Chas. von Weise, being first duly sworn states that as stenographer to the Commission to the Five Civilized Tribes he reported in full all the proceedings in the above cause and that the foregoing is a full, true and correct transcript of his stenographic notes therein.

(Signed) Chas. von Weise.
Subscribed and sworn to before me this the 30th of October, 1901.
(Signed) T. B. Needles,
Commissioner.

Muskogee, Indian Territory, October 13, 1902.

George W. Niemeyer,

Adair, Indian Territory.

Dear Sir:

In response to your verbal inquiry of the 9th inst. relative to your right to enrollment, as a citizen by intermarriage of the Cherokee Nation, you are advised that if you desire to make an application, you will be permitted to do so by appearing in person before the Commission to the Five Civilized Tribes, at its office at Muskogee, Indian Territory, for examination under oath.

You are further advised that such application must be made on or before October 31, 1902.

CHEROKEE GRANTED ENROLLMENT CARDS & DAWES PACKETS 1900-1907 VOLUME I

Respectfully,

Commissioner in Charge.

::

Jesse O. Carr, stenographer to the Commission to the Five Civilized Tribes, being first duly sworn, states that the foregoing is a true and correct copy of the original records of the same on file in said matter.

Jesse O. Carr

Subscribed and sworn to before me this 13th day of November, 1902.

BC Jones
Notary Public.

DEPARTMENT OF THE INTERIOR,
COMMISSION TO THE FIVE CIVILIZED TRIBES.

In the matter of the application for the enrollment of Sarah E. Niemeyer, Ida A. Jones, Charles H. Niemeyer and Robert E. Jones, as citizens of the Cherokee Nation and for the enrollment of George W. Niemeyer, as a citizen by intermarriage of the Cherokee Nation, consolidating the applications of:

Sarah E. Niemeyer, et al.,　Cherokee D　20
George W. Niemeyer,　　　　　　"　　D 3177

D E C I S I O N

(D 20)　The record in this case shows that on July 12, 1900, Sarah E. Niemeyer appeared before the Commission at Fairland, Indian Territory, and made application for the enrollment of herself and her two children, Ida A., and Charles H. Niemeyer, as citizens of the Cherokee Nation. Further proceedings were had in the matter of said application at Vinita, Indian Territory, on October 22, 1901. On June 24, 1902, a marriage certificate was filed with the Commission, showing the marriage of said Ida A. Niemeyer to one J. E. Jones on July 26, 1900, and on October 15, 1902, a birth affidavit was filed for Robert E. Jones, a child of that marriage, and the same is made a part of this record.

(D 3177)　The record in this case shows that on October 9, 1902, George W. Niemeyer appeared before the Commission at Muskogee, Indian Territory, and made application for his enrollment as a citizen by intermarriage of the Cherokee Nation. Under a misapprehension as to the law, his said application was not received nor any record made of the same at that time. On October 13, 1902, the Commission, by letter, notified this applicant that if he desired to renew his application, he would be permitted to do so by appearing in person before the Commission to the Five Civilized Tribes at its office at Muskogee, Indian Territory, and that such application should be made by him on or before October 31, 1902. Owing to a change in his post office address, such letter was not received by the applicant until November 1, 1902, and on November 13, 1902, the said George W. Niemeyer appeared before the Commission at Muskogee, Indian Territory and renewed his application for enrollment as a citizen by intermarriage of the Cherokee Nation.

The evidence in these cases shows that the said Sarah E. Niemeyer is a white woman, but she is identified, under her maiden name of Sarah E. Purcell, on the Shawnee Register, which Register, contains the names of those who permanently located in the Cherokee Nation under the terms of the treaty concluded between the Cherokee Nation and the Shawnee tribe of Indians on June 7, 1869, and approved by the President of the United States June 9, 1869, which said treaty, in part, provides:

"................That the said Shawnees shall be incorporated into and ever afterwards remain a part of the Cherokee Nation, on equal terms in every respect, and with all the privileges and immunities of native citizens of said Cherokee Nation; provided, that all of said Shawnees who shall elect to avail themselves of the provisions of this agreement, shall register their names, and permanently locate in the Cherokee Nation, as herein provided, within two years from the date hereof, otherwise they shall forfeit all rights under this agreement."

The evidence further shows that the said George W. Niemeyer, a white man, was married under a Cherokee marriage license and in accordance with the laws of the Cherokee Nation, on August 22, 1876, to the said Sarah E. Purcell, who, under the provisions of the treaty above quoted, acquired the status of a Cherokee citizen by blood. The said Sarah E. Niemeyer and her two children are identified on the Cherokee-Shawnee pay roll of 1896. Robert E. Jones is identified by a birth affidavit made a part of this record.

The evidence further shows that the said Sarah E. Niemeyer has resided in the Cherokee Nation since 1871; that George W. Niemeyer has resided in the Cherokee Nation since the date of his marriage in 1876, and has been living with his wife, Sarah E., from that time up to and including September 1, 1902. The two children of the said George W., and Sarah E. Niemeyer, being minors, at the date of the application for their enrollment, are considered to have resided in the Cherokee Nation from their birth up to and including June 28, 1898, and the residence of Robert E; Jones, born since 1898, is considered to be that of his mother, the said Ida A. Jones.

It is, therefore the opinion of this Commission that Sarah E. Niemeyer, Ida A. Jones, Charles H. Niemeyer and Robert E. Jones, should be enrolled as citizens of the Cherokee Nation, and that George W. Niemeyer should be enrolled as a citizen by intermarriage of the Cherokee Nation, in accordance with the provisions of Section twenty-one of the Act of Congress approved June 28, 1898 (30 Stats., 495), and it is so ordered.

CHEROKEE GRANTED ENROLLMENT CARDS & DAWES PACKETS 1900-1907 VOLUME I

COMMISSION TO THE FIVE CIVILIZED TRIBES.

<u>Tams Bixby</u>
Acting Chairman.

<u>T.B. Needles</u>
Commissioner.

<u>C. R. Breckinridge</u>
Commissioner.

Muskogee, Indian Territory,
this **JAN 15 1903**

DEPARTMENT OF THE INTERIOR,
Commission to the Five Civilized Tribes,
Vinita I. T. February 5th, 1903.

In the matter of the application of Sarah E. Niemeyer et al for enrollment as citizens of the Cherokee Nation; consolidating the applications of

Sarah E Niemeyer et al Cherokee D 20

George W. Niemeyer   Cherokee D 3177.

Protest of the Cherokee Nation.

Comes now the Cherokee Nation and protests against the Decision of the Commission rendered in these two cases and asks that came[sic] with the records and the protest of the Cherokee Nation filed in D 3177 George W. Niemeyer be forwarded to the Honorable Secretary of the Interior for review.

Respectfully submitted,

W W Hastings
Attorney for the Cherokee Nation.*JCS*

CHEROKEE GRANTED ENROLLMENT CARDS & DAWES PACKETS 1900-1907 VOLUME I

COMMISSIONERS:
HENRY L. DAWES,
TAMS BIXBY,
THOMAS B. NEEDLES,
C. R. BRECKINRIDGE.

DEPARTMENT OF THE INTERIOR.
COMMISSION TO THE FIVE CIVILIZED TRIBES.

REFER IN REPLY TO THE FOLLOWING
Cherokee
D-20 & D3177.

ALLISON L. AYLESWORTH,
SECRETARY.

ADDRESS ONLY THE
COMMISSION TO THE FIVE CIVILIZED TRIBES.

Muskogee, Indian Territory, January 23, 1903.

W. W. Hastings,
    Attorney for the Cherokee Nation,
        Vinita, Indian Territory.

Dear Sir:-

There is herewith enclosed a copy of the decision of the Commission to the Five Civilized Tribes, dated January 15, 1903, granting the application for the enrollment of Sarah E. Niemeyer, Ida A. Jones, Charles H. Niemeyer and Robert E. Jones as citizens of the Cherokee Nation, and for the enrollment of George W. Niemeyer as a citizen by intermarriage of the Cherokee Nation.

You are hereby advised that you will be allowed fifteen days from date hereof, in which to file such protest as you may desire to make against the action of the Commission in this case, a copy of which protest you will be required to serve upon the applicant.

If you fail to file protest within the time allowed, this decision will be considered final.

        Respectfully,
                Tams Bixby   Acting Chairman.

Enc. M-104

CHEROKEE GRANTED ENROLLMENT CARDS
& DAWES PACKETS 1900-1907 VOLUME I

COMMISSIONERS:

HENRY L. DAWES,
TAMS BIXBY,
THOMAS B. NEEDLES,
C. R. BRECKINRIDGE.

DEPARTMENT OF THE INTERIOR,
COMMISSION TO THE FIVE CIVILIZED TRIBES.

REFER IN REPLY TO THE FOLLOWING
Cherokee
D-20 & D3177

ALLISON L. AYLESWORTH,
SECRETARY.

ADDRESS ONLY THE
COMMISSION TO THE FIVE CIVILIZED TRIBES.

Muskogee, Indian Territory, February 21, 1903.

W. W. Hastings,

    Attorney for the Cherokee Nation,

        Vinita, Indian Territory.

Dear Sir:

    You are hereby advised that the Commission has this day transmitted to the Secretary of the Interior, for review, the record of proceedings had in the matter of the application of George W. Niemeyer for the enrollment of himself as a citizen by intermarriage of the Cherokee Nation, and the application of his wife, Sarah E. Niemeyer, for the enrollment of herself and her three minor children, Ida A, and Robert E. Jones and Charles H. Niemeyer, as citizens of the Cherokee Nation, including the Commission's decision, dated 23, 1903, granting said application, and the protest of the Cherokee Nation against said decision, dated February 9, 1903.

    The action of the Secretary will be made known to you as soon as the Commission is informed of same.

                                      Respectfully,

                                      Tams Bixby

                                          Chairman.

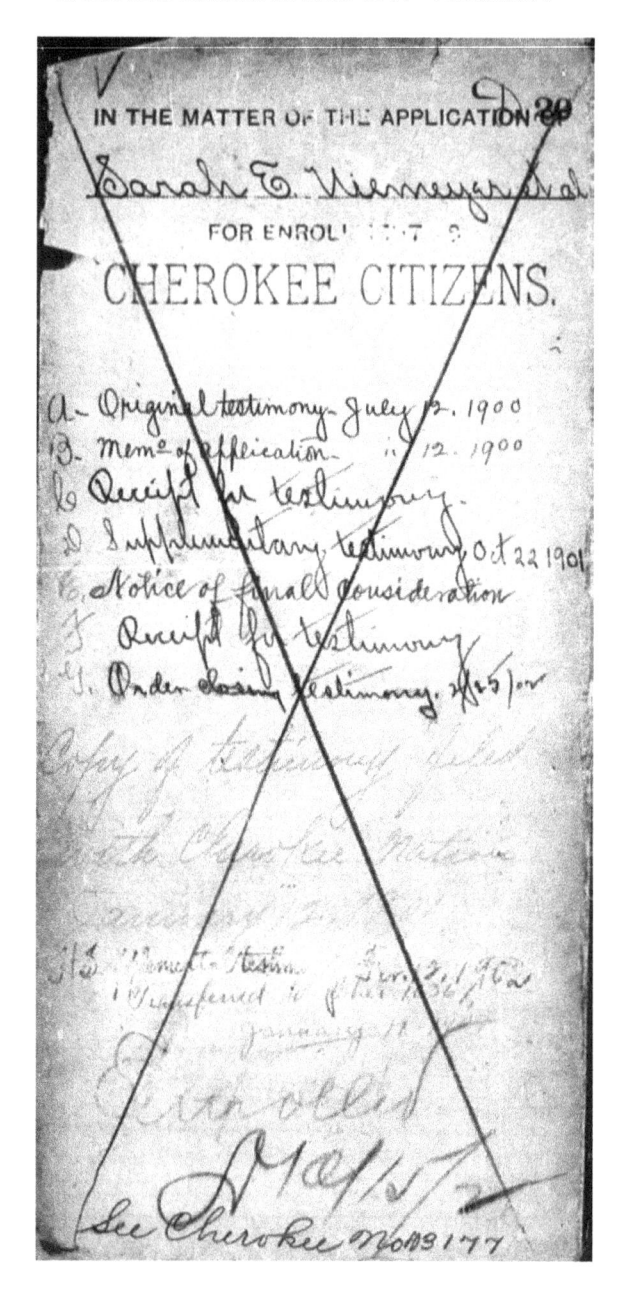

CHEROKEE GRANTED ENROLLMENT CARDS
& DAWES PACKETS 1900-1907 VOLUME I

CHEROKEE GRANTED ENROLLMENT CARDS
& DAWES PACKETS 1900-1907 VOLUME I

CHEROKEE GRANTED ENROLLMENT CARDS & DAWES PACKETS 1900-1907 VOLUME I

Cherokee D24 - Adolphus Washington Dirtseller

212

CHEROKEE GRANTED ENROLLMENT CARDS & DAWES PACKETS 1900-1907 VOLUME I

Department of the Interior,
Commission to the Five Civilized Tribes,
Fairland, I. T., July 12, 1900.

In the matter of the application of Adolphus Washington Dirtseller for enrollment as a Cherokee by blood; being sworn and examined by Commissioner Breckinridge he testifies as follows:

Q   What is your name? A Adolphus Washington Dirtseller.
Q   What is your age? A Twenty-one.
Q   What is your post-office? A Grove.
Q   Your District? A Delaware.
Q   How long have you lived in this District? A I come to Delaware District in 1879 I believe it was.
Q   That was along about the time you were born wasn't it? A Yes sir.
Q   Were you born in the Territory? A No sir.
Q   Are you a Cherokee by blood? A Yes sir.
Q   Have you lived in the Territory ever since 1879? A Yes sir.
Q   You apply for anybody except yourself? A No sir. I won't be found on the 1880 roll as that name it will appear upon the 1880 roll as Adolphus Washington Fox.
    Note: 1880 roll examined, and this name not found.
    1894 roll examined, page 393, #1112, identified on the roll of 1894 as Adolphus Fox, the name he claims to have had at that time.
Q   How does it happen that you bore the name of Adolphus Fox at that time? A I guess that come from a nickname at that time; I couldn't say whether it was Dirtseller or Fox; I was raised an orphan, and I had some friends that advised me to put my name Dirtseller on the 1880 roll.
    Note: 1896 roll, Delaware District, page 463, #959, Adolphus Dirtseller.
Com'r Breckinridge: He is identified on the roll of 1896 under the name given as Adolphus Dirtseller
Q   There is a good deal of variation in the names here, is somebody here that knows you and have known you under all these names?
A   Yes sir, Mr. William Ballard.

--   --   --

William Ballard, being sworn and examined by Commissioner Breckinridge testifies as follows:

Q   What is your name? A William Ballard.
Q   Where do you live? A About ten miles from here.
Q   What is your age? A Forty-eight.
Q   Your business? A Farming.
Q   You know this applicant here who appears under the name of Adolphus Washington Dirtseller? A I have been seeing him for the last ten or twelve years.
Q   Have you known him under that name? A Yes sir.
Q   Have you ever know him under any other name? A No sir.
Q   Did you know him as Adolphus Washington Dirtseller or Adolphus Dirtseller.[sic]
A   When he was put on the '94 roll I think he went on as Adolphus Fox.

213

CHEROKEE GRANTED ENROLLMENT CARDS & DAWES PACKETS 1900-1907 VOLUME I

Q   And you have known him sometimes as Adolphus Fox and as Adolphus Dirtseller? A That is the way he went on.
Q   How have you known him in your personal acquaintance? A Adolphus Fox.

Examined by Attorney Hutchings on part of Cherokee Nation:

Q   When he first came to this country he came here with his mother and grandfather didn't he? A There was a white man and a white woman brought him to this country.
Q   They brought him here from the Choctaw Nation? A Yes sir.
Q   You don't know anything about who his father was? A No sir.

Applicant, Adolphus Washington Dirtseller, re-called, and examined by Commissioner Breckinrdige[sic]:

Q   Do you know who your father was? A I don't remember ever seeing my father at all.
Q   Do you remember your mother? A No sir, I couldn't say I remember.
Q   You can't give, of your own knowledge, either the name of your father or mother? A My father went by the name of John Fox.
Q   Do you know whether he is on the roll of 1880? A No sir, he died before that time.

--   --   --

Thomas Monroe, being sworn and examined by Com'r Breckinridge, testifies as follows:

Q   What is your name? A Thomas Monroe.
Q   What is your age? A Forty-seven.
Q   Where do you live? A Delaware District.
Q   What is your business? A Farming.
Q   You know this applicant, Adolphus Washington Dirtseller? A I don't recognize him, no, but if he is the boy that was with Burks in 1880 I probably knew him.

Commissioner Breckinridge to applicant, Adolphus Washing Dirtseller:

Q   Was you ever with Burks? A Yes sir.
Q   He was your grandfather? A Yes sir.

Commissioner Breckinridge continuing examination of witness Monroe:

Witness: I remember him then as a boy, and I remember his mother. She called him her son; it was my understanding she was a white woman.
Q   You know anything about his father? A No sir.
Q   What did you say his grandmother's name was? A I didn't know his grandmother, I knew his grandfather, Burks.
Q   When did he die? A I don't know whether he is dead or not.

CHEROKEE GRANTED ENROLLMENT CARDS
& DAWES PACKETS 1900-1907 VOLUME I

Commissioner Breckinridge recalls applicant, Adolphus Washington Dirtseller, and examines him as follows:

Q   Do you know anything about your grandfather Burks, is he living?
A   No sir.
Q   When did he die? A   In 1891,
Q   He was a white man? A   Yes sir.

Com'r Breckinridge continuing examination of witness Monroe:

Q   Your understanding was that they came here from the Choctaw Nation?
A   That's what Burks told me.
Q   He was a white man? A   Yes sir.
Q   And stood as his grandfather? A   Yes sir.
Q   Did he tell you anything about the boy? A   I don't remember that he ever told me anything about the boy.

--   --   --

Applicant: I have got some papers that I want to show.
(Produces papers)
Com'r Breckinridge, examining applicant:
Q   This paper is signed by Missouri A. Fox, was she kin to you? A   She was my mother.
Q   This paper is a statement to the following effect: That one Missouri Angeline Fox was duly sworn, and said that she was married to John Fox on the 9th day of September, 1876, and in consequence of said marriage there was one child born to them on the 3rd day of July 1878, and named Adolphus Washington Fox. The above named John Fox was said to be of Cherokee blood, and furthermore, claimed to be himself. This is sworn to and subscribed before H. T. Landrum, Clerk of Delaware District Court, Cherokee Nation, 9th day of March, 1880, and bears the seal of that official. Do you understand that your mother, Missouri A. Fox, was a white woman or an Indian? A   She was a white woman.
Q   And that your Indian blood is through your father? A   Yes sir.

Commissioner Breckinridge: This paper handed to me by the applicant is a statement signed by James A. Moore, sworn to and subscribed before H. T. Landrum, Clerk of Delaware District, Cherokee Nation, on the 9th day of March, 1880, and it bears in addition to the signature, also the seal of that official. It is to the effect that there appeared before him one Olcott Moore, who after being sworn, says, that he was well acquainted with one John Fox, and that he was a Cherokee citizen by blood, and was well acquainted with the family of which said John Fox was a descendant, and he knew the whole family to be of Cherokee blood, and from appearances they seemed to be about full-bloods.
Q   You know whether any of you ancestors are on the old Tribal rolls of the Cherokee Nation? A   No sir, I couldn't say.
Q   Have you ever looked for these names to see it they were? A   No sir.
Q   Have you ever applied for admission to Cherokee citizenship before? A   Yes sir. My mother fixed these same papers out and they was sent to Tahlequah in 1880 when

we came to the Cherokee Nation from the Chctaw[sic] Nation, them papers was sent to Tahlequah.
Q To the Cherokee authorities? A Yes sir.
Q What action did the authorities take? A I couldn't say.
Q You never heard? A No sir. I have always had the rights of a Cherokee.
Q You say you were not born in the Cherokee Nation? A No sir.

Commissioner Breckinridge: I will state to go in[sic] the record that as to the matter of the appearance of the applicant, he looks like a man of Indian blood.

Your case will be put upon what we call the suspended or doubtful list, and will be given further consideration, and when a conclusion is reached you will be informed by mail. If you can get any further information in regard to your rights to enrollment you will be welcome to send it to the Commission and it will be considered in connection with your application.

(Applicant advised to leave his papers with the Commission and to produce further testimony.)

M.D. Green, being first duly sworn, states that as stenographer to the Commission to the Five Civilized Tribes he reported the foregoing case and that the above and foregoing is a full true and complete transcript of his stenographic notes said case.

MD Green

Subscribed and sworn to before me this 13th day of July 1900.

TB Needles
Commissioner.

"R"

Cherokee D-24.

Department of the Interior,
Commission to the Five Civilized Tribes,
Muskogee, I. T., February 14, 1902.

SUPPLEMENTAL TESTIMONY ON BEHALF OF APPLICANT, in the matter of the application of Adolphus W, Dirtseller for enrollment as a Cherokee by blood.

Appearances:
    Applicant in person;
    W. W. Hastings, attorney for the Cherokee Nation.

CHEROKEE GRANTED ENROLLMENT CARDS & DAWES PACKETS 1900-1907 VOLUME I

ADOLPHUS W. DIRTSELLER, being first duly sworn, and being examined testified as follows:
BY COMMISSION:
Q What is your name? A Adolphus W. Dirtseller.
Q How old are you? A 23 years old.
Q Where do you live? A I live five miles west of Grove, in Delaware District.
Q What is the name of your father? A He always generally went by the name of John Fox.
BY COMMISSION: The applicant presents a certificate from J. S. Rice, Superintendent of the Texas State Penitentiary, certifying that John Fox was convicted of Stealing cattle and sentenced on the 6th day of September, 1879 for two years confinement in the penitentiary. He was received at the penitentiary on the 20th day of September, 1879, and served one year, four months and 25 days.
Q Is your father living? A No sir, he is dead.
Q When did he die? A '81 I believe it is.
Q Did he die while he was confined in the penitentiary? A Yes sir.
Q Now where were you living when your father was sentenced to the penitentiary? A We was stopping in the Chickasaw Nation when he was arrested; we wasn't living there; we had started back to this country.
Q Were you born in the Chickasaw Nation? A I was born in the Choctaw Nation.
Q How old were you when you first came to the Cherokee Nation? A I think if I aint mistaken I come here in '79.
Q How old did you say you are now? A 23 years old.
Q You remember the date of your birth? A I will be 24 next July.
Q You will be 24 next July? A Yes sir.
Q Have you always made the Cherokee Nation your home since you came here? A Yes sir.
BY MR. HASTINGS:
Q Where were you when your father was convicted? A I suppose we had stopped there in the Chickasaw Nation.
Q You hadn't as yet gotten up to the Cherokee Nation? A No sir, we had started for the Cherokee Nation, and when we got to the Chickasaw Nation the horses run away, and he started back after the horses and he was arrested, and I suppose we was in the Chickasaw Nation when they sentenced him, and then we come right on to the Cherokee Nation.
Q Had you reached the Cherokee Nation when your father died? A Yes sir.
Q Your mother was a white woman? A Yes sir.
Q Well then you were in the Cherokee Nation as you claim, in '80? A Yes sir.
Q Do you claim to have lived here ever since? A Yes sir.
Q In Delaware district? A No I haven't lived in Delaware district. I used to live down below town here about 15 miles, in Tahlequah and Canadian district both; I have been enrolled in both of them. When I was before the Commission at Fairland I didn't know I was enrolled until after I was with the Commission; I was too small to remember it.
BY COMMISSION:
Q Did you ever go by any other name that John Dirtseller or John Fox? A Yes sir, am on all the rolls as Adolphus Fox, except the 1896, I come as Dirtseller there.

CHEROKEE GRANTED ENROLLMENT CARDS & DAWES PACKETS 1900-1907 VOLUME I

Q What did you call your father? A John Fox.
Q Did they call him anything else? A Dirtseller is what the Indians always called him.
Q What was your mother's name before she married your father? A Birch.
Q Did you ever go by that name? A No sir.
Q Who did you live with after you came to the Cherokee Nation? A I lived with my grandfather.
Q What was your grandfather's name? A Birch.
Q He was a white man, was he? A Yes sir.
Q Any other statement you want to make relative to your enrollment?
A I don't know as there is.
Q Are you willing to submit this case now to the Commission for final consideration[sic]? A I guess so.
BY MR. HASTINGS:
I want to enter protest for the Cherokee Nation against the consideration of the affidavits that have been previously filed in connection with this case; some three or four of them, shown to have been made within the Northern District of the Indian Territory in July 1900, subsequent to the application of the applicant for enrollment, and were therefore living at the time, and accessible.

M.D. Green, being first duly sworn, states that as stenographer to the commission to the he correctly recorded the testimony and proceedings in this case and that the foregoing is a true and complete transcript of his stenographic notes thereof.

_____ *MD Green* _____

Subscribed and sworn to before me this February 15, 1902.

T B Needles

Commissioner.

Cher
Supp'l to D 24

Department of the Interior,
Commission to the Five Civilized Tribes,
Vinita, I. T., February 12, 1903.

In the matter of the application of ADOLPUS[sic] W. DIRTSELLER, for the enrollment of himself as a citizen by blood of the Cherokee Nation.

EDMOND D. CAREY, being first duly sworn, and examined, testified as follows:

CHEROKEE GRANTED ENROLLMENT CARDS
& DAWES PACKETS 1900-1907 VOLUME I

Examined by the Commission:

Q State your name ?   A Edmond D. Carey.
Q How old are you ?   A Seventy years old.
Q What is your post office ?   A Grove.
Q Are you a citizen of the Cherokee Nation ?   A Yes sir.
Q Do you know Adolpus[sic] Dirtseller ?   A I do.
Q How long have you known him ?   A I have known him, I guess, about twenty years.
Q Did you know his parents ?   A I knowed the man he claimed to be his pa.
Q What was his name ?   A His name was Jim Dirtseller.
Q Wasn't it John ?   A No sir, he was raised right down this creek here not more than eight miles from here.
Q Do you know that Jim Dirtseller was his father ?   A I don't know.
Q You are talking now of this boy's father, are you ?   A I am talking of his grandfather.
Q What was his name ?   A They called him Jim.
Q Was he a Cherokee ?   A Yes sir that Jim was a Cherokee, his mammy and daddy were bot full bloods.
Q Did you know John Dirtseller ?   A No sir.
Q What was Adolpus's[sic] mother's name ?   A I didn't know her; I never saw her.
Q Don't know anything about her ?   A No sir.
Q You don't know if this boy's father was married to her or not ?   A No sir.
Q Is this boy's father dead ?   A Yes sir.
Q When did he die ?   A Well he died, it's been just along directly after the war, just a few years; he died in Texas.
Q It couldn't have been right after the war, this boy is only twenty two years old.
A He is nearer thirty. He died while this boy was a baby. That's what they told me; I never saw him after I left Texas; I saw him on Red River in 1867.
Q Do you know where he was living when this boy was born ?   A No sir, I left there in '67, and I never saw him again.
Q Who has this boy been living with ?   A His aunt, and he is living there yet.
Q What is her name ?   A I can't tell you.
Q What district does this Dirtseller live in ?   A Delaware part of the time and in Saline part of the time.
Q When did he die ?   A I don't know when he did die.
Q I mean this boy's father ?   A No, I don't know what time.
Q You say he went away out of the Nation during the war ?   A He was with Watie's regiment, he was a soldier in Watie's regiment.
Q He went out of the Nation ?   A Yes sir, he was in the Choctaw Nation.
Q Did he ever come back here ?   A No sir, he died before he ever got back; he never got back.
Q How long did you say you had known this boy ?   A Well I knowed him, I expect I knowed him about eight or ten years before he died, before I last saw him.
Q Oh no, the boy Adolpus[sic] ?   A I have known him Cherokee like, he was about three years old when they brought him up from Texas.

CHEROKEE GRANTED ENROLLMENT CARDS
& DAWES PACKETS 1900-1907 VOLUME I

Q Who brought him ?   A His aunt that raised him, and he's living with her yet.
Q Has he lived with her all the time from that time up till now ?   A Yes sir.
Q Do you know that to be so ?   A He's living with her yet.
Q How close do you live to them ?   A They live about a quarter from my house.
Q Have you been living there all the time ?   A I have been living there sixty four years except during the war.
Q Have this boy and his aunt been living a quarter of a mile from your place ever since he was three years old ?   A No sir, not all the time.
Q Where has he been gone ?   A He has been there in the neighborhood. He went over into Arkansas last spring and he and his aunt worked a time. That's the only time I have known them to go out.
Q Are you sure this boy and his aunt haven't been out of the Nation since they came back from Texas ?   A They went out last spring.
Q Up to last spring ?   A No sir, I don't think they have, they have lived there in the neighborhood nearly all the time.
Q You would see them frequently, every week would you ?   A No sir, sometimes I wouldn't see them for three months.
Q What is the longest time you have missed them away from there ?   A I missed them last spring about the longest I believe.
Q But before that time ?   A I don't know; they lived down below me on Honey Creek about two miles and lived over across the river in what we called O'Field bottom for a while I didn't see them.
Q How long ago was that ?   A Two or three years.
Q How long would they be away that you wouldn't see them, a year at a time ?
A No sir, I have seen them more than once a year.
Q You have seen them more than once a year during that time ?
A Yes sir.
Q Haven't any doubt about it ?   A No sir.
Q Is his aunt a Cherokee ?   A No sir, a white woman.
Q You don't know, of course, if this Jim Dirtseller was his father ?   A No sir, but he is just exactly like that fellow.
Q Is he a full blood ?   A No sir, he claims to be and he is just like him, and if he was alive you couldn't hardly tell them apart only one would be darker.
Q This boy, then, has lived in Delaware district all the time, him and his aunt ?
A I think he has.
Q How old did you say he was ?   A I don't know exactly, but I would guess him to be about twenty seven or eight years old, and maybe thirty.
Q You say you didn't know John Dirtseller ?   A No sir; well I might have known him. This young fellow had several names, they called him Fox.
Q Who are you talking about now ?   A The one they call Adolpus[sic] father. They had sever names, Indians in them days give a fellow a name, and that was his name.
Q Did old man Jim's father have any other boys ?   A He had one called Chip.
Q Chip and Jim, is that all ?   A That's all I ever knowed of.

CHEROKEE GRANTED ENROLLMENT CARDS & DAWES PACKETS 1900-1907 VOLUME I

E. C. Bagwell, on oath states that, as stenographer to the Commission to the Five Civilized Tribes, he correctly recorded the testimony and proceedings had in the above entitled cause, and that the foregoing is an accurate transcript of his stenographic notes thereof.

EC Bagwell

Subscribed and sworn to before me this March 6, 1903.

Samuel Foreman
Notary Public.

C.D. 24.

Two Miles North of Needmore, Indian Territory,

May 18, 1905.

DEPARTMENT OF THE INTERIOR,
COMMISSION TO THE FIVE CIVILIZED TRIBES.

In the matter of the application of Adolphus W. Dirtseller for enrollment as a citizen by blood of the Cherokee Nation.

John M. Miller, being first duly sworn, testified as follows:

BY THE COMMISSION:

Q What is your name? A John M. Miller.
Q What is your age, Mr. Miller? A 63.
Q What is your post office? A Needmore, I. T.
Q Are you a citizen by blood of the Cherokee Nation? A Yes, sir
Q How long have you lived in Delaware District?
A I was born and raised in Delaware District.
Q Are you acquainted with a young man by the name of Adolphus W. Dirtseller.
A Yes, sir.
Q About how old is Adolphus W. Dirtseller?
A Well, I could not state exactly how old; he was a chunk of a boy when the Cenus[sic] of 1880 was taken, but I could not say how old he is.
Q He is just a young man now?
A Yes,
Q What would be his post office address?
A I guess Echo or Grove, I. T.
Q How long have you known Adolphus W. Dirtseller?
A I have known him ever since the 1880 Census was taken.
Q What was the name of the mother of Adolphus W. Dirtseller?
A She was a Burk before marriage.

CHEROKEE GRANTED ENROLLMENT CARDS & DAWES PACKETS 1900-1907 VOLUME I

Q   Did you know her given name?
A   If I did I have forgotten it.
Q   Was she a white woman?
A   Said to be.
Q   Did you know who the father of Adolphus W. Dirtseller was?
A   I did not know his father.
Q   Are you now acquainted with the father of Adolphus W. Dirtseller at all?
A   No, sir.
Q   Were you acquainted with a brother of Adolphus W. Dirtseller's father?
A   Yes, sir.
Q   What was his name?
A   We called him Chips.
Q   You did not know this boy's father at all?
A   No, sir.
Q   Did you know such a man existed as the reputed father of this boy?
A   Well, I do not remember whether I did nor[sic] not.
Q   Who is the reputed father of this boy - what is his name?
A   John Chips.
Q   Did you ever see John Chips at all?
A   Yes, I saw him in the time of the war.
Q   Where did you see John Chips?
A   Down in the Choctaw Nation.
Q   Was that during the war?
A   Yes, sir.
Q   Was John Chips, who is the reputed father of Adolphus W. Dirtseller, a citizen of the Cherokee Nation?
A   Yes he was a refugee that went from here in the time of the war.
Q   Was he a full blood?
A   Yes, a full blood.
Q   There was no question about his citizenship?
A   No, not that I know of.
Q   Did you serve with John Chips in the war?
A   No, I served with his brother.
Q   Where did you last see John Chips?
A   In the Choctaw Nation on Red River.
Q   What year was that?
A   Some where along in '65.
Q   Was John Chips married at that time?
A   Not when I knew him.
Q   When was the next time you had any account of John Chips?
A   I never had any account of him until this old man drove up here with this child.
Q   What old man was that to whom you refer?
A   Old man Burks.
Q   Do you know old man Burks' given name?
A   Well, no sir, they just called him old man Burks.
Q   Was Burks a white man?
A   Yes, sir.

CHEROKEE GRANTED ENROLLMENT CARDS
& DAWES PACKETS 1900-1907 VOLUME I

Q   Did he have some girls?
A   He had two girls.
Q   Do you remember their names?
A   No, sir, I do not.
Q   Were these girls with Burks when he came to the Cherokee Nation?
A   Yes, sir.
Q   About what year was it he came to the Cherokee Nation?
A   Well, it was some where along in '79 before the Census was taken
Q   Did Burks come from the Choctaw Nation?
A   Yes, sir, that is what he claimed.
Q   Was this Adolphus W. Dirtseller the child of one of these Burks girls?
A   Yes, sir, said to be
Q   Was Adolphus W. Dirtseller with his mother at that time?
A   Yes, sir, when they come here.
Q   Did she say at that time who the father of Adolphus W. Dirtseller was?
A   Well, that was what they claimed; they come to John Chips' sister here for protection, that was Allcut Moore's wife.
Q   When the Burks girl came to the Cherokee Nation about '79 along with this boy, Adolphus W. Dirtseller, you state that they came to John Chips' sister?
A   Yes, sir.
Q   Did the mother of this boy state that John Chips was his father?
A   I do not know whether she did to me or not, but that's what she said to Allcut Moore's wife, and I got this from Allcut Moore and his wife.
Q   Was it generally believed among John Chips' relatives here that this boy was John Chips' son?
A   Well, it was believed in Allcut Moore's family; I do not know how it was believed in the neighborhood.
Q   John Chips' Sister, who was Allcut Moore's wife, was satisfied that this boy was her nephew?
A   Yes, sir.
Q   Did she recognize him as her relative?
A   Yes, I think she did.
Q   Do you know whether or not John Chips and this Miss Burks were ever married?
A   No, sir, I do not.
Q   Have you ever heard whether they were married.
A   Yes, I have heard they were.
Q   Is John Chips dead?
A   They say he is dead.
Q   Why did he not return from the Choctaw Nation with them?
A   Well, they had him in the pen in Texas and he died?
Q   Was he imprisoned just before he expected to return to the Cherokee Nation and died in prison?
A   Yes, sir.
Q   He never came to the Cherokee Nation at all?
A   No, sir.

CHEROKEE GRANTED ENROLLMENT CARDS
& DAWES PACKETS 1900-1907 VOLUME I

Q	Is this Burks woman who is supposed to have been married to John Chips dead?
A	Yes, sir, she is dead.
Q	How long has she been dead?
A	She has been dead several years.
Q	Did she have any other children besides Adolphus W. Dirtseller?
A	She had one.
Q	Whose child was it?
A	It was said to be Chips.
Q	Both of these children were understood to be the children of John Chips, were they?
A	Yes, sir.
Q	Is the other child to whom you refer dead?
A	Yes, sir, she is dead.
Q	How long has she beed[sic] dead?
A	She has been dead several years; did not live long after they moved here.
Q	Is Adolphus W. Dirtseller a Cherokee by blood?
A	Well, if there is any blood in him at all he is a Cherokee by blood.
Q	Does he have the appearance of a Cherokee?
A	Yes, he does.
Q	Since his removal here in '79, has he lived continuously in the Cherokee Nation?
A	Yes.
Q	Has his right as a citizen by blood ever been disputed?
A	Never until the Dawes Commission disputed it.
Q	Is the Dawes Commission the only body that ever disputed his right?
A	Yes.
Q	Did you once represent Adolphus W. Dirtseller before the Cherokee Council at Tahlequah?
A	Yes, sir, I presented a petition in the Lower House.
Q	Were you at that time a member of the Council of the Cherokee Nation?
A	Yes, sir.
Q	Was there a petition presented before the Council for the admission of Adolphus W. Dirtseller?
A	Yes, sir.
Q	Who presented this petition?
A	Judge Landrum.
Q	When was that petition presented?
A	It was just before the Census Roll was taken in '80.
Q	Was that petition acted upon?
A	It was acted upon in the lower house.
Q	Were you a member of the lower house?
A	Yes, sir.
Q	How was it acted upon?
A	I think it went through.
Q	Do you know why his name does not appear on the 1880 Roll?
A	No, sir.

CHEROKEE GRANTED ENROLLMENT CARDS & DAWES PACKETS 1900-1907 VOLUME I

Q You do not know whether the Senate acted upon his application or not?
A No, I do not.
Q Is Adolphus W. Dirtseller a married man?
A He was not the last time I heard from him.

Adolphus W. Dirtseller is identified on the 1896 Cherokee Census Roll, Delaware District, and is listed for enrollment on Cherokee D number 24.
Dock Rattlehead, from whom testimony was sought to be obtained, is dead.

W. P. Covington, being duly sworn, states that, as stenographer to the Commission to the Five Civilized Tribes, he reported proceedings had in the above and foregoing case on the 18th day of May 1905, and that the above and foregoing is a full and correct transcript of his stenographic notes taken in said case.

W. P. Covington
Subscribed and sworn to before me, this June *13th* 1905.

Fred P Branson
Notary Public.

Cherokee D--24.

DEPARTMENT OF THE INTERIOR,
COMMISSIONER TO THE FIVE CIVILIZED TRIBES.
MUSKOGEE, I. T., NOVEMBER 22, 1905.

SUPPLEMENTAL PROCEEDINGS had in the matter of the application for the enrollment of ADOLPHUS W. DIRTSELLER as a citizen by blood of the Cherokee Nation,

ADOLPHUS W. DIRTSELLER, being first duly sworn, testified as follows:

ON BEHALF OF THE COMMISSIONER:
Q What is your name? A Adolphus W. Dirtseller.
Q How old are you? A 26 years old.
Q What is your post office? A Grove, I. T.
Q Are you a Cherokee by blood? A Yes sir.
Q You are an applicant for enrollment as such? A Yes sir.

CHEROKEE GRANTED ENROLLMENT CARDS
& DAWES PACKETS 1900-1907 VOLUME I

Q Have you ever been enrolled or recognized as a citizen of the Choctaw, Chickasaw, Creek or Seminole Nations? A No sir, haven't got any claim whatever in any other nation.

Q Did you ever draw any money or be recognized in any way as a citizen of either of these nations? A No sir.

Q Your former testimony shows that you were brought to the Cherokee Nation about the year 1879 with your mother? A Yes sir.

Q Where have you made your home since that time? A I have been in Canadian District and Tahlequah District.

Q Have you been at any other place besides the Cherokee Nation?

A Not unly[sic] just a little short time, a month or two, two or three months, four months I believe. That has been since I made my application at Fairland.

Q Was that during this past year? A No, that was before that time.

Q That was since you have applied for enrollment? A Yes sir, I went down in Arkansas and worked four months, and then went back to Grove.

Q Have you ever made your home anywhere else besides the Cherokee Nation?

A No sir.

Q Have you ever held any property in the Cherokee Nation? A You mean land.

Q Yes? A I taken up a claim one time and built a house on it, is all the property I ever had.

Q About how long ago was that? A It has been I reckon, It has been about 7 years ago.

Q What became of that claim? A I sold it out to another man there.

Q How long ago? A It has been about 7 years I think.

Q Since you sold it? A Yes sir, I built the house and in a short time I sold it.

Q Is there any one that you know of whose testimony you could get as to the citizenship of your father during his life time? A No sir, there is not any further than what I have done, put in affidavit from Mr. Cary and John Miller, is the only men that lives in our country that knows anything of him.

Q The testimony shows that your father was sometimes known as John Chips?

A Yes sir.

Q Do you know anything about that? A Nothing more than what I have heard them old people say, that is all I know about it.

Q Is Margaret Rattlehead living? A No sir, she is dead.

Q Is John Moore living? A Yes sir, unless he died since I left home

Q Did he know your father during his lifetime? A Claimed to.

Q Could you secure his testimony in this case, could you get him to testify for you?

A I suppose so. Haven't you got one of his affidavits that he made.

Q Who drew your strip money for you? A William Ballard.

Q Is he a Cherokee by blood? A Yes sir.

Q Did you ever draw any money from the Cherokee Nation besides the 1894 payment? A Yes sir.

Q When? A I drew on every payment that was made only the payment that was made in 1880, the payment that was made in 1880 my mother had never applied for citizenship then and I never got that payment

Q Your mother was a white woman? A Yes sir.

CHEROKEE GRANTED ENROLLMENT CARDS
& DAWES PACKETS 1900-1907 VOLUME I

Q The records of the Cherokee Nation as shown by an affidavit signed by J. T. Parks, Executive Secretary of the Cherokee Nation, fails to show that either you or your mother had been admitted to citizenship in the Cherokee Nation. What is your understanding with reference to the residence in the Cherokee Nation of your father prior to the time he was sent to the penitentiary in Texas? A I couldn't tell you one word about it.
Q Do you desire the Commissioner to render a decision in your case on the testimony already introduced? A Yes sir, that is all I am able to furnish you.
Q You don't know of any other evidence you could get? A No sir, I don't.

The applicant announces that he has no further evidence to introduce, this case will be closed, and a decision rendered upon the evidence heretofore introduced.

--------------------------------oOo-------------------------------

George H. Lessley, being first duly sworn, states that as stenographer to the Commissioner to the Five Civilized Tribes, he reported the proceedings had in the above entitled cause, and that the above and foregoing is a true and correct transcript of his stenographic notes thereof.

George H Lessley

Subscribed and sworn to before me this 27th day of November, 1905.

Myron White
Notary Public.

COPY   Cherokee D 24.

DEPARTMENT OF THE INTERIOR,

COMMISSIONER TO THE FIVE CIVILIZED TRIBES.

In the matter of the application for the enrollment of Adolphus Washington Dirtseller as a citizen by blood of the Cherokee Nation.

DECISION.

THE RECORDS OF THIS OFFICE SHOW: That at Fairland, Indian Territory, on July 12, 1900, Adolphus Washington Dirtseller appeared before the Commission to the Five Civilized Tribes and made application for enrollment as a

CHEROKEE GRANTED ENROLLMENT CARDS & DAWES PACKETS 1900-1907 VOLUME I

citizen by blood of the Cherokee Nation. Further proceedings in the matter of said application were had at Muskogee, Indian Territory, February 14, 1902, at Vinita, Indian Territory, February 12, 1903, at Needmore, Indian Territory, May 18, 1905, and at Muskogee, Indian Territory, November 22, 1905.

THE EVIDENCE IN THIS CASE SHOWS: That Adolphus Washington Dirtseller is a son of one John Fox, a Cherokee by blood, and Missouri A. Fox, a non-citizen white woman; that at the date of the birth of said applicant the said John Fox was temporarily absent from the Cherokee Nation; and that while returning to the Cherokee Nation in 1879 he was arrested in the Chickasaw Nation and sent to the Texas State penitentiary, where he died in 1881.

It is further shown that after the incarceration of the said John Fox in the Texas state penitentiary in 1879 the applicant herein, with his mother, came to the Cherokee Nation, where said applicant has since continuously resided, and is duly identified on the Cherokee Strip payment roll of 1894, and the Cherokee Census roll of 1896.

IT IS, THEREFORE, ORDERED AND ADJUDGED: That. under the provisions of Section Twenty-one of the Act of Congress approved June 28, 1898 (30 Stat., 495), Adolphus Washington Dirtseller is entitled to enrollment as a citizen by blood of the Cherokee Nation, and his application for enrollment as such is accordingly granted.

(SIGNED). *Tams Bixby.*
COMMISSIONER.

Dated at Muskogee, Indian Territory
this_____DEC 28 1905_____

REFER IN REPLY TO THE FOLLOWING
Cherokee
D 24

DEPARTMENT OF THE INTERIOR,
COMMISSION TO THE FIVE CIVILIZED TRIBES.

Muskogee, Indian Territory, December 28, 1905.

W. W. Hastings,
    Attorney for Cherokee Nation,
        Muskogee, Indian Territory.
Dear Sir:
        There is inclosed herewith a copy of the decision of the Commissioner to the Five Civilized Tribes, dated December 28, 1905, granting

the application for the enrollment of Adolphus Washington Dirtseller as a citizen by blood of the Cherokee Nation.

You are advised that you will be allowed fifteen days from date hereof within which to file such protest as you desire to make against the action of the Commissioner in this case. You will be required to serve a copy of any protest made upon the principal applicant, and upon your failure to make such protest, this decision will be considered final.

      Respectfully,

        Tams Bixby Commissioner.

Incl. B-90

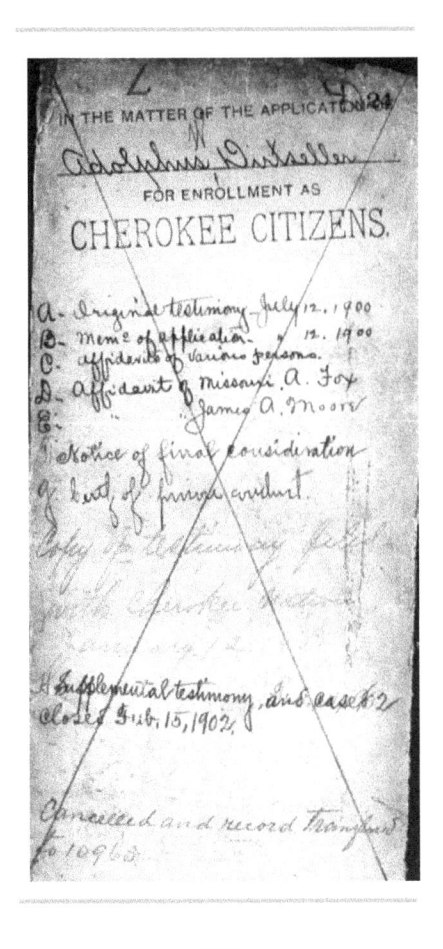

CHEROKEE GRANTED ENROLLMENT CARDS
& DAWES PACKETS 1900-1907 VOLUME I

CHEROKEE GRANTED ENROLLMENT CARDS & DAWES PACKETS 1900-1907 VOLUME I

Cherokee D26 - Charles H. Lasley (Lassley)

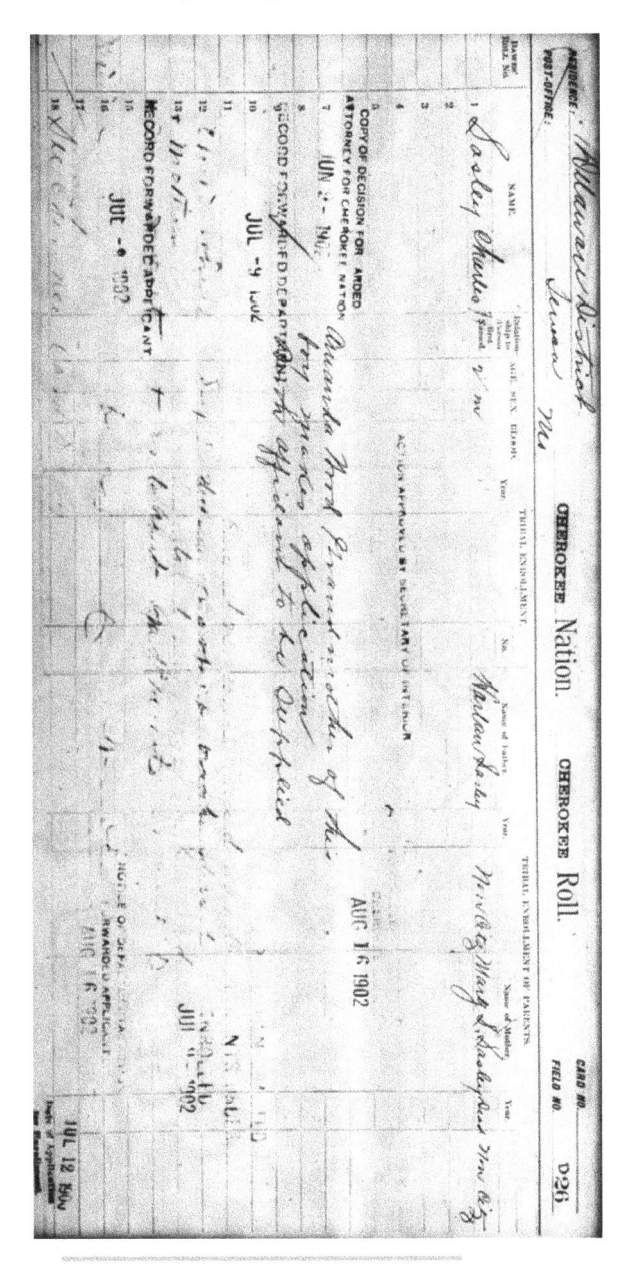

CHEROKEE GRANTED ENROLLMENT CARDS & DAWES PACKETS 1900-1907 VOLUME I

Department of the Interior,
Commission to the Five Civilized Tribes,
Fairland, I. T., July 12, 1900.

In the matter of the application of Charles H. Lassley by his grandmother, Amanda Wood, for enrollment as a citizen of the Cherokee Nation: being sworn and examined by Commissioner Needles she testifies as follows:

Q What is your name? A Amanda Wood.
Q You are the grandmother of Charles H. Lassley? A Yes sir.
Q What was the mother's name of Charles H. Lassley? A Mary L. Boyle before she married Lassley.
Q Does her name appear upon the roll of 1880? A Yes sir.
   Note: 1880 roll examined, Delaware District, page 221, #145, as Mary Boyle, "Adopted white."
Q Is Mary Boyle that is enrolled upon the roll of 1880, is she identified as Mary Lassley? A She never was enrolled under the name of Lassley.
Q I understand, but is the Mary Boyle the mother of this child? A Yes sir.
Q Who did she marry? A Harlin Lassley.
Q What was he, a white man or a Cherokee? A White man.
Q And the mother of this child was a white woman? A Yes sir.
Q Where does this child, Charles H. Lassley, live? A He lives over here in the Wyandotte Nation.
Q Has it ever lived in the Cherokee Nation? A A little while, it was born here.
Q When was it born? A In 1898.
Q Do you know the month in 1898? A June 7th 1898.
Q How long after it was born did it remain in the Cherokee Nation?
A One month.
Q And then was taken to the Wyandotte Nation and has been there ever since?
A Yes sir.
Q Who is it with? A His sister.
Q Is his sister a Cherokee citizen? A No sir.
Q She is a white woman? A Yes sir.

Attorney Hutchings submits law as follows: Section 666.

Applicant: The child's mother died July 22, 1898.
Q Were you present when the child was born? A No sir.
Q Is there anybody living who was there? A Yes sir.

Com'r Needles: The Cherokee Nation, by its representatives, pleading the act of the Cherokee Legislature in regard to citizens marrying white persons, it is the opinion of the Commission that this child, Charles H. Lassley should be placed on what is known as a doubtful card for the consideration of the Commission when the final rolls are made up. The grandmother of this child, or any other person having it in custody or interested in its enrollment can offer in the future any documentary evidence or oral testimony they desire, or can appear before the Commission as its

CHEROKEE GRANTED ENROLLMENT CARDS & DAWES PACKETS 1900-1907 VOLUME I

principal offices in Muskogee at any time in its behalf. The record in regard to the admission of Charles H. Lassley will be forwarded to the Secretary of the Interior. It will be necessary to furnish a certificate of the child's birth, its mother being dead, an affidavit signed by the attending physician or by some one who was present attending at its birth. Blank of this kind will be furnished you to transmit to the Commission.

M.D. Green, being first duly sworn, states that as stenographer to the Commission to the Five Civilized Tribes he reported the foregoing case, and that the above and foregoing is a full, true and complete transcript of his stenographic notes in said case.

M D Green

Subscribed and sworn to before me this 13th day of July 1900.

T B Needles
Commissioner.

File with D card #26.

DEPARTMENT OF THE INTERIOR,
COMMISSION TO THE FIVE CIVILIZED TRIBES,
VINITA, I.T. SEPT. 22, 1900.

Alexander East being sworn by Commissioner Needles, testified as follows:

Q What is your name? A Alexander East.
Q How old are you? A 38.
Q What is your postoffice address? A Senaca[sic], Mo.
Q What district do you live in? A Eastern Shawnee Reservation.
Q Are you a Shawnee? A No sir.
Q Are you a recognized citizen of the Cherokee Nation? A No sir.
Q For whom do you apply? A My child.
Q What is the child's name? A Charles H. Lasley.
Q How old is it? A 2 7 years old
Q What is its mother's name? A Mary L. Boyles.
Q Is she living? A No sir.
Q What is the father's name? A Lasley.
Q What is his first name? A Harland.
Q Where is the father of this child? A He is not in this country.
Q Is the mother of this child dead? A Yes.
    Mother of the child on '80 roll, page 221, number 145, as Mary Boyle.
Q Is she a white woman? A Yes.
Q You know of your own knowledge that this child is her daughter[sic]? A Yes.
Q Have you any proof of its birth? A Yes.

233

CHEROKEE GRANTED ENROLLMENT CARDS & DAWES PACKETS 1900-1907 VOLUME I

Q You so not know where the father is living? A No sir.
Q Is he a native by blood? A No sir, white man.
Q Where is this child living? A With me on the Eastern Shawnee Reservation.
Q Where was it born? A Here in the Cherokee Nation. I have had the child since he was three weeks old.

By W. W. Hastings, Cherokee Attorney:
Q You say its mother's name is Mary L. Lasley? A Yes.
Q Whose maiden name was Mary Boyles--- she is a white woman? A Yes, I suppose so.
Q What is the name of the father of this child? A Harland Lasley.
Q White man? A Yes.
Q Were they ever married? A Yes.
Q Do you know what year she married Harland Lasley? Applicant presents marriage license issued by the Clerk of the United States Court, Indian Territory, certifying that the mother of the child he is applying for, named Mary Boyles, was married to one Harland Lasley. according to the laws of the United States on the 18th day of January, 1896.

The undersigned, being first duly sworn, states that as stenographer to the Commission to the Five Civilized Tribes, he correctly recorded the testimony and proceedings in this case, and that the foregoing is a true and complete transcript of his stenographic notes thereof.

J B McDonald

Subscribed and sworn to before me this 28th day of Sept. 1900.

T B Needles
Commissioner.

Supl.-C.D.#26.

Department of the Interior,
Commission to the Five Civilized Tribes,
Muskogee, I. T., February 15, 1902.

SUPPLEMENTAL in the matter of the enrollment of Charles Lasley as a citizen of the Cherokee Nation:

On the 30th of January, 1902, Mrs. Amanda Wood, the grandmother of Charles Lasley and who made the application for the enrollment of this child, was notified by registed[sic] letter that this Commission would take up this case on the 15th day of February, 1902, for final consideration, and that she would on said date be given an opportunity to introduce such additional testimony as she deemed necessary affecting this case. She has been called three times and fails to respond either in person or by attorney and the case is closed.

T B Needles
Commissioner.

Cherokee D. 26

DEPARTMENT OF THE INTERIOR,
COMMISSION TO THE FIVE CIVILIZED TRIBES.

In the matter of the application of Charles H. Lasley for enrollment as a Cherokee citizen.

Supplemental Statement.

----oOo----

An affidavit of birth duly executed on the 20th day of December, 1900, was received by this Commission on the 18th day of January, 1901, from which it appears that Charley H. Lasley was born to Mary L. and Harlin Lasley on the seventh day of June, 1898, and was living at the date of the execution of said affidavit. The same has been approved and filed with this Commission.

An examination of the authenticated tribal roll of 1880 shows the name of Mary L. Boyle thereon as an "adopted white" two years old.

It is directed that copies of this statement be filed with the testimony in the above case.

T B Needles
Commissioner.

Dated at Muskogee, Indian Territory
this fifth day of March, 1902.

CHEROKEE GRANTED ENROLLMENT CARDS & DAWES PACKETS 1900-1907 VOLUME I

Cherokee D 26

DEPARTMENT OF THE INTERIOR,
COMMISSION TO THE FIVE CIVILIZED TRIBES.

In the matter of the application of Charles H. Lasley, for enrollment as a Cherokee citizen.

On the 12th day of July, 1900, Amanda Wood appeared before the Commission to the Five Civilized Tribes, and made application for the enrollment of her grand-son Charles H. Lasley, as a citizen by blood of the Cherokee Nation.

At the conclusion of the evidence offered at that time the name of Charles H. Lasley was placed upon a "Doubtful" card pending proof of his citizenship.

On the 22nd day of September, 1900, Alexander East appeared before the Commission and mad application for the enrollment of this child.

Upon a consideration of all the evidence the following decision is rendered.

D E C I S I O N.

The evidence in this case shows that Charles H. Lasley was born on the seventh day of June, 1898, to Mary L. Lasley and Harlin Lasley a white man, to [sic] she was married on the 18th day of January, 1896. Mary L. Lasley is identified on the authenticated tribal roll of 1880 under the name of Mary L. Boyle as an "adopted white", two years old. The evidence shows that Mary L. Boyle is the daughter of Amanda Wood and the records of this Commission show that Amanda Wood under the name of Amanda Boyle is identified on a certain register known as the "Shawnee Register" containing the names of those who located in the Cherokee Nation under the terms of a treaty concluded between the Cherokee Nation and the Shawnee Tribe of Indians on June 7, 1869, and approved by the President of the United States June 9, 1869. Amanda Wood is also identified on the authenticated tribal roll of 1880.

Mary L. Boyle died in July, 1898, and was therefore twenty years old and was living in the Cherokee Nation at the time of her decease. Her husband Harlin [sic] Lasley appears to have left the country and is not now living in the Cherokee Nation. Charles H. Lasley is, or course, too young to be upon any roll, but the evidence shows that he was living at the date of this application and was residing with Alexander East in the Eastern Shawnee reservation.

Charles H. Lasley, being the descendant of a person whose name appears upon the authenticated tribal roll of 1880, is considered to be entitled to enrollment as a citizen by blood of the Cherokee Nation under the provisions of paragraph 1, section 21, of the Act of Congress approved June 28, 1898 (30 Stats. 495), and it is therefore so ordered.

Tams Bixby
T B Needles
C. R. Breckinridge
Commissioners.

Dates at Muskogee, Indian Territory,
JUN 9- 1902

DEPARTMENT OF THE INTERIOR,
Commission to the Five Civilized Tribes,
Muskogee, I. T. June 13th 1902.

In the matter of the application of Charles H. Lasley for enrollment as a citizen of the Cherokee Nation.
Cherokee D 25.

Protest of the Cherokee Nation?

The Cherokee Nation desires to respectfully disagree with the decision of the Commission rendered in this case on June 9th 1902 and asks that the same be forwarded to the Honorable Secretary of the Interior for review.

The testimony in this case shows that Charles H. Lasley was born June 7th 1898 and that he is at present living in the Wyandotte country, that both his father and mother were white persons, neither of them having a drop of Indian blood. His father is now living some where in the states and never claimed citizenship in the Cherokee Nation.

CHEROKEE GRANTED ENROLLMENT CARDS & DAWES PACKETS 1900-1907 VOLUME I

An examination of the authenticated roll of Eighteen Hundred and Eighty shows that the mother of the applicant was enrolled upon that roll as an "Adopted White." Her status was determined by the act authenticating the roll of Eighteen Hundred and Eighty; the grandmother of the child admits that its parents were white persons; Alexander East testifies that both were where white persons which shows that the determination of the National Council as to the status of the mother of the applicant in Eighteen Hundred and Eighty was correct. Since that time, in 1896, the mother of the applicant married Harland Lasley a white man, and the Cherokee Nation contends that the mother of the applicant forfeited her right to be enrolled as a citizen of the Cherokee Nation under section 656 of the compiled laws of the Cherokee Nation. You will notice that the applicants[sic] parents were married on the 18th day of January 1895, and the Cherokee 1896 census roll was made subsequent to that time and the name of the applicants[sic] mother does not appear thereon which we cite in support of our contention that the Cherokee Nation had adjudged that the mother of the applicant had forfeited her right to be enrolled as a citizen of the Cherokee Nation by violating Section 666 of the Compiled Laws of the Cherokee Nation.

It was never contemplated or dreamed of by the Cherokee people that the issue of purely white people should be enrolled as citizens of the Cherokee Nation. Throughout all of their legislation they have attempted most jealously to guard against this contingency. Read section 666 and it provided a forfeiture of citizenship where an adopted citizen marries one other than one having rights of citizenship by blood. Here it is confessed that the parents of the applicant are both white and yet the decision of the Commission in the third line from the bottom says that the applicant is "Entitled to enrollment as a citizen by blood of the Cherokee Nation."

It is confessed that this child has not a drop of any kind of Indian blood coursing through its veins yet the Commission comes to the conclusion that this child is a "citizen by blood."

We can not believe that the Honorable Secretary of the Interior will sustain this position. We earnestly contend that Congress intended to confirm the roll of Eighteen Hundred and Eighty, that it made that roll a basis for making this roll; that the status of the names of the persons contained on that roll as fixed and determined by the roll itself and if the Commission takes into consideration that roll and the status of the mother is found on said roll it would seem to us that it must find that the mother lost her citizenship by her marriage with the applicants[sic] father.

Can a white person have any descendible rights, and if the Honorable Secretary of the Interior finds that applicants[sic] mother did not forfeit her right to citizenship in the Cherokee Nation but that she was an adopted citizen certainly the Honorable Secretary of the Interior can not go further than this, and he can not find that the mother as an adopted white could transmit any rights to her child in as much as the father of the child is also a white man. Our contention that this child is not entitled is supported further by the testimony of the grand mother, Amanda Wood who testified that the child was in the Wyandott Nation with his sister and when asked the question, "Is his sister a Cherokee Citizen?" She answered, "No sir.".[sic] Now here is a sister of the applicant living in the Wyandott Country who does not claim to be a citizen of the Cherokee Nation but is a white person; admittedly so; yet the Commission renders a decision admitting the applicant to citizenship in the Cherokee Nation.

But there is another serious question which presents itself for consideration in this case and that is the one of residence. The testimony shows that this child was born on the 7th day of June 1898 and Alexander East testified that he had had the child since it was three weeks old and that it was living in the Wyandott country and not in the Cherokee Nation hence it would seem that on June 28th 1898 that it was not a resident of the Cherokee Nation.

Furthermore, the testimony discloses that the father of this child was a white man and a non citizen and is a resident of some of the outside states; he never acquired citizenship in the Cherokee Nation and having been born a citizen of the United States he must of necessity retained that citizenship; it was not changed, and it is an elementary principle of law that the residence of the child follows that of the father and if the father was a non resident of the Indian Territory on June 28, 1898 the residence of the child being that of the father, the child was a non-resident.

How are you going to classify this child? You can not call it an "Adopted White?" It is not a Cherokee neither is it a Delaware, Shawnee or freedman?

We submit in all sincerety[sic] that we do not believe that the applicant is entitled to be enrolled as a citizen of the Cherokee Nation under the law.

CHEROKEE GRANTED ENROLLMENT CARDS
& DAWES PACKETS 1900-1907 VOLUME I

Respectfully submitted,

W. W. Hastings

J. C. S. Attorney for the Cherokee Nation.

COMMISSIONERS:

HENRY L. DAWES,
TAMS BIXBY,
THOMAS B. NEEDLES,
C. R. BRECKINRIDGE.

ALLISON L. AYLESWORTH,
SECRETARY.

ADDRESS ONLY THE
COMMISSION TO THE FIVE CIVILIZED TRIBES.

DEPARTMENT OF THE INTERIOR,
COMMISSION TO THE FIVE CIVILIZED TRIBES.

REFER IN REPLY TO THE FOLLOWING

Cher. D-26.

Muskogee, Indian Territory, June 9, 1902.

W. W. Hastings, Esq.,

Attorney for the Cherokee Nation,

Muskogee, Indian Territory.

Sir:

Enclosed herewith please find copy of the decision of the Commission rendered June 9, 1902, in the matter of the application of Charles H. Lasley for enrollment as a citizen of the Cherokee Nation.

You are hereby advised that you will be allowed fifteen days from the date hereof in which to file with the Commission such protest as you desire to make against the enrollment of the person above named as a citizen of the Cherokee Nation. If you fail to file the protest within the time allowed this applicant will be regularly listed for enrollment.

Yours truly,

Tams Bixby

Acting Chairman.[ALA]

Encl. D-26.

CHEROKEE GRANTED ENROLLMENT CARDS
& DAWES PACKETS 1900-1907 VOLUME I

COMMISSIONERS:
HENRY L. DAWES,
TAMS BIXBY,
THOMAS B. NEEDLES,
C. R. BRECKINRIDGE.

DEPARTMENT OF THE INTERIOR.
COMMISSION TO THE FIVE CIVILIZED TRIBES.

REFER IN REPLY TO THE FOLLOWING
Cherokee D-26.

ALLISON L. AYLESWORTH,
SECRETARY.
ADDRESS ONLY THE
COMMISSION TO THE FIVE CIVILIZED TRIBES.

Muskogee, Indian Territory, July 9, 1902.

Mr. W. W. Hastings,
    Attorney for Cherokee Nation,
        Muskogee, Indian Territory.

Sir:

    You are hereby advised that the decision of the Commission to the Five Civilized Tribes, granting the application of Amanda Wood for the enrollment of her grand-child, Charles H. Lasley, as a citizen by blood of the Cherokee Nation, copy of which decision was furnished you on June 9, 1902, has this day been transmitted to the Secretary of the Interior for his review and decision.

    The action of the Secretary will be made known to you as soon as the Commission is informed of same.

        Respectfully,

            Tams Bixby
            Acting Chairman.

COMMISSIONERS:
HENRY L. DAWES,
TAMS BIXBY,
THOMAS B. NEEDLES,
C. R. BRECKINRIDGE.

DEPARTMENT OF THE INTERIOR.
COMMISSION TO THE FIVE CIVILIZED TRIBES.

REFER IN REPLY TO THE FOLLOWING
Cherokee D 26.

ALLISON L. AYLESWORTH,
SECRETARY.
ADDRESS ONLY THE
COMMISSION TO THE FIVE CIVILIZED TRIBES.

Muskogee, Indian Territory, August 16, 1902.

W. W. Hastings, Esq.,
    Attorney for the Cherokee Nation,
        Muskogee, Indian Territory.

Sir:

CHEROKEE GRANTED ENROLLMENT CARDS
& DAWES PACKETS 1900-1907 VOLUME I

You are hereby advised that the decision of the Commission to the Five Civilized Tribes, of date July 9, 1902, granting the application of Charles H. Lasley for the enrollment of himself as a citizen of the Cherokee Nation, was affirmed by the Secretary of the Interior on July 31, 1902.

Very respectfully,

Tams Bixby
Acting Chairman.

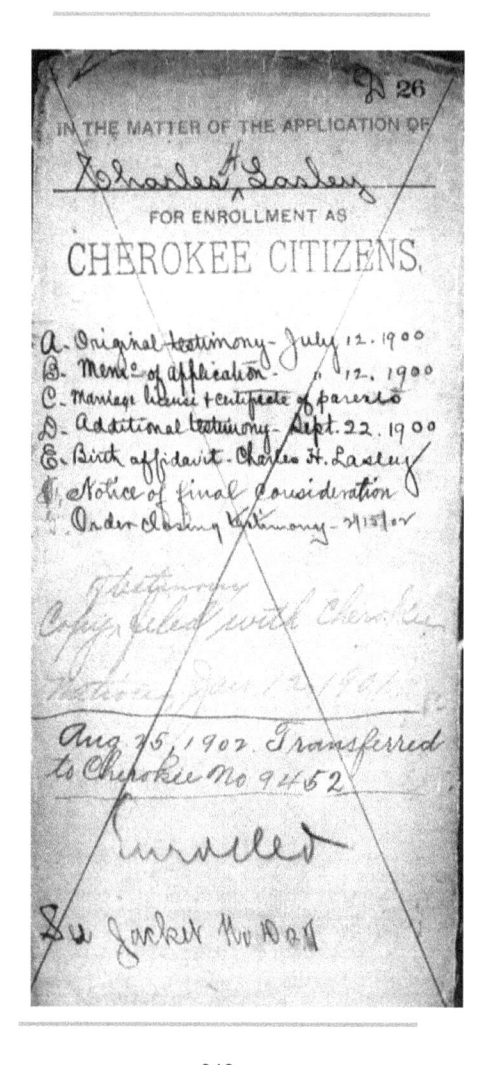

CHEROKEE GRANTED ENROLLMENT CARDS
& DAWES PACKETS 1900-1907 VOLUME I

CHEROKEE GRANTED ENROLLMENT CARDS & DAWES PACKETS 1900-1907 VOLUME I

Cherokee D29 - Lucretia G. Hunter

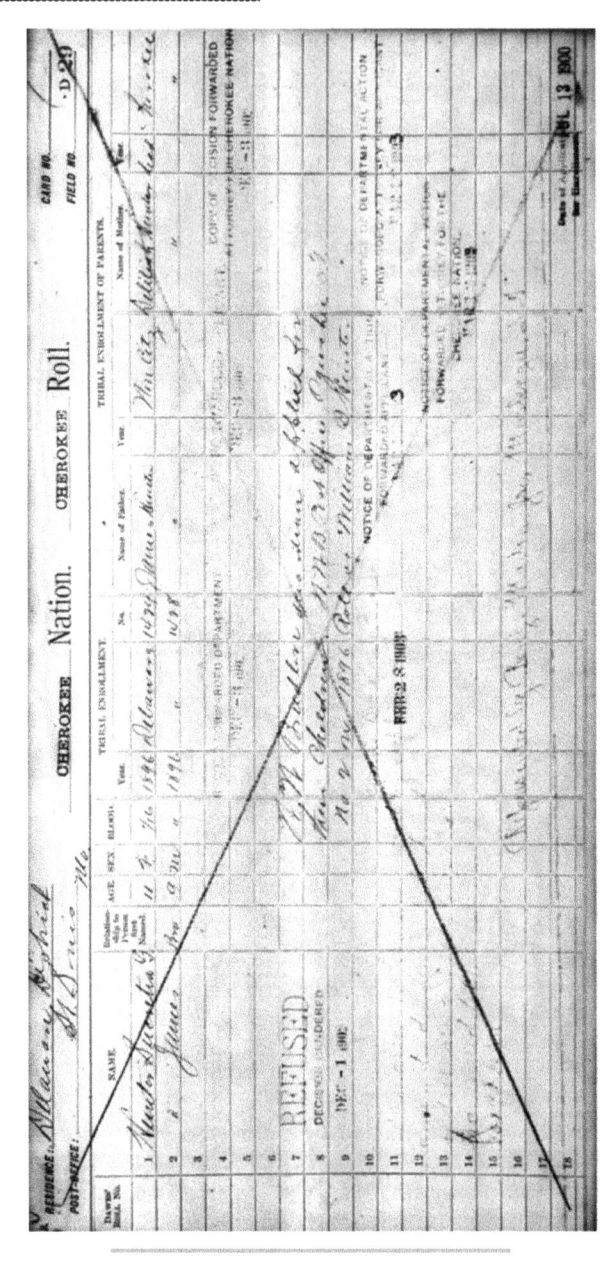

CHEROKEE GRANTED ENROLLMENT CARDS & DAWES PACKETS 1900-1907 VOLUME I

Department of the Interior,
Commission to the Five Civilized Tribes,
Fairland, I.T., July 13, 1900.

In the matter of the application for the enrollment of Lucretia and James Hunter, made by their guardian, Waller W. Breedlove; Waller W. Breedlove, being duly sworn, and examined by Commissioner Breckenridge[sic], testified as follows:

Q What is your name? A Waller W. Breedlove.
Q What is your age? A I am 39 years old.
Q What is your post office address? A Ogeechee.
Q What district? A Delaware.
Q You say you want to apply for some children for whom you are guardian? A Yes, sir.
Q What are their names? A Lucretia and James Wilson.
Q What is Lucretia's age? A She is about 11 years old.
Q What is the age of James? A He is 9 years old.
Q Are these children Cherokees by blood? A Yes, sir.
Q What was the name of their father? A He was a white man.
Q They claim through their mother? A Yes, sir; I made a mistake, their mother's name was Wilson, their name is Hunter.
Q They both claim through their mother? A Yes, sir.
Q What was her name in 1880? A Delilah Wilson; you will find her on the roll, in Going Snake district.
Q When did she die? A I can't say when she did die; they are Jim Hunter's children.
Q Has she beed[sic] dead five or six years? A She has been dead 8 years I reckon.
(On 1880 roll, page 490, No. 1991, Going Snake District, Delilah Wilson.)
Q They were married after 1880? A Yes, sir.
Q When did the father of these children did[sic]? A He is living, as far as I know, in the State of Louisiana.
Q Is he on the roll of 1896? A I can't say whether he is or not; I understand he has been married since in Louisiana; James Hunter his name was.
(The name of James Hunter is not found on the roll of 1896.[sic]
Q Are these children living with you? A No, sir, they are living with an aunt in St. Louis; they were living with their grandmother.
Q Are you their guardian? A Yes, sir.
Q Have you any evidence of guardianship? A I have them at home, I haven't them with me.
Mr. W. T. Hutchings, attorney for Cherokee Nation: Where have they lived since their mother's death? A In St. Louis with their grandmother.
Q Where were they born? A In Cooweescoowee district; their old home was in Going Snake district; I think the youngest was born in Going Snake district. I tried to get the children and their grandmother wouldn't give them up at all.

CHEROKEE GRANTED ENROLLMENT CARDS & DAWES PACKETS 1900-1907 VOLUME I

Q I understand you to say the children are in St. Louis being cared for by their grandmother? A No, sir, they are not now, their grandmother is dead; they are with their aunt now.

Q Do you apply for them simply as a relation, or as a legal guardian?
A As legal guardian.

Q Did you have papers of guardianship? A Yes, sir, I have papers.

Q Is that known by anybody present here? A No, sir, I don't believe anybody can tell here; Judge John Wolff was the man issued the papers.

Q You say that these children were both born in this country?
A Yes, sir, I am pretty sure they were. One of them was born on Prior Creek and I have been told that the woman was over at the old place where she had formerly lived with Bird Wilson when the oldest child was born.

Joel L. Baugh, being duly sworn, and examined by Commissioner Breckenridge[sic], testified as follows:

Q What is your name? A Joel L. Baugh.
Q What is your post office address? A Choteau.
Q What district? A Cooweescoowee.
Q What is your business? A I am a farmer and stock raiser.
Q What do you know about these two children that Mr. Breedlove has applied for here as orphan children? A I knew Mr. Hunter and his wife when they lived on Prior Creek, only 8 miles above me; Mrs. Hunter gave birth to the oldest child while she lived at Prior Creek.
Q Do you know anything about the birth of the younger child?
A No, sir.
Q How long did they live there after the birth of the older child? A I suppose a year or more.
Q And then where did they live? A The went over to what is called the Verdigri[sic] west of there.
Q How long did they live there? A About a year.
Q And then what did they do? A I don't know where they went to from there, that is as far as I know anything about them.

Waller W. Breedlove, recalled:

Q Is there anybody here, Mr. Breedlove, who knows anything about them when they lived over about the Verdigri river? A No, sir, I don't suppose there is.
Q Do you know what became of them after they lived over there?
A No, sir, I do not, I never met Hunter, but it is my understanding that while they were there on the Verdigri river she went back to the old place with Bird Wilson, where he lived, and that she was confined there, and I think she died there either at confinement or right shortly after; I think he kinder[sic] took the child and raised it.
Q Did she die here in the Indian Territory? A Yes, sir, I think she died here in the Indian Territory, I am not sure of it.
Q Do you know whether she ever moved out of the Cherokee Nation prior to her death? A I don't think she ever moved out at all.
Q You think she died in this country? A I am pretty sure she died in the Going Snake district.

CHEROKEE GRANTED ENROLLMENT CARDS
& DAWES PACKETS 1900-1907 VOLUME I

Hutchinson M. Robertson, being duly sworn and examined by Commissioner Breckenridge[sic], testified as follows:

Q What is your name? A Hutchinson M. Robertson.
Q How old are you? A 43 I guess.
Q What is your post office address? A Echo.
Q What is your district? A Delaware
Q What is your business? A Farmer.

Q Mr. Robertson, do you know anything about two children, Lucretia and James Hunter, that are orphans, for whom Mr. Breedlove is now applying for enrollment? A Yes, sir.

Q Did you know their father and their mother? A Yes, sir, I knew them both.

Q Please tell us just what you know about Mr. and Mrs. Hunter living in the Territory at the time of the birth of these children. A One of the children was born about 12 miles from where I live on Spring Creek, the older one, and the other one, I don't know this to be a fact, but I lived there and was at the house, and they moved on Prior Creek and then they moved on Verdigri[sic], and Mrs. Hunter died on Verdigri.

Q How far did they live from you? A They lived, it must have been about 30 miles, I expect, the last time.

Q How long did you know them prior to her death? A I knew here always nearly, I was raised with her.

Q Do you remember when she married Mr. Hunter? A It must have been in 1885, sometime along there.

Q Do you know whether they made their home continuously in the Territory up to the time of her death? A She did, yes, sir; I was at her house a few days after she died, on the Verdigri.

Q And that was her home at that time? A Yes, sir.

Q How long before that do you know they had continued to make the Cherokee Nation their home? A He came to my house and stopped there often, and she made it her home all the time I reckon.

Q During who[sic] long a time? A It must have been about 1886 or 1887 or 1888.

Q Did you know her in her childhood? A Yes, sir, I knew her.
Q You knew her before her marriage? A Yes, sir.
Q And you knew her at the time of her death? A Yes, sir.
Q Did you never know her to live outside of the Cherokee Nation? A No, sir, I never did.

Q Did you ever have any reason to think that she lived out of the Territory? A No, sir.

Q You knew her before her marriage? A Yes, sir.
Q Did you know her off and on all the time after her marriage down to her death? A Yes, sir.
Q Did you ever hear of her living outside of the Territory? A I never did.
Q Do you know where the[sic] lived during the whole time from her marriage to her death? A She married on Spring Creek and moved to Prior Creek.
Q How long did she live on Spring Creek? A She was raised there, she lived on Prior Creek and Verdigri[sic] is all I know after she married.
Q How many years after she married? A About five years after her marriage.

247

CHEROKEE GRANTED ENROLLMENT CARDS & DAWES PACKETS 1900-1907 VOLUME I

Q You saw her off and on during that time? A Yes, sir, she stopped at my house during the whole period of her marriage, on the way to visit her father and mother.

Q And you always understood her to live in the Nation? A Yes, sir.

Waller W. Breedlove, recalled, testified as follows:

Q Mr. Breedlove, is there anyone else here that you think knew this woman during her married life? A No, sir, I know of no one here at all that knew of her, unless it is Mr. Woodall, he use to stop with Bird Wilson's folks.

(1896 roll, page 480, No. 1429 and 1428, Delaware district, the names of Lucretia G. Hunter, and William B. Hunter, aged 10.)

Q You say Mr. Breedlove that Lucretia is the older of the two? A Yes, sir, that is what I think.

Q Then you must have been mistaken in the age of these children?

A Well, I must have been, I got the age from that record. He was named down there after a grandfather and an uncle, and they carried him to St. Louis and they changed the name of the child and called him James all the time. The named him William B. when he was first born, and when the grandmother took him away from this country they changed him and named him after his father, James, and I don't know whether they knocked the B. off or left it on; he goes now by the name of James.

This applicant which you make for these two children will be placed upon a doubtful card, and will be considered further by the Commission, and the decision that is arrived at will be communicated to you by mail. And further evidence which you wish to submit, you can forward to the Commission at Muskogee, and it will be taken into consideration, and its final decision will be forwarded to the Secretary of the Interior for his approval or disapproval.

--------------o--------------

Bruce C. Jones, being duly sworn, says that as stenographer to the Commission to the Five Civilized Tribes he reported the testimony of the above named witnesses, and that the foregoing is a full, true and correct translation of his stenographic notes.

Bruce C. Jones

Sworn to and subscribed before me this the 16th day of July, 1900.

Clifton R. Breckinridge
Commissioner.

CHEROKEE GRANTED ENROLLMENT CARDS & DAWES PACKETS 1900-1907 VOLUME I

"R"

Cherokee D 29.

                Department of the Interior,
             Commission to the Five Civilized Tribes,
                Muskogee, I. T, February 15, 1902.

    SUPPLEMENTAL TESTIMONY AND PROCEEDINGS, in the matter of the application of Lucretia G. Hunter, and James Hunter for enrollment as Cherokee citizens.

        Appearance:
                Benjamin Martin, Muskogee, I.T., Attorney for appl'ts;
                W.W. Hastings, attorney for the Cherokee Nation.

    N.B. MAXEY, being sworn and examined, testified as follows:

    BY MR. MARTIN:

Q What is your name? A My name is N. B. Maxey, I reside at Muskogee, I have resided here for about thirteen years, and I have been engaged in the practice of law during that time.

Q Just go ahead and tell what you know about this matter?

A I am not personally acquainted with the applicants; I only know them in a business way. My first acquaintance with them was through the Mississippi Valley Trust Company, of Saint Louis, which is the curator for these children, appointed by the Probate Court in Saint Louis. There was some money due them. My recollection is it was what was known as the "Old Settler" fund. The Mississippi Valley Trust Company sent me a certified copy of their letters as curator, and a certified copy of the bond, and I filed same with Colonel D. M. Wisdom, who was then Indian Agent, and he paid the Strip money, not the Strip money, the Old Settler money due them to the Mississippi Valley Trust Company. I afterwards brought suit for the Mississippi Valley Trust Company against W. W. Breedlove, in the United States Court at Vinita, to require him as their guardian appointed by the Cherokee authorities, to account for the Strip money. Mr. Breedlove answered in that case, stating-

    BY MR. HASTINGS: I am going to object to that, because the answer would show. I can't see that it's relative.

    BY MR. MARTIN: Mr. Breedlove was notified by the Commission to be here to-day. He has been acting as guardian of these children in the Indian Territory. We ask that we may file a certified copy of the pleadings in the case to which Mr. Maxey refers as evidence in this case; this is the case that is pending on the docket at Vinita, and I can have the clerk at Vinita make up a certified copy of the pleadings and file with the Commission.

    BY MR. HASTINGS: Representatives of the Cherokee Nation object to this evidence, for the reason that it is over the Strip money which belongs to these children, and if that be true their names will appear on the roll o 1894, and those rolls are in the possession of the Commission, and I cannot see that the pleadings and answer in the case over this money would be relative in this case.

BY COMMISSION: This roll will show by show by whom this money was drawn and we can introduce that now. Upon an examination of the Cherokee Strip payment roll, it is found that the name of Lucretia Hunter and Willie Hunter appear upon the Cooweescoowee District roll on page 221, No. 2300 and 2301, respectively; that the sum of $532.40 was paid to W.W. Breedlove, Guardian. The payment was witnesses by J.C. Starr.

BY WITNESS, N.B. MAXEY: I will state that in the investigation in regard to the Old Settler money we found that Willie Hunter and James Hunter was the same person. The mistake occurred by Mr. Breedlove making application for the wrong name, for Willie instead of James.

BY MR. MARTIN:

Q State what you know about these children owning property in the Cherokee Nation.

BY MR. HASTINGS: Do you know this personally or otherwise?

A I only know it through the records of Mr. Breedlove as Guardian, to the Court.

BY MR. HASTINGS: Then I object to your making any statement with reference to it.

BY MR. MARTIN: We think that that would be competent.

BY COMMISSION: Mr. Maxey will be permitted to make the statement; it will be considered for what it is worth.

Answer of witness: Mr. Breedlove reported that he invested the money received for these children known as the "Strip money", in lands in the Cherokee Nation, near Afton, or Fairland, I think it is in between the two, and accounted for the rents off of the land so purchased.

BY MR. HASTINGS: Comes now the representative of the Cherokee Nation and moves to strike out the last part of this testimony, because the records are on file and would show this matter, and that this is not competent testimony.

BY COMMISSION; Objection of the Representative of the Cherokee Nation will be entered.

BY MR. MARTIN:

Q Do you know whether or not he still holds those lands that he purchased with that money as guardian of those children? A Yes sir, he did a short time ago.

These children are in Saint Louis with their aunt. Their father left them with their grandmother when their mother died, and after their grandmother died an aunt has had charge of them. Their father was somewhere in Louisiana last I heard of him. Never paid any attention to the children. That is the only place they have had for a home since their mother's death.

BY COMMISSION:

Q That is in Saint Louis? A Yes sir.

BY MR. HASTINGS:

Q You know about when their mother died? A It was in about 1891, or '2, is my recollection; died when James was born.

Q When the youngest one was born? A Yes sir.

BY MR. MARTIN: I request that as attorney for the applicants I have an opportunity to append certified copies of the proceedings in the case to which reference has been made and as to the acts of Walter W. Breedlove, as guardian of the applicants, and that I be permitted to file the same as a part of the evidence in support of the application herein.

BY COMMISSION: This case is continued by agreement of the attorney for the Nation and the attorney for the applicants, until Wednesday, February 26, at which time the attorney for the applicants will be required to file with the Commission a brief, also a copy of said brief with the Representatives of the Cherokee Nation. Applicant's attorney requests subpoena for Walter W. Breedlove to appear on the 26th of February, which is granted.

M.D. Green, being first duly sworn, states that as stenographer to the Commission to the Five Civilized Tribes he correctly recorded the testimony and proceedings in this case and that the foregoing is a true and complete transcript of his stenographic notes thereof.

MD Green

Subscribed and sworn to before me this February 18, 1902.

T B Needles

Commissioner.

Supl.-C.D.#29.

Department of the Interior,
Commission to the Five Civilized Tribes,
Muskogee, I. T., February 26, 1902.

SUPPLEMENTAL PROCEEDINGS in the matter of the enrollment of LUCRETIA G. HUNTER, ET AL., as citizens of the Cherokee Nation:

Appearances:
    Benjamin Martin, Muskogee, I.T., Attorney for applicant
    Mr. W. W. Hastings, Cherokee representative.

Commission: This case was originally set for final consideration on the 15th day of February, 1902, and by agreement between the attorney for the applicant and representative of the Cherokee Nation present the same was continued until the 26th day of February, 1902, for the purpose of giving the attorney for the applicant an opportunity to introduce further testimony in the matter of said application.

CHEROKEE GRANTED ENROLLMENT CARDS
& DAWES PACKETS 1900-1907 VOLUME I

Mr. Martin: Afforney[sic] for applicants makes return of a subpoena which was issued by the Commission on February 15, 1902, to Walter W. Breedlove, and asks that this subpoena be considered by the Commission for the reason that Walter W. Breedlove fails to appear in obedience thereto.

Also the applicants by their attorney offer in evidence a certified copy of the answer of Walter W. Breedlove in the United States Court for the Northern District Indian Territory, at Vinita, in the matter of his guardianship of said minors.

Commission: By agreement between the attorney for the applicant and representative of the Cherokee Nation present this case will be continued until the 19th day of March, 1902, for the purpose of giving the attorney for the applicant an opportunity to introduce the testimony of Walter W. Breedlove.

---oooOOOooo---

J. O. Rosson, being first duly sworn, states that as stenographer to the Commission to the Five Civilized Tribes, he correctly recorded the testimony and proceedings in this case, and that the foregoing is a true and complete transcript of his stenographic notes thereof.

JO Rosson

Subscribed and sworn to before me this March 1, 1902.

T B Needles

Commissioner.

"R"

Cherokee D 29.

Department of the Interior,
Commission to the Five Civilized Tribes,
Muskogee, I. T., March 3, 1902.

SUPPLEMENTAL TESTIMONY AND PROCEEDINGS in the matter of the application of Lucretia G. Hunter for the enrollment of herself and brother as Cherokee citizens.

Appearances:
Benjamin Martin, Jr., Muskogee, I. T., attorney for the applicants;
W. W. Hastings, attorney for the Cherokee Nation,

BY COMMISSION: The applicant's Guardian, Walter W. Breedlove, was notified by registered letter January 30, 1902, that the case of Lucretia G. Hunter for the enrollment of herself and brother as citizens of the Cherokee

CHEROKEE GRANTED ENROLLMENT CARDS & DAWES PACKETS 1900-1907 VOLUME I

Nation would be taken up for final consideration by the Commission on the 15th day of February, 1902. On said day the applicant appeared before the Commission by their attorney, Benjamin Martin, Jr., Muskogee, I. Y[sic]., and introduced further testimony as regards said application. By agreement between the attorney for the Cherokee Nation and the attorney for the applicant, this case was continued until the 26th day of February, 1902, in order that the attorney for the applicants might introduce testimony of Walter W. Breedlove. Subpoena was issued for said Walter W. Breedlove, and he failed to appear on said day, the 26th day of February, 1902; the applicants appeared by their attorney, and by agreement with the representative of the Cherokee Nation the case was again continued. The applicants this day, to-wit: the 3rd day of March, 1902, appear by their attorney and the case is taken up for consideration.

WALTER W. BREEDLOVE, being first duly sworn and being examined testified as follows:
BY MR. MARTIN:
Q What is your name, age and post-office address? A Walter W. Breedlove, 41 years old, post-office address Ogeechee, Indian Territory.
Q Were you appointed by the district court of the Cherokee Nation as guardian for Lucretia and James Hunter, the applicants herein? A Yes sir.
Q Mr. Breedlove, on or about the 30th of January, 1899, you filed in the United States Court for the Northern District of the Indian Territory at Vinita your answer and report in the matter of the guardianship of the applicants herein a certified copy of which has been introduced as a part of the evidence in this case, in which you stated that you had with the funds received as guardian of the applicants from the Cherokee Nation invested and made improvements upon landsof[sic] the Cherokee Nation and held these improvements for the applicants. Please state whether or not that is correct? A Yes sir.
Q Have you ever since that date and do you now hold these improvements for these applicants? A Yes sir.
Q About where are these improvements located? A They are north, almost due north of Afton in the Indian Territory, I should judge about a mile or a mile and three-quarters just east of that new railroad that runs from Miami down there i[sic]
Q In what district of the Cherokee Nation? A Delaware District.
Q You have those improvements now as the guardian of these children? A Yes sir.
Q Mr. Breedlove, do you remember about the time these children were taken from the Cherokee Nation to the City of St. Louis? A They were taken out, it must have been in '87 or '8.
Q Do you know their respective ages at that time, when they were taken away?
A No, I don't know exactly the time that they were taken away.
Q About how old were they when they were taken away? A About I judge the boy must have been possibly three years old, and the girl was younger, I don't know, hardly a year old I should judge, maybe younger.
Q By whom were they taken? A I understood they were taken by their grandmother; had been down there nursing their mother in her sickness at the time of her death.

CHEROKEE GRANTED ENROLLMENT CARDS & DAWES PACKETS 1900-1907 VOLUME I

Q Their grandmother a citizen of the Cherokee Nation? A No sir.
Q Did you know the name of this Grandmother? A Lucretia Hunter.
Q And I believe she makes her residence in the City of Saint Louis? A She is dead.
Q The grandmother? A That is what I have been informed; I suppose they are living with their aunt now.
Q Have they an aunt in the city of Saint Louis? A Yes sir.
Q What is her name? A Lillie Hunter.

MR. HASTINGS WAIVES CROSS-EXAMINATION.

BY COMMISSION: The attorney for the applicants and the representatives of the Cherokee Nation submit the case and same is ordered closed and reported to the Commission for final decision based upon the evidence now of record. The attorney for the applicants requests and will be granted 15 days in which to file a brief in this case, one copy with the Commission and one copy with the representatives of the Cherokee Nation.

M.D.Green[sic], being first duly sworn, states that as stenographer to the Commission to the Five Civilized Tribes he correctly recorded the testimony and proceedings in this case and that the foregoing is a true and complete transcript of his stenographic notes thereof.

                                                MD Green

Subscribed and sworn to before me this March 4, 1902.

                                          T B Needles
                                          Commissioner.

DEPARTMENT OF THE INTERIOR,

COMMISSION TO THE FIVE CIVILIZED TRIBES.

In the matter of the application for the enrollment of Lucretia and James Hunter as citizens by blood of the Cherokee Nation.

D E C I S I O N.

---oOo---

The record in this case shows that on July 13, 1900, Waller[sic] W. Breedlove appeared before the Commission at Fairland, Indian Territory, and made application for the enrollment of his wards, Lucretia and James Hunter, as citizens by blood of the Cherokee Nation. Further proceedings were had in the matter of said application at Muskogee, Indian Territory, on February 15, February 26, and March 3, 1902.

CHEROKEE GRANTED ENROLLMENT CARDS & DAWES PACKETS 1900-1907 VOLUME I

The evidence shows that Lucretia and James Hunter are the minor children of James Hunter and Delilah Hunter, his wife. Delilah Hunter is identified on the authenticated tribal roll of 1880, under the name of Delilah Wilson, a native Cherokee. It appears that she was married to James Hunter about 1885, that she lived in the Cherokee Nation from 1880 until her death in 1892. James Hunter, the father of these children, appears to have left the Cherokee Nation and that on the death of Delilah Hunter, Waller[sic] W. Breedlove was appointed guardian for the said Lucretia and James Hunter. Said children are identified on the Strip payment roll of 1894, and the Cherokee Census roll of 1896.

The evidence further shows that, since the death of their mother in 1892, the said Lucretia and James Hunter have been living with their aunt in St. Louis, Missouri, and were not residing in the Cherokee Nation on June 28, 1898.

Paragraph 9, Section 21, of the Act of Congress approved June 28, 1898 (30 Stats., 495), provided:

> "No person shall be enrolled who has not heretofore removed to and in good faith settled in the Nation in which he claims citizenship."

It is, therefore, the opinion of this Commission that the application for the enrollment of Lucretia Hunter and James Hunter as citizens by blood of the Cherokee Nation should be denied, and it is so ordered.

COMMISSION TO THE FIVE CIVILIZED TRIBES.

(SIGNED).
Tams Bixby.
Chairman.

(SIGNED).
T. B. Needles.
Commissioner.

(SIGNED).
C. R. Breckinridge.
Commissioner.

Dated Muskogee, Indian Territory,
this ___DEC -1 1902___

DEPARTMENT OF THE INTERIOR,
COMMISSION TO THE FIVE CIVILIZED TRIBES.

-----o-----

In the matter of the application for the enrollment of Lucretia G. Hunter & James Hunter, as citizens of the Cherokee Nation.

----------------------O----------------------

SPECIFICATION OF ERRORS.

CHEROKEE GRANTED ENROLLMENT CARDS & DAWES PACKETS 1900-1907 VOLUME I

Come now the applicants herein and except to the ruling and decision of the Commission with reference to application for enrollment of Lucretia G. Hunter and James Hunter, as citizens of the Cherokee Nation, and for cause thereof, state;

FIRST:- The commission erred in construing paragraph 9, Section 21 of the Act of Congress, approved June 28, 1898 to mean citizens whose names appear upon the Authenticated Tribal Rolls.

SECOND:- The Commission erred in construing said paragraph to exclude citizens who had heretofore settled in the Nation of which he was a citizen.

THIRD:- The Commission erred in finding that the applicants who are minors are non-residents of the Indian Territory.

-------0-------

STATEMENT OF FACTS.

The statement contained in the judgment of the Commission, as to the facts in this case, is substantially correct. The name of the mother of the applicants appears upon the 1880 Authenticated Tribal Roll of the Cherokee Nation. The applicants were born since that time and their names appear upon the rolls of 1894 and 1896. Upon the death of the mother, these applicant, who were very small children, were taken to St. Louis by relatives and have remained there since that time. These applicants, at the time they were taken to St. Louis, from the Cherokee Nation, were and are at the present time, minors. They are the owners of places in the Cherokee Nation purchased with funds received as their annuities, by their guardian who is a Cherokee Citizen. They were taken by relatives to St. Louis to be educated and cared for until they are able to care for themselves.

-------------------0-------------------

ARGUMENT.

ERROR NO. 1. "The Commission erred in construing paragraph nine Section 21 of the Act of Congress, approved June 28, 1898 to mean citizens whose names appeared upon the Authenticated Tribal rolls."

The Act of June 28, 1898 quoted under the decision, had no reference to:

(1) Citizens whose names appear upon the last Authenticated rolls of each Tribe.

(2) Citizens who were admitted by the Tribal Courts or authorities.

CHEROKEE GRANTED ENROLLMENT CARDS & DAWES PACKETS 1900-1907 VOLUME I

(3) Citizens who were admitted by the Commission to the Five Civilized Tribes, under Act of June 10, 1896 and the Act of June 7, 1897.

(4) Citizens who were admitted by the judgment of the United States Courts for the Indian Territory.

(5) In the ~~Creek~~ *Cherokee* Nation ("Act of June 28, 1898), the roll of Cherokee Citizens of 1880 and all descendants born since the date of said roll to persons whose names are found thereon.

An analysis of the Act referred to will make this statement plain.

"No person shall be enrolled who has not <u>heretofore</u> removed to, and in good faith, <u>settled</u> in the Nation in which he <u>claims</u> citizenship."

The word "heretofore" means, " in time past, " (Webster's international Dictionary). The word "settled" means to establish a dwelling place or home, (Webster's International Dictionary.)

A settlement may be obtained by birth, (Bouviers[sic] Law Dictionary) and is prima facie, his place of settlement. (1 Bla. Com. 363) of the legitimate children being really settled in the parish with their parents are settled until they get a new settlement for themselves (1 Bla. 363.)

Thus interpretated[sic], the Act reads, "No person shall be enrolled who has not in time past removed to and in good faith established a dwelling place or home in the Nation in which he claims citizenship."

If Congress had intended this Act to refer to citizens, instead of using the word "CLAIM", it would have said, "in the Nation of which he was a citizen."

The word claim supposes a right heretofore unacknowledged (Crabbs[sic] English Synomys[sic]) a demand of a right or a supposed right (Webster's International Dictionary.)

Mr. Webster defines the transitive verb claim as follows: "To ask for or seek to obtain by virture[sic] of authority, right or supposed right." Mr. Crabb in his work on English Synomys, in distinguishing the verb claim for other words of kindred meaning, says: "Claim supposes a right heretofore unacknowledged."

Words that have no legal definition will be taken in their common acceptation. It is evident that "claim" indicated a right which has been undertermined[sic] or unacknowledged. A person may claim citizenship but after his citizenship has been confirmed by Congress or adjudicated and determined under the provisions of an Act of Congress, the judgment having been affirmed by the United States Supreme Court, he certainly ceases to "claim citizenship" and is "a citizen." Had it been the intention of Congress that this provision should apply to the recognized citizens of the tribes and receive the construction placed upon it by the Commission it would have been worded: "No person shall be enrolled who has not heretofore removed to, and in good faith, settled in the nation of which he is a citizen." To our minds the use of the word "claims" makes the construction of this provision a very easy matter. It cannot be construed so as to effect a recognized citizen of the tribe without giving the language used a strained and unheard of meaning."

The Commission in its effort to construe this act so as to apply to the above five classes, has many times found it necessary to place strained constructions upon words, a few of which are as follows: It does not apply to convicts, fugitives from justice, children who are being educated away from home, persons in the service of the Government, and persons who live on other Indian reservations. The word "NATION" means "Indian Territory." It became necessary to embody in the Creek Agreement of May 25, 1901, a provision for the enrollment of citizens who were non-residents, at the time the Act in question was passed.

If this construction placed on this act by the Commission be true, there is absolutely no authority for construing the word Nation to mean "Indian Territory." It is unwarranted and unnecessary and brought about by trying to strike from the rolls a few whose citizenship is unquestioned. If these applicants are noncitizens, every Cherokee residing in the Creek Nation is a non-citizen. Every Choctaw residing in the Chickasaw Nation and every Chickasaw residing in the Choctaw Nation is a non-citizen. Thus it would lead to striking from the rolls thousands of citizens residing in the Territory.

There is no reasoning around the fact if Congress can pass an Act that would deprive a single Indian Citizen of his rights it could pass an Act depriving all Indian citizens of their rights.

There was no law prohibiting a citizen of an Indian Tribe journeying into a state or even residing there (Act of Congress [illegible] Feb. 8, 188[sic])

CHEROKEE GRANTED ENROLLMENT CARDS & DAWES PACKETS 1900-1907 VOLUME I

"Every Indian born within the territorial limits of the United State[sic], who has voluntarily[sic] taken up, with said limits, his residence separate and a part from any tribe of Indians therein, and has adopted the habits of civilized life, is hereby declared to be a citizenoof[sic] the United States, and is entitled to all the rights, privileges and immunities of such citizens, whether said Indian has been or not, by birth or otherwise, a member of any tribe of Indians within the territorial limits of the United States, without in any manner imparing[sic] or otherwise affecting the right of any such Indian to tribal or other property."

We insist that if these applicants are nonresidents then Cherokees residing in the Creek Nation are nonresidents and must be denied enrollment. If Congress had meant "Indian Territory" it would have said so, and not said "Nation" in which he claims citizenship."

Under the Commission's holding, a citizen may live in another nation and not be a non-resident, because though they live with another tribe. Although the laws of the United States entice a citizen from his native home and permit him to live within the confines of a state, yet Congress says to him (under the Commission's views,) although I have enticed you away and it is not your fault; although I am your guardian and curator; and although you have property and lands and money which is due you from your guardian, I will pass a law that has given you no notice, but which becomes operative at once, whick[sic] will take from you your property and your lands, and will cancel my debt to you.

ERROR NO. 2. The Commission erred in construing said paragraph to exclude citizens who had heretofore settled in the Nation of which he was a citizen.

Under the Act of Congress under consideration, our contention is that any citizen had ever in time past, established a domicile in the Indian Territory, he could not be denied citizenship, although he might have been absent from the Territory at the time of the passage of the Act of June 28, 1898. The said paragraph was inserted for the same purpose, as the Act of May 31, 1900 was passed. viz; to stop the immigration of people who claimed to be citizens, yet who had never been enrolled by the Tribal Authorities and had no right under the existing laws to be enrolled by the Commission to the Five Civilized Tribes. There was a great army of claimants pouring into the Indian Territory who had no right whatever to citizenship, yet in some way had an idea that they could secure lands. The time of the Commission was taken up, by reason of these claimants, and for the purpose of stopping these so that the Commission could proceed with the work for which I was appointed, the clause in question was inserted in the Act of June 28, 1898. It failed to however, for although the Commission knew a claimant was not entitled to enrollment, and would tell him so, he would insist that he had a right to make application so that he could appeal from the decision of the Commission to the Secretary of the Interior. This made it necessary for the Commission to hear his application, in order that he could appeal to the Secretary of the Interior. These cases very often require a great deal of time, because the claimant who did not know what was necessary to establish their right, often had a large number of witnesses whose testimony had to be taken. In order to put an end to this, the Act of May 31, 1900 was passed by Congress. Said Act reads as follows:……

"That said Commission shall continue to exercise all authority heretofore conferred on it by law. But it shall not receive, consider, or make any record of any application of any person for enrollment as a member of any Tribe in the Indian Territory, who has not been a recognized citizen there of and duly and lawfully enrolled and admitted as such, and its refusal or such application shall be final when approved by the Secretary of the Interior."

This Act had the desired effect because it was only necessary to examine the claimant sufficient to ascertain where he had ever been enrolled as required by this Act, and if not, refused to hear further witnesses, making what is called by the Commission a "Memorandum case."

There are several reasons why a citizen duly and lawfully enrolled shall not be stricken from the roll, chief among which are and Act taking from these people their rights without giving them a chance to comply with said Act when they have not committed any act which of itself would forfeit their rights, would be unconstitutional and void. While the Department perhaps does not desire to pass upon the constitutionality of an Act of Congress, yet it ought not in justice to these wards of the Government, construe this Act so as to work a hardship on them; when it can be very reasonably construed so as to preserve their rights. The Department has the right to construe this Act liberally and we believe that any other construction than that herein contended for, will not only work a hardship upon a great many who are citizens without any question, but it will result in the Commission meeting with many cases that will be very embarrassing to them, as they have already may times in the past, and will necessitate their putting a strained and unwarranted construciton[sic] on the Act in question.

ERROR NO. 3. "The Commission erred in finding that the applicants who are minors were nonresidents of the Indian Territory."

It is a well settled principle of law that a minor's first domicile is his place of birth; that he has no power to change his domicile neither can his guardian change it for him. Expecially[sic] is this true where the attempt is made from one state to another and from one nation to another. The applicants are minors, that have a guardian who is a citizen of the Cherokee Nation and he holds property for them in said nation. The fact that these wards have a guardian at the place where they are now staying, even if it could be held to be a residence, does not effect their domicile in the Cherokee Nation.

AUTHORITIES.

And since the law conclusively disables infants from acting for themselves during minority, their domicil[sic] cannot be altered by their own acts.

Woerners[sic] American Law of Guardianship, Sec. 26.

And since minors are not sui juris, they may not change their domicil during minority; though they may when of full age.

Schouler's Domestic Relation, Sec. 230.

The authority of a guardian is not only local but it is also limited. A guardian is but an officer of the court appointing him, is subject to its control and supervision in all things, and has no powers except such as are conferred upon him by his appointment, or by the laws of the place where his appointment is made. The ward is thus under the care of the Court; and that it would, under ordinary curcumstances[sic], decree, or ever sanction a change of his domicil, and thus deliver him over to the jurisdiction of foreign laws, seems doubtful. It will allow him to be taken abroad for the benefit of his health, for education, and sometimes even for nurture; but in some cases only on security being given that he shall be brought back within the jurisdiction when required. It by no means follows that such a change of residence will accomplish a change of domicil.

CHEROKEE GRANTED ENROLLMENT CARDS
& DAWES PACKETS 1900-1907 VOLUME I

Nor will the domiciliary court alone take such view,[sic] The courts of the place where the ward is found, having due regard, however, to the welfare and interests of the ward, will sometimes, even though another guardian has been there appointed for him, restore him to the custody of his domiciliary guardian, in order that he may be returned to his own State or Country, or will under proper circumstances, carry out the directions of the domiciliary court with respect to him, so far as may be consistant[sic] with the laws of their own country.

But as applications in such matters are not grantable of right, but rather addressed to the discression[sic] of the court, it is apparent that conflict may arise between the courts of several states or countries with respect to the guardianship, custody and residence of the same minor, --as actually occurred in the Dawson case between the New York courts and the English Court of Chancery,--and under such circumstances necessity should arise for application of the principle of domicil,--for example, to determine his general testamentary capacity, or in event of his death his personal succession,--conflicting views with regard to his domicil would doubtless be held by such courts.

To avoid such perplexaties[sic], it seems better to hold strictly to the view that an appointed guardian has no power to change the national or quasi-national domicil of his infant ward, without the express direction or consent of the proper domiciliary tribunal appointing him." (Jacob's Law of Domicil, Sec. 262-263.)

CHEROKEE LAWS ON THE SUBJECT. Laws of 1892.

"Sec. 510. The guardian shall have the control and disposal of the ward, with the advice and consent of the district judge who shall appoint him; and, for any gross neglect or mistreatment of any ward the guardian shll[sic] be removed from his trust, etc...."

Sec. 491. None of the rights of any minor or orphan shall be impaired, in any estate or effects that such minor or orphan may be justly entitled to, by the removal if any guardian without the limits of this Nation."

Respectfully submitted this 19th day of Dec., 1902.

_____

_____
Attorneys for applicants.

Service of a copy of the above and foregoing petition and brief accepted this 19th day of December, 1902.

_____
Attorney for Cherokee Nation.

COMMISSIONERS:
HENRY L. DAWES,
TAMS BIXBY,
THOMAS B. NEEDLES,
C. R. BRECKINRIDGE.

ALLISON L. AYLESWORTH,
SECRETARY.

ADDRESS ONLY THE
COMMISSION TO THE FIVE CIVILIZED TRIBES.

DEPARTMENT OF THE INTERIOR,
COMMISSION TO THE FIVE CIVILIZED TRIBES.

REFER IN REPLY TO THE FOLLOWING
Cherokee D-29.

Muskogee, Indian Territory, December 3, 1902.

W. W. Hastings,
    Attorney for Cherokee Nation,
        Muskogee, Indian Territory.

Dear Sir:

    There is herewith inclosed a copy of the decision of the Commission to the Five Civilized Tribes, dated December 1, 1902, rejecting the application of Waller[sic] W. Breedlove for the enrollment of Lucretia and James Hunter as citizens by blood of the Cherokee Nation.

    The decision, with the record of proceedings had in the case, has this day been transmitted to the Secretary of the Interior for his review and decision.

    The action of the Secretary will be made known to you as soon as the Commission is informed of same.

                Respectfully,
                    Tams Bixby Acting Chairman.

Enc. H-25.

CHEROKEE GRANTED ENROLLMENT CARDS
& DAWES PACKETS 1900-1907 VOLUME I

COMMISSIONERS:
TAMS BIXBY,
THOMAS B. NEEDLES,
C. R. BRECKINRIDGE,
W. E. STANLEY.

ALLISON L. AYLESWORTH,
SECRETARY.

DEPARTMENT OF THE INTERIOR,
COMMISSION TO THE FIVE CIVILIZED TRIBES.

REFER IN REPLY TO THE FOLLOWING

Cherokee D-29.

ADDRESS ONLY THE
COMMISSION TO THE FIVE CIVILIZED TRIBES.

Muskogee, Indian Territory, March 12, 1903,

W. W. Hastings,
    Attorney for Cherokee Nation,
        Vinita, Indian Territory.

Dear Sir;

    You are hereby advised that the Commission's decision, dated December 1, 1902, rejecting the application of W. W. Breedlove for the enrollment of Lucretia and James Hunter, as citizens by blood of the Cherokee Nation, was reversed by the Secretary of the Interior on February 28, 1903.

        Respectfully,

           Tams Bixby
              Chairman.

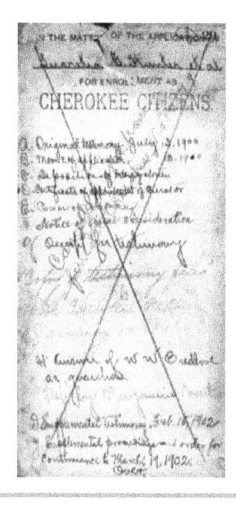

CHEROKEE GRANTED ENROLLMENT CARDS & DAWES PACKETS 1900-1907 VOLUME I

CHEROKEE GRANTED ENROLLMENT CARDS & DAWES PACKETS 1900-1907 VOLUME I

Cherokee D30 - Nancy E. Forbes

CHEROKEE GRANTED ENROLLMENT CARDS
& DAWES PACKETS 1900-1907 VOLUME I

Department of the Interior,
Commission to the Five Civilized Tribes,
Westville, I. T., July 16, 1900.

In the matter of the application of Nancy E. Forbes for enrollment as a Cherokee citizen; being sworn and examined by Commissioner Needles she testifies as follows:

Q What is your name? A Nancy E. Forbes.
Q What is your age? A Sixty.
Q What is your post-office? A Westville.
Q Where do you live? A On Ballard Creek, in Goingsnake.
Q How long have you lived there'? A Seven years.
Q Who do you apply for for citizenship? A Myself.
Q Anybody else? A No, I have got one daughter here and a little baby, but she is twenty years old.
Q How long have you lived in the Indian Territory? A I have been here seven years.
Q Where did you come from? A Georgia.
Q Your name is not on the 1880 roll then? A I guess it is.
   Note: 1880 roll examind[sic], and name not found.
Q Have you any papers of re-admission? A I have got a certificate somwehrer[sic] in this Nation, but I don't know where it is.
Q You have lived in the Nation for the last eight years? A Yes sir, I don't know whether it is seven or eight years, I came here awhile before the payment.
Q Where were you born? A In Georgia.
Q Always lived in Georgia until seven years ago? A Yes sir. My grandfather's father was the first man that ever married a Cherokee Indian in this Nation. I guess I can get my certificate but I haven't got it now. Henry Crittenden had my certificate, and Gabe Morris.
   Note: 1896 roll examined, page 747, #809, Goingsnake District, Nancy E. Forges.
Q What is the name of your father? A Benjamin Dardee.
Q Is he living? A No sir, dead.
Q Was he on the rolls of the Cherokee Nation? A I don't know, he died in the Cherokee Nation. I don't know anything about him, he left home when I was small.
Q You don't know whether he is on the rolls of 1880 or not? A I don't know anything about it. He killed a man in Georgia and come here under a false name and married a woman and went under the name of Dodge, and when their children went to draw their money they had to change their name to Dardee.
Q What is the name of your mother? A Julia Ann Dardee. She has been dead twenty-four or twenty-five years.
Q What proportion of Cherokee blood do you claim? A One-eighth.

Com'r Needles: The name of Nancy E. Forbes appears upon the roll of 1896; she makes proof of the fact that she has been a resident in the Indian Territory for the last eight years; she claims to have been admitted by the Commission, but presents no certificate of admission; her name will be placed upon a doubtful card, and when she presents her certificate of admission she will be admitted to enrollment as a Cherokee citizen.

M.D. Green, being first duly sworn, states that as stenographer to the Commission to the Five Civilized Tribes he reported the foregoing case, and that the above is a full true and complete transcript of his stenographic notes in said case.

___MD Green___

Subscribed and sworn to before me this 16th day of July 1900.
T B Needles
Commissioner.

CHEROKEE D 30

DEPARTMENT OF THE INTERIOR,
COMMISSION TO THE FIVE CIVILIZED TRIBES.
Muskogee, Indian Territory, February 24, 1902.

In the matter of the application of Nancy E. Forbes, for enrollment as a citizen of the Cherokee Nation.

Supplemental Statement.

On the 24th day of July, 1900, there was filed with this Commission a certificate bearing the seal of the Cherokee Nation, and signed by B.W. Alberty, Assistant Executive Secretary of the Cherokee Nation and dated July 21, 1900, certifying that Nancy E. Forbes appears in the records of the Citizenship Commission of the Cherokee Nation as having been admitted to citizenship in said Nation on the 16th day of May, 1888, as a Cherokee by blood; said Record being signed by J. T. Adair, Chairman of the Commission and D. W. Lipe, Commissioner.

It is directed that copies of this statement be filed with the testimony in the above case.

___T B Needles___
Commissioner.

CHEROKEE GRANTED ENROLLMENT CARDS & DAWES PACKETS 1900-1907 VOLUME I

CHEROKEE D 30

DEPARTMENT OF THE INTERIOR,
COMMISSION TO THE FIVE CIVILIZED TRIBES.

In the matter of the application of Nancy E. Forbes, for enrollment as a Cherokee citizen.

On the 16th day of July, 1900, Nancy E. Forbes appeared before the Commission to the Five Civilized Tribes, and made application for her enrollment as a citizen by blood of the Cherokee Nation. At the conclusion of the evidence offered at that time her name was placed upon a "Doubtful" card awaiting proof of her admission to citizenship in the Cherokee Nation as alleged. Further evidence in that matter has been submitted to the Commission and the following decision is rendered in her case.

DECISION
--oOo--

From all the evidence of record in this case it appears that Nancy E. Forbes was admitted to citizenship in the Cherokee Nation on the 16th day of May, 1888, by a Cherokee Commission on Citizenship. She testified that she had lived in the Cherokee Nation for seven years prior to the date of her application for enrollment. She is identified on the Cherokee Census roll of 1896.

In making rolls of citizenship of the Cherokee Nation this Commission is governed by the following provision of the Act of Congress approved June 28, 1898 (30 Stats., 495);

> "That in making rolls of citizenship of the several tribes, as required by law, the Commission to the Five Civilized Tribes is authorized and directed to take the roll of Cherokee citizens of eighteen hundred and eighty (not including freedmen) as the only roll intended to be confirmed by this and preceding Acts of Congress, and to enroll all persons now living whose names are found on said roll, and all descendants born since the date of said roll to persons whose names are found thereon; and all persons who have been enrolled by the tribal authorities who have heretofore made permanent settlement in the Cherokee Nation whose parents, by reason of their Cherokee blood, have been lawfully admitted to citizenship by the tribal authorities, and

CHEROKEE GRANTED ENROLLMENT CARDS
& DAWES PACKETS 1900-1907 VOLUME I

who were minors when their parents were so admitted; and they shall investigate the right of all other persons whose names are found on any other rolls and omit all such as may have been placed thereon by fraud or without authority of law, enrolling only such as may have lawful right thereto, and their descendants born since such rolls were made, with such intermarried white persons as may be entitled to citizenship under Cherokee laws."

In view of the facts and the law in this case it is considered that Nancy E. Forbes is entitled to be enrolled as a citizen by blood of the Cherokee Nation, and it is therefore so ordered.

Tams Bixby

T B Needles

C. R. Breckinridge
Commissioners.

Dated at Muskogee, Indian Territory,

JUN 9 - 1902

COMMISSIONERS:

HENRY L. DAWES,
TAMS BIXBY,
THOMAS B. NEEDLES,
C. R. BRECKINRIDGE.

ALLISON L. AYLESWORTH,
SECRETARY.

ADDRESS ONLY THE
COMMISSION TO THE FIVE CIVILIZED TRIBES.

DEPARTMENT OF THE INTERIOR,
COMMISSION TO THE FIVE CIVILIZED TRIBES.

REFER IN REPLY TO THE FOLLOWING

Cher. D-30.

Muskogee, Indian Territory, June 9, 1902.

W. W. Hastings, Esq.,

    Attorney for Cherokee Nation,

        Muskogee, Indian Territory.

Sir:

Enclosed herewith please find copy of the decision of the Commission rendered June 9, 1902, in the matter of the application of Nancy E. Forbes for enrollment as a citizen of the Cherokee Nation.

You are hereby advised that you will be allowed fifteen days from the date hereof in which to file with the Commission such protest as you desire to make against the enrollment of the person above named as a citizen of the Cherokee Nation.

CHEROKEE GRANTED ENROLLMENT CARDS & DAWES PACKETS 1900-1907 VOLUME I

If you fail to file the protest within the time allowed this applicant will be regularly listed for enrollment.

Yours truly,

Tams Bixby
Acting Chairman.

Encl. D-30.

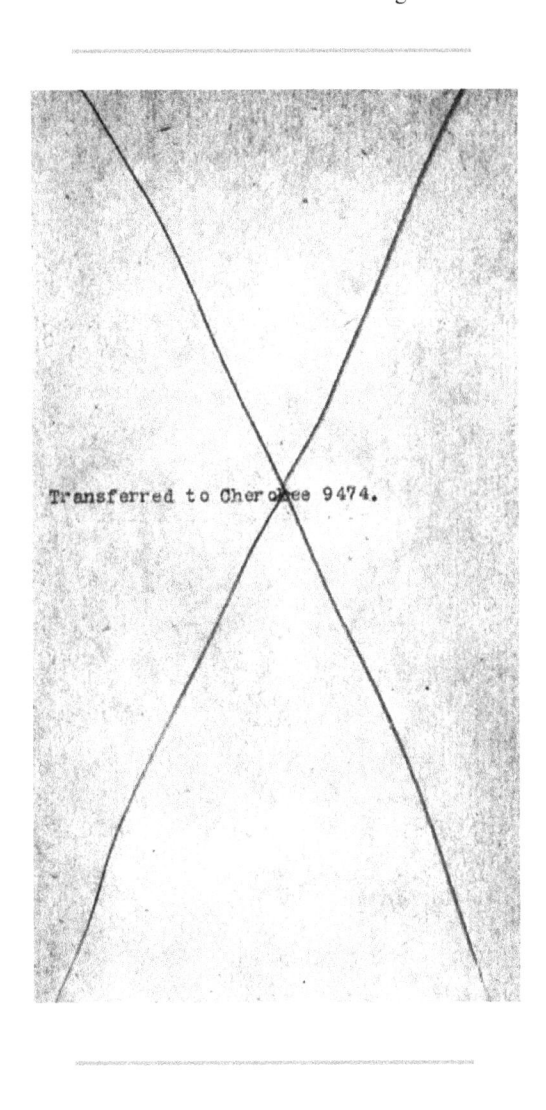

Transferred to Cherokee 9474.

CHEROKEE GRANTED ENROLLMENT CARDS
& DAWES PACKETS 1900-1907 VOLUME I

CHEROKEE GRANTED ENROLLMENT CARDS & DAWES PACKETS 1900-1907 VOLUME I

Cherokee D31 - Susan L. Beavers

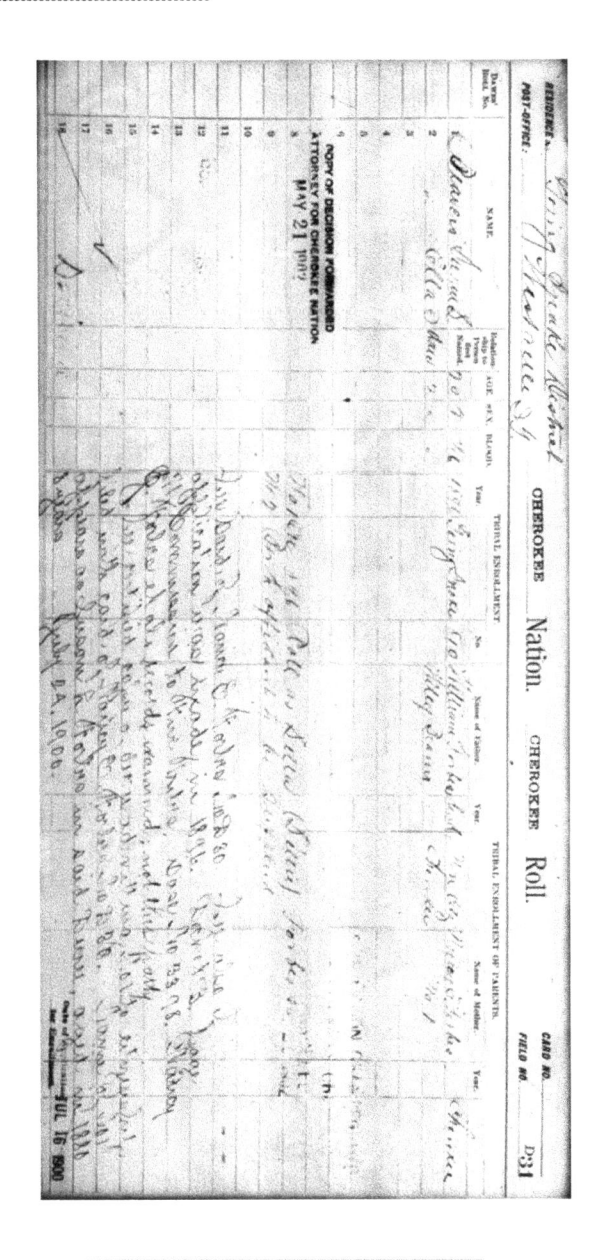

CHEROKEE GRANTED ENROLLMENT CARDS
& DAWES PACKETS 1900-1907 VOLUME I

Department of the Interior,
Commission to the Five Civilized Tribes,
Westville, I. T., July 16, 1900.

In the matter of the application of Susan L. Beavers for enrollment of herself et. al., as Cherokee citizens; being sworn and examined by Commissioner Needles, she testifies as follows:

Q What is your name? A Susan L. Beavers.
Q What is your age? A Twenty.
Q What is your post-office address? A Westville.
Q Where do you live? A About two mile and a half from here.
Q How long have you lived there? A About eight years.
Q Where did you come for there? A Georgia.
Q Who do you aply[sic] for? A For me and my child.
Q What is the name of your father? A William Forbes.
Q Is he living? A No sir he is dead.
Q Is he on the rolls of the Cherokee Nation? A No sir.
Q What is the name of your mother? A Nancy E. Forbes.
Q Is she living? A Yes sir.
Q Is her name on the 1896 roll? A Yes sir.
Q What district do you live in? A Goingsnake.
Q How long have you lived there? A Eight years.
Q Have you been outside the Territory since then? A No sir.
Q You are not upon the rolls of 1880? A No sir.
   Note: 1896 roll examined, no Susan L. Forbes found upon the 1896 roll.
Q How long have you been married? A About three years.
Q What year did you marry in? A 8th of October, 1896.
   Note: 1896 roll examined, page 747, #810, Lilla (Lillie) Forbis, Goingsnake District.
Q What proportion of Cherokee blood do you claim? A One-sixteenth.

Examination by Att'y W. W. Hastings, representative of the Cherokee Nation:

Q What time did you move to the Cherokee Nation? A I don't know, I was married right out here in Westville.
Q Where did your husband live prior to your marriage? A In the Nation.
Q What part of the Nation? A Goingsnake.
Q After you moved here about seven or eight years ago did you ever live out anywhere? A No sir, I have never lived anywhere only right in the Nation.
Q Have you ever been out of the Nation for a month at a time. A No sir, I haven't.
Q You have always lived near Westville? A Yes sir.
Q Lived with your mother up to your marriage? A Yes sir.
Q Since that with your husband? A I am not living with my husband.
Q Where is he? A On Eskoot prairie.
Q You never lived outside the Cherokee Nation? A No sir.
Q You never visited out[sic] A No sir.

CHEROKEE GRANTED ENROLLMENT CARDS & DAWES PACKETS 1900-1907 VOLUME I

Q What is your husband's name? A Wiley Beavers.
Examination by Com'r Needles:
Q Do you claim to have been admitted in 1888? A Yes sir.
Q Have you got a certificate? A No sir.
Q What is your child's name? A Ella Isabelle Beavers.
Q How old is she? A About two years old.

Com'r Needles: The name of Susan L. Beavers appears upon the 1896 roll as Lillie Forbis; she claims to have been admitted in 1888 by the Citizenship Commission, but presents no proof of same. Her name will be placed upon the doubtful list, and the name of her child, Ella Isabelle; upon the filing with the Commission of a certified copy or the original certificate of admission, she will be admitted to citizenship, and her child Ella Isabelle, when proper certificate of birth is filed.

M.D. Green, being first duly sworn, states that as stenographer to the Commission to the Five Civilized Tribes he reported the foregoing case and that the foregoing is a full true and complete transcript of his stenographic notes in said case.

<u>MD Green</u>

Subscribed and sworn to before me this 16th day of July 1900.

TB Needles
Commissioner.

CHEROKEE D 31
DEPARTMENT OF THE INTERIOR,
COMMISSION TO THE FIVE CIVILIZED TRIBES.
Muskogee, Indian Territory, February 24, 1902.

In the matter of the application of Susan L. Beavers, et. al. for enrollment as Cherokee citizens.

Supplemental Statement.
--oOo--

There was filed with this Commission on the 24th day of July, 1900, a certificate under the seal of the Cherokee Nation, signed by B.W. Alberty, Assistant Executive Secretary of the Cherokee Nation and dated July 21, 1900, certifying that Susan L. Beavers appears in the Records of the Citizenship Commission of the

CHEROKEE GRANTED ENROLLMENT CARDS & DAWES PACKETS 1900-1907 VOLUME I

Cherokee Nation as having been admitted to citizenship in said Nation on the 16th day of May, 1888; said record being signed by J. T. Adair, Chairman of the Commission and D. W. Lipe Commissioner.

Applicant's change of name is explained by the fact of her marriage to Wiley Beavers.

From a birth affidavit duly examined on the 17th day of July, 1900, and received by this Commission on the same day it appears that Ella I. Beavers, was born to Susan L. Beavers on the 24th day of July, 1898, and was living at the date of the execution of said affidavit. The same has been approved and filed with this Commission.

It is directed that copies of this statement be filed with the testimony in the above case.

<u>T B Needles</u>
Commissioner.

Cherokee D 31

DEPARTMENT OF THE INTERIOR,
COMMISSION TO THE FIVE CIVILIZED TRIBES.

In the matter of the application of Susan L. Beavers for the enrollment of herself and her minor child Ella I. as citizens by blood of the Cherokee Nation.

DECISION.

--oOo--

The record in this case shows that on July 16, 1900, Susan L. Beavers appeared before the Commission at Westville, Indian Territory and then and there made personal application for the enrollment of herself and her minor child Ella I. Beavers as citizens by blood of the Cherokee Nation. On July 17 and July 24, 1900, the applicant filed with this Commission documentary evidence in the matter of the above application.

From the evidence in this case it appears that Susan L. Beavers under her maiden name of Rogers, was admitted to citizenship in the Cherokee Nation on May

16, 1888. She is identified on the Cherokee Census roll of 1896. Her child Ella I. Beavers was born July 28, 1898 and was living at the date of this application.

The authority of the Commission herein is defined in Paragraph 1, Sec. 21, of the Act of Congress June 28, 1898 (30 Stats., 495).

It is therefore the opinion of this Commission that Susan L. Beavers and her minor child Ella I. Beavers are lawfully entitled to be enrolled as members by blood of the Cherokee Tribe of Indians in Indian Territory, and that the application for their enrollment as such should be granted, and it is so ordered.

COMMISSION TO THE FIVE CIVILIZED TRIBES.

Tams Bixby
Acting Chairman.

T.B. Needles
Commissioner.

C. R. Breckinridge
Commissioner.

Dated Muskogee, Indian Territory, this MAY 20 1902

COMMISSIONERS:
HENRY L. DAWES,
TAMS BIXBY,
THOMAS B. NEEDLES,
C. R. BRECKINRIDGE.

ALLISON L. AYLESWORTH,
SECRETARY.

ADDRESS ONLY THE
COMMISSION TO THE FIVE CIVILIZED TRIBES.

DEPARTMENT OF THE INTERIOR.
COMMISSION TO THE FIVE CIVILIZED TRIBES.

REFER IN REPLY TO THE FOLLOWING

D. 31.

Muskogee, Indian Territory, May 21, 1902.

W. W. Hastings, Esq.,
   Attorney for Cherokee Nation,

Sir:

Enclosed herewith please find copy of the decision of the Commission rendered May 20th, in the matter of the application of Susan L. Beavers for the enrollment of herself and her minor child, Ella I. Beavers, as citizens of the Cherokee Nation.

You are hereby advised that you will be allowed fifteen days from the date hereof in which to file with the Commission such protest as you desire to make against the enrollment of the above persons as citizens of the Cherokee Nation. If you fail to file the protest within the time allowed these applicants will be regularly listed for enrollment.

Very respectfully,

TB Needles

Commissioner in Charge.

Encl. D-31.

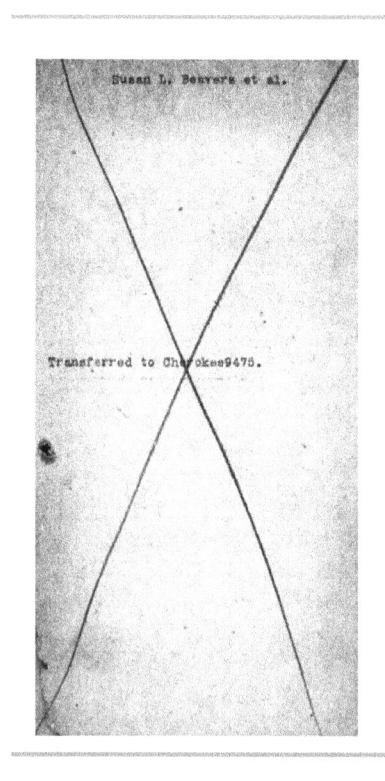

CHEROKEE GRANTED ENROLLMENT CARDS
& DAWES PACKETS 1900-1907 VOLUME I

CHEROKEE GRANTED ENROLLMENT CARDS
& DAWES PACKETS 1900-1907 VOLUME I

Cherokee D32 - Nancy L. Crittenden by Joseph Crittenden

CHEROKEE GRANTED ENROLLMENT CARDS & DAWES PACKETS 1900-1907 VOLUME I

Department of the Interior,
Commission to the Five Civilized Tribes,
Westville, I. T., July 16, 1900.

In the matter of the application of Joseph Crittenden et al for enrollment as Cherokee citizens; being sworn and examined by Commissioner Needles he testifies as follows:

Q What is your name? A Joseph Crittenden.
Q What is your age? A Twenty-seven.
Q What is your post-office address? A Westville.
Q Where do you live? A I live in Goingsnake.
Q How long have you lived there? A About twenty-seven years.
Q Live there all your live? A Yes sir.
Q Never lived out? A No sir.
Q Never resided outside the Nation? A No sir.
Q Who do you apply for? A Me and my wife and child.
Q Are you Cherokee? A Yes sir.
Q Do you make application as a Cherokee by blood? A Yes sir.
Q What is the name of your father? A George Crittenden
Q He living? A Yes sir.
Q What is the name of your mother? A Martha Jane Starr.
Q Is she living? A No sir.
Q Her name on the rolls of the Cherokee Nation? A Yes sir.
Q Does your name appear upon the 1880 authenticated roll? A Yes sir.
　　Note: 1880 roll examined, page 417, #327, Joseph Crittenden, Goingsnake District, as Joe Crittenten[sic].
Q Does your name appear upon the 1896 roll? A I guess so.
　　Note: 1896 roll examined, page 731, #364, Joseph Crittenden, Goingsnake District.
Q What proportion of Cherokee blood do you claim to have? A I don't hardly know - a quarter.
Q Are you married? A Yes sir.
Q Under what law were you married? A Under the Cherokee law I reckon.
Q Where were you living when you were married? A Goingsnake.
Q What was your wife's name before she was married? A Nancy L Forbes.
Q Her name upon the 1880 authenticated rolls of the Cherokee Nation?
A I think so.
　　Note: 1880 roll examined, and her name not found. 1896 roll examined, Nancy L. Crittenden, page 731, #365, Goingsnake.
Q What is the name of your wife's father? A William Forbes.
Q Is he alive? A No sir.
Q Your wife's mother? A Nancy E. Forbes.
Q She alive? A Yes sir.
Q To what district in the Cherokee Nation does she belong? A Goingsnake.
Q What proportion of Cherokee blood does she claim? A About one-sixteenth.
Q Have you a certificate of marriage? A No sir.

Q You claim that your wife was ever admitted as a Cherokee citizen? A I guess she was.
Q In 1888? A I don't know.
Q You have got no certificate of marriage at all? A No, not unless it is in the Clerk's office. We were both Cherokees.
Q Have you any children? A Yes sir.
Q How many? A One.
Q What is its name? A Carl Crittenden.
Q How old is it? A Three years old.
Question by Att'y Hastings, on part of Cherokee Nation: What time in 1895 were you married? A In January.

Com'r Needles: The name of Joseph Crittenden being found upon the authenticated 1880 roll and also identified as being upon the census roll of 1896, both according to page and number as mentioned in the testimony, and he having given sufficient evidence of his bona fide residence in the Territory, he is therefore admitted to citizenship in the Cherokee Nation. He claims for his wife that she was admitted as a Cherokee in 1888, but offers no certificate of admission, nor certified copy of same; she will be placed upon a doubtful list and enrolled as a Cherokee citizen when she files with this Commission either the original or a certified copy of the certificate of admission. His child, Carl, will be admitted when a certificate of birth is forwarded and received by the Commission, and when satisfactory proof is made as indicated herein of the citizenship of its mother; the child will be placed upon a doubtful card with its mother. The name of Nancy L., his wife, appearing upon the roll of 1896, according to page and number as specified in the testimony.

M.D. Green, being first duly sworn, states as stenographer to the Commission to the Five Civilized Tribes he reported the foregoing case and that the above and foregoing is a full, true and complete transcript of his stenographic notes in said case.

MD Green

Subscribed and sworn to before me this 16th day of July 1900.

TB Needles

Commissioner.

CHEROKEE GRANTED ENROLLMENT CARDS & DAWES PACKETS 1900-1907 VOLUME I

CHEROKEE D 32

DEPARTMENT OF THE INTERIOR,
COMMISSION TO THE FIVE CIVILIZED TRIBES.

Muskogee, Indian Territory, February 24, 1902.

In the matter of the application of Nancy L. Crittenden for enrollment as a Cherokee citizen.

Supplemental Statement.

On the 24th day of July, 1900, there was filed with this Commission a certificate, under the seal of the Cherokee Nation, and signed by B.W. Alberty, Assistant Executive Secretary of the Cherokee Nation and dated July 21, 1900, certifying that Nancy L. Rogers appears in the records of the Citizenship Commission of the Cherokee Nation as having been admitted to citizenship in said Nation on the 16th day of May, 1888 as a Cherokee by blood; said record being signed by J. T. Adair, Chairman of the Commission and D. W. Lipe, Commissioner.

Applicant's change of name is explained by the fact of her marriage to Joseph Crittenden.

It is directed that copies of this statement be filed with the testimony in the above case.

T B Needles
Commissioner.

Cherokee D 32.

DEPARTMENT OF THE INTERIOR,
COMMISSION TO THE FIVE CIVILIZED TRIBES.

In the matter of the application for the enrollment of Nancy L. Crittenden as a citizen by blood of the Cherokee Nation.

DECISION.

CHEROKEE GRANTED ENROLLMENT CARDS & DAWES PACKETS 1900-1907 VOLUME I

The record in this case shows that on July 16, 1900 Joseph Crittenden appeared before the Commission at Westville, Indian Territory, and made application for the enrollment, among others, of his wife, Nancy L. Crittenden, as a citizen by blood of the Cherokee Nation. The other parties to the application are differently classified and are not embraced in this decision.

The evidence shows that the said Nancy L. Crittenden, under her maiden name of Forbes, was admitted to citizenship in the Cherokee Nation by the duly constituted authorities of the said Nation on May 16, 1888. She is identified on the Cherokee Census roll of 1896.

It does not appear from the evidence how long the said Nancy L. Crittenden has been a resident of the Cherokee Nation, but it appears that she was married to Joseph Crittenden in January, 1895, and as her said husband has been a resident of the Cherokee Nation all his life, her residence is considered to be satisfactorily established.

It is, therefore, the opinion of this Commission that Nancy L. Crittenden should be enrolled as a citizen by blood of the Cherokee Nation, in accordance with the provisions of Section twenty-one of the Act of Congress, approved June 28, 1898, (30 Stats., 495), and it is so ordered.

COMMISSION TO THE FIVE CIVILIZED TRIBES.

Tams Bixby
Acting Chairman.

T.B. Needles
Commissioner.

C. R. Breckinridge
Commissioner.

Dated Muskogee, Indian Territory,
this   SEP 20 1902

COMMISSIONERS:
HENRY L. DAWES,
TAMS BIXBY,
THOMAS B. NEEDLES,
C. R. BRECKINRIDGE.

ALLISON L. AYLESWORTH,
SECRETARY.

ADDRESS ONLY THE
COMMISSION TO THE FIVE CIVILIZED TRIBES.

DEPARTMENT OF THE INTERIOR.
COMMISSION TO THE FIVE CIVILIZED TRIBES.

REFER IN REPLY TO THE FOLLOWING
Cherokee D 32.

Muskogee, Indian Territory, September 30, 1902.

W. W. Hastings,
Attorney for the Cherokee Nation,
Muskogee, Indian Territory.

CHEROKEE GRANTED ENROLLMENT CARDS & DAWES PACKETS 1900-1907 VOLUME I

Dear Sir:

    Enclosed herewith please find a copy of the decision of the Commission to the Five Civilized Tribes, rendered September 20, 1902, granting the application of Joseph Crittenden for the enrollment of his wife, Nancy L. Crittenden, as a citizen by blood of the Cherokee Nation.

    You are hereby advised that you will be allowed fifteen days from date hereof in which to file with the Commission such protest as you desire to make against the decision rendered in this case. If you fail to file protest within the time allowed, this decision will be considered final.

                  Respectfully,

                    Tams Bixby

Enc. C. No. 87.   Acting Chairman.

CHEROKEE GRANTED ENROLLMENT CARDS
& DAWES PACKETS 1900-1907 VOLUME I

CHEROKEE GRANTED ENROLLMENT CARDS & DAWES PACKETS 1900-1907 VOLUME I

Cherokee D33 - William M. Forbis (Forbes)

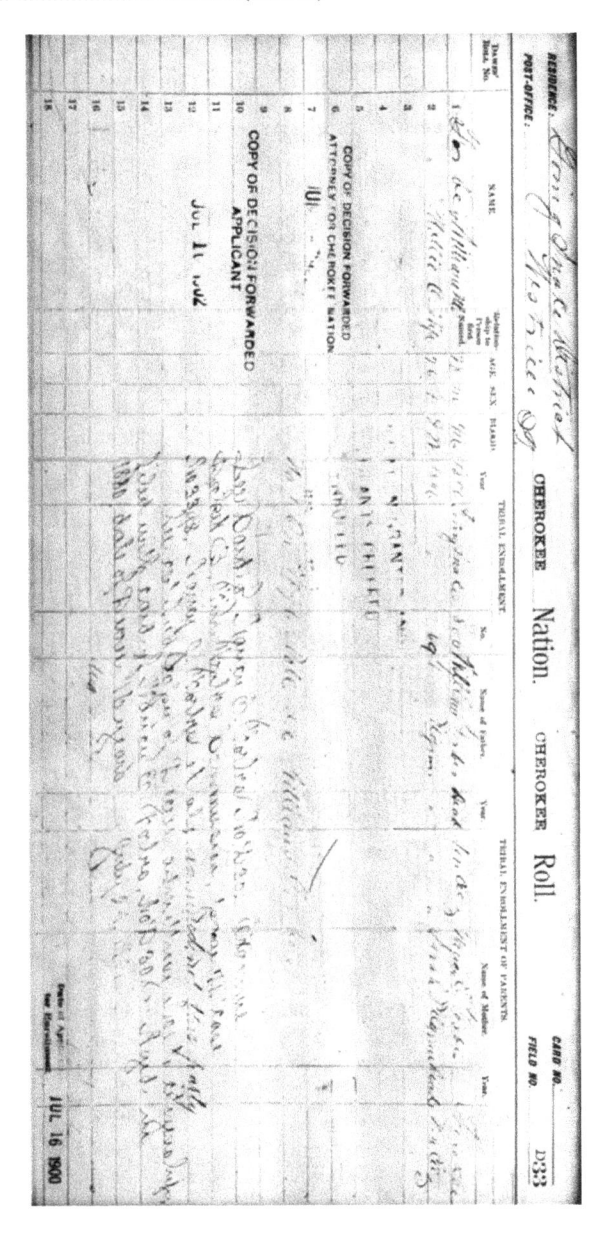

CHEROKEE GRANTED ENROLLMENT CARDS & DAWES PACKETS 1900-1907 VOLUME I

Department of the Interior,
Commission to the Five Civilized Tribes,
Westville, I. T. July 16, 1900.

In the matter of the application of William M. Forbis et al for enrollment as Cherokee citizens; being sworn and examined by Commissioner Needles he testifies as follows:

Q What is your name? A William M. Forbis.
Q What is your age? A Twenty-eight years old, about that.
Q What is your post-office address? A Westville.
Q Where do you live? A I live in here the other side of this prairie, right here close to town.
Q In the Cherokee Nation? A Yes sir.
Q What district? A Goingsnake.
Q How long have you lived there? A About eight years.
Q Where did you live before that? A I lived in Georgia.
Q Have you lived for the last eight years continuously in the Cherokee Nation?
A Yes sir.
Q Never lived out of it? A No sir.
Q Are you a Cherokee? A Yes sir.
Q You make application as a Cherokee by blood? A Yes sir.
Q What proof have you that you are a Cherokee by blood? A My mother's proof; my father was a white man.
Q Is your name upon the authenticated roll of 1880? A Yes sir, I have been here seven years.
Q Your name aint on the authenticated roll of 1880? A I don't know sir.
　　　Note: 1880 roll examined, and name not found thereon.
　　　1896 roll examined, William Forbis, page 747, #800.
Q You claim to be admitted in 1888? Do you, by the act of the Cherokee Citizenship Commission? A Yes sir.
Q Have you a copy of that certificate or the certificate itself? A No sir.
Q Are you married? A Yes sir.
Q When did you marry? A I have been married about five years.
(Produces marriage certificate.)
Q Is your wife a white woman? A Yes sir.
Q What proportion of Cherokee blood do you claim to have? A One-sixteenth.
Q Have you ever applied to the Dawes Commission, the Commission to the Five Civilized Tribes, for admission before? A No sir.
Q You never applied to the Cherokee Tribal authorities for citizenship in the Cherokee Nation? A No sir.
Q Under what law were you married? A Cherokee law.
Q Where were you living at the time of your marriage? A Right over here on Ballard Creek, about a mile and a half from here.
Q Your wife a white woman? A Yes sir.
Q What was her name before she was married? A Mollie C. Pilgram.
Q Her name on the 1896 roll? A Yes sir.

CHEROKEE GRANTED ENROLLMENT CARDS & DAWES PACKETS 1900-1907 VOLUME I

Note: 1896 roll examined, page 821, #69, Mollie C. Forbis, Goingsnake District.
Q Have you any children? A No sir.
Q You apply for yourself and wife? A Yes sir.
Q What is the name of your wife's father? A Tom Pilgram.
Q He is a white man? A Yes sir.
Q What is the name of your wife's mother? A Sarah Pilgram.
Q Is she a white woman? A Yes sir.

Com'r Needles: William M. Forbis applies for citizenship by reason of being admitted by the Citizenship Commission of the Cherokee Nation; he also presents a marriage certificate in due form certifying to his marriage with Mollie Pilgram, a white woman; he also makes proof that he and his wife Mollie Pilgram have lived in the Cherokee Nation for the past eight years continuously; haven't lived out. Said William Forbis fails to present original certificate admitting him by the Citizenship Commission, or a certified copy thereof. His name and that of his wife are also found upon the census roll of 1896, page and number as indicated in the testimony. The name of William M. Forbis and his wife Mollie will be placed upon a doubtful card, and they will be admitted to citizenship when the original certificate r a certified copy thereof filed, he as a citizen by blood and his wife as an intermarried citizen.

M.D. Green, being first duly sworn, states that as stenographer to the Commission to the Five Civilized Tribes he reported the foregoing case and that the above and foregoing is a full, true and complete transcript of his stenographic notes in said case.

MD Green

Subscribed and sworn to before me this 16th day of July 1900.

TB Needles
Commissioner.

Cherokee D 33

DEPARTMENT OF THE INTERIOR,
COMMISSION TO THE FIVE CIVILIZED TRIBES.

In the matter of the application of William M. Forbes, et. al. for enrollment as Cherokee citizens.

The following facts are shown by the records of this Commission.

CHEROKEE GRANTED ENROLLMENT CARDS & DAWES PACKETS 1900-1907 VOLUME I

On the 16th day of July, 1900, William M. Forbes[sic] appeared before the Commission to the Five Civilized Tribes and made application for his own enrollment as a citizen by blood of the Cherokee Nation and for the enrollment of his wife Mollie C. as a citizen by intermarriage of the Cherokee Nation.

At the conclusion of the evidence offered at that time the names of both applicants were placed upon a "Doubtful" card for proof of his admission to citizenship in the Cherokee Nation, and also proof of marriage.

There has been filed with this Commission a certificate signed by B.W. Alberty, Assistant Executive Secretary of the Cherokee Nation from which it appears that William M. Forbes was admitted to citizenship in the Cherokee Nation on the 16th day of May, 1888, as a Cherokee by blood. A marriage certificate was filed with this commission on the 14th day of March, 1902, showing that William M. Forbes and Mollie Pilgrim[sic] were married on the 17th day of January, 1895 by N. O. Sowers, a Minister of the Gospel.

The record in this case shows that William M. Forbes resided in the Cherokee Nation for eight years prior to the date of his application for enrollment. He is identified on the Cherokee Census roll f 1896. He was married to Mollie C. Pilgrim, a white woman on the 17th day of January, 1895. She is also identified on the Cherokee Census roll f 1896.

In making rolls of citizenship of the Cherokee Nation this Commission is governed by the following provisions of the Act of Congress approved June 28, 1898 (30 Stats., 495);

> "That in making rolls of citizenship of the several tribes, as required by law, the Commission to the Five Civilized Tribes is authorized and directed to take the roll of Cherokee citizens of eighteen hundred and eighty (not including freedmen) as the only roll intended to be confirmed by this and preceding Acts of Congress, and to enroll all persons now living whose names are found on said roll, and all descendants born since the date of said roll to persons whose names are found thereon; and all persons who have been enrolled by the tribal authorities who have heretofore made permanent settlement in the Cherokee Nation whose parents, by reason of their Cherokee blood, have been lawfully admitted to citizenship by the tribal authorities, and who were minors when their parents were so admitted; and they shall investigate the right of all other persons whose names are found on any other rolls and omit all such as may have been placed thereon by fraud or

without authority of law, enrolling only such as may have lawful right thereto, and their descendants born since such rolls were made, with such intermarried white persons as may be entitled to citizenship under Cherokee laws."

DECISION
---oOo---

Under the facts and the law in this case this Commission therefore decides that William M. Forbes is entitled to be enrolled as a citizen by blood of the Cherokee Nation, and that his wife Mollie C. Forbes is entitled to be enrolled as a citizen by intermarriage of the Cherokee Nation.

It is therefore so ordered.

Tams Bixby

T B Needles

C. R. Breckinridge
Commissioners.

Dated at Muskogee, Indian Territory,

JUN 9 - 1902

COMMISSIONERS:
HENRY L. DAWES,
TAMS BIXBY,
THOMAS B. NEEDLES,
C. R. BRECKINRIDGE.

DEPARTMENT OF THE INTERIOR,
COMMISSION TO THE FIVE CIVILIZED TRIBES.

REFER IN REPLY TO THE FOLLOWING
Cher. D-33.

ALLISON L. AYLESWORTH,
SECRETARY.

ADDRESS ONLY THE
COMMISSION TO THE FIVE CIVILIZED TRIBES.

Muskogee, Indian Territory, June 9, 1902.

W. W. Hastings, Esq.,
    Attorney for the Cherokee Nation,
        Muskogee, Indian Territory.

Sir:

Enclosed herewith please find copy of the decision of the Commission rendered June 9, 1902, in the matter of the application of William M. Forbes[sic] et al for enrollment as citizens of the Cherokee Nation.

CHEROKEE GRANTED ENROLLMENT CARDS
& DAWES PACKETS 1900-1907 VOLUME I

You are hereby advised that you will be allowed fifteen days from date hereof in which to file with the Commission such protest as you desire to make against the enrollment of the persons above named as citizens of the Cherokee Nation. If you fail to file the protest within the time allowed these applicants will be regularly listed for enrollment.

                                    Yours truly,

                                    Tams Bixby
                                  Acting Chairman.

Encl. D-33.

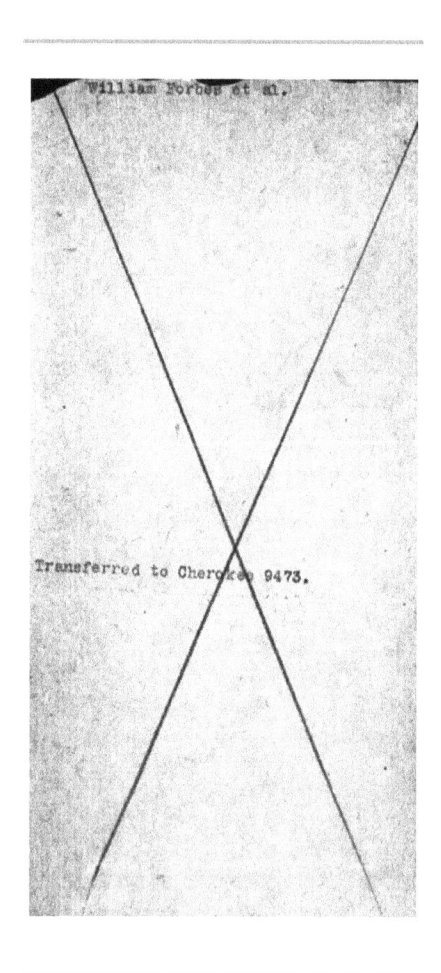

CHEROKEE GRANTED ENROLLMENT CARDS & DAWES PACKETS 1900-1907 VOLUME I

CHEROKEE GRANTED ENROLLMENT CARDS & DAWES PACKETS 1900-1907 VOLUME I

Cherokee D34 - Robert J. Forbis (Forbes)

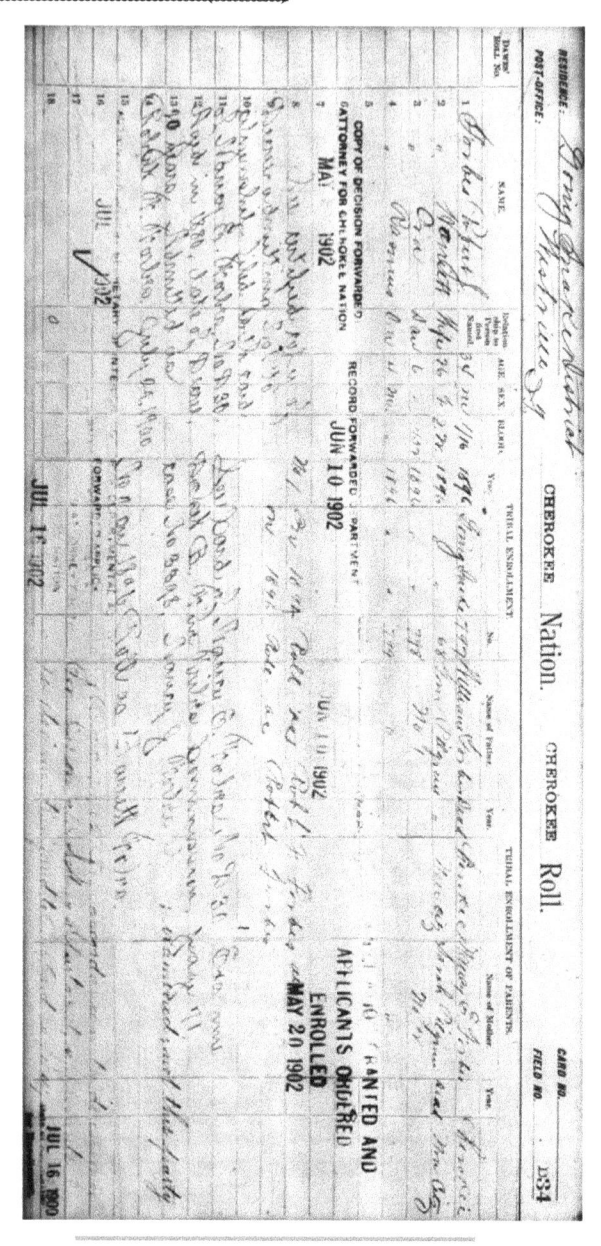

CHEROKEE GRANTED ENROLLMENT CARDS & DAWES PACKETS 1900-1907 VOLUME I

Department of the Interior,
Commission to the Five Civilized Tribes,
Westville, I. T., July 16, 1900.

In the matter of the application of Robert J. Forbis et al for enrollment as Cherokees; being sworn and examined by Commissioner Needles he testifies as follows:

Q What is your name? A Robert J. Forbis.
Q What is your age? A About thirty-four.
Q What is your post-office address? A Westville.
Q Where do you live? A Out west of Westville about a mile and a half or two miles.
Q In the Cherokee Nation? A Yes sir.
Q How long have you lived there? A Seven years.
Q Where did you live prior to that time? A In Georgia.
Q Have you lived here continuously for seven years? A Yes sir.
Q Who do you want to enroll here now? A Myself and two kids.
Q You mean children don't you? A Yes sir.
Q Have you got a wife? A Yes sir.
Q Do you want to apply for her? A Yes sir, she is a white woman.
Q Are you a Cherokee? A Yes sir.
Q You make application as a Cherokee by blood? A Yes sir.
Q What is the name of your father? A Bill Forbis.
Q Is he living? A No sir, he is dead
Q Is he on the rolls of the Cherokee Nation? A No sir, he was a white man.
Q What is the name of your mother? A Nancy E. Frobis[sic].
Q Is she living? A Yes sir.
Q Her name on the rolls of the Cherokee Nation? A Yes sir.
Q To what District does she belong? A Goingsnake District.
Q How long have you lived in the Territory? A Seven years.
Q Have you ever been enrolled by the Cherokee Tribal authorities? A Yes sir.
Q Upon what roll? A On the 1896.
Q Does your name appear upon the 1880 authenticated roll? A I guess it does; I don't know about that.
Q When were you admitted as a Cherokee citizen? A I don't remember how long age it has been; we sent in our application here.
Q Have you any evidence that you were admitted? A I haven't got any certificate.
Q Does your name appear upon the roll of 1894? A (No answer.)
    Note: 1894 roll examined, Robert F. Forbis page 649, #820, Goingsnake District.
Q Is your name Robert F. or Robert J.? A I don't know. They call me Bob.
Q How do you sign your name? A I don't sign it.
Q You never applied to the Dawes Commission before for citizenship? A No sir.
Q Under what law were you married? A Married under the Georgia Law.
Q You were married in Georgia? A Yes sir.
Q When were you married? A In 1887.

CHEROKEE GRANTED ENROLLMENT CARDS
& DAWES PACKETS 1900-1907 VOLUME I

Q   Is your wife living? A Yes sir.
Q   Do you apply for as an intermarried citizen? A I reckon so.
Q   Her name aint on any of the rolls? A I don't know.
Q   What is her name? A Harriet Forbis.
Note: 1896 roll examined, page 821, [illegible]68, Harriet Forbis.
Q   Have you any children? A Yes sir.
Q   How many? A Two.
Q   What is the name of the oldest one? A Ora Forbis, six years old (On 1896 roll, page 747, #798, Ora Forbis.) Rasmus Forbis, four years old. (On 1896 roll, page 747, #799, Rasmus Forbis.)
    Note: 1896 roll examined for applicant's name, page 747, #797, Robert Forbis.
Q   We would like to get your name exactly, is your name Robert F., Robert J., Robert or Bob? A My name is Bob Jefferson.
Q   You have no marriage certificate? A No sir.
Q   When were you married? A In 1887.
Q   You know the date if your marriage, what date in 1887? A It was in October, 1887.
Q   Have you got anybody here you could prove your marriage by?
A   One or two I guess.

        --   --   --

    Evalina Forbis-Folsom, being sworn and examined by Commissioner Needles testifies as follows:

Q   What is your name? A Evalina Forbis Folsom.
Q   What is your age? A Thirty-five.
Q   You know Robert J. Forbis? A Yes sir, he is my brother.
Q   Do you know whether he is married? A Yes sir, I saw him married.
Q   When? A I can't tell you how long ago.
Q   Has he been living with his wife from that time until this? A Yes sir.

        --   --   --

    Frances E. Forbis, being sworn and examined by Commissioner Needles testifies as follows:
Q   What is your name? A Frances E. Forbis.
Q   What is your age? A Forty
Q   Do you know Robert Forbis? A Yes sir.
Q   Do you know whether he was married? A I saw him married.
Q   What was his wife's name before she was married? A Harriet Pilgram.
Q   Do you know when it was? A I disremember the year.
Q   They are living together as man and wife? A Yes sir.
Q   Been living together ever since? A Yes sir.

    Com'r Needles: Robert J. Forbis applies for admission to citizenship as a citizen by blood; upon examination his name is not found upon the authenticated roll of 1880, but is found upon the census roll of 1896, and the authenticated blood roll of 1894, according to page and number as indicated in this testimony. Robert J. Forbis claims that he was admitted to citizenship in 1888 by the Citizenship Commission of the Indian Territory, but fails to present the original certificate or a copy thereof; he claims to have been married to his wife Harriet, but presents no certificate of marriage, the only evidence of marriage he presents is the evidence as set forth in the testimony above; and his wife's name, Harriet, is found upon the census rolls of 1896, page and number as indicated in the testimony. The name of Robert J. Forbis will be placed upon a doubtful or white card, and he will be enrolled as a citizen upon the rolls now being made by this Commission when he presents to this Commission satisfactory proof by certificate or certified copy of certificate of his admission by the Citizenship Commission. His wife's name will also be enrolled accordingly, when the same proof is made as to her being admitted. His two children, Ora and Rasmus, are found upon the rolls of 1896, according to page and number as indicated, and will also be admitted if satisfactory proof is made as to the citizenship of their father and mother.

M.D. Green, being first duly sworn, states that as stenographer to the Commission to the Five Civilized Tribes he reported the foregoing case and that the above and foregoing is a full, true and complete transcript of his stenographic notes in said case.

MD Green

Subscribed and sworn to before me this 16th day of July, 1900.

TB Needles
Commissioner.

CHEROKEE D 34

DEPARTMENT OF THE INTERIOR,
COMMISSION TO THE FIVE CIVILIZED TRIBES.

Muskogee, Indian Territory, February 25, 1902.

In the matter of the application of Robert J. Forbes, et.al. for enrollment as Cherokee citizens.

Supplemental Statement.

--oOo--

On the 24th day of July, 1900, there was filed with this Commission a certificate, under the seal of the Cherokee Nation, signed by B.W. Alberty, Assistant Executive Secretary of the Cherokee Nation and dated July 21, 1900, certifying that Robert J. Forbes appears on the records of the Citizenship Commission of the Cherokee Nation as having been admitted to citizenship in said Nation on the 16th day of May, 1888, as

CHEROKEE GRANTED ENROLLMENT CARDS & DAWES PACKETS 1900-1907 VOLUME I

a Cherokee by blood; said record being signed by J. T. Adair, Chairman of the Commission and D. W. Lipe, Commissioner.

It is directed that copies of this statement be filed with the testimony in the above case.

T B Needles
Commissioner.

Cherokee D 34

DEPARTMENT OF THE INTERIOR,
COMMISSION TO THE FIVE CIVILIZED TRIBES.

In the matter of the application of Robert J. Forbes, et.al. for enrollment as Cherokee citizens.

On the 16th day of July, 1900, Robert J. Forbes appeared before the Commission to the Five Civilized Tribes and made application for the enrollment of himself and his two children Ora and Rasmus as citizens by blood of the Cherokee Nation, and for the enrollment of his wife Harriett as a citizen by intermarriage of the Cherokee Nation.

At the conclusion of the evidence offered at that time all of the parties herein were placed upon a "Doubtful" card awaiting proof of the admission of Robert J. Forbes to citizenship in the Cherokee Nation as alleged. Further evidence in that matter has been submitted to the Commission and the following decision is rendered.

DECISION.
--oOo--

The evidence of record in this case shows that Robert J. Forbes was admitted to citizenship in the Cherokee Nation by a decision of a Cherokee Commission on Citizenship on the 16th day of May, 1888, and that he had resided in the Cherokee Nation for seven years prior to the date of his application for enrollment. He is identified on the Cherokee census roll of 1896 and the Strip payment roll of 1894,

His wife Harriett Forbes is a white woman, married to him in October, 1887. No certificate of the marriage was presented, but the testimony in this particular and the fact that she is identified on the Cherokee Census roll of 1896 is considered satisfactory proof of such marriage, and she and her husband have been living together in the Cherokee Nation ever since. Their children Ora and Rasmus are both identified on the Cherokee Census roll of 1896.

In making rolls of citizenship of the Cherokee Nation this Commission is governed by the follow provisions of the Act of Congress approved June 28, 1898 (30 Stats., 495);

> "That in making rolls of citizenship of the several tribes, as required by law, the Commission to the Five Civilized Tribes is authorized and directed to take the roll of Cherokee citizens of eighteen hundred and eighty (not including freedmen) as the only roll intended to be confirmed by this and preceding Acts of Congress, and to enroll all persons now living whose names are found on said roll, and all descendants born since the date of said roll to persons whose names are found thereon; and all persons who have been enrolled by the tribal authorities who have heretofore made permanent settlement in the Cherokee Nation whose parents, by reason of their Cherokee blood, have been lawfully admitted to citizenship by the tribal authorities, and who were minors when their parents were so admitted; and they shall investigate the right of all other persons whose names are found on any other rolls and omit all such as may have been placed thereon by fraud or without authority of law, enrolling only such as may have lawful right thereto, and their descendants born since such rolls were made, with such intermarried white persons as may be entitled to citizenship under Cherokee laws."

In 1871 the Supreme Court of the Cherokee Nation sitting as a Court of Commission to try and decide the cases of persons of doubtful citizenship, in the case of The Cherokee Nation vs. Nancy Rogers laid down the rule governing the status of white women intermarrying with Cherokee men in the following language:

1st. "That common custom of the Cherokees since their first intercourse with white men made common law upon which most of our statute laws have been founded. White women have been taken as wives by Cherokees from time immemorial, and their rights as Cherokees has never been disputed apart from that of her husband."

2nd. "In all treaties with the United States white women intermarried with Cherokee men have ever been classed as a part of our people."

3rd. "As the Cherokee man is the acknowledged head of the family and white men as wives become subject to him as such and as no special law to regulate the status of white women has been made, nor does the court think it necessary. Therefore, decide: That Nancy Rogers and all other white women married to Cherokee men or the widows of such who have not forfeited their rights under any other law are entitled to such rights and privileges as white men who have been married under

CHEROKEE GRANTED ENROLLMENT CARDS & DAWES PACKETS 1900-1907 VOLUME I

the law regulating intermarriage between white men citizens of the U.S. and Cherokee women."

Fifteen years later the Supreme Court of the Cherokee Nation in the case of Melissa Dawson vs. W. A. Dawson approved the rule laid down in the Nancy Rogers case. Melissa Dawson was a white woman and was married in the State of Texas on the 28th day of September, 1873, to one W. A. Dawson who was admitted to citizenship in the Cherokee Nation on the 14th day of September, 1883. The case herein referred to was a suit brought by Melissa Dawson against her said husband, W. A. Dawson for divorce. A motion was made by the defendant to dismiss the case upon the ground that the plaintiff was a white woman and a citizen of the United States and that she was never adopted by any act of the National Council of the Cherokee Nation or any of the courts of the Cherokee Nation, and therefore was not entitled to be heard in this case. This motion was overruled, the court holding that it saw no good reason for departing from the doctrine laid down in the case of Cherokee Nation vs. Nancy Rogers.

In view of the facts and the decisions of the Supreme Court of the Cherokee Nation herein cited it is the opinion of this Commission that Harriett Forbes, a white woman, duly married to said Robert J. Forbes in 1887, prior to the date of his admission to citizenship in the Cherokee Nation acquired by virtue of such marriage the rights of citizenship in the Cherokee Nation. She has not forfeited such rights under any law of the Cherokee Nation, and consequently is entitled to be enrolled as a citizen by intermarriage of the Cherokee Nation, and it is so ordered.

Under all the facts and the law cited it is also considered that Robert J. Forbes and his children Ora and Rasmus Forbes are entitled to be enrolled as citizens by blood of the Cherokee Nation, and it is so ordered.

Tams Bixby
T B Needles
C. R. Breckinridge
Commissioners.

Dated at Muskogee, Indian Territory,

MAY 20 1902

CHEROKEE GRANTED ENROLLMENT CARDS
& DAWES PACKETS 1900-1907 VOLUME I

COMMISSIONERS:
HENRY L. DAWES,
TAMS BIXBY,
THOMAS B. NEEDLES,
C. R. BRECKINRIDGE.

DEPARTMENT OF THE INTERIOR.
COMMISSION TO THE FIVE CIVILIZED TRIBES.

REFER IN REPLY TO THE FOLLOWING

D 34.

ALLISON L. AYLESWORTH,
SECRETARY.

ADDRESS ONLY THE
COMMISSION TO THE FIVE CIVILIZED TRIBES.

Muskogee, Indian Territory, May 21, 1902.

W. W. Hastings, Esq.,

    Attorney for the Cherokee Nation,

        Muskogee, Indian Territory.

Sir:

    Enclosed herewith, please find a copy of the decision of the Commission rendered May 20, 1902, in the matter of the application of Robert J. Forbes et al. for enrollment as citizens of the Cherokee Nation.

    You are hereby advised that you will be allowed fifteen days from date hereof in which to file with the Commission such protest as you desire to make against the enrollment of the above named persons as citizens of the Cherokee Nation. If you fail to file the protest within the time allowed these applicants will be regularly listed for enrollment.

        Very respectfully,

           T B Needles
                Commissioner in Charge.

Enc. D-34.

COMMISSIONERS:
HENRY L. DAWES,
TAMS BIXBY,
THOMAS B. NEEDLES,
C. R. BRECKINRIDGE.

DEPARTMENT OF THE INTERIOR.
COMMISSION TO THE FIVE CIVILIZED TRIBES.

REFER IN REPLY TO THE FOLLOWING

Cher. D 34.

ALLISON L. AYLESWORTH,
SECRETARY.

ADDRESS ONLY THE
COMMISSION TO THE FIVE CIVILIZED TRIBES.

Muskogee, Indian Territory, July 16, 1902.

W. W. Hastings,

    Attorney for the Cherokee Nation,

        Muskogee, Indian Territory.

Sir:

CHEROKEE GRANTED ENROLLMENT CARDS & DAWES PACKETS 1900-1907 VOLUME I

You are hereby advised that the Commission's decision of date May 20, 1902, granting the application of Robert J. Forbes for the enrollment of himself and his two children, Ora and Rasmus Forbes, as citizens by blood, and for the enrollment of his wife, Harriet Forbes, as a citizen by intermarriage of the Cherokee Nation was affirmed by the Secretary of the Interior on the 2nd day of July, 1902.

>Yours truly,
>
>*Tams Bixby*
>Acting Chairman.

ATTORNEYS
L. B. BELL
W. W. HASTINGS
J. S. DAVENPORT

J. C. STARR, Secretary

OFFICE OF
ATTORNEYS FOR THE CHEROKEE NATION

CHEROKEE FREEDMEN ENROLLMENT

No. F. D. _____

MUSKOGEE, IND. TER. _____ 190_

Protest as to wife only — She is a white woman & not married again — No division of husband property of marriage.

№ 34

IN THE MATTER OF THE APPLICATION OF

Robert J. Forbes et al.

FOR ENROLLMENT AS

CHEROKEE CITIZENS.

a - Original testimony, July 16, 1900
b - Memo of application - " 16, 1900
c - Birth affidavit - Erasmus Forbes

Copy of testimony filed with Cherokee Nation January 12, 1906.

Transferred to Cherokee No. 9447, in accordance with decision of Commission of approved July 16, 1902

voided

CHEROKEE GRANTED ENROLLMENT CARDS
& DAWES PACKETS 1900-1907 VOLUME I

CHEROKEE GRANTED ENROLLMENT CARDS & DAWES PACKETS 1900-1907 VOLUME I

Cherokee D35 - Gideon Graham

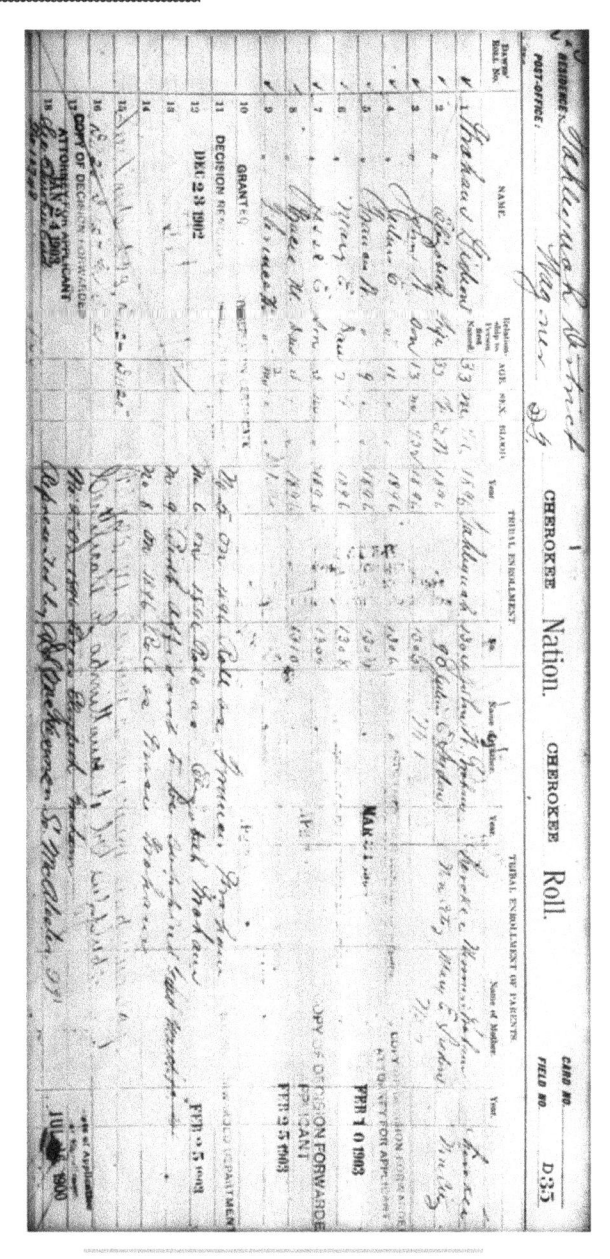

CHEROKEE GRANTED ENROLLMENT CARDS & DAWES PACKETS 1900-1907 VOLUME I

Department of the Interior,
Commission to the Five Civilized Tribes,
Westville, I. T., July 16, 1900.

In the matter of the application of Gideon Graham et al for enrollment as Cherokee Indians; being sworn and examined by Commissioner Needles he testifies as follows:

Q What is your name? A Gideon Graham.
Q What is your age? A Thirty-three.
Q What is your post-office address? A Wagoner.
Q Where do you live? A Wagoner.
Q How long have you lived there? A About eight years.
Q Where did you live prior to that? A In Vinita.
Q About eight years you have been living in the Creek country? A Yes sir.
Q Where did you live prior to that? A I lived near Vinita.
Q How long have you lived in the Indian Territory? A About twelve years.
Q Continuously? A Yes sir, never lived out of it.
Q For whom do you apply? A For myself and family, my wife and children.
Q Are you a Cherokee? A Yes sir.
Q You make application as a Cherokee by blood? A Yes sir.
Q What is the name of your father? A John W. Graham.
Q Is he living? A Yes sir.
Q Is he on the Rolls of the Cherokee Nation? A Yes sir.
Q To what district does he belong? A He formerly lived in Delaware, he is in Canadian.
Q Your mother living? A Yes sir.
Q To what district does she belong? A Canadian.
Q Your name appear upon the 1880 authenticated roll? A No sir.
Q Does it appear upon the 1894 roll? A It appears upon the 1890 roll, Delaware District.
Q Does it appear upon the 1894 roll? A Yes sir, I reckon so
    Note: 1894 roll examined, page 1070, #1280, Tahlequah District, Gideon Graham.
    1896 roll, Gideon Graham, page 1178, #1304, Tahlequah District
Q Did you ever apply to the Cherokee Tribal authorities for citizenship in the Cherokee Nation? A No sir.
Q Did you ever apply to the Commission to the Five Civilized Tribes known as the Dawes Commission? A No sir.
Q Your name does not appear upon the authenticated roll of 1880? A No sir.
Q By what right do you claim citizenship? A By my mother, my ancestors.
Q Your mother's name wasn't upon the roll of 1880? A No sir she was admitted jere[sic] by the properly constituted authorities in 1883.
Q Have you a certificate of that admission? A No sir.
Q Or a certified copy? A No sir, I haven't. But I can get it all right.
Q Are you married? A Yes sir.

CHEROKEE GRANTED ENROLLMENT CARDS & DAWES PACKETS 1900-1907 VOLUME I

Q Under what law were you married? A Under the laws of Texas, I was married in Texas.
Q Have you a marriage license and certificate with you? A No sir.
Q What is your wife's name? A Elizabeth.
Q What was her name before she was married? A Elizabeth Sydow.
Q Does her name appear upon the rolls of the Cherokee Nation? A It appears upon all of them I suppose.
Q Is her name upon the rolls of 1880? A No sir.
    Note: 1896 roll examined, Elizabeth Graham, page 1280, #90, Tahlequah District.
Q Is that the only roll her name appears upon? A No sir, she would be upon the roll of 1890, Delaware District.
Q Her father and mother are both white people? A Yes sir.
Q In what year were you married? A In 1886.
Q You claim your wife as an intermarried citizen? A Yes sir.
Q You being admitted in 1883? A My mother was admitted in 1883.
Q How old were you in 1883? A I was born in 1867, January first.
Q She was admitted in 1883? A Yes sir.
Q That was before you was twenty-one years of age? A Yes sir, I was about sixteen or seventeen.
Q You do not present any copy of the act of admission of your mother? A No sir, I haven't got it here
Q Is your name in the decree? admitting your mother? A No sir it is not.
Q Have you got any children? A Yes sir.
John W. Graham, thirteen years old. (On 1896 roll, page 1178, #1305, John W. Graham, Tahlequah District) Julius E. Graham, eleven. (On 1896 roll, page 1178, #1306, Julius Graham, Tahlequah District.) Francis W. Graham, nine years old. (On 1896 roll, as Francis Graham, page 1178, #1307, Tahlequah District.) Mary E. Graham, seven years old. (On 1896 roll, page 1178, #1308, Tahlequah District.) Jesse E. Graham, five years old. On 1896 roll, page 1178, #1309, Tahlequah District. Grace Graham, four years old. On 1896 roll, page 1178, #1310, as Gracie Graham. Florence Graham, three months old.
Q Are these children all alive and living with you? A Yes sir.

    Examination by Att'y W. W. Hastings, Att'y for Cherokee Nation.

Q Where were you married? A Married in Texas.
Q In what year? A 1886.
Q What is your oldest child's name? A John W.
Q Where was this child born? A In Texas.
Q In what year? A In 1887.
Q What is your second child? A Julius.
Q Where was it born? A In Texas.
Q In what year? A In 1889.
Q Then you never moved to the Cherokee Nation until about 1889? A That's right.

CHEROKEE GRANTED ENROLLMENT CARDS & DAWES PACKETS 1900-1907 VOLUME I

Q You never moved to the Cherokee Nation until you were twenty-two or twenty-three years of age, and had been married three or four years? A No sir, I don't say that.
Q You were married in 1886 and the child was born in 1889? A About two years, I moved here before this second child was born, I left my wife in Texas and came on out here.

  Com'r Needles: Gideon Graham applies for citizenship as a Cherokee by blood, claiming that his mother was admitted by act of the Cherokee Council in 1883 as a Cherokee citizen; he presents no copy of the decree or act admitting him, or certified copy of same; he acknowledges that his name was not included in the act or certificate admitting his mother, but claims as a descendant, by reason of being a descendant. His name is found upon the roll of 1896, page and number as indicated. He claims to have been married to his wife, Elizabeth Sydow, in 1886, but presents no certificate of marriage or proof of same. Her name appears, though, upon the roll of 1896 as per page and number as mentioned herein. Because of the fact that Gideon Graham's name does not appear, according to his own testimony, upon the certificate of admission issued to his mother by the Cherokee authorities, his name will be placed upon a doubtful card; the name of his wife, Elizabeth will also be placed upon a doubtful card, no proof of marriage, or any kind being presented to this Commission. His seven children as named in this testimony will also be placed upon a doubtful card, awaiting proof of citizenship of their father and mother. It will be necessary for Mr. Graham to furnish proof of his marriage to his wife, Elizabeth Sydow, and also certificate of birth as to Florence Graham, she being but three months old, and her name not being found upon the rolls of 1896. The six other childrens' names are found upon the roll of 1896, and identified as stated in the testimony.

  The representatives of the Cherokee Nation protest against the name of Gideon Graham and his family being enrolled even upon a doubtful card, as his name according to his own acknowledgment was not in the decree or act admitting his mother, and he is in no wise a Cherokee citizen and should be rejected by this Commission.

  Statement by Att'y W.W. Hastings, representative of the Cherokee Nation:

  The representatives of the Cherokee Nation also reserve the right to contest the admission of the mother of this applicant, on the ground of fraud, in case proof is subsequently presented of that fact.

  M.D. Green, being first duly sworn, states that as stenographer to the Commission to the Five Civilized Tribes he reported the foregoing case and that the above and foregoing is a full, true and complete transcript of his stenographic notes in said case.

               MD Green
Subscribed and sworn to before me this 16th day of July 1900.
                TB Needles
                Commissioner.

CHEROKEE GRANTED ENROLLMENT CARDS
& DAWES PACKETS 1900-1907 VOLUME I

ATTORNEYS
L. B. BELL
W. W. HASTINGS
J. S. DAVENPORT
J. C. STARR, Secretary

OFFICE OF

ATTORNEYS FOR THE CHEROKEE NATION

CHEROKEE FREEDMEN ENROLLMENT

No. F. D.

C. D. 35.

VINITA, IND. TER._____ 190

Muskogee, I. T., March 14, 1902.

Hon. A. S. McKennon,
   South McAlester, I. T.

Dear Sir :

     Enclosed herewith find a notice for the taking of testimony in that branch of the Dawson family represented by you. Kindly accept service and return one copy of the notice to us. We do not have a separate list of that branch of the Dawson cases that you represent, and we have notified all of them by registered mail, and give you this notice as to those represented by you. We are unable to give you a separate notice in each case for the reason that we do not know exactly which ones you represent. At any rate, we suppose the one notice will be sufficient.

     Kindly let us hear from you with one of these notices duly endorsed showing that you accept service.

              Yours truly,

                        J. C. Starr

BEFORE THE UNITED STATES COMMISSION
TO THE FIVE CIVILIZED TRIBES.

Case No. C. D. 35.

################

    To Gideon Graham, John W. Graham, and others, or to Hon. Archibald S. McKennon, their attorney, NOTICE:

    You, and each of You, are hereby notified that the Cherokee Nation will present before the United States Commission to the Five Civilized Tribes testimony on behalf of the Cherokee Nation tending to disprove the right of all that branch of the

CHEROKEE GRANTED ENROLLMENT CARDS & DAWES PACKETS 1900-1907 VOLUME I

Dawson family represented by the Hon. Archibald S. McKennon, to be enrolled as Cherokee citizens, at the office of the United States Commission to the Five Civilized Tribes, in the town of Muskogee, Indian Territory, on the 17th day of March, 1902, at 8 o'clock A. M., or from day to day thereafter until the same can be heard by said Commission during the usual business hours of said Commission for the taking of testimony, both for and against applicants for enrollment as Cherokee citizens.

IN TESTIMONY WHEREOF, the undersigned representative of the Cherokee Nation has hereunto set his hand this the 14th day of March, 1902.

W W Hastings
Attorney for the Cherokee Nation.

Cherokee D 35.

DEPARTMENT OF THE INTERIOR, COMMISSION TO THE FIVE CIVILIZED TRIBES.
Muskogee, I. T., October 17, 1902.

In the matter of the application of Gideon Graham for the enrollment of himself and his seven minor children, John W., Julius E., Francis W., Mary E., Jesse E., Gracie M. and Florence M. Graham, as citizens by blood, and for the enrollment of his wife, Elizabeth Graham, as a citizen by intermarriage, of the Cherokee Nation.

SUPPLEMENTAL PROCEEDINGS.

GIDEON GRAHAM, being sworn, testified as follows:

By the Commission,

Q   Your name is Gideon Graham? A Yes, sir.
Q   How old are you? A Thrity[sic]-five years old.
Q   What is your postoffice? A Wagoner.
Q   Are you a Cherokee by blood? A Yes, sir.
Q   Your mother was admitted to citizenship in '83? A Yes, sir.
Q   Have you been living in the Cherokee Nation since '83? A No, sir, in '87 or '88.
Q   You came here in '87? A Yes, sir.
Q   Have you been living in the Cherokee Nation since '87? A No, sir.
Q   Have you been living in Indian Territory since '87? A I have been living in Wagoner for the last seven years.
Q   What's your wife's name? A Elizabeth.
Q   Is she a white woman? A Yes, sir.
Q   When were you married to her? A '86.
Q   She your first wife? A Yes, sir.

CHEROKEE GRANTED ENROLLMENT CARDS
& DAWES PACKETS 1900-1907 VOLUME I

Q Have you and your wife been living together since your marriage? A Yes, sir.
Q Never been separated? A No, sir.
Q Living together now? A Yes, sir.
Q How many children have you? A Seven.
Q Are they all living? A Yes, sir.

      Retta Chick, being first duly sworn, states that, as stenographer to the Commission to the Five Civilized Tribes, she recorded the testimony and proceedings in the matter of the foregoing application, and that the above is a true and complete transcript of her stenographic notes thereof.

                                               Retta Chick

Subscribed and sworn to before me this 17th day of November, 1902.

                                               PJ Reuter
                                                 Notary Public.

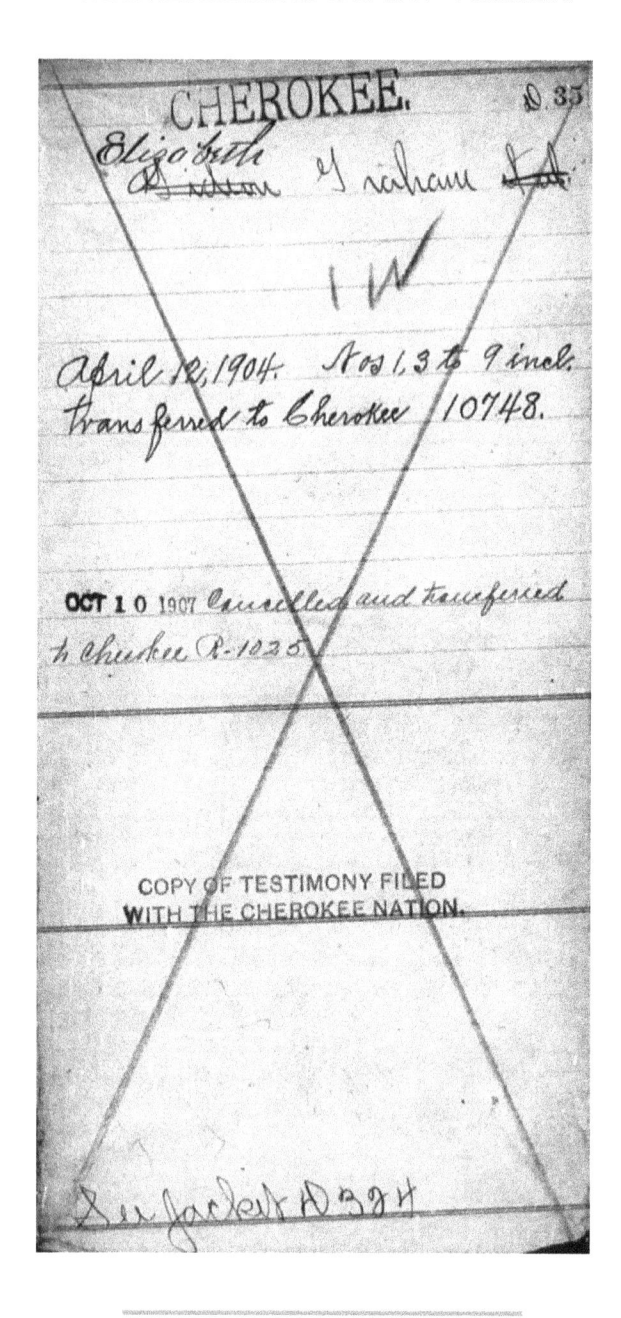

CHEROKEE GRANTED ENROLLMENT CARDS & DAWES PACKETS 1900-1907 VOLUME I

CHEROKEE. D. 35

Elizabeth Grisham

April 12, 1904. Nos 1, 3 to 9 incl. transferred to Cherokee 10748.

OCT 10 1907 Cancelled and transferred to Cherokee R-1025

COPY OF TESTIMONY FILED WITH THE CHEROKEE NATION.

Su Jacket D394

312

CHEROKEE GRANTED ENROLLMENT CARDS
& DAWES PACKETS 1900-1907 VOLUME I

CHEROKEE GRANTED ENROLLMENT CARDS & DAWES PACKETS 1900-1907 VOLUME I

Cherokee D36 - Evaline Folsom by Joel Folsom

314

CHEROKEE GRANTED ENROLLMENT CARDS & DAWES PACKETS 1900-1907 VOLUME I

DEPARTMENT OF THE INTERIOR, COMMISSION TO THE FIVE CIVILIZED TRIBES. WESTVILLE, I. T., JULY 16th, 1900.

IN THE MATTER OF THE APPLICATION OF Joel Folsom et al, for enrollment as citizens of the Cherokee Nation, and he being sworn by Commissioner, T. B. Needles, testified as follows:

Q What is your name? A Joel Folsom.
Q What is your age? A Twenty nine.
Q What is your Postoffice address? A Westville, I. T.
Q How long have you lived there? A About twenty six years.
Q Have you lived in the Indian Territory twenty six years continuously? A Yes sir.
Q Never lived out? A No sir.
Q Are you a Cherokee? A Yes sir.
Q You make application as a Cherokee by blood? A Yes sir.
Q What is the name of your father? A Levi Folsom.
Q Is he living? A No sir.
Q What District did he live in? A Going Snake.
Q What is the name of your mother? A Melvina Folsom.
Q Is she living? A Yes sir.
Q Are you on the authenticated Rolls of 1880? A I think so.
(Roll of 1880 examined, and on Page 430, thereof, #647, appears the name of Joel "Fulsom", Going Snake District)
Q Are you on the Roll of 1896? A Yes sir. (On the Roll of 1896, Page 747, #807, Joel W. Folsom)
Q Is that you? A Yes sir.
Q Is your name Joel W. Folsom? A Yes sir.
Q When you sign you name, what do you sign it, Joel? A Just Joel; yes sir.
Q What proportion of Cherokee blood do you claim to have? A I do not remember whether it is -- I do not remember; I did know.
Q You do not know? A No sir.
Q Are you married? A Yes sir.
Q Under what law were you married? A Cherokee Law.
Q Have you a marriage liscence[sic] and Certificate with you? A No sir, it is at home.
Q Where were you living at the time of your marriage? A Going Snake District.
Q What was your wifes[sic] name before she was married? A Evaline Forbes.
Q Is she a white woman? A No sir.
Q Is her name on the Roll of 1880? A I do not know.
Q When were you married? A I was married in 1893.
Q Is her name on the 1894 Strip payment Roll?
(Roll of 1896 examined, and on Page 747 thereof, #808, appears the name of Evaline (Forbes) Folsom, as Eva Folsom, Going Snake)
Q You say you are an Indian? A Yes sir.
Q You are not upon the Roll of 1880; you do not know what degree of blood you are? A I am on the Roll of 1880.

CHEROKEE GRANTED ENROLLMENT CARDS & DAWES PACKETS 1900-1907 VOLUME I

Q Did you draw the Strip money for your wife? A Yes sir, she gave ne an oreder[sic] for it, and I drew it myself.
(Roll of 1894 examined, and on Page 649 thereof, #823, appears the name of Agnes E. Forbes)
Q Have you any children living? A No sir.
Q You apply only for yourself and wife? A Yes sir.
Q You have no certificate of marriage? A I have at home.
Q You will have to send that to us? A Yes sir.

The name of Joel Folsom being found on the Roll of 1880, satisfactory proof being made as to his residence; and being fully identified on the Rolls of 1896 and 1894, he is admitted to citizenship, and his name is ordered enrolled on the rolls now being made. His wife, Evaline Folsom, having proven her residence to be sufficient to entitle her to citizenship; she will be enrolled upon the rolls now being made by this Commission; she claiming to be a citizen by blood; her name being on a doubtful card, in case it is found that she is not admitted as a citizen by blood by the Commission, when the doubtful cards are taken into consideration. It will be necessary for a certificate of marriage to be furnished between Joel Folsom and Evaline Forbes, his said wife, in order to admit her as an intermarried citizen.

R. R. Cravens, being sworn, states that as stenographer to the Commission to the Five Civilized Tribes, he reported the foregoing case, and that the foregoing and above is a true, full and correct transcript of his stenographic notes in said case.

R R Cravens

Sworn to and subscribed before me this *18th* day of July, 1900.

T B Needles
COMMISSIONER.

CHEROKEE D 38

DEPARTMENT OF THE INTERIOR,
COMMISSION TO THE FIVE CIVILIZED TRIBES.

Muskogee, Indian Territory, February 27, 1902.
In the matter of the application of Evaline Folsom for enrollment as a Cherokee citizens.

CHEROKEE GRANTED ENROLLMENT CARDS & DAWES PACKETS 1900-1907 VOLUME I

Supplemental Statement.

--oOo--

On the 24th day of July, 1900, there was filed with this Commission a certificate, under the seal of the Cherokee Nation, and signed by B.W. Alberty, Assistant Executive Secretary of the Cherokee Nation, and dated July 21, 1900, from which it appears that Evaline Forbes appears in the record of the Citizenship Commission of the Cherokee Nation as having been admitted to citizenship in said Nation on the 16th day of May, 1888, as a Cherokee by blood, said record being signed by J. T. Adair, Chairman of the Commission and D. W. Lipe, Commissioner.

Her change of name is due to the fact of her marriage to Joel Folsom.

It is directed that copies of this statement be filed with the testimony in the above case.

T B Needles
Commissioner.

Cherokee D. 38

DEPARTMENT OF THE INTERIOR,
COMMISSION TO THE FIVE CIVILIZED TRIBES.

In the matter of the application of Evaline Folsom for enrollment as a Cherokee citizen.

On the 16th day of July, 1900, Joel Folsom, appeared before the Commission to the Five Civilized Tribes and made application for the enrollment of himself and wife, Evaline Folsom, as citizens by blood of the Cherokee Nation.

At the conclusion of the evidence offered at that time Joel Folsom was listed for enrollment upon a regular card; the name of his wife Evaline Folsom was placed upon a "Doubtful" card awaiting proof of her admission to citizenship in the Cherokee Nation.

Further evidence in this matter has been submitted to the Commission and the following decision is rendered.

CHEROKEE GRANTED ENROLLMENT CARDS & DAWES PACKETS 1900-1907 VOLUME I

DECISION

--oOOo--

From all the evidence of record in this case it appears that Evaline Folsom, under her maiden name of Evaline Forbes was admitted to citizenship in the Cherokee Nation on the 16th day of May, 1881, by the Cherokee Commission on Citizenship. She is identified on the Cherokee Census roll of 1896.

Her residence in the Cherokee Nation is not specifically established, but it appears that she was married to Joel Folsom in 1893, and Joel Folsom is shown by the evidence has been a resident of the Cherokee Nation all his life, the residence of his wife would therefore appear to be sufficiently established for the purposes of this application.

In making rolls of citizenship of the Cherokee Nation this Commission is governed by the following provisions of the Act of Congress approved June 28, 1898, (30 Stats., 495);

"That in making rolls of citizenship of the several tribes, as required by law, the Commission to the Five Civilized Tribes is authorized and directed to take the roll of Cherokee citizens of eighteen hundred and eighty (not including freedmen) as the only roll intended to be confirmed by this and preceding Acts of Congress, and to enroll all persons now living whose names are found on said roll, and all descendants born since the date of said roll to persons whose names are found thereon; and all persons who have been enrolled by the tribal authorities who have heretofore made permanent settlement in the Cherokee Nation whose parents, by reason of their Cherokee blood, have been lawfully admitted to citizenship by the tribal authorities, and who were minors when their parents were so admitted; and they shall investigate the right of all other persons whose names are found on any other rolls and omit all such as may have been placed thereon by fraud or without authority of law, enrolling only such as may have lawful right thereto, and their descendants born since such rolls were made, with such intermarried white persons as may be entitled to citizenship under Cherokee laws."

In view of the facts and the law in this case it is considered that Evaline Folsom is entitled to be enrolled as a citizen by blood of the Cherokee Nation, and it is therefore so ordered.

Tams Bixby
T B Needles
C. R. Breckinridge
Commissioners.

CHEROKEE GRANTED ENROLLMENT CARDS & DAWES PACKETS 1900-1907 VOLUME I

Dated at Muskogee, Indian Territory,

JUN 9 - 1902

COMMISSIONERS:
Henry L. Dawes,
Tams Bixby,
Thomas B. Needles,
C. R. Breckinridge.

Allison L. Aylesworth,
SECRETARY.

ADDRESS ONLY THE
COMMISSION TO THE FIVE CIVILIZED TRIBES.

DEPARTMENT OF THE INTERIOR.
COMMISSION TO THE FIVE CIVILIZED TRIBES.

REFER IN REPLY TO THE FOLLOWING

Cher. D-38.

Muskogee, Indian Territory, June 9, 1902.

W. W. Hastings, Esq.,
    Attorney for the Cherokee Nation,
        Muskogee, Indian Territory.

Sir:

Enclosed herewith please find copy of the decision of the Commission rendered June 9, 1902, in the matter of the application of Evaline Folsom for enrollment as a citizen of the Cherokee Nation.

You are hereby advised that you will be allowed fifteen days from date hereof in which to file with the Commission such protest as you desire to make against the enrollment of the person above named as a citizen of the Cherokee Nation. If you fail to file the protest within the time allowed this applicant will be regularly listed for enrollment.

                Yours truly,

                      Tams Bixby
                      Acting Chairman.

Encl. D-38.

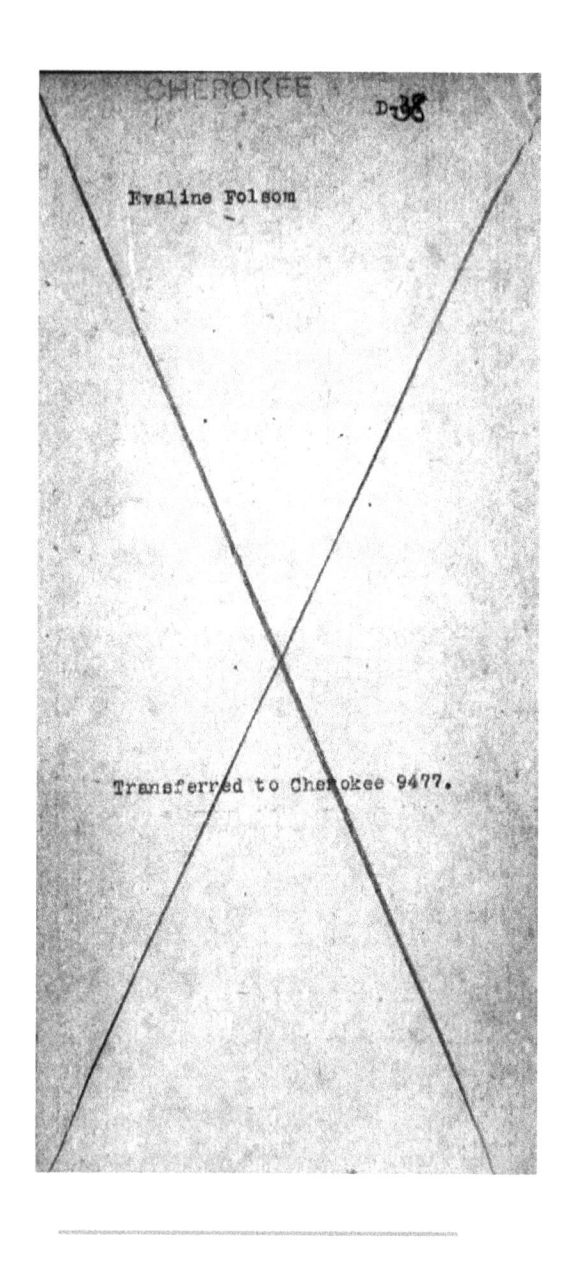

CHEROKEE GRANTED ENROLLMENT CARDS & DAWES PACKETS 1900-1907 VOLUME I

Evaline Folsom

Transferred to Cherokee 9477.

CHEROKEE GRANTED ENROLLMENT CARDS
& DAWES PACKETS 1900-1907 VOLUME I

CHEROKEE GRANTED ENROLLMENT CARDS & DAWES PACKETS 1900-1907 VOLUME I

Cherokee D41 - Maud Hunter by Charles P. Hunter

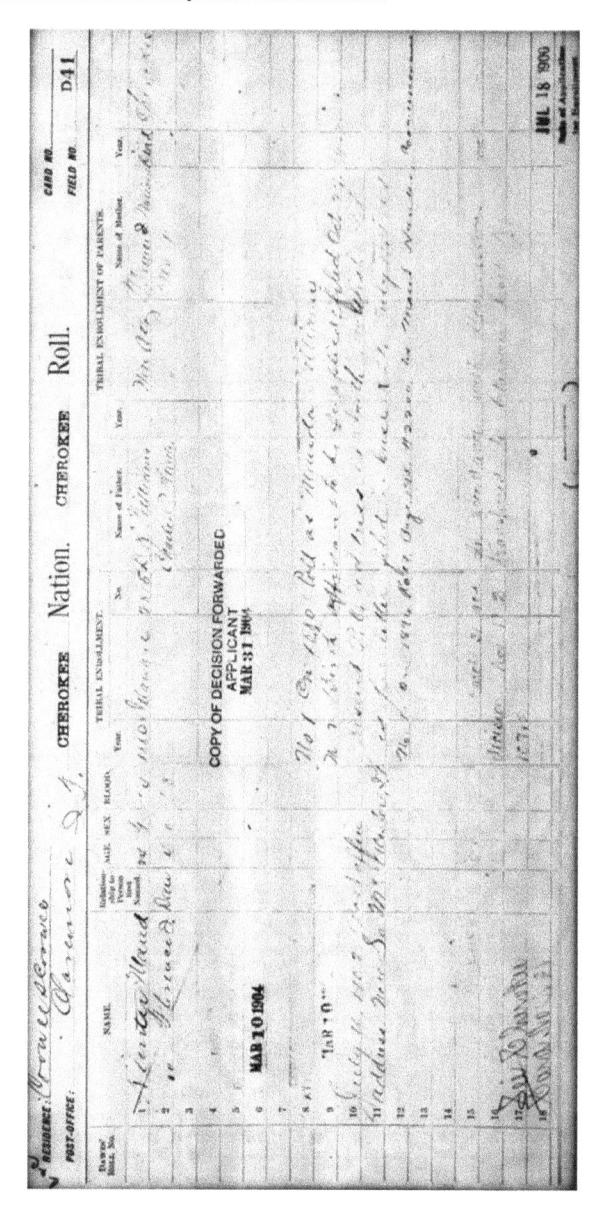

CHEROKEE GRANTED ENROLLMENT CARDS
& DAWES PACKETS 1900-1907 VOLUME I

DEPARRMENT[sic] OF THE INTERIOR.
COMMISSION TO THE FIVE CIVILIZED TRIBES.
WESTVILLE, I. T., JULY 18th, 1900.

IN THE MATTER OF THE APPLICATION OF Charles P. Hunter et al, for enrollment as citizens of the Cherokee Nation, and he being sworn by Commissioner, T. B. Needles, testified as follows:

Q What is your name? A Charles P. Hunter.
Q What is your age? A Thirty two.
Q What is your Postoffice address? A Claremore.
Q Where do you live? A I am here now; moving around.
Q Where is your residence? A Claremore.
Q How long have you lived at Claremore? A I came there in 1894.
Q Where did you live prior to that time? A In the Commanchee[sic] Nation.
Q Are you a Cherokee? A No sir, adopted citizen.
Q You make application then as an intermarried citizen? A Yes sir.
Q How long have you lived in the Cherokee Nation? A Three years.
Q You have lived in the Cherokee Nation three years?
A Yes sir, lived right in it.
Q What year was it you came to the Cherokee Nation, Mr. Hunter?
A 1894, I have not been out of the Territory since 1894, more than just across the river and back again; I have really been in the Territory since 1882.
Q Does your name appear on the rolls of 1880? A No sir, mine does not.
Q Does it appear on the roll of 1896? A Yes sir.
(Identified on the roll of 1896, Page 308, #458, Charley P. Hunter)
Q Did you live in Cooweescoowee District in 1896; Have you ever applied to the tribal authorities for citizenship? A No sir.
Q Have you ever applied to the Dawes Commission before? A No sir.
Q Are you married? A Yes sir.
Q What is your wifes[sic] name? A Maud Hunter, her name was Williams before I married her.
Q When did you marry her? A In 1896 I think.
Q What was her name before you married her? A Maud Williams.
Q Was that her maiden name? A Yes sir.
Q Did she have any name but Maud? A Her christian[sic] name was Maud Medora.
Q Have you been married twice? A Yes sir; under the laws of the Cherokee Nation, and under the laws of the State.

By Mr. W. W. Hastings, Cherokee Represenative[sic]:
Q Where were you living when you married under the laws of the State? A I was living in the Territory, but went to Texas to marry.

By the Commission:
Q You were first married in the State of Texas? A Yes sir.
Q Your wifes[sic] name was Williams then? A Yes sir.

CHEROKEE GRANTED ENROLLMENT CARDS
& DAWES PACKETS 1900-1907 VOLUME I

(Identified on the roll of 1896, Page 175, #2200, Maud Hunter, Cooweescoowee District)
(Identified on the roll of 1894 as Maude Hunter, Page 214, #2127)
Q Have you any children? A Yes sir; one, Florence Isabelle Hunter.
Q How old is Florence Isabelle? A She will be four years old her next birth day.
Q The child is living and living with you? A Yes sir.
Q You say you never applied for citizenship to the Dawes Commission? A No sir.

By Mr. W. W. Hastings, Cherokee Represenative[sic]:
Q Do you know where your wife was born? A Tahlequah.
Q When did she leave Tahlequah? A When she was three years old.
Q How old is she now? A Twenty four I think; born in 1876.
Q She livd[sic] there in 1879? A I think about that time when she left there.
Q Then she was not in the Cherokee Nation in 1880? A She was in Texas in 1880, but her grand mother was there.
Q What is her grand mothers[sic] name? A Mrs. Boynton.

By the Commission.
Q What is her mother's name? A Florence Isabelle Boynton
Q Where did she live in 1880? A I think she was dead in 1880.
Q What would her name be in 1880; your wife's mother? A Her name would be Mrs. Florence Isabelle Williams.

By Mr. W. W. Hastings, Cherokee Represenative:
Q Where were you married the first time? A Henrietta, Texas.
Q When? A In 1893.
Q You met your wife down there? A Yes sir.
Q She lived there from the time she had been taken there until the time you married her? A Yes sir, I brought her here.
Q When? A In 1894.
Q Then from 1879 to 1894, she lived in Texas, according to your testimony?
A Yes sir.
Q She has never been readmitted here? A Yes sir.
Q How; by act of council? A Yes sir.
Q Have you a certificate of her readmission? A No sir.
Q When did you say your wife was born? A In 1876.

By the Commission.
(Roll of 1880 examined, and on Page 333 thereof, #2815, appears the name of applicant's wife, as "Manda Williams", Delaware District)
Q She returned here with you in what year? A 1894.
Q And she has been living here continuously ever since 1894? A Yes sir.
Q Do you apply for citizenship yourself? A As an adopted citizen, yes sir.

The name of Charles P. Hunter is found on the census roll of 1896, according to the page and number as given in the testimony; he applied for citizenship as an inter-married citizen; he presents a marriage liscence[sic] duly authenticated and attested that

CHEROKEE GRANTED ENROLLMENT CARDS
& DAWES PACKETS 1900-1907 VOLUME I

he was married on the 2nd day of May, 1896; the laws of the Cherokee Nation, providing that all persons other than Cherokee citizens, marrying after December 16th, 1895, shall not be entitled to citizenship: The proofs show that said Charles P. Hunter was married to Mrs[sic] Hunter, nee Williams on the 2nd day of May, 1896; consequently his marriage was not solemnized within the time prescribed by the Cherokee law, permitting him to become a citizen by intermarriage, and his application for citizenship is hereby rejected.

His wife, Maud Hunter, nee Williams, appearing on the authenticated rolls of 1880; also upon the census roll of 1896, and the pay roll of 1894, as per page and number mentioned in the testimony now taken; it appears from the testimony that his wife, Maud Hunter removed to Texas with her father in the year 1879, or 1880, and resided there until 1894, when she was married to Charles P. Hunter and returned to the Indian Territory with him; the testimony shows that she has lived continuously in the Indian Territory since 1894. Because of her absence from the Territory between the dates mentioned her name will be placed upon a doubtful card; and also that of her child, Florence Isabelle Hunter, four years if age: It will be necessary for Mrs. Hunter to also present to this Commission as duly certified certificate and proof as to the birth of said Florence Isabelle Hunter. As to the application of the said Charles P. Hunter himself, he will be permitted to file any additonal[sic] evidence in the form of written statements, or affidavits, or other proper papers he may desire to present to the Commission for its consideration, in connection with his application; he being rejected. In the event that this Commission denies the application you make on behalf of your wife and child for citizenship in the Cherokee Nation, you will be so advised in writing, the decision of the Commission being based on the oral testimony given by you at this time, and upon such written testimony as you may now desire to submit for the consideration of the Commission, or shall submit hereafter.

By Mr. W. W. Hastins[sic], Cherokee Represenative[sic]:

Q Where were you during the payment of 1894? A Claremore.
Q Did you draw the money for your wife then? A Yes sir.
Q You were there present yourself and drew it? A No sir, I was not present myself; I turned it over to Mr. Neilson; had traded it out.
Q Have you been back to Texas since 1894? A I have been back on visits; not over a month at a time.
Q How long has your wife been there? A She was just there when I was.
Q Has she ever remained over a month; her father lives in Denton.
Q Where is your home here? A Cooweescoowee District.
Q Have you a farm and improvements there? A I have a claim there and after she died, they got in a squabble about it; I let it go; I moved here from there; I left my furniture and everything at Claremore.
Q When did you get it? A About six months ago.

R. R. Cravens, being sworn, states that as stenographer to the Commission to the Five Civilized Tribes, he reported the foregoing case, and that the foregoing and above is a true, full and correct transcript of his stenographic notes in said case.

<u>   *R R Cravens*   </u>

CHEROKEE GRANTED ENROLLMENT CARDS & DAWES PACKETS 1900-1907 VOLUME I

Sworn to and subscribed before me this 18th day of July, 1900.

T B Needles
COMMISSIONER.

Supl.-C.D.#41.

Department of the Interior,
Commission to the Five Civilized Tribes,
Muskogee, I. T., February 15, 1902.

SUPPLEMENTAL in the matter of the application of Maud Hunter, et al for enrollment as a[sic] citizens of the Cherokee Nation:

On the 30th day of January, 1902, Charles P. Hunter, the husband of the applicant and the father of her child, was notified by registered letter that the application for the enrollment of his wife and child would be taken up for final consideration by the Commission on the 15th day of February, 1902. He was also requested to supply the Commission with an affidavit as to the birth of his daughter, Florence I. Hunter. Applicant has been called three times and fails to respond either in person or by attorney and the case is closed.

T B Needles
Commissioner.

Cherokee D 41.

DEPARTMENT OF THE INTERIOR, COMMISSION TO THE FIVE CIVILIZED TRIBES.

In the matter of the application for the enrollment of Maud Hunter and her minor child, Florence I. Hunter, as citizens by blood of the Cherokee Nation.

DECISION.

The record in this case shows that on July 18, 1900 Charles P. Hunter appeared before the Commission at Claremore, Indian Territory, and made application for the enrollment, among others, of his wife, Maud Hunter, and her minor child, Florence I. Hunter, as citizens by blood of the Cherokee Nation. The application also included the said Charles P. Hunter, but he is differently classified and is not embraced in this decision.

CHEROKEE GRANTED ENROLLMENT CARDS
& DAWES PACKETS 1900-1907 VOLUME I

The evidence shows that the said Maud Hunter is identified by the name of Manda Williams on the 1880 authenticated Cherokee roll that she is also identified on the 1894 Cherokee strip payment roll and the 1896 Cherokee census roll. It further appears that the applicant, Florence I. Hunter, who is identified by a birth affidavit made a part of the record herein, is the child of said Maud Hunter, and was born since 1880.

The evidence further shows that the said Maud Hunter has resided in the Cherokee Nation continuously from 1894 up to and including the date of her application herein; and it is considered that the residence of her said minor child has always been in the Cherokee Nation.

It is, therefore, the opinion of this Commission that Maud Hunter and Florence I. Hunter should be enrolled as citizens by blood of the Cherokee Nation, in accordance with the provisions of section twenty-one of the act of Congress, approved June 28, 1898 (30 Stats., 495), and it is so ordered.

COMMISSION TO THE FIVE CIVILIZED TRIBES.

(SIGNED). *Tams Bixby.*
Chairman.

(SIGNED). *T. B. Needles.*
Commissioner.

(SIGNED). *C. R. Breckinridge.*
Commissioner.

(SIGNED). *W. E. Stanley.*
Commissioner.

Muskogee, Indian Territory,
this   MAR 10 1904

COMMISSIONERS:
TAMS BIXBY,
THOMAS B. NEEDLES,
C. R. BRECKINRIDGE,
W. E. STANLEY.

ALLISON L. AYLESWORTH,
SECRETARY.

DEPARTMENT OF THE INTERIOR,
COMMISSION TO THE FIVE CIVILIZED TRIBES.

ADDRESS ONLY THE
COMMISSION TO THE FIVE CIVILIZED TRIBES.

REFER IN REPLY TO THE FOLLOWING
Cherokee D 41

Muskogee, Indian Territory, March 10, 1904.

W. W. Hastings,
    Attorney for the Cherokee Nation,
        Tahlequah, Indian Territory.

Dear Sir:

There is herewith inclosed a copy of the decision of the Commission to the Five Civilized Tribes, dated March 10, 1904, granting the application of Charles P. Hunter for the enrollment of his wife, Maud, and his minor child, Florence I. Hunter, as citizens by blood of the Cherokee Nation.

You are advised that you will be allowed fifteen days from the date hereof within which to file such protest as you may desire to make against the action of the Commission in this case. If you fail to file such protest within the time allowed this decision will be considered final.

Respectfully,

T B Needles

Encl. V-10   Commissioner in Charge.

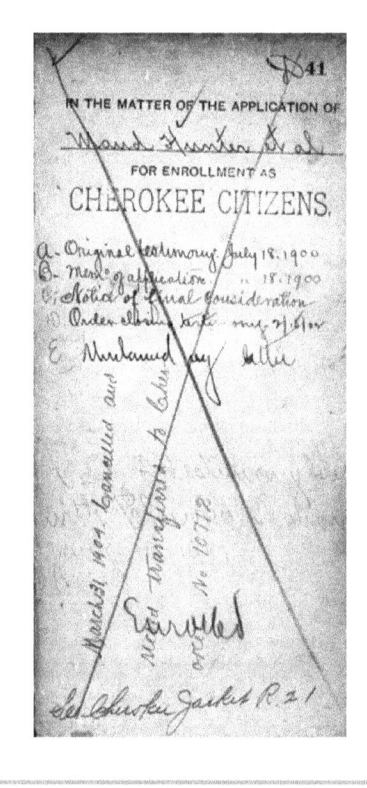

CHEROKEE GRANTED ENROLLMENT CARDS
& DAWES PACKETS 1900-1907 VOLUME I

CHEROKEE GRANTED ENROLLMENT CARDS & DAWES PACKETS 1900-1907 VOLUME I

Cherokee D43 - William Parris by Joseph Weaver

330

CHEROKEE GRANTED ENROLLMENT CARDS
& DAWES PACKETS 1900-1907 VOLUME I

DEPARTMENT OF THE INTERIOR,
COMMISSION TO THE FIVE CIVILIZED TRIBES,
WESTVILLE, I.T. JULY 16, 1900.

In the matter of the application of Joseph Weaver et als., for enrollment as Cherokee citizens, said Weaver being sworn by Com'r Needles, testified as follows:

Q What is your name? A Joseph Weaver.
Q How old are you? A About 70.
Q Where do you live? A Right over here about two miles.
Q How long have you lived there? A About 35 years.
Q Lived there all the time? A Yes.
Q Never lived out? A No sir.
Q Are you a Cherokee? A Yes,
Q Your father not living? A No sir.
Q Nor your mother? A No sir.
        On '80 roll, page 485, number 1851; as Joe Weaver;
        On '96 roll as Joseph Weaver, page 802, number 2264.
Q What degree of blood do you claim? A Full blood.
Q Are you married? A Yes.
Q What is your wife's name? A Mary.
Q When were you married? A I am not married - - we just too up together before the law was in force.
Q Is she still living? A Yes.
Q Is she a Cherokee by blood? A Yes.
Q Is she a white woman? A No sir.
        On '80 roll, page 485, number 1852;
        On '96 roll, page 830, number 201.
Q When did you take up with her-- when were you married? A Just after peace was made-- about '67.
Q Have you any children by her? A Yes. They are all married though
Q Have you any young ones at home? A I have one grand-child.
Q What is his name? A William Paris.
Q What was his mother's name? A Hester.
Q Is she living? A No sir, she's dead.
Q Was she your daughter? A No sir.
Q Who was this William's mother? A Hester.
Q She is a Cherokee by blood? A Yes.
        On '80 roll, page 485, number 1856.
Q Is Hester dead? A Yes.
Q How old is William Parris[sic], this grand-child? A He is going on six years old.
Q Is he living with you? A Yes.
Q How much Indian blood does this boy claim? A About one-fourth, I guess.
Q Who was the mother of this boy? A Hester Weaver.
        On '80 roll, 485, number 1856.

CHEROKEE GRANTED ENROLLMENT CARDS & DAWES PACKETS 1900-1907 VOLUME I

MARY WEAVER, being sworn, testified:
Q What is your name? A Mary Weaver.
Q How old are you? A I am up in 60, I guess.
Q How long have you lived in the Nation? A I was brought here with the old settlers, a baby.
Q You are a citizen by adoption? A Yes.
Q Do you know of your own knowledge that this child, William Paris, is the child of Hester Weaver? A Yes, I was there when it was born--- I was her doctor, and the child has, lived with me ever since it's mother died, right at my house.

By Mr. Hastings, Cherokee Attorney:
Q Did Jack Paris and Hester Weaver live together as husband and wife? A Well, he quit her.
Q Do you know whether they were ever married? A Yes.
Q Were you present at their marriage? A Yes.
Q Who married them? A Adam Lacy.
Q Was this child born to them while he was living with her? A No sir, he had done left her and sent her home.
Q How long after he sent her home before this child was born? A I reckon some three months.
Q How long did they live together as husband and wife? A I reckon about a year. I do not think they lived together over a year.
Q Where is Jack Paris now? A I don't know.
Q Is he living? A I guess he is.
Q Is he a Cherokee? A Yes, he has never proved his right. He was carried out of the Nation when he was small and they never did prove his right up.
Q This woman was staying at your house when the child was born? A Yes, he sent her back home and she was there. I reckon there is a sight of people knows that; they lived right here at the time.
Q You say this child was born in January or February of '95-- how long was it before that they had quite living together? A It was about three months before the child was born.
Q How do you know the woman was a citizen? A I knew all her people-- I knew that they were all Indians only her mother was a white woman.
Q Her father was who? A She was a grand-child of old Uncle Levi Robinson.
Q Do you know who Hester's father was? A It was laid to John Kelly.
Q It was an illegitimate child and laid to John Kelly? A Yes.
Q The mother of Hester was a white woman? A Yes.
Q And John Kelly was a white man? A No sir; but was not married.
Q What did John say about it? A I reckon he can't deny it.

  The name of Joseph Weaver being found upon the roll of '80, and also upon the roll of '96, and his wife Mary Weaver, being found upon the roll of '80 and also '96, and having proven their residence, Joe Weaver is admitted as a citizen by blood, and his wife, Mary, as a Cherokee by adoption. The name of William Paris, great grand-child of Mary Weaver, and Mary Weaver is a white woman, is ordered placed upon a doubtful card. Any further testimony you may desire to

CHEROKEE GRANTED ENROLLMENT CARDS & DAWES PACKETS 1900-1907 VOLUME I

offer as to the rights of this child you may do so at any time, but under the testimony given now it probably cannot be enrolled.

Brown McDonald, being sworn by Commissioner Needles, says as Stenographer to the Commission to the Five Civilized Tribes, he reported in full the testimony of the above named two witnesses, and the foregoing is a full, true and correct transcript of his notes.

Brown McDonald

Sworn to and subscribed before me this 19th day of July, 1900, at Westville, I.T.

T B Needles
Commissioner.

Department of the Interior,
Commission to the Five Civilized Tribes,
Westville, I.T., July 19th, 1900.

In the matter of the application for the enrollment of William Parris as a Cherokee citizen.

Melvina Fulsom, being duly sworn and examined by Commissioner Needles, testified as follows:
Q   What is your name? A Melvina Fulsom.
Q   How old are you? A 56.
Q   Are you a Cherokee citizen? A Yes, sir.
Q   Where do you live? A About 2 miles from here.
Q   What is your post office? A Westville.
Mr. W. W. Hastings, on behalf of Cherokee Nation: Who was the mother of William Parris? A Hester Robbins.
Q   Now Hester Robbins is a grand-daughter to Mrs. Joe Weaver? A No, sir, she is not her granddaughter, she raised the girl.
Q   Who were Hester Robbins parents? A Lucinda Robbins.
Q   Wasn't the mother of this Hester a white woman? A No, sir, she was a Cherokee.
Q   Was she on the rolls? A Yes, sir, she was on the rolls when she died. She has been dead 4 years, I think, seems to me.
Q   When[sic] was her name when she died? A Parris.
Q   What was her name in 1880, the mother of this Hester? A That was Lucinda Robbins, was Hester's mother.
Q   Was her name Lucinda Robbins in 1880? A Yes, sir, I guess it was, her mother has been dead worse than that, she has been dead about 16 years I think.
Q   Isn't Hester's mother dead? A Yes, sir, about 16 years ago.
Q   And her name was Robbins at that time? A Yes, sir.
Q   That was the name she went by? A Yes, sir.

CHEROKEE GRANTED ENROLLMENT CARDS & DAWES PACKETS 1900-1907 VOLUME I

Q Was she a Cherokee by blood? A Yes, sir, that is what she was always called, she drey[sic] money from them.

Q What kin were you to this Lucinda Robbins? A We were brothers and sisters children, and that made me and her second cousins.

Tom Still, being duly sworn and examined by Commissioner Needles testified as follows:

Q What is your name? A Tom Still.
Q What is your age? A About 51 or 52.
Q What is your post office address? A Westville.
Q Are you a Cherokee citizen? A Yes, sir.

Mr. W. W. Hastings: Do you know this child by the name of William Parris that is being applied for enrollment here by Mrs. Weaver? A No, sir, all I know about it, I drawed their money, and that is all I can tell you about it; I don't know whether they are Cherokees of not; the mother, I reckon, of this child she give me an order for her strip money and I drawed it.

Q Do you know what district they were enrolled in in 1894? A No, sir, I don't, I reckon they must have been enrolled in Going Snake.

Q Do you know whether or not the mother of this child was in Going Snake in 1894? A No, sir, I reckon so.

Q You don't know anything more about it? A No, sir.

Q You don't know whether she is Cherokee or not? A No, sir, I cant tell you, all I know she give me the order for that money.

George Critdenten[sic], being duly sworn and examined by Commissioner Needles, testified as follows:

Q Your name is George Critdenten? A Yes, sir.
Q What is your age? A 53.
Q You live in the Going Snake district of the Cherokee Nation? A Yes, sir.
Q You are a Cherokee citizen? A Yes, sir.

Mr. Hastings: You know this child William Parris? A Yes, sir, I know the child that Mrs. Weaver has got.

Q Did you know that child's mother, Hester? A Yes, sir.

Q Did you know Hester's parents, who would be the grandparents of this child? A I don't know about her mother? I recollect Uncle Levi Robbins, that was her grandfather.

Q You say you don't remember who the mother of Hester was, whether a white woman or a Cherokee? A No, sir, I don't.

Q And you don't know whether she was born to the mother as a legitimate or an illegitimate child? A No, sir, only I heard that Uncle Levi gave this lady the child to raise and she raised it, that is all I know about it.

----------o----------

Bruce C. Jones, being duly sworn, says that as stenographer to the Commission to the Five Civilized Tribes he reported the testimony of the above named witnesses, and that the foregoing is a full, true and correct translation of his stenographic notes.

<u>   Bruce C Jones   </u>

Sworn to and subscribed before me this the 20th day of July, 1900.

<u>   Tams Bixby   </u>
Commissioner.

CHEROKEE D 43

DEPARTMENT OF THE INTERIOR,

COMMISSION TO THE FIVE CIVILIZED TRIBES.

Muskogee, Indian Territory, February 25, 1902.

In the matter of the application of William Parris for enrollment as a Cherokee citizen.

Supplemental Statement.

A further examination of the authenticated tribal roll of 1880 shows the name of Hester Weaver thereon, page 485, No. 1856 as a Native Cherokee.

It is directed that copies of this statement be filed with the testimony in the above case.

<u>   TB Needles   </u>
Commissioner.

CHEROKEE D 43

DEPARTMENT OF THE INTERIOR,
COMMISSION TO THE FIVE CIVILIZED TRIBES.

In the matter of the application of William Parris for enrollment as a Cherokee citizen.

On the 18th day of July, 1900, Joseph Weaver appeared before the Commission to the Five Civilized Tribes and made application for the enrollment of William Parris as a citizen by blood of the Cherokee Nation. The application included other parties, but as they were differently classified by the examiner in the field they are not embraced in this decision.

At the conclusion of the evidence submitted in support of the application William Parris was placed upon a "Doubtful" card because the examiner was not satisfied with the proof of citizenship of the child's mother, Hester Weaver. Further evidence on this question has been submitted to the Commission and the following decision is rendered.

DECISION

--oOo--

From the evidence of record in the case it appears that William Parris is the son of one Hester Weaver, sometimes known as Hester Robbins. There is some conflict in the testimony as to whether Hester Weaver was a citizen of the Cherokee Nation and capable of endowing her child with the rights of Cherokee citizenship.

The evidence, however, shows that Hester Weaver is identified on the roll of 1880 as a native Cherokee. For the purposes of this particular case this fact is conclusive as to the citizenship of said Hester Weaver. The child, William Parris, is identified on the Cherokee Census roll of 1896.

In making rolls of citizenship of the Cherokee Nation this Commission is governed by the following provision of the Act of Congress approved June 28, 1898 (30 Stats., 495);

> "That in making rolls of citizenship of the several tribes, as required by law, the Commission to the Five Civilized Tribes is authorized and directed to take the roll of Cherokee citizens of eighteen hundred and eighty (not including freedmen) as the only roll intended to be confirmed by this and preceding Acts of Congress, and to enroll all persons now living whose names are found on said roll, and all descendants born since the date of said roll to persons whose names are found thereon; and all persons who have been enrolled by the tribal authorities who have heretofore made permanent settlement in the Cherokee Nation whose parents, by reason of their Cherokee blood, have been lawfully admitted to citizenship by the tribal authorities, and who were minors when their parents were so admitted; and they shall investigate the right of all other persons whose names are found on any other rolls and omit all such as may have been placed thereon by fraud or without authority of law, enrolling only such as may have lawful right thereto, and

their descendants born since such rolls were made, with such intermarried white persons as may be entitled to citizenship under Cherokee laws."

It is considered by this Commission that William Parris being the descendant of a person whose name appears upon the authenticated tribal roll of 1880 is entitled to be enrolled as a citizen by blood of the Cherokee Nation, and it is therefore so ordered.

_____Tams Bixby_____
_____T B Needles_____
_____C. R. Breckinridge_____
Commissioners.

Dated at Muskogee, Indian Territory,
JUN 9 - 1902

COMMISSIONERS:
HENRY L. DAWES,
TAMS BIXBY,
THOMAS B. NEEDLES,
C. R. BRECKINRIDGE.

ALLISON L. AYLESWORTH,
SECRETARY.

ADDRESS ONLY THE
COMMISSION TO THE FIVE CIVILIZED TRIBES.

DEPARTMENT OF THE INTERIOR,
COMMISSION TO THE FIVE CIVILIZED TRIBES.

REFER IN REPLY TO THE FOLLOWING
Cher. D-43.

Muskogee, Indian Territory, June 9, 1902.

W. W. Hastings, Esq.,
    Attorney for the Cherokee Nation,
        Muskogee, Indian Territory.

Sir:

Enclosed herewith please find copy of the decision of the Commission rendered June 9, 1902, in the matter of the application of William Parris for enrollment as a citizen of the Cherokee Nation.

You are hereby advised that you will be allowed fifteen days from date hereof in which to file with the Commission such protest as you desire to make against the enrollment of the above named person as a citizen of the Cherokee Nation. If you fail to file the protest within the time allowed this applicant will be regularly listed for enrollment.

CHEROKEE GRANTED ENROLLMENT CARDS & DAWES PACKETS 1900-1907 VOLUME I

Yours truly,

Tams Bixby
Acting Chairman.

Encl. D-43.

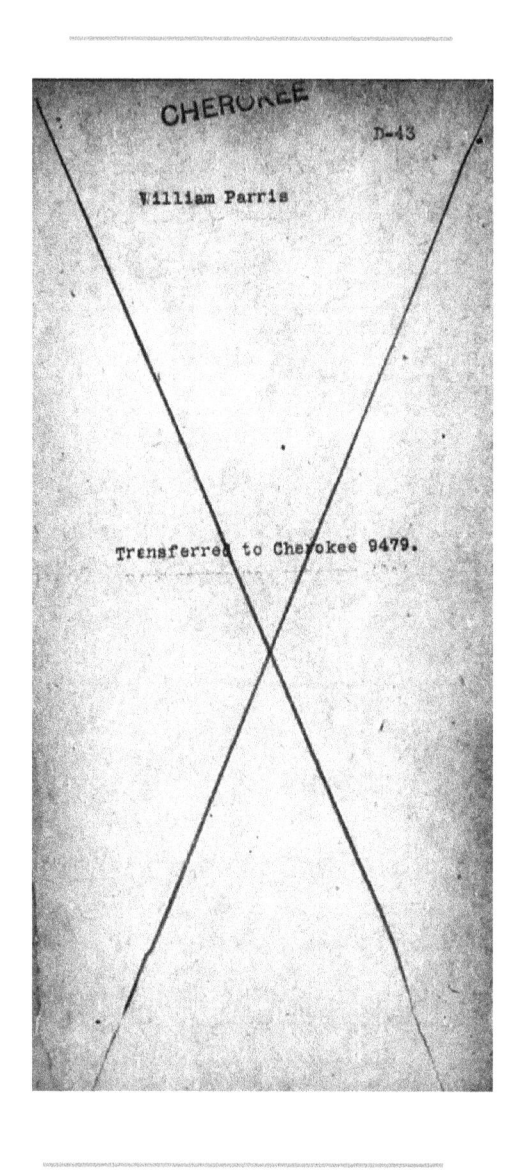

CHEROKEE
D-43

William Parris

Transferred to Cherokee 9479.

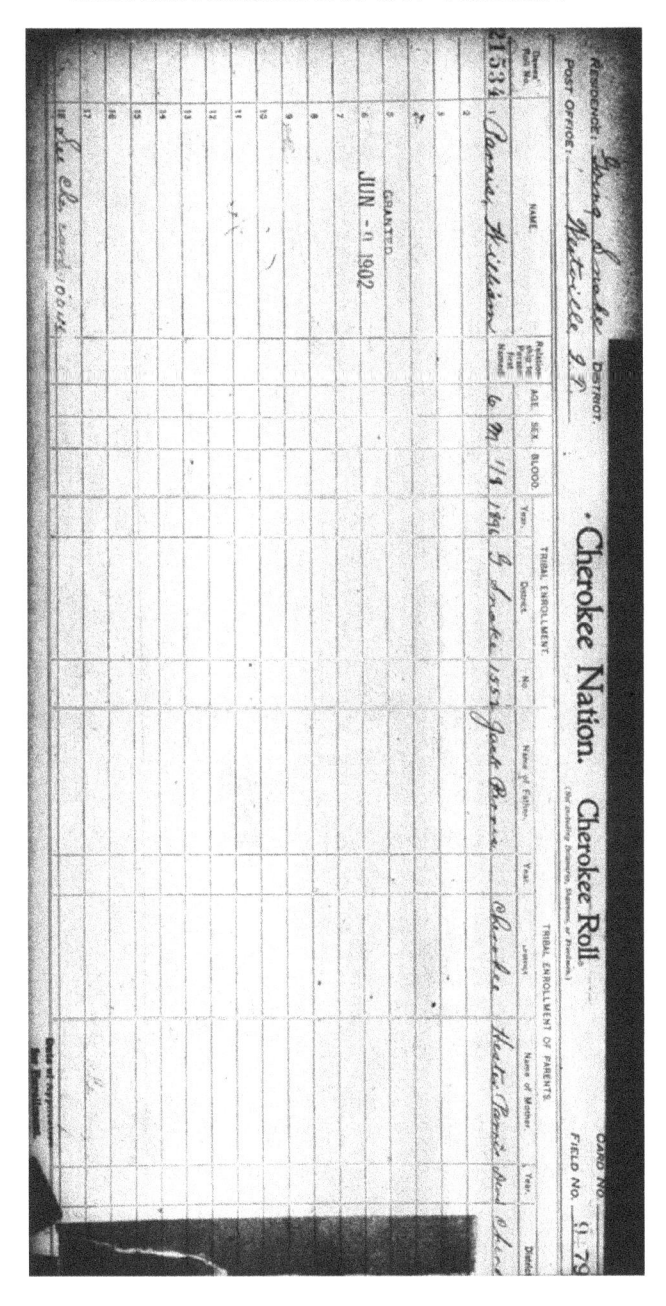

CHEROKEE GRANTED ENROLLMENT CARDS & DAWES PACKETS 1900-1907 VOLUME I

CHEROKEE GRANTED ENROLLMENT CARDS & DAWES PACKETS 1900-1907 VOLUME I

Cherokee D45 - Thomas Devine

CHEROKEE GRANTED ENROLLMENT CARDS
& DAWES PACKETS 1900-1907 VOLUME I

DEPARTMENT OF THE INTERIOR,
COMMISSION TO THE FIVE CIVILIZED TRIBES,
WESTVILLE, I.T. JULY 19, 1900.

In the matter of the application of Thomas Devine et als.[sic], for enrollment as Cherokee citizens, said Devine being sworn by Commissioner Needles, testified as follows:

Q What is your name? A Thomas Devine.
Q Your postoffice? A Westville.
Q Your age? A 39.
Q Where do you live? A Goingsnake.
Q How long have you lived there? A 18 years. I was born in the Cherokee Nation.
Q Lived here all your life? A No sir, my father and mother died when I was quite small and I was carried to the State of Missouri, and came back here about '80 and have been living here ever since.
Q Are you a Cherokee by blood? A Yes.
Q What is the name of your father? A Jim Devine.
Q Is he living? A No sir.
Q Is his name upon the rolls of the Cherokee Nation? A No sir.
Q What's the name of your mother? A Lou Harlan.
Q Is she living? A No sir.
Q Is her name upon the rolls of the Cherokee Nation? A I don't know.
Q Was she a Cherokee by blood? A Yes.
Q Does your name appear upon the rolls of '80? A No sir.
Q Is your name upon the '96 roll? A Yes.
    On '96 roll, page 741, number 644.
Q Did you draw your strip payment fund? A Yes.
    On '94 roll, page 642, number 715 as Thos. N. Devine.
Q If you are a Cherokee by blood why isn't your name upon the rolls of '80?
A That is the year I was in Missouri before I came back here.
Q What evidence have you that you are a Cherokee by blood? A There are several here who know.
Q Have you any documentary evidence? A No sir.
Did you ever apply to the tribal authorities? *A Yes.* Did they reject you? A No sir.
Q Did you ever apply to the Dawes Commission in '96? A No sir.
Q Was your mother a citizen by blood? A Yes.
Q She died before '80? A Yes.
Q When were you born? A '61.
Q When did they take you out to Missouri? A When I was three or four years old.
Q During the war? A Right after the war.
Q How long did they keep you there? A 10 or 12 years. My father and mother both died when I was small.
Q Didn't you know it was necessary for you to be upon the authenticated roll of '80 or have an admission certificate from the Cherokee authorities to be admitted as a Cherokee citizen? A They claimed that I was already admitted-- that I had not forfeited my rights.

CHEROKEE GRANTED ENROLLMENT CARDS
& DAWES PACKETS 1900-1907 VOLUME I

Q Is your mother living? A No sir.
Q Where did she die? A Here in Flint district.
By Mr. Hastings, Cherokee Attorney:
Q You stated something about having property in here at the time of your removal out? A My father had property here.
Q When did your father die? A When I was 4 or 5 years old.
Q In Missouri? A No sir, in Flint.
Q You took you out? A My father's first children.
Q Did you have any property here when you came back here? A Yes.
Q What kind? A I had two improvements.
Q You came into possession of these improvements when you came back here? A Yes.
Q How old were you when you came back from Missouri? A Between 18 and 19.
Q Did you draw money in '80 or '81 that fall payment? A I think I did
Q Did you in '83? A Yes.
Q '86? A Yes.
Q '94? A Yes.
Q Voted here ever since you have been old enough? A Yes.
By the Commission:
Q How much blood do you claim? A 1/16.
Q Your mother was a white woman? A Yes.
Q Are you married? A Yes.
By Mr. Hastings:
Q Was your wife a white woman or a Cherokee? A White woman.
By the Commission?[sic] A[sic] Is she living? A Yes.
Q What year were you married? A '80.
By Mr. Hastings: Where? A In Missouri.
Q Before you came back here? A Yes.
By the Commission:
Q Not according to Cherokee laws? A No sir.
Q You do not claim citizenship for her? A No sir, not unless she is entitled to it.
Q Have you a Certificate of Marriage? A No sir. I did not know it would be required.
Q Have you any children living? A Yes.
Q Under 21? A Yes.
Q What is your wife's name? A Mollie.
Q When were you married to her? A '80.
Q She was a white woman? A Yes.
Q Is her name upon the roll or '80? A No sir.
   On '96 roll, page 820, number 57.
Q Is there no one here knows you were married? A No sir, no on here was present.
Q What is the name of your children under 21 years of age living at home with you?
A James, 14 years old.
   On '96 roll, page 741, number 646.
Q What's the name of the next one? A Joel, 13 years old.
   On '96 roll, page 741, number 647, as Joel M.

342

CHEROKEE GRANTED ENROLLMENT CARDS & DAWES PACKETS 1900-1907 VOLUME I

Q   What's the next one? A William, 10 years old.
        On '96 roll, page 741, number 648.
Q   What's the next one? A Jackson, 8 years old.
        On '96 roll, page 741, number 649, as Jack B.
Q   James, on '94 roll, page 642, number 717.
        Joel M., on '94 roll, page 642, number 718.
        William R., on '94 roll, page 642, number 719.
        Jackson B., on '94 roll, page 642, number 720.

    The name of Thomas Devine appears upon the Census roll of '96, and also upon the pay-roll of '94. Upon the authenticated roll of 1880, on examination, his name is not found. The name of his wife, Mollie, appears also upon the census rolls of '96. Thomas Devine testifies that he was married to Mollie Devine in the year 1880 in the State of Missouri. As The issue of said marriage he had four children, James, Joel, William and Jackson, whose names appear upon the Census rolls of '96 and upon the pay-rolls of '94. Thomas Devine presenting no testimony as to his Cherokee blood, he applying as a Cherokee by blood, other than the fact that his name appears upon the Census rolls of '96, and the pay-roll of '94; his name and that of his wife and children will be placed upon what is known as a doubtful card, and any further testimony that he may desire to present to this Commission as to his citizenship, or as to the legal marriage of his wife and himself, he can do so at any future time. As stated above his name not appearing upon the authenticated rolls of '80, neither does he present any certificate of admission from any citizenship commission or any authorities of the Cherokee Nation.

J. W. ALBERTY, being sworn, testified as follows:
Q   What is your name? A J. W. Alberty.
Q   How old are you? A 66.
Q   Are you a Cherokee citizen? A Yes.
Q   Do you know Thomas Devine? A Yes.

By Mr. Hastings, Cherokee Attorney:

Q   Who was his mother? A His mother was a sister of Dell O. Crittenden's wife and John Harlan.
Q   Where was she living when you know her? A She first lived-before her marriage- just at the foot of ----- mountain.
Q   In Goingsnake district? A Yes.
Q   Was she a citizen of the Cherokee Nation by blood? A Yes, she was recognized as one.
Q   Do you kniw[sic] when she died? A About the commencement of the war. I saw her husband after the war was going on on Red River- he was a widower? I knew the applicant when he was a child, but did not see him any more until '80 or '81.
Q   Do you know whether he had any property here in the Cherokee Nation before '80? A Yes. There was a farm.
Q   Have you known him since '80? A Yes.
Q   How far from you does he live? A He has moved around, but not more than 10 or 15 miles.

CHEROKEE GRANTED ENROLLMENT CARDS & DAWES PACKETS 1900-1907 VOLUME I

Q Has his citizenship been questioned since '80? A No sir.
Q Has he exercised all the priviliges[sic] of citizenship? A Yes.
Q What degree of blood did his mother have? A I don't know.
Q Is Thomas Devine a Cherokee by blood? A He is recognized so.
Q How do you know that this Thomas Devine is the Thomas Devine son of Louisa Harlan? A By John Harlan being appointed his guardian in Missouri. After he returned John Harlan settled with him and --- Adair bought the farm.
Q He got the proceeds from that farm? A Yes.

GEORGE CRITTENDEN, being sworn, testified:

Q What is your name? A George Crittenden.
Q Your age? A 53.
Q Do you know Thomas Devine? A Yes.
Q What do you know about his citizenship? A I know his mother was named Louana Harlan.
Q Do you know whether she was a Cherokee by blood? A She was claimed such.
Q Do you know Thomas Devine to be her son? A I saw him with his father on Red River during the war.

By Mr. Hastings, Cherokee Attorney:

Q There was no question about his mother being a Cherokee by blood? A No sir My sister-in-law claimed him aw her nephew.
Q Have you know him since '80, about the time he came back here? A Yes. He moved out to Saline district and stayed one year.
Q Has he been exercising the rights of citizenship unquestioned by the people of the community? A Did anyone ever question his right to citizenship? A They may have done so, I could not say.
Q Does he own a farm and improvements here? A Yes.
Q How long? A I don't know--- ever since he has been here. He owned a place here and traded it off and then moved back.

By the Commission:

Q Mr. Devine, who told you it was not necessary for you to apply? (to the Cherokee tribal authorities for admission as a citizen by blood?) A Joel Mayes, Sam Mayes and old Uncle Bill Harnage.
Q I understand that since your return here you have exercised all the rights of Cherokee citizenship? A Yes.
Q And drew pay at all different payments? A Yes.

Brown McDonald, being sworn by Commissioner Needles, says as Stenographer to the Commission to the Five Civilized Tribes, he reported in full the testimony of the

CHEROKEE GRANTED ENROLLMENT CARDS & DAWES PACKETS 1900-1907 VOLUME I

above named three witnesses, and that the foregoing is a full, true and correct transcript of his notes.

Brown McDonald

Sworn to and subscribed before me this 20th day of July, 1900, at Westville, I.T.

T B Needles
Commissioner.

"R"

Cherokee D-43.

Department of the Interior,
Commission to the Five Civilized Tribes,
Muskogee, I. T., February 14, 1902.

SUPPLEMENTAL TESTIMONY ON BEHALF OF APPLICANTS, in the matter of the application of Thomas Divine[sic] et al., for enrollment as citizens of the Cherokee Nation.

Appearances:
Applicant in person;
W. W. Hastings, attorney for the Cherokee Nation.

THOMAS DIVINE, being sworn and examined, testified as follows:
BY COMMISSION:
Q What is your name? A Thomas Divine.
Q Where do you live, Mr. Divine? A Goingsnake District, Cherokee Nation.
Q What is your post-office address? A Westville.
COMMISSION: The applicant was notified by registered mail on the 30th day of January, 1902, that his case would be taken up for final consideration by the Commission on the 15th day of February, 1902, and that he would at that time be given an opportunity to appear before the Commission in person or by attorney, when an opportunity would be given him to introduce any additional testimony affecting his application. He this day appears before the Commission in person and requests that this case be taken up.
Q Were you ever admitted to citizenship by the Cherokee National Council or commissions on citizenship? A I suppose that I was; I didn't know at the time I was at Westville; I had no certificate.
Q Did you ever make application for admission? A To a citizenship court, yes sir.
Q About what year was that in? A About '81 I think.
Q Have you any middle name? A Yes sir.
Q What is it? A Thomas Nelson Divine.

345

CHEROKEE GRANTED ENROLLMENT CARDS & DAWES PACKETS 1900-1907 VOLUME I

BY COMMISSION: It appears from the records of the Cherokee Nation in the docket of the Cherokee Commission on citizenship, page 100, No. 94, that Thomas N. Divine[sic] was admitted to citizenship in the Cherokee Nation on the 23rd day of September, 1881, by the Cherokee commission on citizenship, - Roach Young, President, of the Commission; William Harnage, and G.W. Mayes, Assistant Commissioners, and J.B. Mayes, clerk.

NO CROSS EXAMINATION.

Q   Do you submit this case to the Commission now for final consideration?   A   Yes sir.
BY MR. HASTINGS:
The Cherokee Nation submits this case.

M.D. Green, being first duly sworn, states that as stenographer to the Commission to the Five Civilized Tribes he correctly recorded the testimony and proceedings in this case and that the foregoing is a true and complete transcript of his stenographic notes thereof.

MD Green

Subscribed and sworn to before me this February 15, 1902.

T B Needles
Commissioner.

Cherokee D 45

DEPARTMENT OF THE INTERIOR,

COMMISSION TO THE FIVE CIVILIZED TRIBES.

In the matter of the application of Thomas Devine for the enrollment of himself and his minor children, James, Joel M., William, and Jackson Devine as citizens by blood of the Cherokee Nation, and for the enrollment of his wife Mollie, as a citizen by intermarriage of the Cherokee Nation.

D E C I S I O N.

--oOo--

The record in this case shows that on July 19, 1900, Thomas Devine appeared before the Commission at Westville, Indian Territory, and then and there made

CHEROKEE GRANTED ENROLLMENT CARDS & DAWES PACKETS 1900-1907 VOLUME I

personal application for the enrollment of himself and his minor children, James, Joel H[sic]., William and Jackson Devine as citizens by blood of the Cherokee Nation, and for the enrollment of his wife Mollie as a citizen by intermarriage of the Cherokee Nation.

On February 14, 1902, the principal applicant appeared before the Commission at its office in Muskogee, Indian Territory, and submitted further evidence in the matter of the above application. From the evidence in this case it appears that Thomas Devine was admitted to citizenship in the Cherokee Nation on September 23, 1881. He has resided in the Cherokee Nation ever since and is identified on the Strip payment roll of 1894 and the Cherokee Census roll of 1896. His wife Mollie was lawfully married to him on April 11, 1880; she is also identified on the Cherokee Census roll of 1896.

Her status is defined by the decisions of the Cherokee Supreme Court in the cases of Cherokee Nation vs. Nancy Rogers and Melissa Dawson vs. W. S. Dawson, which hold that a white woman married to a Cherokee at the time of his admission to citizenship, acquires thereby, the rights of citizenship in the Cherokee Nation. The children, James, Joel M., William and Jackson Devine are the issue of said marriage, and they are identified on the Cherokee tribal rolls of 1894 and 1896.

The authority of the Commission herein is defined in Paragraph 1, Sec. 21 of the Act of Congress June 28, 1898 (30 Stats., 495).

It is therefore the opinion of this Commission that Thomas Devine and his minor children James Devine, Joel M. Devine, William Devine, and Jackson Devine are lawfully entitled to be enrolled as members by blood of the Cherokee Tribe of Indians in Indian Territory, and that his wife Mollie Devine is lawfully entitled to be enrolled as a member by intermarriage of the Cherokee Tribe of Indians in Indian Territory, and that the application for their enrollment should be granted, and it is so ordered.

COMMISSION TO THE FIVE CIVILIZED TRIBES.

Tams Bixby
Acting Chairman.

CHEROKEE GRANTED ENROLLMENT CARDS & DAWES PACKETS 1900-1907 VOLUME I

_____T.B. Needles_____
Commissioner.

_____C. R. Breckinridge_____
Commissioner.

Dated Muskogee, Indian Territory,
this _____MAY 20 1902_____

COMMISSIONERS:
HENRY L. DAWES,
TAMS BIXBY,
THOMAS B. NEEDLES,
C. R. BRECKINRIDGE.

ALLISON L. AYLESWORTH,
SECRETARY.

ADDRESS ONLY THE
COMMISSION TO THE FIVE CIVILIZED TRIBES.

DEPARTMENT OF THE INTERIOR,
COMMISSION TO THE FIVE CIVILIZED TRIBES.

REFER IN REPLY TO THE FOLLOWING

D. 45.

Muskogee, Indian Territory, May 21, 1902.

W. W. Hastings, Esq.,
    Attorney for the Cherokee Nation,
        Muskogee, Indian Territory.

Sir:

    Enclosed herewith please find copy of a decision of the Commission rendered May 20th, in the matter of the application of Thomas Devine for the enrollment of himself, his wife, Mollie Devine, and their minor children, James, Joel M., William and Jackson Devine, as citizens of the Cherokee Nation.

    You are hereby advised that you will be allowed fifteen days from date hereof in which to file with the Commission such protest as you desire to make against the enrollment of the above named persons as citizens of the Cherokee Nation. If you fail to file the protest within the time allowed these applicants will be regularly listed for enrollment.

                Very respectfully,

                    T B Needles

                    Commissioner in Charge.

Encl. D-45.

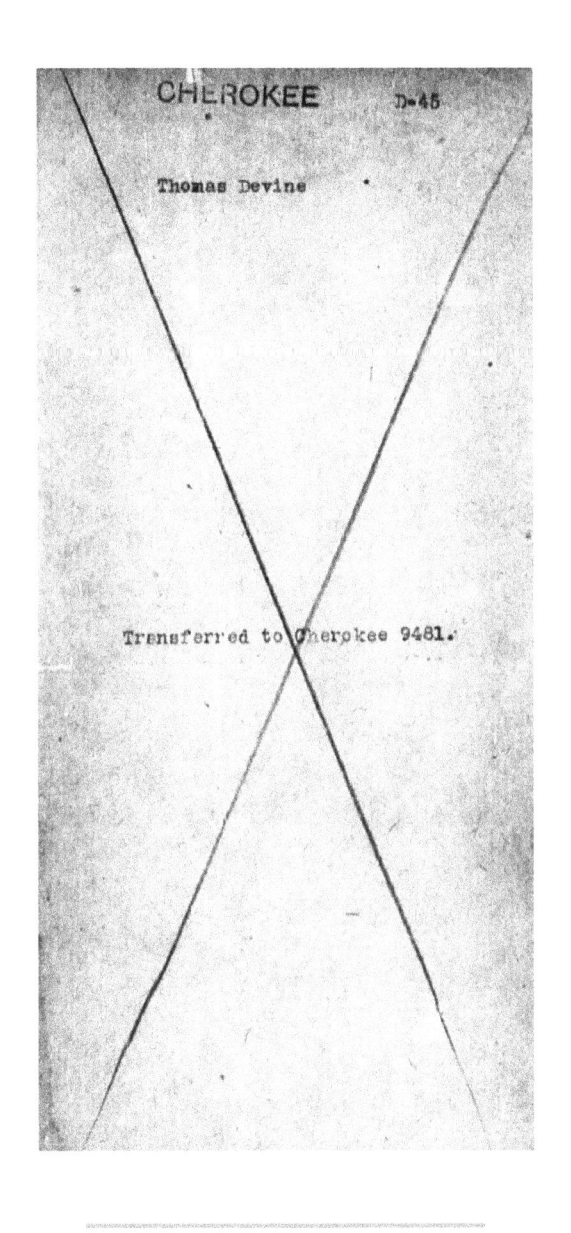

CHEROKEE GRANTED ENROLLMENT CARDS & DAWES PACKETS 1900-1907 VOLUME I

CHEROKEE D-45

Thomas Devine

Transferred to Cherokee 9481.

CHEROKEE GRANTED ENROLLMENT CARDS & DAWES PACKETS 1900-1907 VOLUME I

Index

ADAIR 344
  J T 4,268,276,283,298,317
ADOLPUS 220
ALBERTY
  Alexander 168
  B W 268,275,283,290,297,317
  J W 343
BAGWELL, E C 221
BALLARD
  Mr 153,159
  William 213,226
BAUGH
  J L 179,192,202
  Joel L 246
  Mr 180,181,192,193,202,203
BEAVERS
  Ella I 276,277,278
  Ella Isabelle 275
  Susan L 273,274,275,276,
 277,278,279
  Wiley 275,276
BIRCH 218
BIXBY
  Commissioner 167
  Mr 11
  Tams 26,63,77,78,100,109,112,
  113,114,131,134,136,137,138,157,
  162,164,167,169,184,185,207,208,
  209,228,229,237,240,241,255,263,
  264,270,271,277,284,285,291,292,
  300,302,318,319,327,335,337,338,
  347
BLAINE 144
BLEVINS
  Allen 74,77
  Laura 74,77
  Mike 72
  Minnie 69,70,71,72,73,74,75,
 76,77,79,80
  Minnie Lee 74,78
  Nellie 69,70,71,72,73,74,75,
 76,77,79,80
  Nellie May 74,78
BLUEJACKET, Charlie 197
BLYTHE 160
  Aubrey A 151,152,154,156,157,
 158,165,166
  Aubrey Allen 144

Charles F 151,152,154,156,
.... 157,165,166
Charles P[sic] 158
Erma Lolla 144
Ermer L 154,157,165,166
Ermer Lolla 144
Ermer[sic]L 151,152,156,158
Farry A 151,152,154,156,157,
.... 158,165,166
Farry Alpha 144
Jesse L 151,152,154,156,157,
.... 158,165,166
Jesse Louie 145
John E 131,132,136,137,138,
.... 165,166
John Ellis 144
Lolla 144
Luella ... 142,143,145,152,153,156,
  157,161,162,166,167,168,169,170
Lueller 142
Mary Ann 153
Mary J .. 151,152,154,156,157,158,
.... 165,166
Mary Jane 144
Mr 144,145
N B 142,143
Napoleon B 141,142,143,146,
  147,150,151,152,153,154,156,157,
  158,161,162,163,164,165,166,167
Orberry Allen 144
Suella[sic] 151,152
William H 151,152,154,156,
.... 157,158,165,166
William Henry 144
BOB 295
BOUDINOT, W P 172,175,178,
.... 190,197,200
BOUVIER 257
BOYLE
  Amanda 236
  Mary 233
  Mary L 232,235,236
BOYLES
  Mary 234
  Mary L 233
BOYNTON
  Florence Isabelle 324
  Mrs 324

Index

BRADY, William 97
BRANSON, Fred P 225
BRECKENRIDGE[sic], Commissioner
.... 247
BRECKINRIDGE
   Att'y 90
   C R 26,74,77,93,100,109,131,
      134,157,184,207,237,255,270,277,
      284,291,300,318,327,337,348
   Clifton R 120,248
   Commissioner 82,87,89,91,174,
   175,213,214,215,216
   Com'r 86,87,90,91,92,182,
   213,214,215
BREEDLOVE
   Mr 246,248,249,250
   W W 250,264
   Waller W 245,246,248
   Waller[sic]W 255
   Walter W 251,252,253
BROWN, Lewis 168
BURK 221
BURKS 214,215,222,223,224
   Miss 223
CAMP, Ora M 77
CAREY, Edmond D 218,219
CARR, Jesse O ... 98,152,154,198,205
CARY, Mr 226
CHICK, Retta 311
CHIP 220
CHIPS 222
   John 222,223,224,226
CHISHOLM, Lucy 168
CLARK, Clement G 110
CLARKE, Clement G 109
CLEAVELAND[sic] 144
COLLINS, Frances 168
COVINGTON, W P 225
CRABB 257
   Mr 257
CRAVENS, R R 120,145,316,325
CRITDENTEN, George 334
CRITTENDEN
   Carl 282
   Dell O 343
   George 281,344
   Henry 267
   Joseph ... 280,281,282,283,284,285

   Nanch L 284
   Nancy L 280,282,283,285,286
CRITTENTEN, Joe 281
CRONINGER, Arthur G 182
CUNNINGHAM, J T 196
DARDEE
   Benjamin 267
   Julia Ann 267
DAVENPORT, Mr 72,73
DAWSON 262,309,310
   Melissa 300,347
   W A 300
   W S 347
DEVINE
   Jack B 343
   Jackson 343,346,347,348
   Jackson B 343
   James 342,343,346,347,348
   Jim 341
   Joel 342,343
   Joel H[sic] 347
   Joel M 342,343,346,347,348
   Mollie 342,343,346,347,348
   Thomas 340,341,343,344,346,
   347,348,349,350
   Thos N 341
   William 343,346,347,348
   William R 343
DIRTSELLER 218
   Adolphus 213,214,217
   Adolphus W 216,217,221,222,
   223,224,225,229
   Adolphus Washington 212,213,
   214,215,227,228,229,230
   Adolpus[sic] 219
   Adolpus[sic]W 218
   Jim 219,220
   John 217,219,220
DIVINE
   Thomas 345
   Thomas N 346
   Thomas Nelson 345
DOUGHERTY, Thomas 180,192,
.... 203
DOWNING, Lewis 122,125
EAST, Alexander 233,236,237,
.... 238,239
EDWARDS 83

352

Index

Alice N 99
ELK, John 126
ELK V WILKENS 126
ELK VS WILKENS 129
ENGLAND, Benjamin C 151
EUGENE 93
FITE
   Dr 40
   F B 10
   Francis B 9,22,37,51,61
FOLSOM
   Eva 315
   Evalina Forbis 296
   Evaline 314,315,316,317,318,
  319,320,321
   Joel 314,315,316,317,318
   Joel W 315
   Levi 315
   Melvina 315
FORBES
   Agnes E 316
   Evaline 315,316,317,318
   Harriet 302
   Harriett 298,300
   Mollie C 290,291
   Nancy E
   266,267,268,269,270,272,274,281
   Nancy L 281
   Ora 298,299,300,302
   Rasmus 298,299,300,302
   Robert J 294,297,298,300,301,
  302,303,304
   Susan L 274
   William 274,281,292
   William M 287,289,290,291,293
FORBIS
   Bill 295
   Bob 296
   Bob Jefferson 296
   Frances E 296
   Harriet 296,297
   Lilla 274
   Lillie 274,275
   Mollie E 289
   Ora 296,297
   Rasmus 296,297
   Robert 296
   Robert F 295,296

Robert J 294,295,296,297
William 288,289
William M 287,289
FOREMAN, Samuel 41,76,221
FOSTER, Hannah 82
FOX 213,220
   Adolphus 213,214,217
   Adolphus Washington 213
   John 214,215,217,218,228
   Missouri A 215,228
   Missouri Angeline 215
FRANCIS, David R 147
FROBIS[sic], Nancy E 295
FULSOM
   Joel 315
   Melvina 333
G T THOMPSON & SONS 9
GIBSON
   H A 163
   Mr 146
   Mr N A 146
   N A 150
GOOSEBERG, Don 123
GRAHAM
   Elizabeth 307,310,312
   Florence 307,308
   Florence M 310
   Francis 307
   Francis W 307,310
   Gid 311
   Gideon .. 305,306,308,309,310,313
   Grace 307
   Gracie 307
   Gracie M 310
   Jesse E 307,310
   John W 306,307,309,310
   Julius 307
   Julius E 307,310
   Mary E 307,310
GREEN
   M D 3,14,16,19,21,22,23,31,34,
   35,36,37,38,45,47,48,49,50,51,55,
   58,59,60,61,66,92,146,182,216,218
   ,233,251,254,268,275,282,289,297,
   308,346
   Mr 105
HAINES, Mr 5
HALL

353

Index

Alice Nancy 83
Blanch 99,108
Blanche 84,87,91,92,109
Blanche E 92,99,109
Eugene 84,86,87,96
Eugene J 87,99
James Eugene ... 84,85,87,97,98,99,
  100,101,102,103,108,112,113,114
Jesse Swan 90
Jessie 84,87,89,90,108
Jessie M 90,99,109
Jessie Mae 108,109,110,111,
  115,116
Jessie May 108
Jessie Swan 99,109
Joe Ann 93
Joseph Ahh 114
Joseph Ann .. 81,82,83,93,94,95,97,
  . 98,99,100,101,102,103,107,108,
  111,112,113,116,117
Josie Winters 88,89,95,97,98,
  99,100,101,102,103,108,112,113,1
  14
Mae E 84
Mae Evelyn 84,98,99,100,101,
  102,103,108,112,113,114
Mrs 88,93,94,96,104,106
Mrs Joseph Ann 92
William B 96
William O 87,99
William Oscar 84,85,86,87,88
Willie Oscar 98
Willis Oscar ... 87,88,97,98,99,100,
  101,102,103,107,111,112,113,114
HARD, Elizabeth H 143
HARLAN
John 343,344
Lou 341
Louana 344
Louisa 344
HARNAGE
Uncle Bill 344
William 346
HASTINGS
Attorney 85,86,87,89,90
Att'y 84,91,282
Att'y W W 274
Mr 5,15,16,19,22,34,37,50,
  57,60,95,96,97,105,106,121,122,
  123,195,196,197,198,217,218,249,
  250,254,332,342,343,344,346
Mr W W 4,121,137,138,251
W W 14,17,22,24,25,27,28,
  32,37,39,45,51,52,56,61,62,63,72,
  73,74,78,94,103,110,112,113,114,
  115,116,120,132,135,136,146,151,
  156,160,163,164,165,166,169,185,
  194,207,208,209,216,228,234,240,
  241,249,252,263,264,270,277,284,
  291,301,307,308,310,319,323,324,
  325,327,333,334,337,345,348
HAWKINS
Charles 9,22,37,51,61
Chas 10
W S 162
HESTER 334
HILL, Martha 26
HORTON, John H 143
HOUSE, Ethal Mary 168
HUNTER 245,246
Charles P 322,323,324,325,
  326,328
Charley P 323
Delilah 255
Florence I 326,327,328
Florence Isabelle 324,325
James 245,247,249,250,
  253,254,255,256,263,264
Jim 245
Lillie 254
Lucretia 245,247,250,253,254,
  255,263,264
Lucretia G 244,248,249,251,
  252,256,265
Maud 322,323,324,325,326,
  327,328,329
Maude 324
Mr 246,247
Mrs 246,247,325
William B 248
Willie 250
HUTCHINGS
Attorney 214,232
Mr 174,175
Mr W T 178,190,201,245
HUTCHINS, Mr 144

Index

IRONSIDE
  Charles T 163
  Robert 197
JACOB 262
JAMES, Manchie 168
JEFFERSON, Charles E 111
JIM 220
JONES
  B C 98,198,205
  B O 152
  Bruce C 13,72,176,179,
  191,201,248,334,335
  Ida A 205,208
  J E 205
  Robert E 205,206,208,209
KELLY, John 332
LACY, Adam 332
LADD, Joseph B 155
LANDRUM, H T 215
LARRABEE, C F 167
LASLEY
  Charles 234
  Charles H 231,233,235,236,
  237,240,241,242,243
  Harland 233,234,238
  Harlin 235,236
  Mary L 234,235,236
LASSLEY
  Charles H 231,232,233
  Harlin 232
  Mary L 232
LESSLEY, George H 162,227
LIPE
  C C 4
  D W 268,276,283,298,317
LITTLE, William A 147
MADDEN, George E 168
MARKS
  Lemuel W 93,101
  Mr 87,95,96
MARSHALL, Mr 95
MARTIN
  Benjamin 249,251
  Benjamin, Jr 252,253
  Mr 249,250,252,253
  Mr W N 5
MARY 331
MAXEY
  Mr 249,250
  N B 249,250
MAXWELL
  Mabel F 40,106,107
  Mable F 76
MAYES
  G W 346
  J B 4,346
  Joel 344
  Sam 344
MCDONALD, J B 234
MCDONALD, Brown ... 333,344,345
MCKENNON
  Archibald S 309,310
  Capt 10,12
  Commissioner 2,13,31,44,55,66
  Com'r 13
  A S 13,309
MELLETTE, Mr 121,122,123
MELLETTE & SMITH
  121,124,128,135
MIELENG, Ella 10,19,21,22,34,
  36,37,48,49,50
MILLER
  John 226
  John M 221
  Willie 93
MONROE 215
  Thomas 214
MOORE, Olcott 215
MOORE
  Allcut 223
  James A 215
  John 226
MORRIS, Gabe 267
MORRISON
  Blanch E H 97,99,100,108,109,
  110,113,114,115,116
  Blanch Hall 114
  Blanche E H 98,100,103,105,
  107,109,111,112
  Blanche Evelyn Hall 91
  Lewis F 99,100
NEEDLES
  Commissioner 232,233,267,274,
  281,288,295,296,344
  Com'r 232,267,275,282,
  289,296,308,331

T B 3,5,6,17,19,21,22,23,24, 25,26,27,34,36,37,38,48,49,50,51, 58,59,60,61,62,72,73,77,92,94,100, 109,115,116,123,131,134,143,145, 146,157,165,166,176,179,181,182, 183,184,191,194,202,204,207,216, 218,233,234,235,237,251,252,254, 255,268,270,275,276,277,278,282, 283,284,289,291,297,298,300,301, 308,315,316,317,318,325,326,327, 328,333,335,337,345,346,348

NEILSON, Mr 325
NEIMEYER
    Alfred Cope 173
    Charles H 205
    George W 208
    Mr 173
    Sarah E 173
~~NICKEL~~, Mary Elizabeth 2
NIEMEYER
    Alfred C 183,184,185
    Charles H .... 177,190,198,200, ... 208,209
    Eliza 184
    George 178,190,200
    George W .... 194,195,198,199, ... 204,205,206,207,209
    Ida A 177,190,198,200,209
    Mr 174,195,196
    Mrs .... 178,180,191,192,201, ... 203,204
    Mrs Sarah E 174
    Sarah E 176,177,179,180,181, 182,183,184,188,189,191,192,193, 194,198,199,202,203,205,206,207, 208,209,210,211
    William W .... 171,172,175,176, ... 182,183,184,185,186,187
OSCAR 93,102
PARIS
    Jack 332
    William 332
PARKS
    J T 227
    Mr 180,181,193,203
    S F 179,192,194,202
PARR, Mollie E 164
PARRIS, William ... 330,331,333,334, ... 335,336,337,338,339
PILGRAM
    Harriet 296
    Mollie 289
    Mollie C 288
    Sarah 289
    Tom 289
PILGRIM, Mollie 290
PURCELL 181,204
    Charlie 197
    Ida A 197
    Latham 197
    R W .... 174,175,177,178,189, ... 190,199,200,201
    Robert 180,192,193,203
    Robert W 180,192,202
    Sarah E 172,173,174,175,178, 180,184,190,192,195,196,197,200, 201,202,206
    Sarah M 178,190
    Wesley 197
    William 197
    William W 196
RANDALL
    Mr 122
    William P 118,119,120,121, 125,128,129,130,131,132,133,134, 135,136,137,138,139,140
    Wm P 124
RATTLEHEAD
    Dock 225
    Margaret 226
REAVES
    Charles B 164
    John A 163,164
RED BIRD
    Daniel 162
    Danile[sic] 167
REUTER, P J 154,311
RICE, J S 217
RISSER, Mary B 111
ROBBINS
    Hester 333,336
    Lucinda 333,334
    Uncle Levi 334
ROBERTSON
    Hutchinson M 247
    Mr 247

Index

ROBINSON, Uncle Levi 332
ROGERS
  Joseph 82
  Nancy 299,300,347
  Nancy L 283
  Susan L 276
ROSS, Harriett 181,193,203
ROSSON
  J O 5,73,97,111,123,252
  John O 106,108
ROTHENBERGER, E T 94
RYAN, Thos 137
SCHOULER 261
SMITH, Edgar 137
SORTER
  John H 143
  Mary Ann 153
SORTORE, Mary A 161
SOWERS, N O 290
STANDING BEAR VS CROOK 148
STANLEY, W E 26,109,134,157,327
STARR
  J C 40,97,132,133,151,
  152,250,309
  Martha Jane 281
  Mr 153
STILL, Tom 334
STOVAL, K T 311
SWAN
  Jessie M H 97,98,99,100,103,
  104,106,107,111,112,113,114
  Jessie Mae Hall 89,90,108,111
  Jessie May[sic]Hall 114
  Mark E 99,100
  Mr 111
SYDOW, Elizabeth 307,308
THOMPSON
  Allison 23,24,25,26,27,28,
  30,31,37,38,39,41,42,51,61
  Allison Archibald 25,26,27,39
  Allison G 25,27,44
  Cleo 13
  Earnest W 39
  Ernest 23,24,25,26,27,28,38,
  43,44,50,51,52,53,61
  Ernest T 25,26,27,44
  Ernest W 25,27,31
  Ernost[sic] 44

G T 17,22,32,37,45,51,61
Gilbert T 8,10,13,14,16,
.... 23,24,25,38,51,61
Gilbert T, Jr 14,16,26,27
Gilbert T, Sr 22,25,26,27,
.... 29,37,51,61
Gilbert Taylor 15
Gilbert Taylor, Jr 15
Gilbert, Jr 13,16,25
Hugh C 25,26,27
Hugh G 44
James 57
James K 17,19,20,21,23,25,26,
  27,32,33,34,35,36,38,45,47,48,49,
  ... 51,54,55,56,58,60,61,62,63,64
James L 28
Jimmie G 44
Joseph G 25,26,27
Josephine A 13,15,17,32,45,56
Josephine Amanda 14
Mamie 25,27,31,39
Mamie A 31
Matthew 13,25,26,27
Milton 66
Milton K 22,37,51,61,65,67,68
Mr 16
TRAHERN
  Al 111
  Albert C 111
  Albert L 111
VANN
  Katie 168
  Lucile 168
VON WEISE, Chas 181,182,194,204
WARD
  George M 69,70,76
  John 75
  Laura 70,72
WARREN, J R 195
WATIE 219
WAYBOURN, Ada A 168
WEAVER
  Hester 331,332,335,336
  Joe 331,332
  Joseph 330,331,332
  Mary 332
  Mrs 334
  Mrs Joe 333

Index

WEBSTER 257
   Mr 257
WHITE, Myron 227
WICKET
   Bettie M 5
   Charles 3
   Mary E 3,5,6
   Mary Elizabeth 1,2,3
WIDKED[sic], Mary E 4
WILKENS 127
WILLIAMS
   Manda 324,327
   Mary Elizabeth 4
   Maud 323,325
   Maud Medora 323
   Mrs Florence Isabelle 324
WILSOM, Delilah 255
WILSON 245
   Bird 246,248
   Delilah 245
   James 245
   Jesse E 168
   Lucretia 245
WISDOM, Colonel D M 249
WOERNER 261
WOLFF, Judge John 246
WOOD
   Amanda 232,236,239,241
   Mrs Amanda 234
WOODALL, Mr 248
WORTHINGTON, J L 132
YEARGAIN 110,132,160
   Joseph D 26,109,134,157
YEARGAIN CASE 131
YOUNG, Roach 346
ZIMMERMAN, K G 132,133

358